THE COMPLETE CHRISTMAS BOOK

The Complete Christmas Book

Edited by Franklin Watts

Illustrated by William Ronin

REVISED EDITION

FRANKLIN WATTS, INC.

575 LEXINGTON AVE.
NEW YORK 22, N. Y.

ACKNOWLEDGMENTS

In collecting material used in this anthology, every effort has been made to locate the copyright owners. If anyone has been overlooked, please notify the editor and proper acknowledgment will be made.

The help of Dennison is appreciated, especially with the section on gift wrappings. This material is copyright © by Dennison.

Dick Ashbaugh for "A Merry, Scary Christmas" by Dick Ashbaugh. Copyright ©, 1950, by the Curtis Publishing Company.

Eleanor Alletta Chaffee for "Week Before Christmas" by Eleanor Alletta Chaffee. Copyright ©, 1951, by the Curtis Publishing Company.

The Estate of Robert P. Tristram Coffin for "Christmas in Maine" by Robert P. Tristram Coffin. Copyright ©, 1945, by the author.

Curtis Publishing Company for "Christmas Feast on Fewest Calories." Copyright ©, 1956, by the Curtis Publishing Company.

Coningsby Dawson for "When Father Christmas Was Young" by Coningsby Dawson. Copyright © by the author.

Stephen Daye Press for "How I Spent My Million" by Edgar J. Park. Reprinted from *Christmas Tales for Reading Aloud* compiled by Robert Lohan. Copyright ©, 1946, by the Stephen Daye Press.

Doubleday & Company, Inc. for "The Gift of the Magi" from *The Four Million* by O. Henry. Copyright ©, 1906, by Doubleday & Company, Inc.

Doubleday & Company, Inc. for "Gates and Doors" from *Poems, Essays and Letters* by Joyce Kilmer. Copyright ©, 1914, 1917, 1918, by Doubleday & Company, Inc.

E. P. Dutton & Co., Inc. for "Christmas Everywhere" from *Christmas Songs and Easter Ballads* by Phillips Brooks. Reprinted by permission of the publisher. Copyright ©, 1903, by E. P. Dutton & Co., Inc.

E. P. Dutton & Co., Inc., J. M. Dent & Sons Ltd. and the Trustees of the G. K. Chesterton Estate for "A Christmas Carol" from *The Wild Knight and Other Poems* by G. K. Chesterton. Reprinted by permission of the publishers.

Eldridge Publishing Company for "A Card for Christmas" by Agnes Curtis from *My Good Christmas Book.*

Esquire, Inc. for "When Christmas Went Outdoors" by Grady Johnson. Reprinted from *Coronet*, December 1953. Copyright ©, 1953, by Esquire, Inc.

The Estate of Hamlin Garland for "My First Christmas Tree" by Hamlin Garland. Copyright ©, 1911, by the Curtis Publishing Company.

Good Housekeeping Magazine for "The Year There Was No Christmas" by Samuel Grafton. Copyright ©, 1952, by the Hearst Corporation.

CONTENTS

THE COMPLETE CHRISTMAS BOOK

THIS WOULD I KEEP

by Grace Noll Crowell

This would I keep forever in my heart
Among the things the ruthless years may leave:
The glad excitement, wonder, and delight
Of Christmas Eve;

This would I hold untarnished through the years,
Although the roads I take may lead me far:
The radiant molten glory of the light
From one white star.

And oh, to keep the breathlessness, the thrill,
The heart's swift running out to meet surprise,
Never to lose entirely the light
Of childhood from my eyes;

Never to lose the Christmas morning joy,
And never the quick bright eagerness to give —
God, someway let my spirit keep the shine
Of Christmas while I live.

What Do You Know About Christmas?

THERE is no festival on earth like Christmas, none so vital or universal, none celebrated by so many people for so many centuries in so many lands. Around the season, exulting in its meaning and demonstrating its joyfulness, great numbers of rituals and legends and customs have developed, both religious and secular. Some are as old as the pagan rituals which celebrated the sun's closer approach to the earth after the shortest and coldest days of the year. Some are as new as the singing of "White Christmas," as the lighting of a giant Christmas tree in the middle of town.

What do candles in a window mean? Where do manger scenes come from? Why do children hang up their stockings, and since when have we been kissing under the mistletoe? Sometimes we cannot be sure of the facts; sometimes we can. It makes Christmas richer if we understand what is known of its glorious history.

THE BIRTH OF JESUS FROM THE GOSPELS ACCORDING TO ST. LUKE AND ST. MATTHEW

In the days of Herod the king of Judaea, the angel Gabriel was sent from God to a city of Galilee, named Nazareth, to a virgin espoused to a man whose name was Joseph, of the house of David; and the virgin's name was Mary. And the angel came in unto her, and said,

Hail, thou that art highly favoured, the Lord is with thee: blessed art thou among women.

And when she saw him, she was troubled at his saying, and cast in her mind what manner of salutation this should be. And the angel said unto her,

Fear not, Mary: for thou hast found favour with God. And thou shalt conceive and bring forth a son, and shalt call his name JESUS. He shall be great, and shall be called the Son of the Highest: and the Lord God shall give unto him the throne of his father David: and he shall reign over the house of Jacob for ever; and of his kingdom there shall be no end.

And Mary said,

Behold the handmaid of the Lord; be it unto me according to thy word.

1

And it came to pass in those days, that there went out a decree from Caesar Augustus that all the world should be taxed. And all went to be taxed, everyone in his own city. And Joseph also went up from Galilee, out of the city of Nazareth, into Judaea, unto the city of David, which is called Bethlehem — because he was of the house and lineage of David — to be taxed with Mary his espoused wife, being great with child. And so it was that, while they were there, the days were accomplished that she should be delivered. And she brought forth her firstborn son, and wrapped him in swaddling clothes, and laid him in a manger; because there was no room for them in the inn.

And there were in the same country shepherds abiding in the field, keeping watch over their flock by night. And lo, the angel of the Lord came unto them, and the glory of the Lord shone round them: and they were sore afraid. And the angel said unto them,

> Fear not: for behold, I bring you good tidings of great joy, which shall be to all people. For unto you is born this day in the city of David a Saviour, which is Christ the Lord. And this shall be a sign unto you; Ye shall find the babe wrapped in swaddling clothes, lying in a manger.

And suddenly there was with the angel a multitude of the heavenly host praising God, and saying,

> Glory to God in the highest, and on earth peace, good will towards men.

And it came to pass, as the angels were gone away from them into heaven, the shepherds said one to another, Let us now go even unto Bethlehem, and see this thing which is come to pass, which the Lord hath made known unto us. And they came with haste, and found Mary, and Joseph, and the babe lying in a manger.

And the shepherds returned, glorifying and praising God for all the things they had heard and seen.

Now there came wise men from the east to Jerusalem, saying, Where is he that is born King of the Jews? For we have seen his star in the east, and are come to worship him.

When Herod the king heard these things he was troubled. He called the chief priests and the scribes together and demanded of them where Christ should be born. And they told him in Bethlehem of Judaea. Then Herod sent the wise men to Bethlehem, and said, Go and search diligently for the young child; and when ye have found him, bring me word again, that I may come and worship him also.

When they had heard the king, they departed; and lo, the star which they saw in the east, went before them, till it came and stood over where the young child was.

And when they were come into the house, they saw the young child with Mary his mother, and fell down and worshipped him: and when they had opened their treasures, they presented unto him gifts; gold, frankincense, and myrrh.

And being warned of God in a dream that they should not return to Herod, they departed into their own country another way.

And behold, the angel of the Lord appeared to Joseph in a dream, saying, Arise, and take the young child and his mother, and flee into Egypt, and be thou there until I bring thee word: for Herod will seek the young child to destroy him. When he arose, he took the young child and his mother by night, and departed into Egypt.

Then Herod, when he saw that he was mocked of the wise men, was exceeding wroth, and sent forth and slew all the children, from two years and under, that were in Bethlehem and in all the coasts thereof.

When Herod was dead, the angel of the Lord appeareth in a dream to Joseph in Egypt, saying, Arise, and take the young child and his mother, and go into the land of Israel: for they are dead which sought the young child's life.

And then he arose and took the young child and his mother, and came into the land of Israel, and they returned into Galilee to their own city Nazareth.

And the child grew, and waxed strong in spirit, filled with wisdom: and the grace of God was upon him.

IS THERE A SANTA CLAUS?

(This famous editorial first appeared in the New York Sun, September 21, 1897)

We take pleasure in answering at once and thus prominently the communication below, expressing at the same time our great gratification that its faithful author is numbered among the friends of *The Sun:*

Dear Editor:

I am 8 years old.

Some of my little friends say there is no Santa Claus.

Papa says "If you see it in *The Sun* it's so."

Please tell me the truth, is there a Santa Claus?

Virginia O'Hanlon
115 West 95th Street

Virginia, your little friends are wrong. They have been affected by the skepticism of a skeptical age. They do not believe except what they see. They think that nothing can be which is not comprehensible by their little minds. All minds, Virginia, whether they be men's or children's, are little. In this great universe of ours man is a mere insect, an ant, in his intellect, as compared with the boundless world about him, as measured by the intelligence capable of grasping the whole of truth and knowledge.

Yes, Virginia, there is a Santa Claus. He exists as certainly as love and generosity and devotion exist, and you know that they abound and give to your life its highest beauty and joy. Alas! how dreary would be the world if there were no Santa Claus! It would be as dreary as if there were no Virginias. There would be no childlike faith then, no poetry, no romance to make tolerable this existence. We should have no enjoyment, except in sense and sight. The eternal light with which childhood fills the world would be extinguished.

Not believe in Santa Claus! You might as well not believe in fairies! You might get your papa to hire men to watch in all the chimneys on Christmas eve to catch Santa Claus, but even if they did not see Santa Claus coming down, what would that prove? Nobody sees Santa Claus, but that is no sign that there is no Santa Claus. The most real things in the world are those that neither children nor men can see. Did you ever see fairies dancing on the lawn? Of course not, but that's no proof that they are not there. Nobody can conceive or imagine all the wonders there are unseen and unseeable in the world.

You tear apart the baby's rattle and see what makes the noise inside, but there is a veil covering the unseen world which not the strongest man, nor even the united strength of all the strongest men that ever lived, could tear apart. Only faith, fancy, poetry, love, romance, can push aside that curtain and view and picture the supernal beauty and glory beyond. Is it all real? Ah, Virginia, in all this world there is nothing else real and abiding.

No Santa Claus! Thank God he lives, and he lives forever. A thousand years from now, Virginia, nay, ten times ten thousand years from now, he will continue to make glad the heart of childhood.

GOLD, FRANKINCENSE AND MYRRH

by Donald Culross Peattie

Beneath the fragrant Christmas tree lie piled the gifts in their gay wrappings. Eager hands reach for them, and the children seize their own with innocent greediness. But in this first glow of the holy morning, before we tear at the bright papers and ribbons, let us pause to remember the meaning of presents on Christmas Day. It is very ancient, as old as the gospel itself. A Christmas gift symbolizes the love that Christians bear to one another, in the name of One who loved them all.

Wise men indeed were they that first intended this, and wise men were the first Christmas givers. Only in St. Matthew's Gospel do we read about them, and he tells it in this wise:

Now when Jesus was born in Bethlehem of Judaea in the days of Herod the king, behold, there came wise men from the east to Jerusalem, saying, Where is he that is born King of the Jews? for we have seen his star in the east, and are come to worship him.

Thus begins the second chapter of Matthew; and later the apostle adds:

When they saw the star, they rejoiced with exceeding great joy. And when they were come into the house, they saw the young child with Mary his mother, and fell down, and worshipped him: and when they had opened their treasures, they presented unto him gifts; gold, and frankincense, and myrrh.

How strangely scented and melodiously ringing are those three names! All the distant East, all the splendor of kings, the mystery that lies in things faraway and long ago, come to us in those syllables. Myrrh, and frankincense, and gold! Why were they chosen? Whence did they come? And what, in actuality, are they?

They are emblems of princely generosity, costly now as in ancient times, and still surviving at many a Christian altar. The Magi brought their best to the Newborn. They must have felt that nothing poor earth could offer to the King of Heaven would be more appropriate than gold. Well may we agree with them today, for gold is one of the noble metals. No single acid can destroy it, nor will it rust away, like iron or tin. As a consequence, it is almost never found as a compound, but in free nuggets or as dust, or alloyed with such metals as mercury or silver. No one can successfully imitate or fake gold, so heavy and incorruptible is it. And it is a metal easily turned to the uses of beauty. It has been woven into fabrics at least since Biblical times (Exodus 39:2-3), for its ductility, as chemists say, is so great that a single grain of fine gold may be drawn out into a wire 1/1000 of an inch in diameter, extending for a

length of about one mile. Pure, supple, almost indestructible, gold is indeed a royal metal among all the base ones.

The expert hammer of a goldbeater, whose ancient art is referred to by Homer, can beat an ounce of gold into a sheet two hundred feet square, a mere shimmering film. Ordinarily, such beaten gold is made into "books" containing twenty-five leaves apiece, each 3¼ inches square. When pure gold becomes this thin, it will transmit light almost like glass, but dimly, letting only the green rays through. With this gold the artist gilds his statue, the bookbinder stamps the title on his fine volume.

In the ancient world into which Christianity was born, gold was far rarer than now; the golden ornaments retrieved by archaeologists from graves in Troy or Crete or Egypt were royal or noble treasures exclusively. Not every wife, then, could wear a precious little band on her fourth finger. But as gold became a medium of exchange, it traveled the world. It came to Palestine from Egyptian Nubia, which we call the northern Sudan; also from the Midianites, who wandered through what is now central Jordan, south and east of the Dead Sea. Where did the Three Wise Men get it? As we are not sure where they themselves came from, we can but guess that — if they truly were "kings of Orient," as the old carol calls them — they may have brought their gold from the mines of Indian Mysore. In any case, it was in love and reverence that they offered to the Christ Child the most precious stuff the ancient world knew.

Since those same ancient days, also, many have believed that "incense owns a Deity nigh." No one knows who first lit incense to his God, but doubtless he who did it reasoned that, since all of us enjoy agreeable smells, God probably liked them too. So as times grew less savage and the rituals of worship more spiritualized, burning incense was substituted for the smoke of sacrificial flesh upon the altar. But that sweet reek was not common until the time of Jeremiah. After his day, it was made from an expensive and elaborate formula, containing sixteen different ingredients, with only priests allowed to concoct it. And the chief element in this holy recipe was frankincense, the second gift of the wise men to the Child.

Frankincense is a resin, from a kind of tree held so sacred of old that in southern Arabia and Ethiopia, where it grew, only a few particularly pure persons were allowed even to approach it. Legends told that the precious trees were guarded by winged serpents. All this makes the tree sound fabulous, but it does indeed exist in Nature, and botanists have named it. It belongs to the genus *Boswellia*, and is a member of the torchwood family. This means little to most of us, unless we happen to have seen the rare elephant trees that grow in the Gila and Imperial valleys in our own far Southwest — the only members of the family in the continental United States.

To conjure up a frankincense tree, think of a tree about fifteen feet high, with a patchy bark like a sycamore's. It is as crooked as a snake and all but leafless. The few leaves are compound, like those of an ash, and they sprout at the end of the crazy twigs. The flowers and fruit vaguely resemble a cherry's, although this tree is neither sycamore nor ash nor cherry; indeed, the scaly bark and contorted limbs remind one more of some archaic reptile than of the pleasant shady comfort that we call a tree.

To obtain the precious frankincense itself, an Arab cuts a slash in the trunk, as a Vermonter cuts a maple, and then strips off a narrow piece of bark, about five inches long, below the cut. The sap slowly oozes out and is allowed to harden for about three months. At last it is collected in lumps, to be shipped from such strange places as Berbera, Aden, and Bombay. These lumps are yellow or colorless, dusty-looking, with a bitter taste. But they burn with a bright white flame, and then there arises to heaven that sweet, heavy perfume of mystery the Wise Men thought pleasing to God.

This ritual of burning frankincense had been beloved of the Old Testament worshipers long before the night of the Star and the journey of the three wondering Magi toward it in the dark. But Christians did not adopt frankincense till five whole centuries after the Nativity. It is, however, approved for use in the New Testament. Today it finds a place chiefly in the Catholic Church, whose shrines are still full of its perfume. Incense today is compounded partly of the real frankincense and partly of the resin of a very different tree, the spruce fir of northern Europe. And nowadays the source of true frankincense is not so much Arabia and Ethiopia as the island of Socotra off Africa's eastern tip — a remote, mountainous, harborless island of stones and thorny thickets, where the frankincense trees are guarded by the subjects of an Arabian sultan.

From this same distant part of the world comes the last of the gifts of the Magi, myrrh, a shrub related to frankincense, of the genus *Commiphora*. The sap of myrrh is extracted in the same way as that of frankincense, and it comes in small lumps of reddish-brown resin. But its symbolism is more somber. The word myrrh comes from the Hebrew mar, meaning "bitter." The ancient Egyptians used this resin in embalming, and hence its connection with solemn occasions. Was this a strange gift for an Infant King? Not for one destined to die for his people.

Such were the first of all Christmas presents, birthday presents to the little Lord of Light. They were offered in a spirit of wondering humility and love. In all that we ourselves may give, gaily in the modern manner, may there linger too some sweet savor, some hidden glint, of the greater love that gives Christmas its real meaning!

WHERE DOES CHRISTMAS HAPPEN?

by Margaret Lee Runbeck

The house is full of it again. The streets are full of it, and shops and trees and churches all speak of it in different ways. Even strangers' faces are advertisements showing the transforming power of it. An old Montana friend of ours says, "Ever notice how much purtier people look around Christmas?" And then he goes on, "Even real mean people think about somebody else at Christmastime."

If there were nothing more to Christmas than each of us thinking about somebody else and trying to find some little object to express our affection, that would make it worth celebrating. But there is more to it. So very much more.

Christmas happens to us on three levels of experience: First, riding on the busy surface of the calendar, is the Christmas we're getting ready for right now. Next, we remember other Christmases, even more precious now than when they happened. And then, so still we may easily miss it, there is the deep private miracle that cannot be seen or shared or even made to come, for it is a divine event that can happen only in the heart.

The three levels of Christmas are like the three layers of our very selves: the physical, the mental, and the spiritual. We have the whole of Christmas, as we have the whole of ourselves, when we accept each layer, and love it, and make it rich in meaning.

The top-layer Christmas is the shimmering, exciting one, compounded of surprises and sentiment and rapturous nonsense. It has lists and recipes and timetables all twisted into it, plans scribbled, erased, and improved. We go about our daily business, and sometimes we even grumble over what a lot of work Christmas is. But underneath everything (even the grumbling and the work), we're wistful children, still believing in revised versions of Santa Claus. We know he doesn't exist, but we believe in him anyway, in one form or another. We know he's real because now we have found out that he is *us*, as recklessly generous as we dare to be, as flagrantly sentimental as we are.

So we believe in him, and we contract to pay his bills quite cheerfully through "January, February, June and July."

We have, in fact, two budgets — the long list of people we want to remember, and the short list of money we ought not to spend more than. When we talk about making both ends meet, we mean we're trying to fit the long budget of fondness within the short budget of funds. We know it can't be done, but it's fun trying; and it takes one into a realm of economics that boldly declares that loving is worth whatever you dare to spend on it.

And while you're running about, clicking off errands like a human taximeter, you're remembering other gifts and other Christmases: the gift from an original friend that provided your first painting lesson, then widened out to become a lifelong delight; the expensive wrist watch that *wasn't* an engagement ring; the lovely, lumpy homemade gifts your child creates each year. And the card your father always gave your mother, which said something like, "How could I give you anything now, when everything I have belongs to you?" — and the year she rebelled and announced two weeks before Christmas, "Will, I expect a piece of jewelry this year. No more highfalutin laziness out of you." (He looked shocked, and then burst out laughing and said, "By golly, you're right! You've found me out"; and the bracelet he gave her she never took off.)

You remember hundreds of Christmas moments, and you laugh to yourself, or weep with the dearness of them. You take this Christmas on the run, and you live a score of other Christmases while you shop and wrap and bake and bedeck until the whole house — and the whole heart — is filled with gaiety.

And with something else. *That* comes to you silently, without warning, as quiet as a star rising in the sky. You know the pattern well, the babe and the star, and the bright meaning shining down through the centuries. You know that the world began counting time from the rising of that star. And yet it cannot be said that the babe and the star happened only once; they happened millions of times, and will happen millions of times again as long as the world lasts.

For that star rises across the sky of a human heart, and that babe is born in a manger that only humility can know.

There are no mass-production miracles. They come intimately to one and to another until across the tired darkness of this world there is, *from within,* peace on earth, good will to men.

That is the miracle we famish for today. So let the star rise in you. Let the babe be born, not at the gaudy inn, but in the quiet manger of your heart. Never mind when; never mind how. Only welcome it, and let it happen.

INASMUCH

by Heywood Hale Broun

Once there lived near Bethlehem a man named Simon and his wife Deborah. And Deborah dreamed a curious dream, a dream so vivid that it might better be called a vision. It was not yet daybreak, but she roused her husband and told him that an angel had come to her in the vision and had said, as she remembered it, "Tomorrow night in Bethlehem the King of the World will be born." The rest was not so vivid in Deborah's mind, but she told Simon that wise men and kings were already on their way to Bethlehem, bringing gifts for the wonder child.

"When he is born," she said, "the wise men and the kings who bring these gifts will see the stars dance in the heavens and hear the voices of angels. You and I must send presents, too, for this child will be the greatest man in all the world."

Simon objected that there was nothing of enough value in the house to take to such a child, but Deborah replied, "The King of the World will understand." Then, although it was not yet light, she got up and began to bake a cake, and Simon went beyond the town to the hills to get holly and made a wreath. Later in the day husband and wife looked over all their belongings, but the only suitable gift they could find was an old toy, a somewhat battered wooden duck that had belonged to their eldest son, who had grown up and married and gone away to live in Galilee. Simon painted the toy duck as well as he could, and Deborah told him to take it and the cake and the

wreath of holly and go to Bethlehem. "It's not much," she said, "but the King will understand."

It was almost sunset when Simon started down the winding road that led to Bethlehem. Deborah watched him round the first turn and would have watched longer except that he was walking straight toward the sun and the light hurt her eyes. She went back into the house and an hour had hardly passed when she heard Simon whistling in the garden. He was walking very slowly. At the door he hesitated for almost a minute. She looked up when he came in. He was empty-handed.

"You haven't been to Bethlehem," said Deborah.

"No," said Simon.

"Then, where is the cake, and the holly wreath, and the toy duck?"

"I'm sorry," said Simon, "I couldn't help it somehow. It just happened."

"What happened?" asked Deborah sharply.

"Well," said Simon, "just after I went around the first turn in the road I found a child sitting on that big white rock, crying. He was about two or three years old, and I stopped and asked him why he was crying. He didn't answer. Then I told him not to cry like that, and I patted his head, but that didn't do any good. I hung around, trying to think up something, and I decided to put the cake down and take him up in my arms for a minute. But the cake slipped out of my hands and hit the rock, and a piece of the icing chipped off. Well, I thought, that baby in Bethlehem won't miss a little piece of icing, and I gave it to the child and he stopped crying. But when he finished he began to cry again. I just sort of squeezed another little piece of icing off, and that was all right, for a little while; but then I had to give him another piece, and things went on that way, and all of a sudden I found that there wasn't any cake left. After that he looked as if he might cry again, and I didn't have any more cake and so I showed him the duck and he said 'Ta-ta.' I just meant to lend him the duck for a minute, but he wouldn't give it up. I coaxed him a good while, but he wouldn't let go. And then a woman came out of that little house and she began to scold him for staying out so late, and I told her it was my fault and I gave her the holly wreath just so she wouldn't be mad at the child. And after that, you see, I didn't have anything to take to Bethlehem, and so I came back here."

Deborah had begun to cry before Simon finished his story, but when he had done she lifted up her head and said, "How could you do it, Simon? Those presents were meant for the King of the World, and you gave them to the first crying child you met on the road."

Then she began to cry again, and Simon didn't know what to say or do, and it grew darker in the room and the fire on the hearth faded to a few embers. And that little red glow was all there was in the room. Now, Simon could not even see Deborah across the room, but he could still hear her sobbing. But suddenly the room was flooded with light and Deborah's sobbing broke into a great gulp and she rushed to the window and looked out. The stars danced in the sky and from high above the house came the voice of angels saying, "Glory to God in the highest, and on earth peace, good will toward men."

Deborah dropped to her knees in a panic of joy and fear. Simon knelt beside her, but first he said, "I thought maybe that the baby in Bethlehem wouldn't mind so very much."

CHRISTMAS WITHOUT PRICE

by Victoria Lincoln

Is there anything in the world more delightful than being able to give someone you love a thing he's wanted for a long time? Something ridiculously expensive, perhaps, or ridiculously hard to find? The construction set that Jimmy broods about; not the one almost as good, but the one that would knock a horse's eye out. The shaving mug (and why, in a world of brushless creams and electric razors should it be

your husband who loves and uses his grandfather's shaving mug and then breaks it?); the mug that you've tracked hopelessly through countless antique stores, and suddenly come upon, sitting in a junk-store window, white ironstone, unchipped, price fifty cents.

It feels wonderful, doesn't it? But you only found that mug by an outside chance. And our expenses have such an astounding way of keeping one jump ahead of our incomes.

"But he's been so good, Dave. And he wants it so much."

"You know we can't afford it."

"I know."

Though you both probably go right ahead anyway, and I'm glad you do. Even though January bills get a peculiarly unpleasant look by the first of March. Oh, if everybody had a Fortunatus' purse, what a Christmas it would be!

Or would it? On the December twenty-sixth when all the cleaning women came to work in mink coats, would it be only snobbery that created that run on Harris tweeds?

I think not. For a gift of value is purchased at expense, whether of money or effort or taste or imagination. The little engagement ring that cost a young lover's vacation and the diamond bracelet that demonstrates a smart girl's hold on a gentleman's checkbook are both valued for something beyond themselves; and something that the possessor recognizes as hard to get.

For the delight of both giving and receiving is bound up with the fact that we are somehow, for good or ill, for motives of love or of power, giving ourselves; receiving each other. And without that delight any gift becomes as meaningless as those interoffice presents that the big executive commonly turns over to the care of his secretary.

But anyway, there never was a Fortunatus' purse. If your husband really has his heart set on that springer pup whose bloodlines go back some two hundred years, you can either pull yourself together and be sensible, or shoot the works, glory in Christmas morning, and pin your ears back for the first of March.

And still, in spite of that, you have it in your power to give everyone you love the present he wants most.

And of course you know it already, so that I would feel pompous and silly pointing it out to you, if it weren't that so much of the excitement of our great voyage of discovery through life is simply the firsthand rediscovery, the sudden leaping into life, of familiar platitudes. You know it, and I have known it, too, for a long time; but now that the year is coming on for Christmas, I suddenly discover it in a new way. And I want to share the richness with you; the joy of giving our dearests, each one of them, the present they want most.

Yes, he wants the springer pup, too, and it would be dishonest nonsense to deny it; I hope, I do hope, he will get it. But no matter how you have to decide on that score, you can still give a bounty.

For your purse is the open heart.

What do we want most, all of us? We want to be loved, not blindly or for an illusion that we have to scheme and struggle to maintain, "He'd be so nice, except . . ."

Yes, there it is, the chief lock upon our heart's purse. We have lost the disposition to be pleased. I don't mean the disposition to be a Pollyanna. The disposition to be pleased is no enemy to the honest mind. It is only a courteous direction of attention to the gifts of living which we have fallen into so ungrateful a habit of taking for granted.

What is the open heart? It is the heart that knows how to receive as well as to give. It is the heart that opens its presents from life with grateful attention, and then goes on to put its pleasure into words. That is important: into words, the actual, spoken words which are the chief human instrument by which we are truly made very members of one another.

Who could sit under the tree on Christmas morning, unwrapping her presents without a word, or letting them lie unwrapped at her feet while she talked about the bad weather and that discourteous checker at the supermarket? Who, indeed! And isn't that why Christmas morning is so loved, so anticipated?

For the children the material fact of the presents is still the big thing, yes; but for them the chief lessons of joy are yet to be learned. Don't envy them; childhood is a more narrow time than we remember. For us, the big ones, Christmas morning is wonderful because it is an island in the year when we are all paying attention to delight; an island when we are, for once, all receiving from one another with active, open, spoken affection and appreciation. Yes, for that little time out of the year, at least, everyone is giving everyone else the present he wants most; the present of attention, of admiring pleasure, of warm, outspoken love.

Does it have to be an island? Are we condemned for the rest of the year to turn our attention so promptly to the fog, this discourteous checker, the galoshes on the hall floor; and to unwrap so slowly, so grudgingly the . . . well, yes, I'm going to use a phrase that you will think is sentimental and old-fashioned . . . the day's blessings?

Watch their faces now, this Christmas morning. Don't you see what you are giving them? What a bounty if we were to go on giving it from this Christmas to the next! A bounty beyond Fortunatus' purse; for it is one that the whole world could give without ever making it common.

And it is within the purchasing power of us all.

You love them already; that is the great down payment that can't be faked. Anyone can smell out the hypocritical praise, the false warmth that comes from the desire to get something in return; and don't you let either the cynical or the pseudo-religious boys tell you otherwise. But you have the love; even on the days when you're too hurried and worried to remember it, it is there, waiting to be used. Your first down payment is made.

Only remember: this is a present that cannot be bought for cash down. Even for the saints, the great gifts of the heart are only to be had on the purchase plan, payments due daily, sometimes hourly. And the bank won't send you a reminder.

But don't be discouraged. The remembering

is all that will come hard, even at first. Once remembered, the installments are easy to meet. For they take only a deliberate turn of the head, and a few words.

A turn of the head in the direction of Jimmy's smile, not Jimmy's galoshes (oh, you've got to see them, too, but afterwards, afterwards). Or at Dave's beautiful honesty, not his tactlessness. Or even — little things and big are part of life's pattern — at Sue's nice hat and not the way she lets her heels get run over.

And then, right in that moment of attention, speak out. Don't be afraid of embarrassing casual friends; don't take it for granted that your nearest and dearest understand without words. If your first essential down payment is made, if your perception is honest, whether it is of a grace of spirit or of a becoming dress, nobody will be put off. They'll be too warmed, and glad, and grateful, opening their present. And no love, from the lightest to the deepest, was given to us to be taken for granted. Why does a girl read and reread the closing phrases of a boy's clumsy letter? Why did David write his Psalms?

The open heart sees, and it speaks. Love isn't a duty, a call to self-immolation. Love is delight in the beloved, and in the beloved's delight. Blessed are they who receive with delight, children, for they shall give the greatest gift.

We'll forget, sometimes, at first. But we'll get better at remembering as we go on. And what a present it will be! Come to think of it, why do we wait for Christmas morning? I feel rich, don't you?

AMAHL AND THE NIGHT VISITORS

by Gian-Carlo Menotti

Cast of characters:
    AMAHL — *a lame shepherd boy*
    HIS MOTHER
    KASPAR — *king bringing incense*
    BALTHAZAR — *king bringing myrrh*
    MELCHIOR — *king bringing gold*
    PAGE — *the kings' attendant*
    SHEPHERD AND SHEPHERDESS

(The curtain rises. It is night. The crystal-clear winter sky is dotted with stars, the Eastern Star flaming amongst them. Outside the cottage Amahl is playing his shepherd's pipe. Within, the Mother calls.)

MOTHER: Amahl! Amahl! Time to go to bed.

AMAHL: Coming! *(Amahl does not stir.)*

MOTHER: Amahl! How long must I shout to make you obey?

AMAHL: Oh, very well. *(Amahl takes up his crutch and hobbles into the house.)*

MOTHER: What was keeping you outside?

AMAHL: Oh, Mother, you should go out and see! There's never been such a sky! Hanging over our roof there is a star as large as a window, and the star has a tail and it moves across the sky like a chariot on fire.

MOTHER: Oh! Amahl, when will you stop telling lies? All day long you wander about in a dream. Here we are with nothing to eat, not a stick of wood on the fire, not a drop of oil in the jug, and all you do is to worry your mother with fairy tales.

AMAHL: Mother, I'm not lying. Please do believe me. Come and see for yourself.

MOTHER: Why should I believe you? You come with a new one every day!

AMAHL: But there is a star and it has a long tail.

MOTHER: Amahl!

AMAHL: Cross my heart and hope to die.

MOTHER: Poor Amahl! Hunger has gone to your head. Unless we go begging how shall we live through tomorrow? My little son, a beggar! *(She weeps.)*

AMAHL: *(Amahl goes to her.)* Don't cry, Mother, don't worry for me. If we must go begging, a good beggar I'll be. I know sweet tunes to set people dancing. We'll walk and walk from village to town, you dressed as a gypsy and I as a clown. At noon we shall eat roast goose and sweet almonds, at night we shall sleep with the sheep and the stars. I'll play my pipes, you'll sing and you'll shout. The windows will open and people will lean out.

The King will ride by and hear your loud voice and throw us some gold to stop all the noise.

MOTHER: My dreamer, good night! You're wasting the light. Kiss me good night.

AMAHL: Good night. *(Amahl goes to his pallet of straw at one side of the fireplace. The Mother secures the door, then lies down to sleep. The lights die from the room except for a faint glow through the window.)*

KASPAR, MELCHIOR, BALTHAZAR: *(The voices of the Three Kings are heard very far away.)* From far away we come and farther we must go. How far, how far, my crystal star? *(Amahl listens with astonishment to the distant singing.)* Frozen the incense in our frozen hands, heavy the gold. How far, how far, my crystal star?

(Leaning on his crutch, Amahl hobbles over to the window. Outside appear the Three Kings: first Melchior bearing the coffer of gold, then Balthazar bearing the chalice of myrrh, and finally Kaspar bearing the urn of incense. All are preceded by the Page, carrying a rich Oriental rug, and an elaborate jeweled box.)

KASPAR, MELCHIOR, BALTHAZAR: How far, how far, my crystal star? *(The travelers approach the door of the cottage and King Melchior knocks upon the door.)*

MOTHER: Amahl! Go and see who's knocking at the door.

AMAHL: *(Amahl goes to the door.)* Mother, Mother, Mother, come with me. Outside the door there is a King with a crown.

MOTHER: What shall I do with this boy? If you don't learn to tell the truth, I'll have to spank you!

AMAHL: Mother, Mother, Mother. Come with me. If I tell you the truth, I know you won't believe me.

MOTHER: Try it for a change!

AMAHL: But you won't believe me.

MOTHER: I'll believe you if you tell me the truth.

AMAHL: The Kings are three and one of them is black.

MOTHER: Oh! What shall I do with this boy?

I'm going to the door myself and then, young man, you'll have to reckon with me! *(The Mother moves to the door. As it swings open, she beholds the Three Kings. In utter amazement, she bows to them.)*

KASPAR, MELCHIOR, BALTHAZAR: Good evening! Good evening!

BALTHAZAR: May we rest a while in your house and warm ourselves by your fire?

MOTHER: I am a poor widow. A cold fireplace and a bed of straw are all I have to offer you. To these you are welcome.

KASPAR: Oh, thank you!

MOTHER: Come in! Come in!

(The Mother makes way for the Kings to enter first. The Page enters first. Almost immediately King Kaspar proceeds at a stately march to one side of the fireplace. Balthazar enters and proceeds to a place beside him. Melchior is the last to take his place. Amahl watches the procession with growing wonder and excitement.)

MELCHIOR: It is nice here.

MOTHER: I shall go and gather wood for the fire. *(The Mother goes to the door.)*

MELCHIOR: We can only stay a little while. We must not lose sight of our star.

MOTHER: Your star?

MELCHIOR: We still have a long way to go.

MOTHER: I shall be right back.

AMAHL: *(The moment his mother is gone, Amahl goes to Balthazar.)* Are you a real King?

BALTHAZAR: Yes.

AMAHL: Where is your home?

BALTHAZAR: I live in a black marble palace full of black panthers and white doves. And you, little boy, what do you do?

AMAHL: I was a shepherd; I had a flock of sheep. But my mother sold them. I had a black goat who gave me warm sweet milk. But she died of old age. But Mother says that now we shall both go begging from door to door. Won't it be fun?

BALTHAZAR: It has its points.

AMAHL: *(Pointing at the jeweled box)* And what is this?

KASPAR: This is my box. I never travel without it. In the first drawer, I keep my magic stones. One carnelian against all evil and envy. One moonstone to make you sleep. One red coral to heal your wounds. One lapis lazuli against quartern fever. One small jasper to help you find water. One small topaz to soothe your eyes. One red ruby to protect you from lightning. In the second drawer I keep my beads. Oh, how I love to play with all kinds of beads. In the third drawer, I keep licorice — black, sweet licorice. Have some. (*Amahl reaches for the candy as his mother enters, bearing a few sticks.*)

MOTHER: Amahl, I told you not to be a nuisance.

AMAHL: But it isn't my fault! They kept asking me questions.

MOTHER: I want you to go and call the other shepherds. Tell them about our visitors and ask them to bring whatever they have in the house, as we have nothing to offer them. Hurry on!

AMAHL: Yes, Mother. (*Amahl hurries out as fast as his crutch will carry him.*)

MOTHER: (*The Mother crosses to the fireplace. Suddenly she sees the coffer of gold and the rich chalices of incense and myrrh.*) Oh, these beautiful things, and all that gold!

MELCHIOR: These are the gifts to the Child.

MOTHER: The child? Which child?

MELCHIOR: We don't know. But the Star will guide us to Him.

MOTHER: But perhaps I know him.

MELCHIOR: Have you seen a child the color of wheat, the color of dawn? His eyes are mild, His hands are those of a King, as King He was born. Incense, myrrh and gold we bring to His side, and the Eastern Star is our guide.

MOTHER: Yes, I know a child the color of wheat, the color of dawn. His eyes are mild, his hands are those of a King, as King he was born. But no one will bring him incense or gold, though sick and poor and hungry and cold. He's my child, my son, my darling, my own.

MELCHIOR, BALTHAZAR: Have you seen a Child the color of earth, the color of thorn? His eyes are sad, His hands are those of the poor, as poor He was born.

MOTHER: Yes, I know a child the color of earth, the color of thorn. His eyes are sad, his hands are those of the poor, as poor he was born. He's my child, my son, my darling, my own.

MELCHIOR: The Child we seek holds the seas and the winds on His palm.

KASPAR: The Child we seek has the moon and the stars at His feet.

BALTHAZAR: Before Him the eagle is gentle, the lion is meek.

KASPAR, MELCHIOR, BALTHAZAR: Choirs of angels hover over His roof and sing Him to sleep. He's fed by a Mother who is both Virgin and Queen. Incense, myrrh and gold we bring to His side, and the Eastern Star is our guide.

MOTHER: The child I know on his palm holds my heart. The child I know at his feet has my life. He's my child, my son, my darling, my own, and his name is Amahl!

MOTHER: (*The call of the shepherds falls sharp and clear on the air.*) The shepherds are coming!

SHEPHERDS: All the flocks are asleep. We are going with Amahl, bringing gifts to the Kings. (*The shepherds stop in the door, struck dumb by the sight of the Kings. Amahl, however, slips in to take his place beside his mother.*)

SHEPHERDS: Oh, look! Oh, look!

MOTHER: Come in, come in! What are you afraid of? Show what you brought them.

SHEPHERD: (*The shepherd boldly marches forward and lays his gift before the Kings, then, bowing shyly, he retreats to his place.*) Olives and quinces, apples and raisins, nutmeg and myrtle, medlars and chestnuts, this is all we shepherds can offer you.

KASPAR, MELCHIOR, BALTHAZAR: Thank you kindly.

SHEPHERD: Citrons and lemons, musk and pomegranates, goat cheese and walnuts, figs and cucumbers, this is all we shepherds can offer you.

KASPAR, MELCHIOR, BALTHAZAR: Thank you kindly.

SHEPHERDS: Take them, eat them, you are welcome.

BALTHAZAR: (*Balthazar rises.*) Thank you, good friends. But now we must bid you good night.

We have little time for sleep and a long journey ahead.

SHEPHERDS: *(The shepherds pass before the Kings, bowing as they depart.)* Good night, my good Kings, good night and farewell. The pale stars foretell that dawn is in sight. The night winds foretell the day will be bright. *(Having closed the door, Amahl and his mother bid the Kings good night. While the Mother prepares herself a pallet of sheepskins on the floor, Amahl seizes his opportunity to speak to King Kaspar.)*

AMAHL: Excuse me, sir. Amongst your magic stones is there . . . is there one that could cure a crippled boy? *(Kaspar does not answer. Amahl goes sadly to his pallet.)* Never mind. Good night . . . *(The Mother and Amahl have lain down. The Kings are still sitting on the rude bench. They settle themselves to sleep leaning against each other. The Page lies at their feet, beside the rich gifts.)*

MOTHER: *(The Mother cannot take her eyes from the treasure guarded by the Page.)* All that gold! I wonder if rich people know what to do with their gold! Do they know that a house can be kept warm all day with burning logs? All that gold! Oh, what I could do for my child with that gold! Why should it all go to a child they don't even know? They are asleep. Do I dare? If I take some they will never miss it. They won't miss it. *(Slowly she creeps across the floor.)* For my child . . . for my child. *(As the Mother touches the gold, the Page is aroused. He seizes her arm, crying out.)*

PAGE: Thief! Thief!

MELCHIOR: What is it?

PAGE: I've seen her steal some of the gold. She's a thief! Don't let her go. She's stolen the gold!

KASPAR, MELCHIOR, BALTHAZAR: Shame!

PAGE: Give it back or I'll tear it from you!

KASPAR, MELCHIOR, BALTHAZAR: Give it back! Give it back!

AMAHL: *(Amahl awakens. When he sees his mother in the hands of the Page, he helps himself up with his crutch and awkwardly hurls himself upon the Page.)* Don't you dare! Don't you dare, ugly man, hurt my mother! I'll smash in your face! I'll knock out your teeth! *(Rushing to King Kaspar)* Oh, Mister King, don't let him hurt my mother! My mother is good. She cannot do anything wrong. I'm the one who lies, I'm the one who steals! *(At a sign from Kaspar, the Page releases the Mother. Amahl staggers toward her, sobbing.)*

MELCHIOR: Oh, woman, you may keep the gold. The Child we seek doesn't need our gold. On love, on love alone, He will build His Kingdom. His pierced hand will hold no scepter. His haloed head will wear no crown. His might will not be built on your toil. Swifter than lightning He will soon walk among us. He will bring us new life and receive our death, and the keys of His city belong to the poor. *(Turning to the other Kings)* Let us leave, my friends.

MOTHER: *(Freeing herself from Amahl's embrace, the Mother rushes after the Kings.)* Oh, no, wait. Take back your gold! For such a King I've waited all my life. And if I weren't so poor I would send a gift of my own to such a child.

AMAHL: But, Mother, let me send him my crutch. Who knows, he may need one and this I made myself. *(The Mother moves to stop him as he starts to raise the crutch. Amahl lifts the crutch. He takes one step toward the Kings, then realizes he has moved without the help of his crutch.)*

MOTHER: But you can't, you can't!

AMAHL: I walk, Mother. I walk, Mother!

BALTHAZAR, MELCHIOR, KASPAR: He walks!

MOTHER: He walks, he walks, he walks!

KASPAR, MELCHIOR, BALTHAZAR: He walks! It is a sign from the Holy Child. We must give praise to the newborn King. We must praise Him. This is a sign from God. *(Having placed the crutch in the outstretched hands of the King Kaspar, Amahl moves uncertainly. With growing confidence, Amahl begins to jump and caper about the room.)*

AMAHL: Look, Mother, I can dance, I can jump, I can run! *(Amahl stumbles.)*

MOTHER: *(She lifts Amahl from the floor.)* Please, my darling, be careful now. You must take care not to hurt yourself.

MELCHIOR, BALTHAZAR: Oh, good woman, you must not be afraid. For he is loved by the Son of God. Oh, blessed child, may I touch you? *(One by one, the Kings pass before Amahl and lay their hands upon him. Then each with his gift to the Child begins to depart.)*

AMAHL: Oh, Mother, let me go with the Kings! I want to take the crutch to the Child myself.

KASPAR, MELCHIOR, BALTHAZAR: Yes, good woman, let him come with us! We'll take good care of him, we'll bring him back on a camel's back.

MOTHER: Do you really want to go?

AMAHL: Yes, Mother.

MOTHER: Yes, I think you should go, and bring thanks to the Child yourself. What can you do with your crutch?

AMAHL: You can tie it to my back.

MOTHER: So, my darling, goodbye! I shall miss you very much. Wash your ears!

AMAHL: Yes, I promise.

MOTHER: Don't tell lies!

AMAHL: No, I promise.

MOTHER: I shall miss you very much.

AMAHL: I shall miss you very much.

MELCHIOR: Are you ready?

AMAHL: Yes, I'm ready.

MELCHIOR: Let's go then.

SHEPHERDS: Come, oh, come outside. All the stars have left the sky. Oh, sweet dawn, oh, dawn of peace. *(Led by the Page, the Three Kings start their stately procession out of the cottage. Amahl rushes to his mother, bidding her goodbye, then hurries to catch up with the Kings. Amahl begins to play his pipes as he goes. Outside dawn is brightening the sky. The Mother stands alone in the doorway of the cottage, waving to Amahl. The curtain falls very slowly.)*

2

Gifts

THE HAPPY ART OF CHRISTMAS GIVING

by Dorothy Wilson

GIVE *yourself* at Christmas; there really is no more wonderful gift. Out of the pretty box you give can fly all sorts of rare intangibles, once the ribbon is off and the lid is lifted. Affection, nostalgia, laughter, shared memories — all these can crackle in the tissue paper along with grace and generosity. *I was watching,* a gift can say: last summer I could see you needed a better tennis racket. *I was listening,* a gift can tell: I heard you say you liked old cars . . . or Beethoven . . . or adventure stories. A gift can remember something delicious that once happened, and a gift can speculate: *I am aware,* it can imply, that you wear simple dresses, but here's one astounding ruffled nightgown; I think you have a bit of ruffle hidden in you somewhere. A gift can make promises for the future: the first five books for a boy's library, with a thousand bookplates; the first silver spoon for a teen-ager's hope chest.

Perhaps the art lies in the word itself. To "exchange gifts" at Christmas is an expression we might well drop into the sea. *Exchange* smacks of barter; *giving* smacks of love. Give usefully and generously, yes, but give hyacinths as well as biscuits. Give fun: laughter is beyond price. Open up a door on the world, for a child. Polish up the existing landscape a little, for an adult. Give courage, or leisure; give intimate-

ly. A gift can show that you honor someone's achievements, or his heart's desire. Stimulation is far better than a box of socks.

The art is to put into every package more than the gift itself. We should think to ourselves that *any* gift will rattle around in *any* box unless the box is stuffed with human values, with joy and smiles and loving-kindness. Put yourself in every Christmas package.

CHRISTMAS COMES BUT HALF THE YEAR

Stretch your Christmas shopping out a bit: if you see something in September that's just right for somebody, buy it or order it; Christmas will always come along, every year.

Keep your eyes open all during the year, during sales, off-seasons, general shopping, for the odd, delightful, pertinent gifts that are so meaningful at Christmas; buy them, tag them, and store them away.

When you travel during the year, anywhere, buy for Christmas gifts as well as for souvenirs.

Think well in advance of the gifts that take a whole year to accomplish: a year's collection of the college newspaper for a son at an Army camp; pictures taken the same day of every month of the new baby, for grandparents far away, to be given in an album.

Have a notebook or card index to jot down hints during the year of things that other people would like; be alert to the wishes expressed idly by your family and friends.

Well ahead of the holiday make whatever discreet inquiries are necessary about size or taste, etc.

Mark a calendar for the days when materials for fruitcake, etc. need to be purchased; have some foolproof reminder for whatever takes many weeks before Christmas to do.

Investigate Christmas Clubs, and decide whether they suit your family's buying and spending habits.

GIVING TO CHILDREN

Consciously take notes during the year; many a real desire is forgotten or overlooked by the child in the dazzle of Christmas stores.

Take the children with you, once, early in the shopping season, to the biggest store in your city; say that it is *not* a trip to buy, and stick to it. Let it be just for looking, and allow time for the children to see and think about everything they see.

For very young children, do not buy for Christmas a gift that is out of season; a fishing rod he longed for at the beach last August will have little meaning for the very small boy when he sees it under the tree at Christmastime.

Avoid at all costs the gift a child is not yet ready for; a stamp album given half a year too soon may set up boredom where a little later a lasting interest might have developed.

Wrap everything. Wrap lots of little presents, too, and disguise packages that might be obvious. Under no circumstances tease the child by withholding the one present he has counted most on, if you have bought it for him.

If there is not time to set up a complicated toy on Christmas morning, put it away some-

where safely until that can be done; many a fine gift does not survive the early hours, and pieces are stepped on or thrown away accidentally, and directions are lost.

If there are children of different ages, take pains to protect all their gifts from each other's ravages, and to protect the younger children from harm.

Try to include in every child's Christmas a gift for the day itself, such as a Christmas book to be read or a record to be played.

GIVE A CHILD A COLLECTION
OF RELATED GIFTS

Turn a child into a magician. Find an inexpensive folding tray (or paint one that you already own) to serve as the magician's table; add a big scarf, to confound his audience; and then get as many little tricks and jokes from the novelty store as you can. If you include a top hat (from the party hat counter), the illusion will be complete and the child will be delighted.

Let a little girl become a model. Starting with a paper or plastic hatbox, fill it as full as you can with feminine nonsense for dressing up. It will not matter whether things are old or new, but include if you can feathers, flowers, veils, scarves, and big pins, a fake chignon (made of inexpensive fiber), red candy lipstick, a pretty fan, strings of beads — anything you have or can think of to dress a little girl up as ornately as her heart desires. Even the little girl who lives in dungarees will surprise you with her delight.

Set a little boy on the track of pirate treasure. If the weather at Christmas is anything short of deep snow, bury the treasure; otherwise, hide it above ground somewhere. Make as detailed a map as you can and present it at Christmas; have an actual treasure buried or hidden where the map shows it will be. Start with a metal candy or cookie box (or anything that will suggest a chest) and inside the box have gold-wrapped candy coins, or a hundred shiny pennies, or bunches of glass jewels and pearls and rhinestones pried out from broken jewelry — or all of these.

Save, for a little girl, every bit of glitter, sequins, and unset stones and pearls that you can accumulate; dazzle her with the possibilities of making beautiful fashions at home. Take the trim from dresses, hats, and bags before you discard them; save one-of-a-kind earrings; and add as much as you can find of gilt and decoration from notion counters (fringe and tassels are wonderful). Include all these, plus the right glue and big needle and thread, with a bright red apron for the little girl to decorate, or a doll's evening coat, or a square of felt for a banner that will sparkle on her wall at night.

Pick up, during the summer, all the sea shells you can find. Give them at Christmas to a boy or girl, along with several empty, partitioned boxes (from candy, for instance) into which the child can place the shells when they are identified; include a book describing shells. Send along the right glue, and, if the child is quite young, include the typewritten tags he will need to paste under each shell. Be sure to give him more spaces in the boxes than there are shells, to make it clear that he is just at the beginning of a collection that he can continue himself.

Collect stones in much the same way, or buy a beginner's collection in a hobby store. Include a book, some unidentified stones, and spare boxes, glue, and tags.

Give a child an entire assortment of letter writing materials; paper and envelopes with his name imprinted, stick-on tags with his name imprinted, ball-point pens in different colors, a booklet of stamps and a small address book. Include a book on letter-writing and, for the older child, perhaps a sealing-wax kit with a seal.

Make a boy a private detective, with many disguises. Almost anything that suits your fancy and would serve as a disguise will do. Start with the standard fake mustaches and beards in novelty stores and add things from party counters — silly noses, rubber masks, funny hats, crazy glasses with the eyes painted on the lenses, caps and hats with hair attached, masks

for the eyes. Add to all this whatever you might have in the house, such as empty eyeglass frames, slouchy caps, old raincoats, gloves, an inexpensive magnifying glass, an old fedora.

Give a city child a "green thumb" collection. There are all sorts of things in the stores today that grow almost magically fast: little pieces of log that sprout quickly, beans that grow beanstalks inches in days, flowers that bloom overnight in water, "stones" that unfurl in glass jars in all the prettiest colors. For the city child especially (but also for any child in the very middle of winter) all this sprouting and blooming is the greatest fun, and happens quickly enough to suit the most impatient little gardener. It would be nice, too, to include some narcissus bulbs in stones in a bowl. This will convince him there are ordinary flowers that grow too, as well as chemical miracles. With whatever you select, however, include a metal watering can, the proper pots and jars, and perhaps some gardener's gloves.

If a child you know has started some disordered collection of any of the odd things children seem to like to gather, give him a dignified apparatus for it. Beginning with an album or notebook of sufficient size and durability, arrange a way for him to keep his baseball cards, or bottle tops, or matchbook covers. Give him supply tags, glue, an impressive title or introduction, an inexpensive magnifying glass if it seems suitable to the collection and, of course, if you can, add a batch of objects for the collection itself.

If you know the child has his first camera, give him all the paraphernalia for making and keeping a photographic album. (It seems surprising how seldom this is included at the time the camera is given.) A very inexpensive album can be made handsome if covered with wallpaper and shellacked. Present the album, extra sheets of black paper or pliofilm, all the necessary tags and corners and hinges and, by all means, the proper glue, since the wrong kind can seep through the picture itself. A beginning book on photography included with this album would start the child off well on what might be a joyous, lifelong hobby.

MAKE A CHILD FEEL VERY GROWN UP

Give a very little boy his first wallet, stuffed with a million dollars' worth of play money. If you fill out the identification card in the glass window with his own particulars, and even enclose a picture of his mother and father, he will feel practically old enough to vote, even if he's only three.

A little girl will love her first real package of bubble baths; these come in brilliant, colored, jewel-like discs, very attractively packaged and very grown-up for a girl just big enough to take a bath by herself.

A strongbox in which a little boy or girl can keep all sorts of desperately private objects is a wonderful gift. Paint the child's name on it with nail polish — perhaps with the warning KEEP OUT: PRIVATE — and deliver the key that comes with it on a long chain or string. (Note: these boxes generally come with two keys; better give the second key to the child's mother for safekeeping, since even on a long string keys somehow get lost now and then.)

A small girl would love her first manicure set. These sets come in little kits with colorless polish and with all the necessary gadgets. You might also include cotton squares and a form for holding her hand steady as she dabs.

A child's first address book is a novel idea to him, usually. Fill it out as completely as you can beforehand with the names of all his relatives and friends, his school address, his doctor's telephone number, his church and pastor, his dentist. Most children are wonderfully impressed to see that they have such a wide and complicated social life. (Note: a set of two such books, one for the child's desk at home and a small one for his pocket or her pocketbook, will make a child feel more than ever like an individual of affairs.)

Both boys and girls like rubber stamps made with their name and address, or their name and their school address and room number. A red ink pad as well as a black one, and perhaps ten or twenty little scratch pads in assorted colors, make a bulky, welcome package. (Note: stationers and office supply houses take orders for rubber stamps, and any kind of legend can be made up — nicknames, jokes, or straightforward information.)

As flashy a flashlight as you can manage is always a particularly welcome gift for a boy; the more switches, gadgets, hooks, etc., the better. (Note: of course fill it with batteries, and perhaps include the first refills.)

For the child who has learned to tell time, an inexpensive alarm clock for his own room is a gift he receives with grown-up pleasure. Even if he doesn't always set it (and doesn't always want to get up when it rings) he nevertheless considers it a great forward step in his life and will wind it and be proud of it. (Note: it seems that few children, even though they might have a wristwatch, have a clock in their bedrooms.)

For the child advancing into the years when he has homework, a fine gift is an efficient, workmanlike pencil sharpener for his own room. A child accepts it as a token of confidence in the importance of his work, and it is truly handy; most children by this age have experienced all the frustrations of the tiny, plastic sharpeners that sell for a nickel or so and are rather messy and only moderately good at the job. A good solid sharpener that screws to the wall or the desk is a joy.

For the boy at an age when he suddenly decides life is a busy matter, give a kit that will make him feel as important as the foreman of an engineering gang. A clip board, a ream of paper, carbon paper (which children love to use), two dozen pencils, a box of clips, an inexpensive stapler and a box of staples, a paper punch, calipers — anything, in short, which will allow a little boy to emulate his Daddy and carry on the world's work.

Although toy carpentry kits have their usefulness for very young children, you will make a man of the boy to whom you give his own real tool chest. Give a big, empty chest, and just start to fill in the contents for him; a folding rule, boxes of nails and screws, a screw driver, sandpaper, a C-clamp, bolts and nuts, and a couple of wrenches that fit them. These should not be toys, but standard hardware tools (although perhaps small and light versions of them if the boy is small), which can be the beginning of a respect for, and interest in, tools that will carry through the years.

RIGHT TOYS, WRONG TOYS

Everyone loves to give toys to children, and children certainly love to receive them. The Christmas tree looks rather sedate, and not so magical, when everyone in the family has grown up enough to have presents only in neat boxes. Toys can be wonderful; nevertheless, thought should be given to their selection.

Giving the biggest teddy bear you could find, or the fanciest doll you could afford, is not the whole story. A wagon, for instance, that's too big, may spell absolute frustration for a boy who wants to dominate and manage it. One that's too small will show him that you think he's still a baby. Try to determine his current need; does he want to carry blocks in it? or his sister? Does he perhaps want only to be pulled in it? Is he old enough to scoot down the street, steering, and pumping with one leg? Serve his present interests, and perhaps those he will very soon grow into. If, in the interest of practicality, everything is bought too large (to last for years ahead), a child may well get discouraged in grappling with toys that tax him and thwart him.

Of course, be conscious of safety. Check for smooth edges, on wood as well as metal. Any toy that must bear weight should be sturdily constructed; on the other hand, watch out for toys so substantial that, in tipping or falling, they might hurt a child. The lid of a toy chest, for example, should not be made of wood unless there is some safeguard to prevent smashed fingers. All toys should be painted with non-toxic paint, even things that are larger than bite-size, and therefore might seem unsuitable for chewing. Use discretion in buying toys with small pieces if there's a baby in the house who might swallow them. If you give an electrical gadget, check to see if the wiring is approved, and be very certain that the child is old enough to recognize the power of electricity and behave accordingly.

By all means get together with relatives and friends about what toys to give to children. It's more than all right to suggest the very thing your child would like. This will stop the flow of similar games and oddments, which mean very little, and will save the hurt Grandma will feel if her tiny, china tea set (which she herself loved), goes untouched and unappreciated.

Let it be known if you feel strongly about certain kinds of toys. If you would rather your three-year-old did *not* receive six-shooters, say so. Guns and other weapons for small fry cause uneasiness among many parents; if you yourself give them, be sure that they will be welcome in the family's scheme of things. Some gifts for little girls, also, are thought to be rather worldly, so be certain you're right if you decide to give your five-year-old niece an imitation mink stole.

Give toys that a child can handle by himself, or with another child. Any toy so expensive or complicated that it requires an adult to sit down with it is unsuitably advanced for the child. In a busy household it's not fair to demand that mother or father supervise a game at beck and call. The only exception might be a gift that relates to an abiding hobby of their own, such as a fine rod and reel for a boy who trots along on his father's fishing trips.

A child measures himself in play, to an extent we do not always realize. Although gifts may be stimulating and even reasonably challenging, it is not a kindness to give a toy so far above the child's capacities, either in mental skills or in physical coordination, that he must give up, privately deciding that he is either stupid or weak.

Be patient, when the gifts have been given, for the youngster to settle with his favorites. One always despairs a bit to watch a child on Christmas morning, sitting in the middle of all his many, shiny presents and playing only with the ten-cent whistle from his stocking. If there are fond grandparents about, we feel embarrassed, and if we've given him precisely what he said was his heart's desire, we're exasperated. But the right toy, after all, is the toy that occupies and pleases him, and (in all the hustle-bustle), it may be right that the piping of a whistle will most absorb him and lift his spirits.

A lunch box for a little girl

Here's an idea for a little girl on your list.

Directions: Start with a lunch box without decoration. If you can't find one, paint over the one you have with a pleasing color. Cut out pretty pictures from toy catalogs, gardening catalogs, or magazines. Glue them on the box in an all-over design. When dry, cover with a coat of clear shellac. Wind the lunch box handle tightly with heavy twine.

A wicked wolf from a cotton sock

Could anything be nicer and funnier? This crazy wolf will bring hours of laughter, and stimulate inventive play; it's inexpensive and can be made in a jiffy. It's the perfect thing if you have many children on your list.

Directions: Use a brilliant cotton sock in boys' sizes. Make a center cut, up the foot; line the opening with red felt for the mouth. Add four white felt teeth, and a wicked red felt tongue. For the eyes, glue on an eye-shaped piece of white felt, and on top of this sew on a smooth black button. Nose and ears are of felt, too, and he's ready to scare three little pigs anywhere.

A baby's quilt, easily made

There's probably a very special baby on your list, and if you had the time for quilting, a very special present would be an old-fashioned baby quilt. If, however, you start with an ordinary crib mattress pad of quilted cotton as a base, you can simulate such a quilt in a very charming way.

Directions: Buy 1/2 yard of nursery rhyme chintz and cut out the prettiest figures for appliques. Sew and re-embroider them, by hand, to give dimension. The binding is pink-and-white gingham — or blue-and-white, if that's the story!

There surely can't be a little girl in the whole world who wouldn't love this cuddly pillow, to play with or curl up and sleep on.

Directions: Make the adorable sleepy-head from two 13-inch circles of Dynel and Orlon fleece. Braid a skein of jumbo Orlon yarn for the hair, and attach, pigtail fashion. Save a few strands of unbraided yarn to cut into short lengths and attach as ruffly bangs. The features are made from scraps of felt, glued on; the eyelashes are simply a curve of black felt with the fringe standing free so that a little girl can tickle herself with it. Tie perky bows at the bottom of the braids. Or you might start with any round, plump pillow in a suitable shade for a face, and proceed as above. Or make your own pillow from foam rubber scraps and the palest pink or cream-colored cotton, for the face. But be sure to make it big, and make its face almost beatific.

TOKEN GIFTS

Sometimes the urge to give is simply overpowering. We feel that we *must* do something about the season, however small; *must* send along some tangible object to our friends, along with our greetings; or have a wrapped-up parcel with a ribbon on it to pass by hand with an affectionate smile.

Yet — even though we're tempted — we can't throw our budgets over the Christmas tree. With a fairly large family the list can be mighty long, if you count all the kissin' cousins and the children's best friends at high school.

Dozens! What can we do? Token presents may be the answer. Here, as elsewhere, the general principles apply. Something that you've made yourself has value that's unrelated to its cost. If you've cooked it, it goes out with a bit of your heart in it. If it's wrapped with a dash of spirit and attentiveness, it states happily what it is: a token of your *need* to give a present at Christmas.

Remember that it can be trifling: one large, large, sugar cookie with a child's name written on it, and wrapped up with a jingle bell in the bow, for instance.

Or choose a gift that tucks into an envelope with a Christmas card. A fat little card is always fun to receive: it takes on the aspect of something that's more-than-a-card rather than

A sleepy-head pillow

less-than-a-gift. It seems, as we open it, to be bursting its envelope with the affection that comes with it. (Take care, of course, to see that the envelope is really large enough, and that there is adequate first-class postage on it. Postal authorities suggest that all such envelopes be marked PLEASE CANCEL BY HAND. Otherwise the gift may be damaged or the envelope torn by the cancellation machine.)

The kinds of things that go along well with a card are: a handkerchief, sachet, a veil, a packet of seeds for the garden, neck ribbon. And for children: a baby bib, a batch of bright balloons, a hair ribbon, a bow tie.

Decorated matchboxes

used, or not. Glue in place with fabric glue. For the man-size box, glue on simple shapes of felt in bold colors, such as stripes, diamonds, or triangles. Trimming the tiny ones can be pure invention; use sequins, pieces of lace paper doily, bits of greenery, ribbon, floral or metallic tape, just anything pretty.

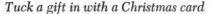

Tuck a gift in with a Christmas card

Matchboxes, sporting the finery of the season, make good, little token gifts. They add a bit of useful decoration to every table in the house all through the season. If you know someone who smokes a pipe or cigar, chances are he uses kitchen matches, and a big box, covered appropriately, would be appreciated.

Directions: Cut felt the correct size to wrap around three sides of the matchbox, whether large or small. Leave exposed, of course, the functional, abrasive side. Pinking shears may be

PERSONALIZING YOUR GIFTS

Ordering commercial monograms takes time; allow for it.

Remember that a lesser gift, when personalized, seems greater and brings greater pleasure, since the recipient knows that more time and forethought went into the gift.

Give a whole stationery outfit: letter paper, envelopes, postal cards, informals, calling cards, labels, and, perhaps, the copper plate if you have had the gift engraved.

Towels and linens, when monogrammed during summer sales, are far less expensive and greater variety is offered.

Many objects are made with a whole name already woven or printed: towels for children, shirts, aprons, handkerchiefs, scarves. Dozens of the most commonly used names are available, but stocks deplete early.

Do the personalizing yourself: a simple gift, such as a child's pair of mittens, is more fun to receive when there are big fat embroidered initials on it.

Put the name of the person on the package itself, in big or fancy letters: spell it out in sequins, or ribbon, or tape, or nail polish. It makes the gift more intimate and warm even before it is opened.

Places Where You Can Buy Initials for Monogramming

Initials made of all kinds of materials, to dress up either the gift itself or the package, can be found in the following places: *Hardware store* — 1. plastic 2. wooden 3. brass 4. luminous 5. nickel. *Variety store* — 1. candy 2. felt 3. gilt 4. silver finish 5. stamped-out shiny paper.

And you can make initials from many, many kinds of material, of which these are only a few: 1. sequins 2. fake fur 3. strings of dime store pearls 4. ribbon and adhesive tape 5. tiny artificial flowers.

GIFTS FROM CHILDREN

Take care to explain to a child how much a gift he made himself means to the person who receives it. Young children don't by any means automatically realize that Grandma would rather have one of their finger paintings than anything else she'll receive.

Decide early if the child shall spend his own money or not. If so, help him to save enough ahead of time; if not, make it clear that he will be giving a gift that Daddy buys, for instance.

If a child is to give anything to anyone, be certain that he has seen it and knows what it is, and if possible, has had a hand in the wrapping, selecting, etc. It is confusing to the child's

sense of Christmas if he "gives" what he has not ever seen before.

If a child wants to give something wonderful to his mother, father, or best friend, help him buy some large, durable, tangible object and decorate it. A big wastebasket, painted for Daddy, or a tray with stars pasted on it for Mommy, will be a far more satisfying gift for the child to give than something of more real value, and less size and "importance."

Encourage the child to give something that lasts for some time and is worn or displayed in the open; it is discouraging for him to give what is only another bottle of cologne, or another pair of socks.

Let the child do his own wrapping, no matter how much better you could do it yourself; and make no patronizing apologies when the gift is presented. However he has overdone it, with whatever horrible color scheme, every sticker was pasted on with the real feeling for what Christmas is.

As far as is possible, keep from the child the swapping principle; do not let him hear you say, for instance, "I don't think he'll give to you." Let him make as generous a list as he wishes, and work it out for him in some practical way.

GIVE A GIFT THAT REFLECTS AN INTEREST OR A HOBBY

If someone you know is from another town or state, but still has family ties with it, a subscription to his home town newspaper would be a delightful batch of nostalgia for him every week for a year.

A person with fond memories of his home town would enjoy a map of it — mounted, framed, and shellacked — especially if you decorate the map with signs and notations of his home address, birthplace, school, and anything else you know about him.

Someone recently graduated from a school or college — or even not so recently, if he has a continuing interest in it — would love a sub-scription to his school paper or magazine.

If you know that there is a certain place close to the heart of someone you know — a building, a city, a monument, a landscape precious be-cause, for instance, of a honeymoon spent there — an enlarged, framed photograph of it or the reproduction of a print, matted, would be a tender gift. (Art shops, chambers of commerce, bookstores, and travel agencies can help you find just the right thing.)

Try to find a baby picture of someone you'd like to give a gift to — or such a picture of someone dear to him. Have the picture en-larged, if necessary, and framed; it will become a priceless memento. (Relatives will have such a picture; or go to grade school annuals for pictures of an older child.)

Make a small album of pictures that you know will mean something to someone; we all have unsorted pictures of family members and friends that could make a sentimental record if enclosed in an appealing way. Give to Grand-father, for instance, a little album with a legend that says "Here are six pictures in which the children remind me of you," or, to Grand-mother, "All these pictures of the girls show them wearing the pretty dresses you made them."

If someone you know is a collector, or has an avid interest in such things as pewter, or old ships, or dolls, a framed print of such an object will be as rewarding as an addition to the collection. (Try art shops, libraries, book-shops, and second-hand bookstores for such prints).

For a person you know who has a deep inter-est in some special field — archaeology, or pearl-diving, or flying saucers — make a scrapbook for six months or a year of every clipping that you see in your daily reading of newspapers and magazines. It will make fascinating read-ing for the person you give it to, and will also show your abiding, attentive affection.

People who have professions or hobbies that have a written history from long ago will love to look through, and own, old books on the subject. Wander through old bookstores, go to auctions and rummage sales and bazaars. With care and a little time you are sure to discover some old work on boating, or home medicine, or law, or many another subject, as a particular-ly personal gift for someone you know.

Add to someone's collection; many people collect things of little intrinsic worth, such as trivets, or old pipes. By keeping your eyes open, you might easily find such a thing at very little cost — yet saving it for Christmas can make it a fine gift.

Gather recipes for someone who has a cook-ing specialty; sometimes the woman at home doesn't realize the fascinating variety of cook-books that exist from other countries and other times. Go to the library and copy from rare or old or expensive cookbooks those particular recipes your friend would be most interested to try; write them neatly on cards and present them in a decorated recipe file.

LITTLE GIFTS FOR DAD

Little gifts for the man of the house are al-ways difficult, it seems. Aside from major, im-portant gifts, there seem to be few little extras, such as there are for women and children. Dad seldom gets lots of little packages — unless they're all ties or socks.

But there is always his car, and lots of inter-esting and useful odds and ends exist which would be perfect for a little mound of presents on Christmas morning. Some are particularly nice if there's a family joke involved. Many of these are inexpensive enough for a child to pay for out of his own allowance.

And, for anyone with a new car, or a first car, or a better car — or anyone you know who's about to take a long trip by automobile — here's a list of gadgets that make nice and appropriate remembrances. Think of them for neighbors, or as under-the-tree presents for people who drop in during the holidays, or for the children to give as tokens to older cousins and uncles and aunts.

The list:

A backing light.

An upholstery brush and spot cleaner.

A raincoat that folds into a pocket.

Cotton gloves with plastic palms (practical and most inexpensive).

A magnetized metal box to hold an extra set of keys. This goes under the fender for use if one set is lost.

Half a dozen railroad flares, to be placed in the road in case of car trouble after dark.

An eyeglass case that clings to the dashboard by means of suction cups or with the aid of a magnet.

An armrest.

An outside rear view mirror.

Travel books, especially those listing places to stay and sights to see.

A cooler.

A book of maps.

A steering-wheel cover (pleasant in very hot or cold weather; helps driver to keep a firm grip).

A luggage-holder for the roof of the car.

Snack trays (one type fits over a lowered window; another is permanently attached and swings under the dashboard when not in use).

A "trouble" light.

A book in which to record trip itineraries, expenses, mileage, etc.

A vacuum bottle.

A nighttime rear view mirror, which cuts down the glare from car lights behind.

A gas-tank lock.

A utility tray for the dashboard, to hold pencils, loose coins, cigarettes, matches.

A coin-holder that clings to the dashboard by means of a magnet or suction cup.

A silicon-treated dustcloth.

An extra-large rear view mirror.

Curb-finders (little gadgets that send out a warning when the car is close to the curb and thus prevent scraping tires).

An anti-fog cloth (as it is wiped over the windshield, it deposits a chemical to keep the glass clear).

A license-holder that fastens to the steering-wheel column.

Safety locks for car doors.

A tobacco pipe with a special top to keep it from blowing out (for owners of convertibles).

Car-washing and polishing materials.

A monogrammed key-holder.

An extra ash tray (attachable).

A spinner, for easy wheel-turning.

An auto compass.

A first-aid kit.

An altimeter (it attaches to the windshield molding, shows the height of hills, the depth of valleys).

A wind silencer (it snaps on the front-door lip, cuts down wind roar).

Sun visors.

A map-holder.

GIFTS TO MAKE

Scrapbooks can be used for many different collections — postcards, matchbook covers, baseball cards; any likely (or unlikely) thing that someone collects. *(See illustration, page 26.)*

Directions: Use heavy cardboard for the covers. So that the finished scrapbook will open easily, score the covers 1½ inches from the edge with a scissors blade, holding it against a ruler *(Fig. A).* Bend cardboard on the scored lines. Cover with gummed crepe paper. Glue an appropriate design on the cover; this can be cut from a magazine or can be made up of several pictures of the items to be collected. Letters can be bought already punched out; or they can be painted on with attractive bold color.

Use construction paper for the inside. This should be cut ½ inch smaller than the covers *on three sides only.* When the scrapbook is assembled, the sides of the pages with the holes should be *flush or very nearly flush* with the back edges of the covers *(Fig. B).*

Use a paper punch to make the holes.

Punch two holes along the scored and bent side of each cover, about ¾ inch in from the edge, and tie covers and pages together with ribbon, leather thongs, twine, golf shoelaces, or braided holiday string.

To make looseleaf scrapbooks, proceed in the same way, but do not score the covers.

Practically everybody has a telephone and almost nobody has a cover for the telephone book, so it's highly safe to give this unusual, practical gift. One made of felt can be turned out in minutes, and will delight the person who has it whenever she looks up a number.

Directions: Three pieces of felt make this cover in the correct dimensions of the telephone book for your friend's community (*Fig. A*). If it's a different size from your own, be sure to check it.

A collector's scrapbook

Start the scrapbook with a few samples. To hold photographs or cards of any kind, use photo corners. To hold matchbook covers, cut slits in the pages and slip the covers into place (*Fig. C*).

A felt cover for the telephone book

Sew around edges.

Cut out letters and design in a contrasting color and glue on. Trim in any fashion that suits you: perhaps with sequins on the letters, or with pasted-on gold twine for the cord *(Fig. B)*.

You'll be blessed by any book-lover for this felt book jacket — and doubly blessed if he's the kind of person who's always misplacing his reading glasses. (And that means nearly everybody.)

A felt book jacket

You'll be blessed by the whole family if you make this cover, with a pocket for a magnifying glass, for a family book, which has small print, such as a dictionary, atlas, or again, the telephone book. Looking things up becomes a pleasure, even if the light is poor, or you're in a hurry, or you can't find your glasses.

Directions: Make a jacket from felt, as in making the jacket for the telephone book.

Sew on the front a piece of felt, in a contrasting color, big enough to hold a magnifying glass. (Include a glass, if you can, and if the family hasn't one.)

Pink around the edges, for trim. If you've included a glass, attach a tassel to its handle, for a pleasing effect.

A felt eyeglass case

Trim the case to suit the person who will receive it. You might make a lavish one for a grown-up young lady, covered with beads, sequins, jewels, and golden rickrack. Make funny ones for the high school set; glue on two white eye-shaped pieces of felt and sew a button (preferably the color of her eyes) in the corner of each. Top with an extravagant fringe of black felt, for eyelashes. Or make a roguish wink, with one button eye open and the other closed, with the eyelash-fringe glued down instead of up.

Here's a lovely apron that will take only fifteen minutes or so to make, and — airy and fancy as it is — it will *really* wash just like a hanky, since that's just what it is.

Directions: Find four beautiful large-sized handkerchiefs, all the same pattern and colors. Stitch them together so that they make a large square; shirr and sew at the top to a length of nylon velvet ribbon.

An apron from four handkerchiefs

Easy-to-make picnic tablecloth

With so many people eating out-of-doors, surely you know someone who'd love this tablecloth that won't blow off a picnic table, no matter what.

Directions: With a pinking shears, cut out a large piece of colored plastic or oilcloth, square, circle, or oblong. Decorate with Contact paper, in cut-out shapes or objects such as houses, cars, anchors, or boats. For a barbecue family, try cutting out everybody's name from Contact paper, in big letters, to serve as a happy seating arrangement.

On the underside of the cloth, sew two-ounce weights at intervals, enough to hold down the sides of the cloth in a pretty strong wind.

Mittens made of toweling are easy to make and fun to use. They substitute in the shower or bath for washcloths, and a pretty one, trimmed with nylon lace at the cuff and a big glass bead sewed at the ring finger, will delight any girl.

For the man of the house, make a pocket in the palm for a cake of soap, and use a bold color, such as bronze, navy, or dark green. Boys may not even fight off the use of soap, if it's in the pocket where they don't have to look at it.

Terry cloth bath mitts

Directions: On paper draw an outline of your hand, allowing a half inch all around for the seam, keeping your thumb away from your fingers as you do. (For a child's mitt, of course, allow for the difference in size.) Use three or four thicknesses of terry cloth for the palms, one for the back of the hand. Open a pocket in the top layer of cloth, and sew down to palm, leaving room for a cake of soap. Buttonhole-stitch or crochet around seams and at pocket edge. Add elastic at the wrist, and trim.

Here's an apron that is made in a jiffy and put on and off in a jiffy, too. Clip-on aprons are quick to sew up and a novel little present to give.

Directions: Buy one curved plastic ring (most notion counters and sewing centers have them). Use ½ yard of fabric for each apron you make. If you use seersucker or any of the new drip-dry cottons, there'll be no ironing involved. One ring and several aprons — both plain and fancy — make a very nice gift, especially for the young homemaker.

A sewing kit

An apron on a plastic ring

GIFTS FOR CHILDREN TO MAKE

Everyone feels the pleasure of giving to a loved one something he has made himself; this is particularly true of children who have little to give in the material sense.

From the time a child first comes home with a grubby bookmark from kindergarten, his eyes alight with joy, he loves to give what he has made. It may be hard for a young child to start a gift from scratch without considerable help from a grownup, but it's easy to improve on something inexpensive that he can buy out of his allowance.

Variety store gifts (a watering can, a tobacco pouch, a plain pot of ivy) can be painted or decorated with things that are glued on, so that the child will feel both the pride of workmanship in his gift and the sweet, sensible idea that he has given something of usefulness and durability otherwise beyond his power to create.

Supply the children with ideas, basic gifts perhaps, and the magic extras that enhance the offering in his own eyes and make it seem worthy for Mother or Dad.

Very small children can make a creditable stamp container; however odd-looking, it will be an endearing and sentimental attraction on any loved one's desk.

Decorated stamp containers

Directions: Paint the metal containers that have held cellophane tape or typewriter ribbons.

Decorate with seals, gummed dots, stamped-out letters — all sorts of things.

Finish with clear spray-on lacquer.

Starting with an inexpensive snap-on iron holder, a child can make a fine and useful cookbook holder.

Directions: First paint it in a cheerful kitchen color; then, when dry, decorate with gummed tape, colored nail polish, or even so happy a legend as "For Grandma."

The wire clips of the holder will keep the

pages of the book open while in use, and fold flat later.

A tissue box can find a place in almost every room in the house; the children can settle down to making them more personal and pretty. Use the kind that has a lid that comes off, so young fingers can work from underneath, for neatness. Matching oilcloth to cover a box for the kitchen is one idea, and a lovely brocade for an aunt's bedroom is a project for a slightly older girl.

Directions: Cut cloth larger than necessary, smooth out over fabric glue, and turn up over

A handy cookbook holder

all edges. From kindergarten on, kids learn to make good squared corners. A little help with the slit may be needed, but if the job isn't perfect, glue down rickrack to conceal untidy edges. Gummed tape and gummed paper are also possibilities, and a name can be spelled out in variety-store gilt initials.

Here's a fine job for a boy, and a great gift for him to give his mother. He'll be proud of it and its substantial size; he may *even* keep on being proud as he carries it out as his chore, during the year.

Directions: Paint a covered outside garbage pail some bright, unusual color. Paint on a name, address, or monogram in a contrasting color. The child will need help with this part; stencils will make it easier.

Even very young children like to draw houses; this house, cut out of felt, opens up into a pretty little sewing kit.

Directions: After the youngster has drawn the

A decorated garbage pail

A tissue box can be beautified by covering

house on paper, cut the shape from a double thickness of felt, taking care not to cut through the fold, since you want the kit to open like a book. A door and windows may be cut from another color of felt, and glued on the inside. Pin little, gold safety pins, crosswise, on one window, regular safety pins crosswise on another, and needles on the third. Secure two large needles vertically on the door, and wind a length of black thread around one, white around the other.

Finish with straight pins, points up, along the bottom edge, like tall grass against the house. A thimble may be added, held in place by a sewed-on curtain ring of the right size.

A youngster still too young to manage a real hammer and nails can make a spool holder that's so ingenious and useful that any woman who sews will be pleased by it.

Directions: Start with a piece of pegboard; 10 x 10 inches is a good size, but it could be larger. With a strong wood glue, attach four,

small, empty spools to the underside (not the shiny side) to serve as legs. Paint an attractive color; two coats are best.

Have a supply of round-head bolts, with nuts, on hand, ⅛ x 1½ inches in size. Push the bolts up through the holes from underneath, and spin the nuts down from the top to hold the bolts securely. Spools of thread will slip down on the bolts neatly and easily.

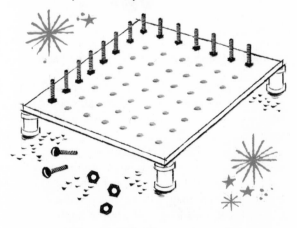

An ingenious spool holder, made without nails

Kitchen salt and pepper shakers are a fine gift from the boy who has learned how to hammer a nail.

Directions: Using two bouillon-cube cans, the first job is to punch holes in the lid — one in the center and six more around it. The lid should be removed from the can for this, and a dowel of proper size held under the lid to prevent it from denting. Be sure that the cans are clean and dry; then paint them with two coats of enamel. They should be bright contrasting colors, so that it is easy to see at a glance which is salt and which is pepper.

Sleek salt and pepper shakers for the kitchen

House numbers for the front lawn make a proud and welcome gift, and it's another good job for a manly boy who can work a bit with tools.

Directions: Start with the numerals that are needed; hardware stores have luminous and light-reflecting letters as well as metal ones. The wood to which they will be tacked should be ¾ inch thick, and long and high enough to accommodate the numerals. For the post, cut an 18-inch-long piece of 2 x 2 inch lumber. From a point five inches up from one end of the post, saw the post and file to a point, so that the sign may later be driven into the earth. Patient whittling will do the trick, also. Sand well, then nail sign to post with two large nails. Shellac and paint; now tack on the numerals.

A house number sign for the front lawn

ADD YOUR OWN TOUCH

Add the touch of your own handiwork to a gift, and you increase its value far beyond anything that is tangible. If you're too busy to make a gift from scratch, or if your money is too limited to buy lavish things for everybody, buy a starter gift and tinker with it, making it uniquely your own, and spiced with your own particular friendliness.

Trays and lamp bases and wastebaskets can be made far more beautiful with decorations cut from wallpaper. This is easy to do and you can decorate several objects from one roll of paper.

Directions: Start with a plain object, without decoration — or paint over existing colors. Choose a wallpaper with a self-contained design, rather than an all-over pattern. You'll find many to choose from in modern wallpapers. Here is a perfect opportunity to recognize a person's hobby: birds, flowers, old cars, ships, dogs, etc. Cut out decorations and arrange on object pleasingly; glue on; let dry. Finish with several coats of clear spray-on lacquer.

Or, for the book-lover, why not a large waste-basket decorated with glued-on book jackets? Use only the front cover design and the lettered backbone.

Too, to decorate small individual cocktail trays, a surplus of colorful foreign postage stamps might be used, arranged helter-skelter or in a simple pattern. They show up brilliantly against a black background.

An apron, made from a bath towel

Decorate a wastebasket or a tray

A perfect small gift for the mother of a young baby is a big practical apron for all the wet jobs there are to do — and there seem to be many of them.

Directions: Start with a big bath towel. A front fold forms three pockets for working supplies. To fold the towel first measure 21 inches from the top and fold right sides together. Bring up the short edge to form a 9½ inch pocket strip. Pin across the width of towel at that point. Stitch in the pockets with the point of the V exactly centered, then sew across the width of the towel 1 inch below the top, forming a slot for a rope-cord tie to be run through.

For the pretty teen-age girl who has just started putting up her hair two or three times a day (or so it seems), make up a set of these glittery hair clips. They'll be much better to look at than bobby-pins.

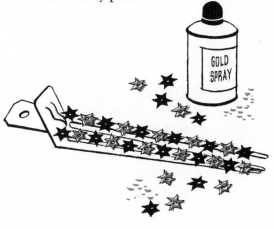

Sequinned hair clips

Directions: Start with a suitable number of metal clips, bought at any variety store counter. Spray with gold or silver paint, or use as they are. Let them dry, and glue on star sequins (the tiny size).

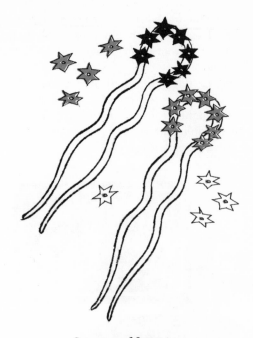

Sequinned hairpins

A planter, made from a bread tin

A bread tin, costing only pennies, becomes an attractive planter when sprayed with gold. Give it with greens already planted, and given a head start under your care. It will make a thoughtful gift that's beyond the consideration of price.

These holiday hairpins will be a tender little gift for anyone you know who has long hair and pins it up in a bun or chignon.

Directions: Buy several large amber-colored hairpins, or those of the tortoise-shell type. Glue tiny star sequins, of an harmonious color, around the head of each. (If you buy these hairpins in plastic, be sure you use a glue meant for plastics. Some standard glues have no holding power when applied to plastic;

others badly mar plastic or eat it away altogether unless used with special care.)

For a high school or college girl, or any girl with a beau away in the Armed Forces, make a treasure box with sentimental decorations. (Especially if she has a rambunctious little brother!)

Directions: Paint an ordinary strongbox (the kind found in hardware and dime stores), and choose for this a feminine color in a pastel shade. Glue on red hearts, a golden arrow, a key, the words LOVE LETTERS in gold, and other decorations from lace doilies or shiny foil fringe. Tie a red ribbon on the actual key.

If the girl lives in a family really *full* of curious younger brothers, better get the kind of strongbox for which you buy a combination lock.

Have you ever watched the brilliant colors in a driftwood fire — the yellows, blues, violets, greens, and reds? You remember, then, how compelling and enchanting a thing they are to see. One of the most exciting and unusual presents you can give your friends at Christmas is a big bag of pine cones, or a Yule log, treated to burn in many colors. Anyone you know who

A treasure box for a girl

has a fireplace will bless you all through the holidays for this unique gift.

And surely it is one of the most inexpensive gifts in the world. If you live in the country, there are pine cones close by; if in the city, head some week end in the car for the nearest pine grove. Children will love to help gather the cones, and this can be a happy family outing. Take several large baskets or corrugated paper boxes for bringing the cones home. You can sort them out as you find them.

Directions: All you need in addition to the cones are ordinary chemicals which could be bought at any drugstore. (You may find some difficulty in finding them *all* at a single drug store, but you'll surely find some of them; if possible try several sources.) Some are even simple kitchen staples, like salt and borax. The following substances produce flames of the specified colors; choose your favorites.

Strontium nitrate — red
Borax — vivid green
Calcium chloride — orange
Copper sulphate — blue
Copper nitrate — emerald
Lithium chloride — purple
Potassium nitrate — yellow
Barium nitrate — apple-green
Common table salt — yellow

These chemicals are safe to use as directed, but like many household items they should be kept out of reach of small children or pets who might taste them. *Another note of warning:* Don't mix them in your metal utensils; use crockery containers or a wooden bucket because many of these chemicals are corrosive to metals. Also, when treating the pine cones, protect your hands with a pair of household rubber gloves.

Pick the color you want and mix the particular chemical in water — about a half-pound of chemical to half a gallon of water. *Don't mix the various chemicals together.*

Chemicals for a colorful hearthfire

Put a few cones in cheesecloth bags, dip them into the liquid, and soak them thoroughly. Drain them well and spread them out to dry on thick newspapers. Sometimes it takes them three or four days to dry thoroughly.

Package the cones for giving in strong bags which are tied with ribbons. The bright red mesh bags that apples and onions and potatoes are often packaged in also make just-right containers.

For the Yule log, paint a small apartment-sized log with a chemical solution made of two parts chemical to five of shellac, or soak the log in a solution of one pound chemical to one gallon of water. Let the log dry for at least forty-eight hours.

The Yule log could be tied round with a big red-ribbon bow, with a couple of treated pine cones tucked in.

If the idea appeals to you but you haven't the cones or the log — or must send gifts quite far — there's another way to produce the same effect.

Mix the chemicals and salt, one at a time, with sawdust as a filler, to be sprinkled directly on the fire for a burst of color.

Pack this mixture in cellophane bags and tie each with a ribbon to show the color that the mixture will produce in the fire.

Nobody is too busy to add this touch of thoughtful hand-made trim. It would take only five or ten minutes. The result is a glamorous and different tablecloth, or apron, or scarf.

Directions: Start with a simply designed object, made of material which is not a print. Buy, too, in a suitable color, magical plastic mending tape; it come in strips. Then cut out large coin dots and merely iron them on. Use your own artistic sense: blue and green dots on a white organdy scarf would be highly chic, for instance *(Fig. A);* and red and black dots would dress up an apron *(Fig. B),* or a luncheon set *(Fig. C).* Have fun with it; it's a device that's quick, imaginative, inexpensive, and personal.

Sometimes the difference between the look of an inexpensive stole and an expensive one is merely the difference between a skimpy fringe and a lavish one.

Use plastic mending tape for decoration

Directions: Starting with a scarf or stole, add a thick and handsome fringe, in a striking, contrasting color. Investigate jumbo Orlon yarns, metallic yarns, and those with a high nap or rich gloss.

The woman of the house will wonder how she ever got along without this practical apron idea — and you can make it as short or as long a job as you like.

An apron and a towel, joined for keeps

Add a rich fringe to any stole

The ingredients are a fingertip terry towel and an apron; you can make them both, or buy them both, or make one and buy the other. The idea is to sew, permanently, into the waistband of an apron, a terry towel of a harmonizing color. This simple innovation is just wonderful: how *many* times in the course of making dinner or tending the baby or washing up the dishes we have occasion to wipe our hands. No more searching for a towel, just think, and not ever again a wet apron! The towel's also handy as a built-in hot pad, and fine for mopping up small spills the minute they happen.

This could be an excellent project for a class of girls making gifts for their mothers, since the sewing job can be tailored to fit the sewing skills of various ages.

The basic materials here — just handkerchiefs — are transformed into a feminine nosegay that

A nosegay, made of handkerchiefs

pays a compliment to any woman, and speaks of thoughtfulness beyond the mere purchase of a gift.

Directions: Use one pink hanky, two red ones, and two green ones. Knot loosely the corners of the pink one; knot tightly the corners of the reds. Gather with the green ones, for leaves, into a nosegay. Circle the whole with a paper doily and wrap the "stem" in foil.

GIVING TO THE PEOPLE WHO HAVE EVERYTHING

Get something brand-new, something you have never seen before in your life, if it is being talked about.

Give the biggest of anything: the biggest paper clip, the biggest straw bag or straw hat, the biggest decanter, the biggest scarf, the biggest apron.

Be funny: fill an apothecary jar with a thousand aspirin tablets for the harried businessman; or do some other pertinent thing that will make comment on what you know of him.

Give the most expensive of anything: one cake of fabulous soap, a gold house key, or some such thing.

Give something of nostalgic value: an old book, an old poster for a play, penny candy in a jar, or a similar thing.

Package whatever it is with wit and imagination.

Search the small advertisements in the back of magazines and newspaper supplements for unusual or funny gifts; one such item, sold for a trifling sum, is $1,000,000 worth of actual Confederate money.

TIPPING AT CHRISTMAS

It may be the custom in your community to give remembrances at Christmas to those people who serve you in one way or another. If you're new in town, ask a neighbor what the practice is. Generally it is more in cities than in towns that small gifts of money are given some people at the holiday season. If it is customary where you live, what should be given? And to whom?

As regards such people as the mailman, who may be someone you never see at all or on the other hand may be someone who's a cheery friend waited for each day, little helpful advice can be given. Each of us knows best what place the mailman plays in his life. If you receive fifteen heavy magazines a week in the course of your work at home, for instance, you'll want to give a generous thank-you gift of money to the mailman. If you've been exchanging flower bulbs with your mailman, and the children run down to the gate to meet him, you will give something based on a friendly relationship like any other.

But always give money, rather than something else. It can always be assumed, with someone who is of service to you but whom you do not know in a social way, that he is a far better judge of what would please him than you could possibly be, and so you give him the opportunity to spend your gift as he sees fit. For many persons who do not receive a bonus from their employer at Christmas, the accumulation of Christmas tips constitutes such a bonus.

If you live in an apartment building, there'll be a staff to remember. In some buildings there is a fund set up by the management, to which tenants contribute a sum. The management then distributes the money to everyone; this is probably the only way the people you seldom see, such as the furnace man, would get as fair a share as the doorman whose daily smile you know so well. If, however, you have really received unusual service from these people you see every day, their share of the fund should be supplemented by you with a gift of money commensurate with their value to your well-being.

If there is no such fund, your gifts will depend very generally upon the rent you pay and the service you receive. Take care to remember everybody. Distribute the money as justly as possible; if the shares are small, get crisp new bills from the bank and enclose them in a tasteful Christmas card.

If you're in the dark about how much, a rule you might use is this: settle on a figure which is about 2 or 2½ per cent of your annual rent, and distribute this among the staff. Whether or not you do this will depend on your being able to afford it, but this is the general rule.

As far as delivery men are concerned, try to determine whether your milkman or diaper-service man is an owner-driver or an employee. Owner-drivers do not expect tips. Employees should receive a nominal amount, based largely on the degree of service or friendly contact that exists.

Other people you tip regularly, such as the barber, beauty-shop employee, and shoeshine boy, can receive a larger tip on the occasion nearest Christmas that you see them, but not necessarily a separate gift of money with a card.

By and large, give in keeping with your actual ability to be generous. Try not to be parsimonious, but on the other hand don't feel any need to be flashy. Do as you do in other Christmas situations: give in friendliness and good will.

HOW TO GIVE BOOKS

Books have advantages at Christmastime that few other gifts can equal. Books first of all bring pleasure, in what is the most joyous season of the year. They pay a certain compliment to both the recipient and the giver, in implying that both are aware of the delights to the eye and the stimulation to the mind to be found in books as in nothing else. They are a gift of permanence: a book that is loved never need disappear from a person's life. Books are not consumed in use. They are never out-of-date: when the world changes enough to pass beyond a book, the book becomes history, and is valued

in a different way. Books can bring pleasure to more than one person; they do not go into a closet but remain in the family rooms, to be enjoyed by the whole family. Long after the season is past they can offer laughter, hope, or challenge to a widening group of family members and friends.

In addition, books have purely practical qualities as well. They are extremely easy to wrap attractively, and they pack and mail easily and inexpensively. They do not damage if given reasonable care, and they are not perishable. There are interesting books available at almost any price you wish to spend, and books on every topic and subject on earth.

When you know a specific book you want to buy for someone, your shopping is most simple. As long before you need it as possible, go to your bookstore, or the book section of a department store. You might need this extra time because the bookseller may not have an unusual book in stock; or he may be temporarily out of a popular title. He can order it for you, however, and will be glad to do so. If you don't know the name of a local bookstore, write to The American Booksellers Association at 175 Fifth Avenue, New York, New York. Ask for a list of booksellers near you. Any one of them will be happy to welcome you in person or fill your mail-order requests. Many stores have fine book catalogs, so that a wide range of good books is as near at hand as your mailbox.

If you don't know a particular book that you want, go to a bookstore and look around, or go through a catalog at your leisure. If you have little to go on in choosing a title, buy something that is good to look at. Every Christmas season there are new and attractive books in the stores that have been produced specifically for the gift market, for both adults and children. Choose books that more than one member of the family will enjoy, such as the various readers and books of cartoons that are new each year.

In general, women like books with a nostalgic element; those that evoke a far-off time are always popular. A sprightly cookbook that is different is always welcome; even if it is not used often as a cookbook, it makes pleasant browsing.

For men there are many handsome, interesting books on sports, science, travel, and history which have been written and illustrated for the general reader rather than for the expert or scholar. Stay away from controversial subjects unless you are absolutely *sure* that the person to whom you are giving the book will appreciate the subject you choose.

Just about the only other rule in giving books to adults is to stay away from books in the expert's field when giving to an expert. Otherwise, you may run into unknown hazards: you may give a book to the expert that he has already read or, on the other hand, a book he already knows but does not care to read. There are different schools of thought in each scholastic or technical field, and it is safer not to give the physician a book on medicine, or the teacher one on pedagogy.

Books for children have never been better than now. There are more titles than ever before, and they are beautifully illustrated and well written. Children love to get books; and if you write a child's name and the date on the flyleaf he will regard his book with extra pride.

For children who are quite young — say, up to eight or nine years old — it is better to give several books of lesser value than to try to settle on just one more expensive one. If you are going to spend five dollars, for instance, it would usually be better to give two two-dollar books and one one-dollar book than one five-dollar book. The young child would appreciate the variety of books more than he would a single de luxe volume. If your budget is larger, include beautiful reference books, such as dictionaries, or encyclopedias. Children of all ages value them, delight in them, and find them exceptionally useful.

Shop early for books, then; give yourself enough time to enjoy dallying in a bookstore or perusing a catalog; wrap books with imagination (see page 48 for ideas); and mail them early. In giving books, you give treasure.

3 Christmas Packages

WRAPPING AND MAILING

WRAP IT RIGHT

It isn't magic! Wrapping a gift so that it is handsome, tasteful, and secure really isn't a trick at all, though it takes a little practice at the beginning. The basic procedures which follow are simple and foolproof.

One helpful tip is to keep all your wrapping materials together, throughout the year. Have a drawer or shelf or box that's handy, and stow them away. Get together a supply of paper, ribbons, tape, tissue, and gift cards (plus a pair of scissors that's attached to a long string, perhaps, so that it stays put and doesn't wander off on a dozen other errands). In addition, collect trimmings: fake flowers, a broken string of dime-store pearls, feathers, odds and ends of notions. You'll be surprised at the way they can spark up a gift wrapping.

That professional look which some packages have when we open them often lies in the fresh crispness of their tissue. All your gifts can have this look if you line the box with tissue in the following manner. Pleat each of two sheets of paper through the center: one to fit the length of the box and extend beyond it at each end, the other to fit the width.

Fit one sheet into the box, and lay the other across it, allowing the ends to extend equally on both sides.

Pleat fresh tissue to fit the box

Now add the gift. If it is fragile, or is to be mailed, gather extra sheets of tissue lengthwise and place them around the object, to keep it

Fit one sheet into the box; lay the other across it

41

from shifting. Finish by folding the extended tissue inside. Write a card with your name, place it on top, and close the box.

Fold the extended tissue inside the box

Try these ideas with tissue.

Line the box in a color to match the contents, or the color of the outer wrapping paper. Tissue is available in pastels and in red, green, and bright blue.

Use tissue that is dusted with sparkle in confetti colors, or in gold or silver.

Sprinkle sachet into the surrounding tissue on gifts of lingerie, hosiery, or gloves, for a personal, feminine touch.

Paste on bright stars or colorful seals.

Fringe or cut with pinking shears the tissue edges in lining boxes for smaller gifts.

Now for the outer wrapping.

Measure the wrapping paper and cut it to fit the box. Follow the accompanying diagrams closely, since they apply to a *rectangular box* of any dimensions.

Measure the paper around the box, allowing about an inch for overlap. Fold back excess, and cut off.

Measure the paper up three-quarters of the box's depth at each end, and cut off excess.

At each end, the paper should measure three-quarters of the box's depth

Seal paper at the box's edge with cellophane tape. Tape may be concealed by overlapping the ends of a small piece of tape, then folding, keeping the sticky side out. Place the tape between the edges to be sealed, and press them together firmly.

Tuck in paper at each end of the box, crease sharply, add tape (concealed in the same way

Measure the paper around the box, and cut off

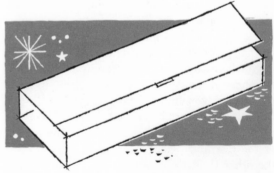

Seal the edges of the wrapping with cellophane tape

as above), and press the end flaps against the box.

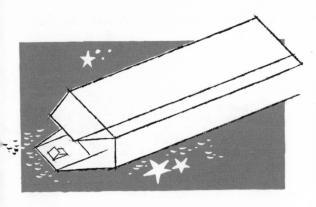

Tuck in paper at each end of box, and seal

To wrap a *circular box,* measure and cut the wrapping paper as for a rectangular one. Place the box on its side and roll the paper around it. Seal the paper with cellophane tape.

For wrapping, place a circular box on its side

Pleat the ends down flat and secure with matching seal or tape.

Pleat the ends down flat, and seal

For a fitted wrap, trace the ends of the cylinder on the wrapping paper and cut out two circles. After the overlap is pleated, spread paste on the edges of the circles and attach one to each end of the cylinder.

For a fitted wrapper, finish the ends with cut-out circles

How can a gift be wrapped if the box is too big for a sheet of gift paper? One way — and it can produce striking results — is to wrap the lid and the bottom of the box separately. Use two different papers that will harmonize or contrast attractively. Cut one sheet of paper to a size that will fold over the ends and the sides of the lid. Fold the paper over the sides

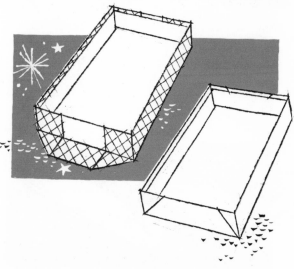

Use two contrasting papers to wrap a too-large package

and secure with cellophane tape. Fold the remaining flaps up and over the ends of the lid. The bottom of the box is wrapped in the same manner with the other sheet of paper.

Ribbon and decoration can be used as desired, secured to the underside of the lid with tape.

Use tape to secure ribbon and decoration to underside of lid

Another treatment for a big box — such as a coat box — is to use two sheets of paper and wrap half of the closed box at a time. Start from either end, attaching the paper to the box, and join securely in the middle with tape. Cover the joined edges with ribbon.

To give a cylindrical package the look of a snapper — the kind used at parties — roll the box in paper which is long enough so that the ends may be gathered and tied. Use ribbon to tie the ends, and cut them in a fringe.

Wrap a cylindrical package to look like a snapper

The easiest way to wrap round gifts is to use the shape, rather than disguising it. Cover with paper, securing the overlap with tape. Don't tuck the paper ends in; tie them off with ribbon and cut them to make a spaghetti fringe.

Wrap round gifts to show their shape

What can be done with a boxless bottle of perfume? Cut the wrapping paper in two squares large enough so that the four corners reach well above the height of the jar or bottle. Place one

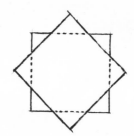

Try an eight-pointed star to wrap a perfume bottle

square over the other so that they make an eight-pointed star. Center the bottle on this star, and bring the paper up to the bottle top. Fasten with a ribbon and fluff out the points of the star.

Ribbon can be used in many ways, now that cellophane tape does so much of the job of holding the paper on the box. Choose a color of ribbon that enhances the paper, and try these decorative ideas.

Wrap around. Wind the ribbon around the gift box once. Cut and secure.

Basket weave. Wind three ribbons around the height of the box. Fasten the ends. Weave

three ribbons between the stationary ones, around the length of the box. Secure.

Crisscross. Hold one end of the ribbon at one end of the box. Wind the ribbon around lengthwise, cross the ribbon at the starting point and wind around the width. Fasten at starting point.

Double crisscross. Follow instructions given above, and repeat, forming two crisscrosses.

Single hourglass. Wind two or more bands around box. Tie together and separate the bands at the edges of the box.

Double hourglass. Follow instructions given above, then wind the ribbons around in the other direction. Fasten the bands together at one end of the box, and separate at the outer edges.

Corner cross. Hold the end of the ribbon at one corner. With the other hand, wind the ribbon in a clockwise direction . . . over a corner, under the next, over, then under and back to the starting point. Secure the ends.

Use ribbon to fasten the star at top of bottle

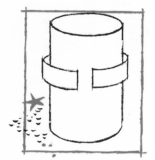

Wrap ribbon around the box once

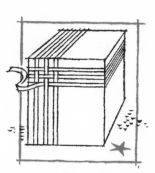

Weave ribbon around a package

Crisscross ribbon around a box

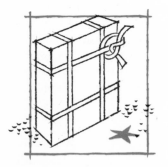

Try a double crisscross

Tie the ribbon in an hourglass shape

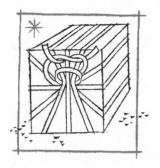

Try two hourglasses

*Cross the ribbon over
the corners*

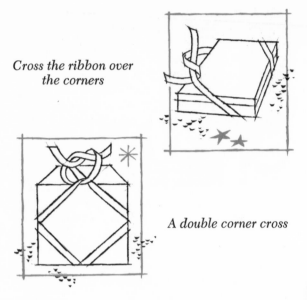

A double corner cross

Double corner cross. Tie the ends for a single corner cross. Reverse the direction. Wind the ribbon around the box in a counter-clockwise

Making a basic bow

direction. Secure the ends at the starting point.

Add a bow for the finishing touch that will beautify your gift, but *always* make it separately. Never try to tie the bow from the same piece of ribbon you're tying up the box with. Tie the finished bow to the package with the knotted ends of the ribbon already in place.

Learn the basic bow, pretty in wide or narrow ribbon.

In making a bow, remember to pinch the ribbon tightly between thumb and fingers as the loops are formed and secure them with spool wire. Bend a short piece of wire round the center of the loops and twist the wire ends together tightly.

A pinwheel bow saves ribbon

The ribbon-saver! Save all the short lengths for this easy, attractive pinwheel bow. Cut ribbon into strips 4 inches to 6 inches long, and tie together with spool wire. Use several different colors for one bow; or combine wide and narrow ribbons in contrasting colors for another.

For a rosette bow, use the same beginning technique as in the first basic one, making about 3 loops on each side. For variations: try placing contrasting colors one over the other; or use one color for half the loops, cut the ribbon off, and join in a second color to complete.

Some bows that are different.

Open a pair of scissors or use a kitchen knife to pull narrow ribbed ribbon into colorful curls. Do it either of two ways. Curl a yard or two, then gather it into casual loops and tie to the

A rosette bow

Pull narrow ribbon into curls

Make a small circle of ribbon around the thumb.

Add other circles, each slightly larger, until the bow is the desired size.

Pass a short strip of ribbon through the center loop and secure on the back.

Use crisp ribbon, and this will make a shimmering and unusual bow.

For a poinsettia, cut three red petals from crisp ribbon. Make one of each of these three sizes: 3 inch, 2½ inch, and 2 inch. *(See page 48.)*

Arrange petals one on top of another, with the largest on the bottom. Tie a knot in a strip of yellow ribbon. Cross two sets and tie together with the ribbon, placing the knot in the center.

Tie on the third set of petals.

Separate all the petals by tying across the flower in all directions. Lift all the small petals,

package; or tie on several shorter lengths and curl them individually.

Ribbon looped in circles makes an unusual bow

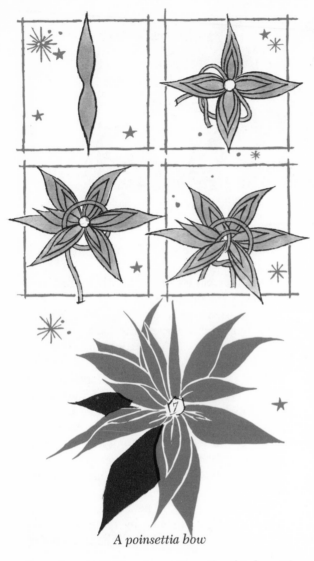

A poinsettia bow

then the next larger layer, then the third, until they all stand up. Add green leaves, made of ribbon.

The beautiful poinsettia which is the result will be taken off the gift and cherished — the nicest kind of Christmas bow.

WRAP A GIFT WITH IMAGINATION

Gift wrappings can be more than practical, and even more than beautiful. They can be, as well, intimate, funny, teasing, ingenious, or sentimental. They can reflect the gift inside or they can be deliberately misleading. They can make an inexpensive gift seem more substantial, since they speak so eloquently of the affection and thoughtfulness of the giver. Homely gifts, staples, necessities, all can become light-hearted. They say, far more than the words could say, "What fun I had, what care I took, how *nice* it is to give you a present!"

Allow time for this kind of gift wrapping. Manage some privacy away from the family and sit down with room, lots of materials of all kinds, and a devil-may-care spirit. Be as different as you like; anything goes. Finish wrapping as long before the holiday itself as you can; it's great fun to look at pretty, amusing packages and joke about them and guess. Pile them on a hall table, except those for little children who might not be able to bear the suspense, and those that would too clearly reveal what is inside. The following ideas may only start you on your own; sit down and wield your scissors and your imagination!

Don't overlook all the following aids to package wrapping that you'll find in the stores: cellophane tape; spool wire; casein glue; nonwoven ribbons; tissue in many new colors; crepe paper in every shade; seals of many kinds; made-up ribbon bows; tiny painted wooden angels; sequins in many sizes, shapes, and colors; spray-on paint, in a large variety of colors, metallic and otherwise.

Commercial packaging is so handsome these days that all through the year you can acquire good-looking containers without thinking much about it. Find a spot in a closet in the kitchen, and start saving them, even though at the time you can't imagine what use you would ever put them to. Jars, bottles, glasses, berry baskets, plastic containers of all kinds, as well as boxes, can be spruced up with paint or gilt or glitter at Christmas and can make a package more handsome than one you might contrive out of the materials of the moment.

A book or the first magazine of a year's subscription, packed as shown in the illustration, is simple to manage and fun to receive. Cover

An unusual wrapping for a book or magazine

in this kind of wrapping. Put green paper underneath the outside decorative paper. Cut from the outer wrapping the shape of a golf green, so that the green paper shows. For the flagpole, twist white paper in a tight roll, or use a drinking straw. Add a triangle of red paper for the flag, wads of paper for golf balls; and a bow, if you like.

the gift with real newspaper, except for a white strip at the top which will show, when the eyes are cut out. Then wrap the gift in red. Cut out eyes and an opening for the newspaper; paint on spectacle frames with ink marker; and paste on shiny black eyes.

Everyone can always tell a record; here the decoration makes a happy admission of the contents. White and black paper are attached to a box top, then the box is wrapped in gold. Cut out the drum, and paste on diamond shapes in vivid colors, and black dots. Drumsticks are plastic drinking straws, with crushed foil tips.

Any gift for the golfer, whether or not it's a golfing gift, would bring smiles when given

A wrapping for a golfing gift

Almost anything could be in this clock-box; whatever gifts come in round tins or boxes would be charming, wrapped this way. But you might use powder boxes for small gifts and hat boxes for larger gifts of any shape, and so puzzle everybody. You might even package a clock this way, since nobody will think you would be so obvious. Start as you would with any cylindrical package, then paste on a black paper ring to indicate the face. Paste on twelve dots, or gilt numerals. Attach gold or silver foil hands and a bow. *(See page 50.)*

If there's anything a child would like more than a present (aside from two presents), it would be a present with candy, too. This simple gift wrapping will be greeted with cries of delight, and many a child will feel compelled to try one of the lollipops even before he opens the package. Draw up your own design, start-

A drum wrapping for a record

A clock wrapping for a small gift

ing with lollipops, a candy cane (or any other cellophane-wrapped candy), and dark shiny paper, ribbon, gummed tape, and stars to hold everything together.

Candy decorates a child's package

Santa Claus is always a happy fellow for us to find on a package, no matter what our age. Here pieces of construction paper are pasted on a solid-colored paper to make a raffish Santa. A gift to Dad might well be wrapped in this way, for he'll be sitting there near the

tree feeling just right to play the part of Saint Nick, himself.

Santa Claus appears on this wrapping

A jack-in-the-box Santa is made of a ping-pong ball, covered with pink gummed crepe paper and bearded appropriately with cotton. Bash in the back of the ball a little so that it will attach to the box better, and improvise cheerfully for the rest of this boisterous fellow.

Many a funny face can be made up out of a package, and it strikes a cheery note every time one sees it. This one is a pirate, but try others. Always start the face with the box tilted up into a triangle, and place the hat in one corner. Construction paper makes all the features; the earrings are gilt paper; our pirate has a brown-paper face. Suit the color of your wrapping to the clown, cowboy, or Indian that you've dreamed up.

For a gay package that is great fun to make, and easy enough for children, too, wrap the box

A pingpong ball is the start of this Santa jack-in-the-box

Confetti forms a gay wreath

A funny face makes an ingenious wrapping

first in a bright, solid-colored paper, the shinier the better. Spread on a thick coating of glue in whatever design you choose: a wreath, a tree, or a star. Sprinkle on multi-colored confetti, more than seems enough, and when the glue has dried, shake off the excess. Decorate the wreath with a ribbon bow, or the tree with a gilt star.

Perhaps you're giving a man a shirt or ties and though you feel sure it's what he wants and needs, it still seems a little un-Christmasy. Try a funny wrapping that will turn the gift into a happy package. After making the wrapping paper secure with cellophane tape, tie wide ribbon around the package in a regular four-in-hand knot. Add anything that tickles your fancy; use a little ball ornament for a stickpin; or make a white paper collar, or a loud vest of striped paper. A bow tie is fun, too; if your man wears them you might use a real one on the outside, as a little extra gift. If the gift is for a woman, the package motif can be a blouse. Use a bright solid, or lively printed, paper for the wrapping. Then cut out a peter-pan collar of crisp white paper. It can be plain, scalloped, or frilly, as your imagination dictates. Paste the collar to the top of the package and fasten a row of ribbon roses, paper discs, or candy dots down the center to the bottom to suggest buttons.

For the golfer the trimming on the package can be an extra gift. In giving golf balls or any other equipment or accessory for the sport, punch a pattern of golf tees on the lid of the box.

Decorate a gift for a bridge enthusiast with a perfect bridge hand of actual playing cards. Fan out the cards and glue them down; a cut-out hand in paper of another color (traced from your own hand), appears to hold the cards. Decorate one finger with a ring made of a seal, or the wrist with a paper bracelet or lace-doily ruffle.

A winning way to wrap a bridge-player's gift

A very fancy package for a very important person can be wrapped in this simple, elegant way. Using a bold checkerboard or striped design in the paper, trim the box with a row of

Add a little fun to a prosaic gift

For the golfer, this package's trim is an extra gift

Stars add elegance to this package

stars stuck out from the box on colored tooth-picks. Attach the toothpicks to the box with more stars. Be sure to have two stars fastened together over each toothpick tip.

Any gift about the sea around us — from a book on fishing to a pair of skin-diving goggles — could be charmingly wrapped in this fishy wrapping. Use blue paper, and glue onto it a tin or plastic fish from the dime store; add horizontal strips of blue ribbon to show water levels; and tiny Christmas balls, in ascending sizes, to show the fish's bubbles.

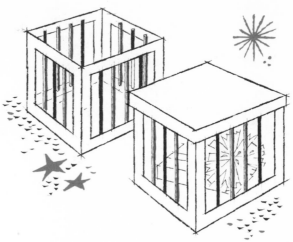

A soda straw cage for a child's tiny gift

To add a marine touch

Maybe your gift to a child is rather small even though it's just what he wants — and you are giving his brother a pogo stick or something else enormous. You can catch his envious eye right away by using the right packaging.

Put the real gift inside a soda straw cage; it's simple and effective made with brightly colored sippers and a gift box. Cut out large windows in four sides of the box, leaving intact, the four corners, and a strip at the top and bottom of each panel. Glue soda straws to these strips from the inside, put your little gift inside (glued, so that it won't slide), and put on the lid.

HIS and HERS wrappings are entertaining for the couple's first Christmas and suitable for

many a pair who've been married much longer. One easy way to make them is with pipe cleaners pasted onto bright gift paper; one in the shape of pants and one in the shape of a skirt. Spell out HIS and HERS in ribbon or tape.

Someone who knits or sews will be pleased with pretty little trifles that acknowledge her skill. A bright red pincushion in the middle of green leaves is charming: stick sequins all over

His *and* Hers *wrappings made with pipe cleaners*

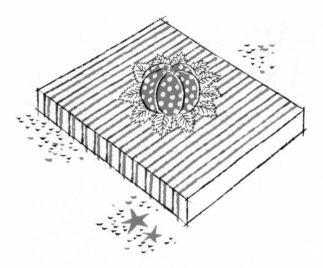

A sequinned pincushion for one who sews

it with straight pins. Wind the wrapping round and round with red and green wool, for a different effect. Or, make rosettes of embroidery floss or, string tiny, shiny nylon thread spools across the package, in unusual colors. To start a young girl on her first sweater, give her the skeins of wool and secure the needles on the outside, tucked into the bow.

For the handy man of the house, push nails (with large heads) right through the lid of the box, to spell out his name. Take care that the gift inside is protected from the points. Tie with wire or twine and — especially if there's a family joke about it — finish off with a crisp rosette of packaged bandages and a bow.

A wrapping for a handyman's gift

Adorn a gift for a student, from kindergarten to college age, with a row of red and green colored pencils. For boy or young man add a pocket, and clip a couple of ball-point pens inside. Out of white paper cut a pocket that is deep enough. When you glue it on be sure you don't press it flat — have the pocket curve up, off the wrapping paper, enough to accommodate the thickness of the pens.

Pencils mark the gift for the student

Games are a favorite gift at Christmas, for young and old alike. For fun, let your outside wrapping give a hint of what's inside. Using checkered paper, which you can make or buy, set up a checker game, in progress, with wrapped candy mints for checkers. Even though you glue them on, you'll be surprised how soon the tasty checkers disappear!

Try a package wrapped with different papers, half and half. This has a practical side, too, since it will use up odds and ends of papers and it's excellent for large or ungainly boxes. Make it dramatic, with bold contrast between the papers, or with one solid color and one plain white. Put seals in a strip down the joined edge; in the illustration we have snowmen.

Last year's Christmas cards can be used as a source of exciting decoration for packages. Cut out a Santa, or a resplendent, glittering tree, or

Use cutouts from Christmas cards as decoration

A tasty hint of the gift inside

There can't be a woman anywhere who wouldn't delight in frothy lace-paper snowflakes on her gift package. Cut out circles of various

Wrap with contrasting papers — half and half

balls, bells, snowflakes; anything beautiful will be fine. Make paper strips that measure ½ by 2 inches and pleat them. Attach the cutout design to the wrapped package by gluing one end of the paper strip to the design and the other to the package.

White snowflakes are pretty against a bold background

sizes from a doily and paste them here and there on a package wrapped in brilliant red, or green, paper. Tie the ribbon around the edge of the lid so that nothing interferes with seeing the pretty white flakes.

When a gift fails to arrive, has to be installed, or is too big for the Christmas tree, give a promissory note. Get a clip board from an office-supply house; cover with gold paper; fasten a decoration to the top. With pinking shears, cut out a sheet of white paper; glue to a 1 inch larger colored sheet; add ribbon, seal, star. Clip note to board.

A promissory note tells of a gift to come

When the gift is large, another way to preserve a surprise around the house (from Mother, especially, who knows everything that goes on) is to buy and wrap a miniature of the gift to come; doll furniture provides stoves, refrigerators, washing machines, television sets — everything. Wrap it tastefully as the small gift that

it is, and keep the guessing going until the very last moment on Christmas Day.

If you find yourself on Christmas Eve, after the last delivery truck has come and gone, in that awful position of a person who counted on something that didn't come, there is something to do besides weep. Wrap a picture. Go through magazines for a picture in color of what you were waiting for; put it in a frame (even if you have to oust another picture for the day); and wrap the whole thing as gaily and lavishly as you can, with a note or card explaining what the picture represents.

This package can be opened without spoiling the decoration, so make it as pretty as you can. Mementos, letters, almost anything can be kept in it on the closet shelf, and the person you give it to will have a year-round reminder of you. One possible color combination follows;

This box will be perfect for keepsakes

try any that you like. Cover 2 sides of a hatbox with black paper, 2 with white, and the lid with turquoise. Cut Christmas-ball shapes from colored paper; glue to sides. Above each ball, punch a hole; tape yarn end inside. To open box, just untie the yarn bow on the top.

Be the first one you know to make penny paper wraps for children's packages. Fifteen or twenty cents' worth of brand new pennies from the bank, glued at random on solid-colored paper, will make any child's eyes shine and will very nearly divert him from the gift inside while he unsticks the pennies for his pocket. Such a wrapping will make any gift more memorable, whether it is a token gift or an important one.

An engaging clown will delight children of all ages. Cut a circle, 3 inches in diameter, from shiny white paper. Slash from the outside

pensive, and they solve the paper problem handsomely for large pieces of luggage. Almost any size box, or book, can be made up to look like luggage, if you tie on the ribbon to look like suitcase straps. With luggage itself, let the handle come through the map.

A clown wrapping for a child's gift

to the center; overlap edges slightly to form a shallow cone. For eyes and mouth, use gummed seals. Glue cone to box; add ears and hat. To make ruffle, cut circle of gold paper, 8 inches in diameter; slash to center; pleat like a fan.

If you're going to visit a whole family — or a family is coming to you — make a merry package family. It's hardly any effort, particularly since the children will help on a project this engaging. The packages are first wrapped in plain white tissue paper, then colored papers (or use paint or crayon) are added to make clothes and features. Hold extra pieces in place with cellophane tape and decorate with bows of non-woven ribbon. You can have the most fun if you try to make the packages distinctly feminine or masculine.

A map! What could be more fitting as a wrapping for any travel gift, such as luggage, a cosmetic case, a man's toilet kit, or even books on travel. Maps are easy to find and free or inex-

Package families are fun

Travel is the theme of both gift and wrapping

A way to wrap your gifts with great unusual-ness and no money — except for the extras — is to use the pages from the large-sized wall paper sample books. Many stores give these books away after they've become outmoded, and you might try your luck at securing one.

A house gift couldn't be better wrapped than in this little house. It would be particularly appreciated by a young couple in their first home at Christmas, and it's very easy to make. Cut off the two long flaps of a shipping box. Cut the short flaps to points. With a dull knife crease a piece of cardboard in the center. Cover with plain paper for roof. Cover the box in patterned paper. Paste on windows and door. Cut wedge shapes in the bottom of the chimney (small box) to fit the bridge of the roof.

Just about as easy as a package can be is one with a taped-on tree, yet it conveys Christmas equally as much as one with many more holi-day props. Use green sticky tape for the tree, and decorate with shiny paper dots and the little colored bells that actually jingle.

This inspired gingham package is for a truly kitcheny gift: herbs, a pepper mill, spices. Cover

A shipping box makes a little house

Sticky green tape makes this tree

A gingham-covered box for a kitchen gift

If there is the slightest interest in your house in arts and crafts, making your own wrapping paper is a fine family project during December evenings. Start with sheets of plain paper in various colors; tissue, shiny, metallic, even butcher or shelf paper, is fine. Have poster or finger painting colors handy, also plastic sponges, a scrub brush, a clothes sprinkler, various sizes of jelly glasses, spools, potatoes and a sharp knife. Block prints are made by carving a design on a potato cut in half. (The V-shape shown here makes stars). The raised design is pressed against a sponge dampened with the paint, then onto the paper. Jelly glasses and spools dipped in color form snowmen; faces are added by hand. Spatter is done with a clothes sprinkler; plaids and stripes with the scrubbing brush. One color should be completely dry before another is applied.

the bottom and the sides of the box with red-and-white checked gingham, the top with bright green paper. Glue on the kind of gilt initials you can buy in sign shops and hardware stores, and the receiver may well be able to use the box for a long time to come for kitchen odds and ends.

Crisp fabrics of any kind make a gift outstanding; glazed chintz, for instance, is perfect. Always cover the top and the bottom of the box separately *(see page 43)* so that the box may be opened without damage to the wrap.

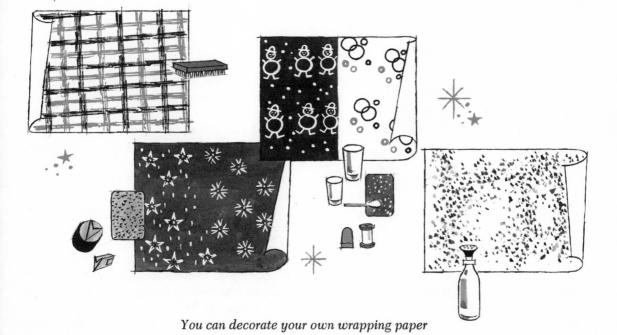

You can decorate your own wrapping paper

In this way the box may be used long after Christmas.

There's a simple way to wrap a tall bottle, such as an unusual herb vinegar for a friend who loves to cook gourmet foods. Set the bottle into a small, closed box with the lid cut out to fit the bottle's base. To enclose the rest of the bottle, twist a cone of stiff paper (colored, gold, or silver), and leave a small opening at the top. To transform this simple cone into a pretty princess' wimple, let an inexpensive chiffon scarf drift out from the top opening and paste gummed stars or sequins at random on the cone. Or, create a gay Mardi Gras hat with confetti streamers or shredded crepe paper spurting forth from the top and a few brightly colored seals or paper cutouts pasted near the bottom.

Christmas bags are festive for hard-to-wrap items

A cone makes a wrap for a tall bottle

PACKAGES FOR FOOD GIFTS

Simple gifts to a neighbor, containing jars of the family's best barbecue relish or perhaps a few flower bulbs are sometimes difficult to wrap,

especially when you have no box. A good solution: Christmas paper bags, which come in a wide assortment of colors. Put your gift in a red bag and spread a generous border of glue around the bottom. Stick wads of cotton batting to the glued area. Then fold the top over on one side, secure, and glue on a white cotton pompom. You have a jaunty Santa's hat. Or, paste on some reindeer cut out from old Christmas cards, fasten a row of bells a few inches from the bottom of the bag, and a bow through the top.

A thoroughly nice way to give your Christmas cookies is to package them as candles; flat candies, too, can be managed this way. For each candle use only as many cookies or candies as you can hold easily in the span of your hand, about 15 or 20. Cut out 3 circles of cardboard the size of your largest piece of sweet. Put one circle on the bottom, one in the middle, and one on top. Roll the stack of candies or cookies securely in aluminum foil. Wrap this cylinder in heavy gift paper, allowing enough extra fold-over at the top and bottom to fold and tape these ends. Cut out a flame-shaped piece of construction paper and attach to one end with clear tape.

A chimney wrapping is good for sweets

Wrap cookies in a candle-shaped package

Cookies, fudge, or brownies, overflowing from an open chimney top, are almost irresistible to the eye. Cut out the top of a box lid; cover both lid and box with chimney crepe paper. Glue the rim of the lid to the box, upside down. Then fill with something good to eat and tie up with clear freezer wrap; it makes a perfect token gift. It's ideal if you have lots of children you wish to remember with goodies.

Save your coffee tins a long time before Christmas. They make fine packages for gifts of cookies and candies. Decorate them first by painting a good, bright color. Play around with decoration; one idea is to tape onto the lid a

Decorated coffee tins are good containers for cookies

ring of colored pipe cleaners. Paste a star or sequin at the end of each pipe cleaner, then bend them all gently toward the center until you have a domelike effect. Tie a shiny ribbon in a contrasting color over the tape.

Start again with a painted coffee tin; cut several strips of ribbon, long enough to hang from the center of the lid to halfway down the sides. Attach a tiny Christmas bell to one end of each ribbon. Then paste the ribbons from the center of the lid outward, like the spokes of a wheel. Fasten a star to the center of the lid where the ribbons meet; the bells against the tin will make a racket, but children will love it!

Children will love the noisy bells on this coffee tin

You can give honey away complete with bees. Make a stylized flower of gold-paper stars and a small gold ball ornament, or use an artificial flower. To top it, attach by fine wire the bees to be found in notion departments or variety store jewelry sections.

Give honey away, complete with bees

If you prefer making your own bees, twist fuzzy black and yellow pipe-cleaners into a

body; fasten on wings cut from clear acetate; and add wire legs.

Place jars of jam or jelly on large sheets of red, pink, and pale green tissue. Draw them all up and tie with ribbon; fluff out the layers of tissue at the top.

Wrap jam or jelly in flowerlike colored tissue

An oatmeal box, filled with cookies or candy, can be wrapped as a great big Christmas candle. Use tinsel, signal dots, sequins perhaps, and the bow described on page 47, pinched a bit at the top to resemble a flame.

If you'd like to give some of your favorite cheese spread, or jelly or jam or relish, pack it in a little individual casserole that comes with a matching tile. Wrap the tile in Christmas paper, and attach the unwrapped casserole to the top, with ribbon.

Give a Yuletide coffeecake placed on a round breadboard, wrapped whole in clear freezer wrap, and tied with red ribbon.

Leave a loaf cake or nut bread in the baking pan (after having bought a brand new shiny one for the purpose) and wrap in wax paper

Use an oatmeal box to make a huge candle package

harden. Make a cone from construction paper, and staple, or seal with cellophane tape. Hang the thimble-sized mints on it. Put the large mints in an olive bottle. Stand the tree cone on top of the bottle; secure with tape. Stick

and a box; decorate as you would any other package.

Give cookies in a cookie jar: the nicest, most traditional one you can find. Especially in a family of children it will become the focal point of the kitchen for years to come.

Give fruit frosted in sugar *(see page 166)*, arranged in a basket. Wrap in clear freezer wrap, tie with a silver ribbon. It couldn't be a more sophisticated gift. It looks lovely as a centerpiece and it's good to eat, too.

Make Christmas mint trees: they're a wonderful way to package candy as gifts for children. They are an especially good idea if you have many children (such as a Sunday School class) on your list. They're also an excellent project for children to undertake, since both the recipe for the mints *(see page 165)* and the packaging are simple and fun to do. While the thimble-sized mints are still soft, press a 2 inch piece of wire into each one. (One end of each wire should be bent into a hook before the other end is inserted in the mint.) Let all mints

Mints are the start of this Christmas tree

two gummed stars together at the top of the tree. (The recipe on page 165 makes enough mints for two trees.)

Here's an easy, basic wrap; the children can make it. Fill a clean, washed rectangular carton (from ice cream or potato chips) with home-made candy. Cover the carton with gummed crepe paper of any color. Cut strips of plain crepe paper, of a different color, 2 inches wide and as high as your carton. Fringe each strip on each edge. Glue the fringe to the corners of the package. Tie on a bright ribbon and make a bow on top.

A clean carton is the start for this simple wrapper

If you have little girls on your list, there's no sweeter way to package Christmas treats for them than this. Pack candy or cookies, your homemade kind or any other, in a box. Cover the box with pink gummed crepe paper. Add gummed stars for eyes, and a heart mouth. Braid 3 long strips of crepe paper, preferably matched to the color of each little girl's hair. Tie the braids around the box with ribbon. A hair ribbon on top completes the package, so pretty that even a hungry little girl anxious for the sweets inside will linger over it.

A wrap especially for a little girl's gift

IF YOUR GIFT MUST TRAVEL

Lots of packages must travel across the miles at Christmas — gifts lovingly chosen, fancily wrapped, and carrying as well a precious bur-den of affection for someone. Yet millions of these packages travel at a time of year when the post office facilities are extremely overtaxed, help is often inadequately trained, and weather conditions are, in general, poor. How can we be sure our packages will get there on time, and in good condition?

Start with a packing plan. Make a list of the packing supplies that you'll need — string, tape, labels, cartons — and buy them all in one trip to the stationery store.

The very best container for a Christmas gift that must be mailed is a fresh new cardboard carton. Sometimes you can obtain from local merchants cartons which are in excellent condition, with firm corners and intact flaps. Or they can be bought; buying a carton is well worth while if it protects a valuable present.

If there is even a remote chance that a gift could be broken or crushed, use *two* cartons, one inside the other. The inner carton should be big enough to allow at least a 2 inch clearance all around the package enclosed — on all four sides as well as at the top and bottom.

Don't let a present rattle around in a carton, whether you use two, as recommended, or one. The best, cheapest cushioning is *shredded* newspaper; crumpled newspaper doesn't have enough give to protect the gift from the shock of handling. Use enough shredded paper so that there is no rattling or shifting when the package is shaken back and forth.

It is not necessary to wrap a carton in heavy wrapping paper, whether you mail it or send it by express. Paper does not add to the strength of the carton, and if it is torn in transit there is the possibility of the label's being lost.

For the utmost safety, make out two labels: one for the outside and one to be placed *inside* the carton. The post office objects to more than one label on the outside, but if you express the package, use two outside labels.

Remember to remove or cover up all the old labels on a carton, if you're using a secondhand one. Write your labels in permanent ink or crayon. If you have any doubt, wet and smudge a test label after you've made it out, and see what snow, rain and friction would do to it under poor circumstances.

Use the full names and addresses of yourself and the recipient of the package; don't use abbreviations. And even if you feel you write a good hand it is always better to print than to use handwriting.

Tie up your carton with medium-heavy cord, wound tightly around the entire package at least two or three times and knotted with simple double knots. Very heavy twine is not as safe, strangely enough, because it is too heavy to pull tight and therefore slips off the package more easily.

Regulations governing packages to be mailed within 150 miles are different from those for packages to be mailed farther than that, as far as the weight permitted is concerned. There is another regulation for the weight of packages which have an APO address. Check these rules with the post office if you want to send heavy packages, since the rules may change from time to time. You may express a package of any weight, no matter how heavy.

The post office strongly advises December 1 as the deadline on mailed packages. It's better to chance their arriving a bit early, with a DO NOT OPEN UNTIL CHRISTMAS sticker, than to run the slightest risk of their not arriving until the day after The Day.

Expressing by rail or air are quicker methods, of course, than mailing a package; be sure to investigate these ways if you've let an important package slip past December 1.

In addition to these general rules, here are hints for packaging a variety of objects.

Flat, nonbreakable objects, such as books, need a double corrugated-paper covering. Envelop the book lengthwise in a corrugated strip, seal with gummed tape. Wrap a second strip around the width and seal. Use heavy brown paper for outer wrapping.

If you are sending a very small package in a box of its own, you must enclose it in a larger carton to be sure of its safe delivery, and cut down the danger of loss.

Pictures, mirrors, and wood articles are best protected from scratches when wax paper is placed directly over the glass or wood, followed by a double corrugated-paper covering. Place the wrapped object in a box; pack space around it with shock-absorbing material.

For sending cookies, there's no safer or nicer package stuffing than popcorn — all around the cookies and between the boxes, if you use two.

Double corrugated paper for flat objects

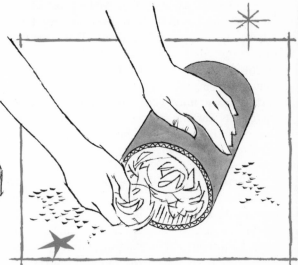

Fragile objects need very careful packing

Fragile objects without a box of their own should be packed inside a corrugated paper sleeve, and all spaces filled with shredded newspaper or crumpled tissue paper. If the object is hollow, fill it with the same material. For absolute safety, place this container inside a carton for mailing.

(Or, use popcorn as an added treat in sending a child any kind of breakable object.)

Other good insulating materials are hay, straw, and ground corncobs, if available. Shredded newspaper is always handy; it's a good thing to put the youngsters to work on, too.

Use wax paper to protect objects from scratching

Popcorn is fine for filling space in packing

Cut folded newspaper into strips about a half-inch wide, toss them about to separate them, and then lightly crush them between your hands. Cutting, tossing, and crumpling are activities you'll always find little hands eager to do.

Shredded newspaper is excellent for packing

4 Christmas Cards

YOUR OWN CHRISTMAS CARDS

F there's anything that brings out the creative urge in us, it's Christmas. Even if we don't bake, or sing, or sew, or paint much during the year, we find ourselves cheerily making cookies, singing carols, running up little gifts on the machine — and making Christmas decorations. And as for Christmas cards, well, everyone at some time or another is tempted. Without question, the cards we look at longest, and remember most, and can't bear to throw away, are the cards we receive that friends have made themselves.

A Christmas card with a photograph of our family is usually the first kind of handmade card we think of, and rightly so; it's intimate and unique. No one else can send it, nor would we send it to anyone except warm friends and relatives. It therefore carries with it a mark of affection that is special to itself.

The first thing to do is plan your picture carefully. If you have a fine picture of the family taken one Christmas, it's quite sensible to save it for the following year's cards. The picture has the spontaneity of having been taken at the right moment, and holiday spirit shines out of it. The house is trimmed, the tree is up, and there are unmistakable evidences in the background of the season. For these reasons, it's a good picture to select for your card, and it precludes the necessity of setting the stage for a Christmas picture in November, in time for processing. Where there are young children in the family, however, who grow and change so much in a year (or, even more so, where there is a new member of the family), the good picture from the year before seems outdated, and you'll want to prepare a new one.

It's possible, of course, to simulate a holiday picture with decorations or wreaths that are saved from year to year, and arranged to form a background that seems authentic. This kind of picture, when successful, can be very effective. But if you'd rather not pretend that it's Christmas a month ahead of time, snap a good scene of Christmas preparations; the children writing a letter to Santa Claus, everyone in the kitchen making gingerbread cookies, Dad and the children checking strings of tree lights

68

(which are lit) to see if they're ready for the big day.

A snow scene of your house or, in any climate, a shot of your front door wreathed for the holiday, is an excellent idea for a card-picture. Let your photographic imagination guide you, and take a picture that speaks best of your own family life.

Once you have your picture, take the negative to your camera store. If you want a printed card, ask to see samples of photographic printing paper on which holiday messages are already printed. They are designed in such a way as to show your picture to good advantage.

You can order almost any number of these cards, and they are not very expensive.

If you'd rather design your own card, remember the precaution for all handmade cards: buy your envelopes first, as soon as you've determined the size of your card but before you've made any of them. Pretty envelopes for cards come in several standard sizes, and it's easier to make your cards to fit the envelopes you've decided upon than the other way around.

For your own snapshots, a card of folded paper with a cutout window shows them in an interesting way *(Figs. A, B, C)*. Use construction paper, parchment, or fairly stiff gift-wrapping paper (not tissue wrap). Use a razor blade to cut out the window; try different shapes of window to find the one that frames your picture best. The window needn't expose the entire picture: if your picture is a little off center or has uninteresting areas, arrange the window to make it appear centered, or to show only its best features. The window can be round, too; use a compass for this. Make slits to hold the picture, or use hinges.

Simple designs are also very good as the background for a picture. Make a tree shape *(page 70)* of strips of colored tape *(Fig. D)*. Or daub green finger paint to suggest a wreath on a card with a round cutout *(Fig. E)*.

You have the entire assortment of paints, seals and tapes to choose from in decorating your card, but take care that you do not in your enthusiasm overwhelm your picture with a too-fancy card. The picture itself is precious

A folder for your own snapshots

to your friends and family, so let it stand out.

Use colored inks, or silver or gold paint on a fine brush, for your message and signature.

If you're not used to handling a brush, or think that you might have difficulty with one, excellent brushlike effects can be obtained easily by using a broad-nibbed pen (the Speedball type, for poster work). To simulate brush

Design a simple background for your picture

strokes in script or lettering, choose one of these pens with a beveled nib. Anyone who can write can be successful with such pens.

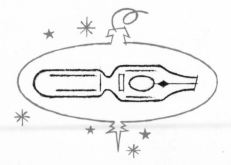

A beveled nib will simulate brush strokes

Handmade cards with stained-glass windows: doesn't the idea sound beautiful? A truly unusual card can be created by sprinkling shavings of colored crayons between two pieces of waxed paper and then pressing with a warm iron. Use colors separately, with plenty of space between them, and let cool and harden. Cut in sizes to your own design, and paste behind an opening in your card that's cut out in the shape of a Gothic church window. Don't try to manage a representational picture; make a design of pleasing shapes and colors in harmony. The effect of stained glass will convey the church-window concept.

Another material which can be used is the waxed paper in candy boxes, which sometimes comes with a frosted glass effect or with a spiderweb-like design in it. If such paper has been saved through the year, it would come in handy here for making very unusual "stained glass."

A "stained glass window" card

The card itself, cut out of construction paper in the shape of a Gothic window, can have the simplest message written on it, in white or silver paint.

Making Christmas cards shouldn't be reserved for artists and the kindergarten set, although sometimes the rest of us are a little shy about it. We needn't be, because delightful and artistic cards can be made by anyone, even those people who confess that they can't draw a straight line.

The use of interesting materials is one answer. Ferns, for instance, make perfect little Christmas trees. Snip off the fronds from the left side of a fern, leaving the main stem intact to serve as a little lane at the base of the trees. (It is the right side of the fern that you will use, but save the individual left-side fronds; you might use them on other cards, or on place cards for a party.) Glue to a folded parchment card, and stick little gold or silver stars at the tip of each frond.

A

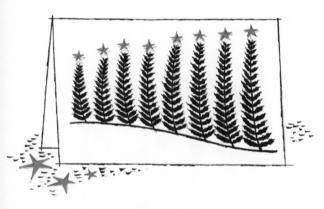

Fern leaves make little Christmas trees

A fern tip makes a pretty Christmas tree

One pressed fern tip is pretty used as a tree, mounted on a scrap of velvet or a heavy-textured paper. Use it in its original green *(Fig. A)*, decorated with sequins, or spray in white or gold, sprinkle it generously with sequins or glitter, and use a dark-colored velvet for mounting *(Fig. B)*.

Felt and pinking shears can produce striking cards very, very easily. Felt comes in vivid colors and needs no hemming; the pinked edge is attractive and finished-looking.

One very pleasing design is a boot; just one thickness of felt, cut in a boot outline, is all

Use felt to make unusual cards

you need to use. Try your own color combinations; one idea is a white book, trimmed with red or gold rickrack and topped with a pipe cleaner candy cane in red and white. Tie the cane with a narrow bit of green ribbon. Attach the cane with a few spots of casein glue, being careful not to use too much or press down too hard, since the glue will soak through and spoil the nap.

Another shape easy to cut in outline is the outline of mittens, which are wintry, Christmasy, and cute. Make glittery, fancy ones for big girls and bright red ones for little boys and girls; perhaps their initial or name pasted on, in white felt, would add a perfect touch.

Green felt Christmas trees make brilliant cards

Almost any design you see that catches your fancy can be simplified enough to be cut out of felt and be pretty — as pretty as a Christmas card.

Felt mittens are attractive cards

Green felt Christmas trees can be brilliant; let the children, who won't want to stop, paste on all the tiny baubles that the tree will hold.

Once everyone gets involved with felt in all its tempting colors, new ideas will just grow out of the cutting. Wreaths, snowmen, fireplaces, chimneys, Santas, all are fun and easy. Make vivid poinsettias with yellow sequin centers, or a sweet little angel face made of pink felt for the face, white wings with silver sequins and yellow-fringed felt for the hair.

Felt has endless possibilities for cards

Construction paper and pipe cleaners are another happy set of materials for Christmas cards. Follow these designs, making up your own color combinations, and probably before you're through you'll have half a dozen ideas of your own.

These are wonderfully simple to do, especially since the pipe cleaners can be bent and rebent until the design is satisfying.

Pipe cleaners can be bought in a wide variety of colors; they can also be dyed to any shade. When they are ready to be attached to the card, use a bit of casein glue here and there. Press down gently, and don't use too much glue, or you will soak the nap of the cleaners and make them less pretty.

Paper, of course, is an old standby for making designs on greeting cards; perhaps you don't realize how many new kinds of paper products are added each year to the supplies in stationery stores and party counters.

Clear a good-sized working space and spread out construction paper in several colors, metallic papers, gummed crepe, gummed paper, cellophane tape in colors and in designs, luminous dots, seals, stars and Christmas seals of all kinds. Begin with simple notions and improvise as you go along. Test the look of everything before you stick it down. Use unusual shapes for the card itself, always remembering first to have an envelope that fits.

Since paper is so wonderfully inexpensive as a material, snip and experiment to your heart's content.

A simple card from construction paper

Make a top-fold card from construction paper; cover the front of the card with gummed crepe of another color.

Pipe-cleaners can be used in making cards

Try three trees of identical size, the two on the outside the same color as each other, the one in the middle different. (They can be cut out all at once so that they are exactly the same in shape.) Sprinkle with dots and stars; cut the front of the folded paper a bit shorter than the back so the card has trim when closed.

Two little gingerbread boys can be cut out of brown gummed crepe, snipped double, like paper dolls, so that they hold hands. Button them down the front with dots, and make their white icing of white gummed crepe. Swing them from the bough of the green crepe evergreen, tied with red gummed crepe.

Gingerbread boys make this card

Paper can do very nearly everything. Make silver-foil bells (cut in many thicknesses, folded like paper dolls) and string them across a deep royal blue card. Letters can be cut from foil or bought, ready made.

Paste vertical strips of red foil on a white card; attach a bright green foil Christmas ball in the center.

Cut out one big green foil tree, or a row of smaller ones; cut canes from red-striped paper; make chimney tops cut from brick-patterned paper. Keep your eyes open for interesting paper, save pieces of gift wrapping paper that are different. And let the children cut and paste without hindrance! They're so much closer to their kindergarten days that they

plunge in with a bravado that's worth copying, when you make your own original designs.

Cut out your own original designs

A rich source of decoration for making your own cards are the cards you receive, yourself, other years. We often receive cards we think too pretty to throw away. Designs are often especially appealing for one reason or another; sometimes a painting or etching is reproduced that is a little work of art.

Cut out such beautiful portions of old cards and build a new card of your own around them. Trim in a way that you feel is appropriate and will enhance the cutout. In adding your time and thought to it, you've made something new and made it your own.

Odds and ends from your sewing cabinet can make cards that will be remembered, too. Buttons, ribbons, bias tape and rickrack all lend a nice feel and style to the basic parchment or construction paper card.

When using buttons on a card, place the card in the envelope so that buttons are not in the upper right-hand corner where the cancellation machine will crack them. Better mark on the envelope PLEASE CANCEL BY HAND.

A piece of inch-wide red satin ribbon makes a glowing Christmas candle. The flame is aluminum foil, the leaves are foil, also, jaggedly cut to resemble pine needles or holly.

To make, cut out an 8¼x6 inch piece from gray or green paper. Measure off 3¾ inches on the top and bottom of the long side. Fold. Then measure off another 3¾ inches and fold again. This will leave a ¾ inch flap to overlap the folded card.

with five rows of ½ inch green or yellow rick-rack in increasing lengths. Space the rows about ¾ inch apart. Line up colored sequins between the rows so that they seem to hang from the rickrack points. Make the trunk and tip with sequins, too. Write the greeting on the left side of the card; decorate the message with more sequins.

A card that's intended to hang from the tree is this clever Christmas ball; it folds over and becomes its own envelope, too.

A candle from satin ribbon

Make the candle from a 3 inch strip of red satin ribbon. Paste down, and add the aluminum foil flame and leaves. Decorate with a few sequins. Print the greeting with black ink on the left side of the card; punctuate *i*'s with sequin dots.

Rickrack makes a modern Christmas tree; you may find that the people who receive it will hang it from the tree or give it first spot in a display — it's that sparkly.

From red or yellow paper, cut a strip 9½x6 inches. Fold it in half crosswise. Form the tree

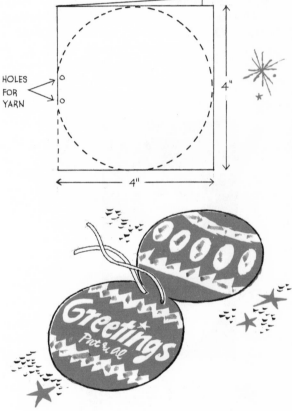

A card for hanging on the tree

Start by folding an 8x4 inch strip of black or red paper in half crosswise. Starting at the folded edge, cut out a circle about 4 inches across, leaving about 1 inch on the folded area uncut so that the ornament opens up to two circles without falling apart.

Rickrack forms this Christmas tree

From aluminum foil, cut out zigzag and other designs to decorate the tree ball; paste onto the card. Make two tiny holes on the fold and pull a short length of red, green, or yellow yarn through; knot the ends.

For mailing, the card should be folded with the design and yarn hanger inside. (When received, it will be opened with the design outside, and the yarn hanger will be pulled through the holes, for proper hanging on the tree.)

Print the greeting with white ink, fold and seal.

Here's a card that has the look of luxury, but is actually simple enough for a child to make.

Directions: Cut and fold a card of solid-colored paper. On the front of the card, spread a thick layer of glue in the shape of a bell, a tree, a star, or a wreath. While the glue is still wet, sprinkle on a handful of sequins, enough to completely cover the glued area. (Glass beads or multi-colored confetti can be used in place of the sequins, if you wish.) Set the card aside, and when it is dry, gently shake off any excess sequins. Use colored-paper tape to make a bow for your bell or wreath or a base for your tree. Then write your greeting under the design in a contrasting-colored ink.

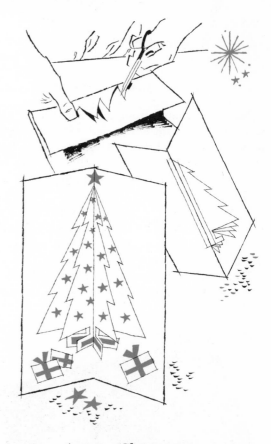

A pop-up Christmas tree

Handmade pop-up cards are impressive and make you appear very skilled, yet they're also in the "easy-to-make" category. Color combinations can be your own; work with construction paper, handsome foils, or stiff, gift paper.

Directions: Fold a sheet of paper and cut out a tree shape, either saw-edged, to show branches,

A penny tree and a rich snowman, for youngsters

or straight-edged, like a tall, stately triangle. Include a simple base for the tree *(Fig. A)*.

˙ Make another tree just like it and then place the folds of the two trees together, joining them from the back with transparent tape. Decorate with gummed stars, sequins, or snips of gummed tape. Again from the back, tape the tree to the center fold of the paper you have chosen for the card itself *(Fig. B)*.

Fold and unfold a few times, to be sure your pop-up is popping easily. Write the message on the front and add, if you like, some paper gifts under the tree, tied up with gummed tape.

Coins stuck on a card for a child will tickle him far more than a ready-made card that costs the same; somehow the shiny pennies given this way take on more value in his eyes than pennies usually have. These cards couldn't be simpler to make, and ideas will come as you work along. They're a happy idea for a child to make for his little friends, too, when there would otherwise be no gift.

Directions: Supply yourself with brand-new pennies and, if you like, bright new dimes. Use heavy construction paper, in colors that will show off the coppery and silvery colors of the coins. Fold over, so that the message may be

Even a child can make this dazzling sequin card

written inside. Then just glue on the coins; the penny tree will make itself as you fit the coins together. Finish with paper-tape trunk and base.

For the snowman, mount two circles of white construction paper on a bright color; then cut a hat, smiling mouth, and belt from black paper. Glue on pennies for buttons, and perhaps two glittering new dimes for his eyes.

GOOD MANNERS IN CHRISTMAS CARDS

Each year we send out Christmas cards to our family, friends, and business associates in what always seems to be a growing number. We sometimes speak of it as a chore: "I haven't sent out my cards yet. I *must* sit down and do it." Yet essentially, and in our hearts we know it, it is one of the pleasantest chores of the year. It gives us a chance to remember and reach old, old friends, who may be far away and whom we seldom see. School friends, remote members of the family, people we do not correspond with for the rest of the year, all can be shown that we do not forget them and do not want ever to forget them.

New acquaintances and neighbors can be reached, too, with a card, in an opening gesture of friendliness. Often relationships that are tentative are established at Christmas by the sending of a greeting card, for the heart of the matter is that we are saying: "I feel warmly toward you, I have placed you inside my world of people, I wish you well, and I want you to know all this."

And people we know only at work, with whom we have little social contact during the year, can be told in this simple way of our regard and responsiveness to their person.

So when we, with a counterfeit sigh, sit down to send out greeting cards, we are in reality assembling those people who make up our own corner of the world, and offering each the open hand of friendship in the name of the very day that means love and peace among people.

Are there, then, rules for this? There are not any rules which interfere with the spirit of well-wishing, no. But there are rules that implement this spirit, and help us to communicate more perfectly what we wish to imply.

Choose a card, or cards, which reveal you. Do this consciously; take the time to look at many, many cards of all kinds, and select those which say the most to you and which you feel most drawn to. Don't buy cards because they seem fashionable to you, or modern, or for any consideration but your own pleased reaction to them. Don't try to be brilliant or offbeat — unless that happens to be your total personality and is exactly what you want to convey.

Choose different groups of cards; you'll probably want to send to friends a different kind of card from the one you send to fellow workers. Cards with the name printed or engraved are entirely correct; as a matter of taste, however, some people feel that only a card signed by hand is proper. There is one rule here, though: printed cards should have printed names, engraved cards engraved names. On either of these, of course, a handwritten signature is correct.

Many people use a Christmas card as a kind of once-a-year letter to those far away, and write a long note on it. All authorities agree that this is perfectly correct to do, a wonderful expression of the true meaning of the season.

Send a card to anyone your feelings urge you to remember; don't stifle any impulse along this line. In most cases it will be a mutual exchange by the automatic fact of friendship, and you needn't say, "Will they be embarrassed if they aren't sending me one?" In that rare case where someone you didn't remember sends a card to you, if there is still time to do so, send a card in return. If there is not time before Christmas, write a note saying thank you for the card, or buy a card which says this. Or send a New Year's card.

Aside from subject matter, let your card in other ways reflect your thoughtfulness. Send it out in plenty of time before the holiday so that it cannot be misconstrued as an afterthought. If you blot the ink or make a messy mistake, discard the envelope or card. Stick the stamp on neatly, squared with the envelope, and not helter-skelter as though you had sent out your cards in a harried, belt-line way. Remember that a sealed envelope with a four cent stamp does seem more gracious than a tucked-in flap, and seal envelopes if you can afford it. Take care that the postage is correct on heavy cards, or cards going to foreign countries, so that no one need pay for it at the other end.

If your cards are hand-signed, and therefore your full name does not appear anywhere on them, by all means put your full name on the envelope with your return address. Your card may be signed "Mary and George" but you have no way of knowing, in most cases, how many other Marys and Georges your friend knows; nor of knowing how little he recognizes handwriting. It can be perplexing — and vexing — in the extreme to receive a card meant to convey good wishes and not be able to tell where they came from.

If you decide to have your cards this year imprinted with your name, first consider the degree of formality or informality you desire. The cards you send to relatives and friends will naturally be in an informal vein, and should be imprinted as follows:

Anne and Mark Carey
or
The Careys
Anne and Mark

It is a matter of personal taste, which name comes first, the man's or woman's.

For business associates, the formal imprint is preferred as follows:

Mr. and Mrs. Mark Carey

Listing each member of the family: Use a comma to separate each individual in the family or use "and" before the last member listed.
The Barkers
Alice, Henry, Kathy and Susan
or
The Barkers
Alice, Henry, Kathy, Susan

Order of children's names: Children are listed according to age, regardless of sex.

The single girl: She usually uses the informal style:

Penny Marsh

The single man may use:

Stuart Martin   Stu Martin   Stuart M. Martin

Use of Jr.: The use of Jr. as an addition to a boy's name is not separated from the boy's name if the boy is mentioned within the series, for example:

Helen, Paul, Anne, Paul Jr., Robert

If the Jr. belongs to the youngest member of the family who is naturally listed last, the boy's first name and the Jr. are separated by a comma, as follows:

Helen, Paul, Nancy, Eric and Paul, Jr.

The forming of plurals: Names ending in *s* add *es*. Never form the plural of names with an apostrophe *s*. Family names ending in *ch, sh, s* or *z*, add *es*.

| Harsh | Church | Knox | Markowitz |
| Harshes | Churches | Knoxes | Markowitzes |

If adding *es* is not desirable to you or sounds clumsy, use the surname followed by the word "Family."

The Forester Family

To form the plural of all other family names, add *s*.

The Careys
Anne and Mark

Names followed by Jr. or II: The plurals of names followed by Jr. or II may be correctly formed in two ways as shown below. In either case, the first example of each is the preferred use of the plural.

The Mark Careys, Jr.   The William Fentons, II
or   or
The Mark Carey, Jrs.   The William Fenton, IIs

Engaged couples: It is quite proper that engaged couples jointly send an informal card, imprinted simply *Barbara and Jim*, etc.

Officers in the Army, Marines, or Air Force use their titles if they hold the grade of Captain or higher. For other grades, "Mr." is preferred. Naval officers use titles with the grade of Lieutenant Commander or higher. Never use both "Mr." and title. It is permissible for noncommissioned officers to use their titles, but "Mr." is generally considered correct.

5

Have a Christmas House

DECORATE THE OUTSIDE

Let your home, your door, your windows, call out the Christmas message. For family, for friends, for strangers passing by, you can set the joyous mood of the season days before the Day itself. It's always such a pleasant moment when we see the first lighted wreath, the first evergreen sparkling at night on a lawn. Christmas can begin at that hour for us, and extend all through the holidays.

You can decorate in such a way that you share your Christmas happiness. An outside tree, the rim of a porch, windows, gables, archways — almost anything — can be strung with colored lights, and nothing could be gayer. Greens and wreaths, decorated with pine cones and holly and red bows, are signs for all the world to see that you are ready to welcome the holidays and all those who come to your door to help celebrate them.

If you have a lamppost on your front lawn, what could be a more natural way for it to appear at Christmas time than as a giant candle? All you have to do is to surround the post from base to lamp with corrugated cardboard or chicken wire, then cover the tubelike enclosure with bright red or green foil or oilcloth. Or, if the weather is really rugged, you can cut a strip of red or green linoleum to the height needed to form the candle tube. Spray the top of the candle with gold glitter. The "flame," of course, will be the lamplight itself, softened by surrounding it with a cloud of angel hair.

A lamppost becomes a magnificent Christmas candle

When you are planning decorations for your lawn, or for the planting next to the house, don't forget your bird and squirrel friends. Offer them holiday hospitality by hanging, from a tree or shrub, bright tarlatan bags filled with suet, nuts or other tasty bits. Stitch up only one side of the bag, leaving the other side open for easy access. Or, if you buy the bags, make a long slit in one side.

Outdoors, a birds' Christmas tree

If you don't have a living tree, buy a small tree on a stand, shiny cornucopia cups, birdseed, and chunks of suet. The children will love to string necklaces of raisins, cranberries, and popcorn. Hang the garlands on the tree as you would tinsel, and tie the cups of birdseed and suet on with red and green ribbons. The nicest kind of bird-tree is just outside a window, where everyone can watch the birds come and go.

Even your garage door can be decked out in Christmas finery. Decorate it with a wreath, a few sprays of evergreen tied with bright bows, colored aluminum cutouts, or any other adornment that seems appropriate and durable. If

Junior keeps his tools and bike in the garage, he might claim this project for himself.

Massive porch columns can be handsomely covered with large, bold motifs. Here's an idea that you can try when you decorate yours: Cut oversized holly leaves from green aluminum foil and arrange them in clusters, attaching red Christmas balls for berries. Then string the clusters of leaves on a wire and wind them round and round the porch column, in a climbing vine fashion.

Giant holly leaves climb a porch column

Don't forget your window box at Christmas time. It can be decorated in many different ways — inexpensively and easily — and will add its own bit of festivity to your house. One very striking and effective box arrangement is made with evergreen boughs, or just twigs and branches, sprayed white or gold, and set off by a few stately, red candles. The candles are cardboard tubes (the kind that serve as the roll for wax paper or aluminum foil) covered with red foil; the "flame" is angel hair stuffed into the top of the tube. Incidentally, boughs or branches sprayed white or gold can be arranged in an attractive sheaf, trimmed with ornaments, and tied with a red or green oilcloth ribbon to make an eye-catching decoration that's sturdy enough to withstand the stormiest elements.

Fill your window box with Christmas

For the door itself, try your hand at an asymmetrical arrangement to distinguish *your* entrance from that of every other house in the block. Mass greens, balls, and stars at one corner, letting the composition trail down one side and across the top of the entryway.

A door arrangement that is different

Large gold bells on your door will ring out Christmas cheer to all who ring your doorbell. You can buy them, or make them of papier-mâché (see instructions on page 94). If you buy your bells, weatherproof them by crushing gold aluminum foil around them. Papier-mâché bells can be painted gold, or likewise covered with gold aluminum. Use a bright-colored ornament for the clapper. Then make a bow of bright red oilcloth (an excellent material for outdoor decorations exposed to winter weather) and attach with the bells and a spray of pine to your door.

Gold bells on your door signal a gay welcome

Another durable door motif is a star full of greens and Christmas balls. It's easy to fashion by cutting a section of mesh chicken wire in a star shape, filling it with greens and ornaments, and trimming it with tinsel, gold glitter, or artificial snow.

A star of greens and glitter

Red tape creates a striking effect on this paneled door

A plain paneled door can be strikingly decorated, and all it takes is a pair of scissors and brightly colored gummed tape. Outline each panel of the door in tape and also accent the handle. Then add just a small wreath or spray of greenery — not too much, for the beauty of this door lies in its simplicity.

Vary the shape of traditional door decorations this year. For example, instead of hanging evergreens in the usual round wreath or vertical cluster, try a crescent shape. One that almost completely covers your door will be particularly impressive. Wire evergreen boughs together and bend the wire into a large curve. Then place multi-colored clusters of Christmas balls at intervals along the crescent.

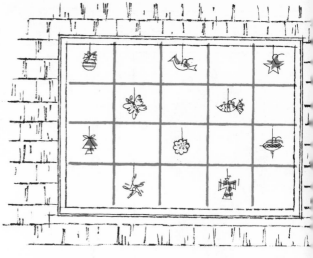

*A picture window becomes old-fashioned
and colonial*

Decorate a Christmas tree of felt

Hang huge artificial poinsettias on copper wires from the top of your windows on the inside, between the panes and your curtains.

Here's a handy tip for hanging holiday decorations on metal or glass-door panels, or even on wooden doors and walls, when you don't want to damage the surface with nails: use paste-up type picture hangers. These can be found in hardware stores and can be fastened to any surface by moistening the back. They can be completely removed by carefully scraping with a razor blade and soaking with water.

If your front door is sheltered from the weather, a delightful idea is a felt tree, decorated with all the imagination your family can muster. With pinking shears, cut two pieces of felt 14 x 20 inches into a tree shape. Paste cardboard to back of one piece, leaving a margin all around for stitching. Then stitch together bottoms and sides of the two trees, but leave an opening of 5 inches on both sides to hold a few evergreen boughs. About an inch in from the edges, fasten an inside border of gummed ribbon, heavy gold twine, or contrasting rickrack. Trim tree with small Christmas balls, all the same size, arranged in symmetrical pattern.

Artificial poinsettias hung on wire

Just for the holidays, turn your modern picture window into an old-fashioned colonial window by subdividing it into small, equal-sized squares with strips of gummed tape attached horizontally and vertically on the pane. To decorate the window, cut out small ornaments of various shapes and motifs from bright construction paper, or cut ready-made patterns from old Christmas cards. Make this a family project, with each member contributing a few paper ornaments. Then hang pretty ornaments on strings in every other square of the window, securing ends of strings under tape.

A strip of felt, hung with bells

A crescent wreath, for variety

AND ALL THROUGH THE HOUSE

Once inside, your family and friends can smell and see and hear the essence of Christmas. Fill the house with it; have a little of the holiday in every room.

Hang fragrant pomander balls in a foyer or hallway to lend a delicious, spicy aroma to your house, and when festivities are over and your guests leave, give one to each guest to take home and hang in a linen or clothes closet.

To make the pomander balls, wrap firm, perfect oranges with narrow cotton tape, forming four equal sections. Then stick whole cloves closely together until the entire exposed surface is covered. Sprinkle with orris root and let stand a few days. Shake off surplus powder and replace the tape on each ball with red or green ribbon. Have enough ribbon so that the pomander balls will hang in a long, graceful cluster. Tie the ribbons together and top with a big red or green bow and a spray of greens.

Silk upholsterer's rope in green and white adds a sophisticated note to a colonial mantel decoration of greens, plastic foam stars, white wax roses, and a cherub, or some other pretty object with a seasonal motif. You may have a plaster-of-Paris angel, or a garland of bells, or

Pomander balls are fragrant decorations

a figurine or piece of statuary that would look equally attractive in this slightly formal and elegant setting.

Silk upholsterer's rope adds a bright note

A handsome poinsettia arrangement for the mantel will last throughout the holidays if made of foil. The flowers are made of 5 inch circles, wrinkled, smoothed out, and then sprayed red *(A)*.

Fold smoothed-out circles into halves *(B)*, then into quarters *(C)*, then into eighths. Cut the two corners off the folded circle so that you have a rounded diamond shape before unfolding. Be sure to leave the narrow point uncut *(D)*. Unfold, and you have a poinsettia bloom of eight sharp-pointed petals. Glue tiny yellow beads to the center.

Make your own poinsettias from foil

Cut wire into stem lengths. Form a little circle on one end and glue a circle to the back of each poinsettia.

Cut out foil leaves; crinkle, smooth out, and spray green. When dry, add straight wire for stems. Arrange flowers and leaves against a background of pine.

Lanterns, used with caution, add to a mantelpiece

to have on hand in emergencies.) Use extreme caution, always, in using actual flame; be sure that no part of the lanterns touches the green-

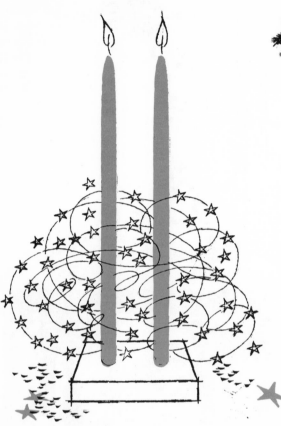

Stately candles in a cloud of stars

Wire is also the mainstay of another decoration that will add charm to a mantle, table, or the top of the television set. Set two tall candles into a styrofoam block. Attach gummed gold stars, back to back, at random along lengths of fine flexible wire. Next, wind the wire loosely around the candles, until you have the effect of a floating cloud of stars.

To lend an old-time touch to a mantel arrangement centered with polished red apples, greenery, and pine cones, set on each side a miniature fire-engine red lantern. (This kind of lantern burns kerosene and is even helpful

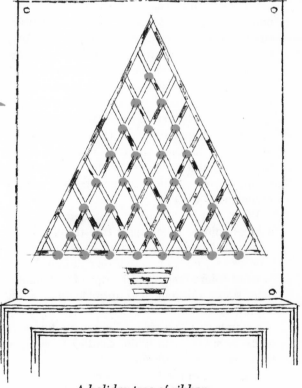

A holiday tree of ribbon

ery, and never leave the lanterns burning when you are not in the room.

If you have a large mirror, try a striking symbol of a tree made of brilliant ribbon streamers. Start with the outside triangle, using gummed ribbon or transparent tape, sticky on both sides, under regular ribbon. Inside the triangle, add parallel diagonal strips, first in one direction and then in the other, so that the strips crisscross. For the base use three short horizontal strips. Fasten small Christmas ornaments, all the same size, at points where the ribbons cross.

Milk cartons in the kitchen, naturally; but *such* milk cartons! These cute and chunky trees will make a cheerful lineup on the window sill above the sink or on the kitchen table. There's no end to the basic material, and the trees are durable and easy to make.

Directions: Cut the top from a carton, wash out and dry. Cut down the carton at the four corners; cut each panel into a triangle which slopes to a point at the top. Bring the four points together and tape them, making a steeple shape. (Before the final side is taped in, add a bunch of shredded crepe paper or confetti streamers, to spray out of the tip of the tree.) Cover the tree next, with gummed crepe paper, and add whatever trimmings you have at hand. Round seals could march up the panels; you'll get a rakish effect if you glue the panels and sprinkle confetti over them. For a neat and crisp pattern, stick gummed tape in horizontal strips all around the tree. Outline the edges of the tree with tinsel, or cover the tree with leftover scraps of your prettiest gift paper; stick a small ornament at the top.

When you have finished your tree, glue it to a large painted spool, for a tree trunk.

Spangled chains to brighten an inner doorway are easy even for very little children. Make loops of colored tapes. Add strips of cellophane tape, sticky side out, and sprinkle them with sequins or glitter.

A simple wreath is always impressive. Sprayed white or silver, with white candles flanking it on a mantel, it is extremely effective.

A graceful open stairway becomes a holiday aisle with little trees in pots on each step.

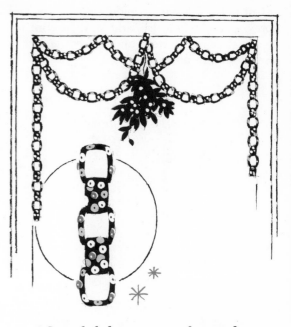

Spangled chains are simple to make

A simple wreath is always effective

Watch your window, in any room, come alive with color by creating a stained glass effect; a star design lends itself well to this technique. Tape onto the windowpane eight triangles of brilliant cellophane, in a pinwheel design. The long side of the triangle is the spoke of the wheel, and all triangles should face in the same direction. With transparent gift tape, outline each triangle in a contrasting color, and make

Tiny Christmas trees for the steps

on the pane an identical triangle, facing the colored triangle. This will make eight diamond- or kite-shaped segments of your sun-catching star.

A stained glass window with cellophane

A beribboned window box or rattan basket wears a new holiday look when filled with pine

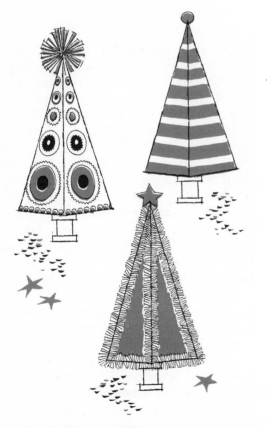

For the kitchen, milk-carton trees

Gold foil stars have a holiday look

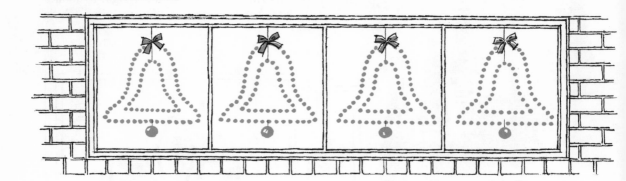

Bells of cranberries

boughs and cones and garnished with clusters of gold-foil stars attached to flexible wire.

Candles represent Christmas; the more of them the better. Let them be the entire motif for your mantle, a chest or sideboard, or the tops of bookcases. Use many of different sizes, each size and color bound together with ribbon, and arranged among greens and bright ornaments. Or, make candle groupings that resemble huge peppermint sticks; start with two of the thickest, largest, red candles you can find. Set each into a separate blob of clay, and surround each with narrow white tapers, arranged with a narrow space between each taper and placed an inch or so out from the red candle. Light the inner candle first, and as it burns, the tapers, still unlit, will cast pretty shadows.

Windows can be dressed up by the children by stringing cranberries on wires, which can be bent to form bells. Suspend a small cranberry bell inside a larger one by looping a thread through the small bell and tying the ends to the larger one. Tie a gold, or green, Christmas ball to bottom of outside bell and a bright contrasting bow to the top. Then hang the decoration from the window moldings.

Candle groupings give the feeling of Christmas

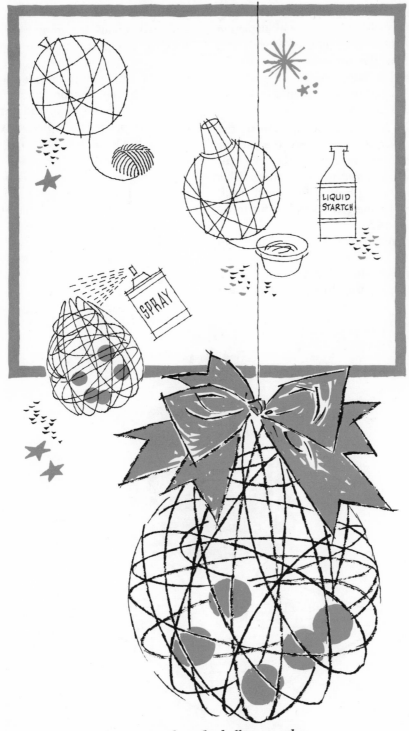

*String, starch, and a balloon are the
basic ingredients here*

A novel mesh balloon hung from the ceiling or in a doorway will be the center of attraction during the holidays. Your amazed friends will want to know how the ornaments got inside the starched string. It's simple, really; all you need is a balloon, some brightly colored yarn or string, and a bottle of liquid starch.

Directions: 1. Inflate the balloon and tie the neck. Starting from the stem, wind the yarn or string at random around and around the balloon until you've covered it with a mesh. This is for testing the length of string you'll need; unwind it now, having left enough extra to be sure, and put it aside.

2. Put some small ornaments in a paper cup and glue the cup, bottom side up, to the neck of the balloon. Set aside to dry.

3. When the glue has dried, coil the string you've measured into a bowl of liquid starch, and soak about ten minutes. Next, wind the starched string around both cup and balloon, being sure the mesh openings are smaller than the ornaments you put inside the paper cup.

4. Hang the balloon up to dry overnight. Burst the balloon then, and carefully remove it and the paper cup. Spray on snow, or brush with glue and glitter. Tie a bright red bow at the top, and hang.

A living tree for your breakfast table can be supplied from the boxwood shrubs on your terrace. A small one will readily withstand a few weeks in the house. Pot it temporarily in any handsome bowl or compote, and tie the branches with red and silver ribbons. Tuck in some white roses, either fresh or artificial.

A living Christmas tree of boxwood

Garlands of holly are a universally appealing symbol of the holiday, and making them is a happy project when the day draws to a close. The accompanying pattern can be adapted to any size, and a garland of large holly leaves would make an effective, beautiful decoration for a church hall or school.

Lastly, don't be put off by the feeling that the papier-mâché technique is difficult or complicated. It is somewhat time-consuming, that is true, but the rewards are great. It produces handsome, unbreakable objects which will last

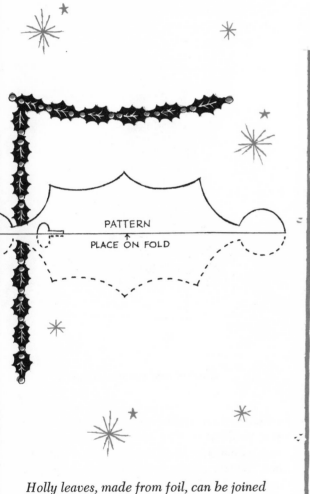

Holly leaves, made from foil, can be joined into garlands

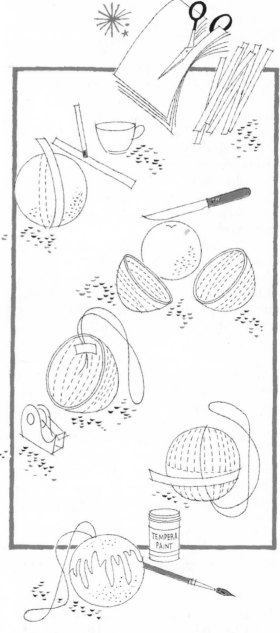

Paint veins on each leaf and add a bright holly berry at each end made with deep red nail polish or paint. The leaves are easily locked together, as illustrated, through the slot in each one. They can quickly be taken apart and stored for use another year.

Steps in making a hanging papier-mâché ball

for many years; and it is unusually inexpensive. The satisfactions from papier-mâché are great, and, once undertaken, it's a technique that will stand by in many school, church, and family projects. To make a hanging ball:

1. Cut newspaper into strips about ½ inch wide and 7 to 8 inches long. Cut several thicknesses at once. If you're making a larger object, like the snowman on page 82, you'll need wider and longer newspaper strips.

2. Cover fruit that has a waxy surface (apple, orange, pear, or gourd) with wet newspaper strips. Paste one strip at a time, vertically. Cover surface, pasting each strip in the same direction. Keep the strips moist. Smooth the surface by rubbing your fingers over the paper.

3. Continue pasting until you have 5 or 6 layers over the whole surface. Set aside to let form dry. When dry, cut through the center with a knife or saw, from top to bottom, until you reach the fruit. The two half shells pull apart easily.

4. Take a piece of cord about 12 inches long, double it, and make a strong knot at the end. Place the knotted end into the inside top center of the paper shell. Paste it into the shell with a strip of newspaper or with cellophane tape. The string acts as a hanger when the ball is hung on a tree.

5. Match the two shells together. Take small strips of the moistened newspaper and paste over the incision so that they overlap and stretch horizontally. Keep the string hanger on the outside. When the ball is thoroughly dry, it's ready for the fun of trimming.

6. White tempera paint is best for the base coat. After the base coat dries, decorate with a colored design. Paint the ornament any color. Bejewel with sequins or rhinestones to make a sparkle.

DECORATE WITH CHRISTMAS BALLS

Of all the objects that can be used for decorating every room in the house, none are more festive than colored glass balls. The possibilities for arrangement are endless.

Before you start, check your ornaments from previous years. If any seem dusty, and some with rough surfaces might, restore them to their original sparkle by gentle cleaning. Dip cotton sticks into solution of detergent and water, and carefully clean all crevices.

Elegant and easy-to-make

Start with a square styrofoam block, to serve as a pedestal for the tree. Trim in an elegant way, rather than haphazardly, so that full attention focuses on the tree. Gold paper rickrack and metal foil flowers, or seals, are effective. Then, in the center of the foam block, insert the head end of a knitting needle, the 13¾″ size. Use four glass balls of each size, from large to small. With the largest at the bottom, slip their wire hangers over the needle, setting four upon four until you reach the top. At the top, place a tiny ornament, or a tiny star, upside down. This is a fine idea for the top of the television set.

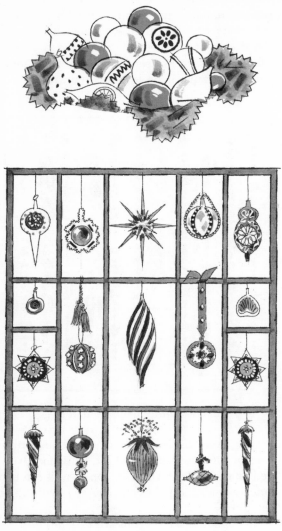

Candelabra can be used to hold glass balls

provide a focal point. Greens and tiny stars of coiled wire fill in the gaps and add sparkle.

Stand large clear glass jars on mantels, shelves, the television set, or console table, and fill them with brilliant ornaments of different sizes.

*Christmas tree ornaments have a
variety of uses*

Instead of using candles in the candelabra, fill each holder with florist's clay, set a knitting needle firmly into it, and string it with pink and silver balls in graduated sizes. Stick silver tinsel in between the balls and top the "candles" with silver Christmas bugles.

Another simple but very effective arrangement is a group of balls either placed freely on a mantel or tabletop, or held in a shallow tray. A sun ball brought in from the garden might

Group balls on a tray or tabletop

Fill clear glass jars with colored balls

Or fill that treasured epergne that has been passed down in your family for generations with tiny red balls stacked to look like cherries.

Stack tiny red balls to look like cherries

Glass curtains at the window can serve as an airy and dramatic backdrop for brightly-colored ornaments of many different sizes and colors and shapes. String them on gold twine (knotted where necessary to keep ornaments from slipping), and tape or tie to the curtain rod.

An enchanting winter window

Hang from the molding, or the ceiling, ribbons of different lengths with a Christmas ball tied on each one. A large section of wall can be quickly and inexpensively covered with this gay device.

Any small basket becomes a decoration if it is lined with pinked aluminum foil and filled with gay balls whose color is enhanced by a light bulb placed underneath.

Save your plastic strawberry baskets — they make charming containers for colored ornaments. First spray the baskets gold or a bright color. Then make the containers by placing one basket upside down on another and joining them with bright ribbon where their rims meet. You can put the ornament in first, or, if it's easier, just before you completely close the baskets. Place the filled baskets on a mantle or table, or hang them with wide ribbon from the rafters or the molding of a doorway.

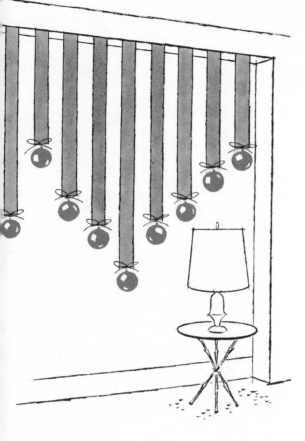

Balls hanging by ribbons — a good wall decoration

Hang gay baskets filled with ornaments

Heirloom candelabra sparkle the more brilliantly if balls, all of the same color and preferably wound with tinsel, are suspended from the arms. *(See picture, page 98.)*

For a country dining room, why not make a Christmas mobile? Suspend a graceful artificial branch from the ceiling with a fine dark wire, and wire small bright balls to its twigs. Every current of air will set it revolving. *(See page 99.)*

Hang small brilliant ornaments, possibly in one of the fluorescent colors, from the rim of a glass-topped table. Any size or shape of table will do. Use narrow ribbons for hanging.

Rim the edges of café curtains with dozens of tiny glass ball ornaments, all one color. This decoration is as easy and charming as can be, particularly effective in the dinette or the

Fill a foil-lined basket with colored balls

nursery, or on sheer white tier curtains in a bedroom.

Always remember, when using glass ornaments, to hang them high, and well out of the reach of children. Very young children, unwatched for a moment, might be tempted to sample their flavor, with truly disastrous results. This caution applies also to the home with a dog.

There are on the market now quite handsome ornaments made of plastic. They resemble the glass ornaments and are far sturdier, and safer to use, in any place where children and dogs can possibly reach them.

Make the most of any permanent wall decoration in your entrance hall or foyer. Hang evergreen roping gracefully over wall light fixtures, and fill the lavabo with colored ornaments. (Securing the ornaments with modeling clay will keep them from falling out.)

Houses have hanging lights again. Whether you have an old-fashioned chandelier or a bright brass pulley lamp, hang small glass balls on gilded string from the rim of it. On a modern lamp it can take on the nostalgic look of a beaded fringe.

Hang glass balls from the candelabra

A stylized tree for the teen-ager's room

Decorate a desk in a study or a teen-ager's bedroom with a stylized tree. It's small and simple enough not to interfere with working space, yet it serves as a pleasant reminder of Christmas whenever the student looks up from reading. The tree is made from a gilded dowel set into a dirt-filled, gold-sprayed container, such as a flower pot or refrigerator container. The tree itself is a jumbo Christmas ball, perhaps in a favorite color, and studded with beads, sequins, stars, and glitter. Set it, upside down, on the dowel.

In some families, particularly fine Christmas tree ornaments have been preserved through the years. An imaginative way of displaying them safely is to put them in a shadow box that may be hung in a window or against a wall. The box is made of dowels or lath crossbars in a frame; this itself may be a prized family possession. *(See picture, page 100.)*

Whenever you're not using your serving pieces during the holidays, make them festive. Fill a tiered piece with tinsel or greens, and glass ornaments. Place your prettiest stemmed glass on the top tier, also filled with greens, and crown with a top-of-the-tree ornament. If you have a handsome lazy susan, make it even more decorative (when it's not in use), by filling each section with Christmas balls of different colors and shapes.

Make a mobile for the dining room

Ornament a glass-topped table

Hang small glass balls from ceiling lamps

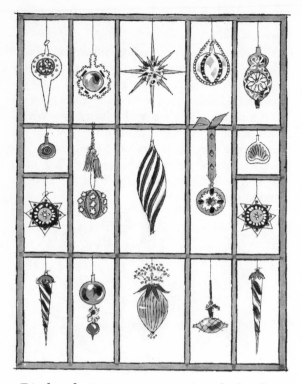

Display choice tree ornaments in a shadow box

A few ornaments on a very large scale make an impressive decorative accent, yet they simplify the problem of what to do with a bare wall, or a mantel-less fireplace. Hang the very largest you can find at different heights from the ceiling.

DECORATE WITH GREETING CARDS

Greeting cards not only bring messages from loved ones at Christmastime, but can be made into a holiday display themselves. Share the gayest ones with everyone who comes into your house!

Cards may be arranged on a mantel, on bookshelves, or in fireside niches. Greens in the background make the display into a decoration.

If some of your shelves have knickknacks on them during the year, you might consider moving them for the holidays so that there will be enough room for everyone to see and fully enjoy your cards.

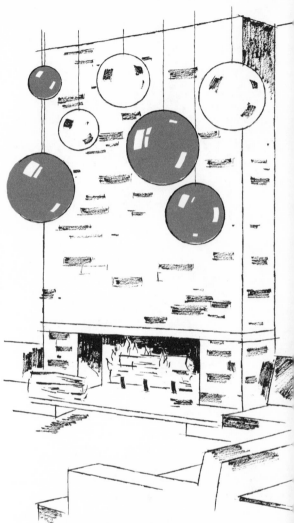

Huge ornaments suspended from the ceiling are impressive

Christmas cards can also be displayed in tree form. One way that allows for the steady increase in mail is to tape the cards together in a vertical line of six or eight. Use two more of these lines to outline your tree on a wall, then fill in the center as more cards arrive.

Your cards can make a charming welcome, if you have a glass door. Arrange them carefully against the panes.

Christmas cards make decorative displays

A tiered serving piece can be used for decoration

A wreath for your cards — from your circle of friends — seems the perfect shape in which to hang them. If there's an old hula hoop in your house, suspend it with bright ribbon against a wall, tape your cards as you receive them, from the back of the hoop with transparent tape. Or have the man of the house make a wire hoop, of wire strong enough to hold its form. You might wind the hoop with greens, ribbon, expandable metal foil or crushed foil in colors, cotton batting, or anything your fancy dictates. If there's a youngster in your family especially thrilled by his Christmas mail, put up a smaller wreath, lower-hanging on the wall, for his cards only.

A wreath of friends, big and small

In your cellar or attic, you might have an old picture frame, or the gilt frame of a useless mirror, which could be used to make the very picture of Christmas, for your cards. Cover the picture, or mirror, with corrugated paper or construction board; then cover this with gold, silver, or any solid-colored paper. If you decide to keep the frame only for Christmases, you might spray it with gilt paint, or snow, or bright glitter. Cards can be fastened with map tacks, thumbtacks, or tape.

Arrange Christmas cards in a glass doorway

Hang cards from red ribbon Christmas tree branches

A permanent card tree, for use year after year with just a change of ribbon, is simple to make from moderately heavy wire, or wooden dowels, or garden stakes; with whichever material the handy person in your house works most comfortably. From the back, tape on bright lengths of stiff ribbon, metallic tape, or heavy foil. Tape, glue, or pin your cards onto tree.

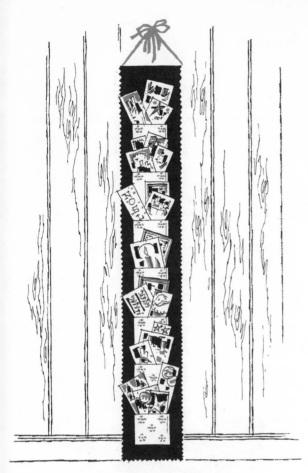

A card pocket for everyone

The very picture of Christmas

A long, long piece of felt, attached to the molding near the ceiling and stretching down to the floor, makes a card holder for the whole family. Father's the only one who can reach the top pocket, and the bottom pocket is reserved for the littlest one in the house.

Directions: With pinking shears, cut a strip of felt six inches wide and as long as necessary. (Of course, you may buy a yard, cut it into strips and sew the strips together at the ends.) Sew on in a contrasting color, as many pockets of felt as you will need for your cards. To give the panel body turn over a one-inch hem at the top and insert a pencil. Slide ribbon or gold twine through the hem, for hanging. Trim with rick-rack or sequins, if you wish.

Over the hall table, or the console in the foyer, put up a lacy, shiny mesh tree, made of strips of perforated plastic ribbon. It's pretty even when it's empty; as cards arrive they can be attached with straight pins through the holes. Cut out and cover cardboard in the shape you desire, or use heavy construction paper reinforced with a "tree trunk" of corrugated cardboard attached from the back. Turn an inch of the perforated ribbon around the edges of the tree, and tape from the back, as you place the ribbon in strips, horizontally. Top with a star, and don't forget to add a piece for the base.

DECORATE WITH LIVING PLANTS

All through the holidays your house can have new beauty and meaning if you decorate with living flowers and greens. You don't need many — it's where you put them that counts most, and rangements of plants and objects that convey the holiday story.

See what you can do with your prize ivy plant, and candles. Try special Christmasy flower-pot wrappings for house plants that you've nurtured through the year, and see what perfect decorations they make for your mantel or bookshelf. Place flowers or plants in front of mirrors, and stand around them candles to blend with their colors.

Dracaenas, sansevierias, aspidistras, dieffenbachias, azaleas, and begonias are all good plants for the season.

Of course the first plant of Christmas is the poinsettia. It is a perfect symbol of the holiday, and almost anywhere in the house is the right place for it; a modest pot with two blooms in the kitchen and a giant plant inside the front door will both call out "Merry Christmas" every time you pass them by.

Perforated plastic ribbon, ready for pinning

how you combine the new ones with those you have.

The results are so right, so in tune with the new life that Christmas ushers in, that you'll want to continue the practice each year. You can arrange them gaily, or make them reverent. Either way, live and growing plants will bring something fresh to these happy days.

Make your own experiments; the ideas that follow are intended to inspire your own ar-

A poinsettia — first of all Christmas plants

The first Christmas came to the world in a far-off land and a warmer climate, far from snow and spruce trees. A beautiful way to remember this holy time is with small crèche fig-

A lovely nativity scene

*Azalea and peperomia plants make an
interesting grouping*

ures in a living, green surrounding.

Use any plants that resemble palm trees, with long stems and a sheltering leaf. *Philodendron dubium* is a good choice, or any other available plant like it. Wrap two pots in gold paper; stand one tall candle behind them higher than the "trees," to symbolize, when lit, the star. Place the simplest group of figures together, and your lovely nativity scene is complete.

One fine red azalea may be sufficient, among the pretty clutter that fills the house during the holidays. Azaleas need quite a lot of water at a time. So set the pot — it will be a big one — on a large plate or tray.

You can add small pots of variegated peperomia to wreathe your azalea and furnish interest before the stockings are emptied and ribbons and wrappings tossed about. Short poinsettias can be just as decorative.

Christmas begonias stay covered with flowers for several weeks, given plenty of water. But enjoy their gorgeous color while you can. When it's through, it's through. Place them against a wall where their contrast will be vivid — not too close to the Christmas tree where nearness would waste their extravagant beauty.

The Star of Bethlehem is a cut flower growing in popularity at Christmastime. Shipped by air from Africa, and available in department stores and through mail order houses, it arrives in a budded state, and with proper care will open and bloom for about six weeks. In order to have it at its peak at Christmas it is necessary to order it early, since it must be kept in the dark for about two weeks. This lovely and unusual white flower will arrive complete with explicit directions for its care and best display.

An amaryllis adds dramatic shape and color anywhere at all in the house, since it can

Christmas begonias are vivid decorations

Amaryllis plants lend a dramatic touch

flourish in a dark corner as well as on a sunlit window sill. The flowers will open and remain lovely for a week or more.

A new hybrid amaryllis will add excitement, too. As the big stems rise and the 6- to 8-inch flowers unfold, everybody watches. They can't help it, once the performance starts. For Christmas, the best colors are the scarlet, salmon, white, or rich crimson.

Do you know the luxurious feeling that flowers in the house in the cold of winter give you? With potted plants, that feeling can be extended long past Christmas, if you know a few simple rules. Perhaps you've bought something you're not familiar with, or have received as a gift a variety of plant you've never owned before. Either way, it will arrive from the florist's trained, well-fed, pampered, and trimmed in such a way that you can enjoy it at the peak of its perfection.

Some plants, with proper care, can brighten your house for days or weeks; some for extra

years. For the holiday season itself, it is important to remember that all plants must be kept in a cool room, no higher than 75°, no lower than about 55-60°. Keep them out of drafts. Water them regularly — as soon as the soil surface gets dry — even though you'll be busy with a hundred other things.

The following plants most commonly associated with Christmas will give bloom at other seasons — with proper care.

Azaleas. After the blossoms fade, feed once a month with a balanced plant food. Water every two weeks — not oftener — with acidified water. This water is made by adding ½ teaspoon of vinegar to a quart of water. In the spring, move to a pot that is a size larger. Use pure peat — no soil — to fill around the soil ball. Grow in a sheltered, shady spot outdoors until fall.

Poinsettia. Keep constantly moist until the blooms fade. Stop watering when the leaves drop. Store in a cool spot until mid-spring. Cut the stems back to 4 or 5 inches. In the North, sink the pot in an outside border when the soil warms up. Bring inside before frost. In mild areas of the South, plant directly in the garden.

Amaryllis. Cut off faded flowers, and continue to water until spring. Sink the pot into soil outdoors in summer. Pick a spot in partial shade. Bring inside before frost, and water once a month until new growth starts. Then feed and water regularly.

Begonias. The showy, large-flowered Christmas begonias bloom for several weeks, but do not make good permanent plants for the home. The smaller, everblooming begonias should grow and bloom all year. Pinch the tips and feed regularly to keep compact.

Cyclamen. These big-leaved plants need lots of water and good ventilation. Keep in a cool room in a sunny window. Feed with liquid plant food. Keep water off crown as much as possible. Keep in shady spot outside through the summer.

Christmas roses are a gift that will make many, many Christmases beyond this year more beautiful. Planted in the spring or fall, they will bloom through the snow, providing flowers to cut and bring indoors: a lovely, living gift with enduring white flowers and shiny, leathery green leaves. Order *Hellebrous orientalis* or *Hellebrous niger;* delivery follows at planting time in the spring. If you have a similar plant of your own, announce your gift with blossoms of your plant.

DECORATE WITH CANDLES

Be original and make your own holiday candles. The molds and decoration can be found at home. Just save up your old candles, or collect them from friends, get out some kitchen equipment, and you're set for the fun of making candles for the holidays. Your imagination can be the springboard for unusual and original ideas for candles — from decorating tapers for the dinner table to making flat ones that float in a pretty tray or bowl for a special luncheon centerpiece.

To ornament candles, drizzle wax down the side, use colored cellophane tape or sequins, or sprinkle them with brilliant gold or silver sparkle dust. A used candle that has become crooked may be straightened by putting it in hot water for 5 to 10 minutes and hanging it up with a safety pin through its wick. All these decorations are easy to make and the children will love to help. In all of the following wax-pouring projects, give the molds a thin coating of mineral oil before you start. It will keep the wax from sticking and will make it easier to remove the molds when you are through.

Boots, houses, and bells can be made from plastic tree ornaments. The bells are open at the bottom, of course, or, you can cut out the bottom with a razor. Slice the bottom carefully so that you will have an opening for the wax. Stick the wick from a small candle through the hole at the hanging-top of the ornament, and secure with a little softened wax. Turn the ornament upside down, in a glass (to hold it steady), and pour in wax, making sure the wick remains

Plastic tree ornaments make good candle molds

vertical. Allow the wax to cool a little before pouring, so that it does not cause the plastic to melt out of shape. When candle is thoroughly hardened, remove the plastic mold.

Make funny-face candles, using a stemmed glass for the squat shapes; then make sequin — or button — faces. Suspend the wick as shown, tied around a soda straw, and dip in warm water to loosen the candle from the glass when it has completely hardened. Gelatin molds may be used also, for fancy candles.

A festive bottle-shaped candle makes a pretty memento when decorated with Christmas legends, glitter, and ribbon. Make it with a soda bottle as the mold, again holding the wick out carefully. When the candle is hard, put the bottle inside a paper bag, for safety, and hit just hard enough to crack, break, and remove bottle.

Gay candles are fun to make and give

A treasured candle, to burn from year to year

With a large rubber ball, the kind with which a young child plays (eight to ten inches in diameter), you can make an imposing and beautiful candle that can be saved from year to year. Burn it only for a few hours each year, perhaps on Christmas Eve; it will become a treasured object and a beloved custom.

DECORATIONS WITH A TRADITION

For tradition, for decoration, and for kisses, too, hang an English kissing ball. Suspend it in the hallway, or over the stairs, and it will quickly become an American custom in your house.

Fill two plastic berry containers with Oasis (available at florists). Invert one basket and wire both together, as in tying a package, and leave a long piece for hanging. Soak in water. Thrust small sprays of boxwood or pine into Oasis through the basket mesh, forming a ball; trim evenly. Tuck in sprays of mistletoe. Wire a ribbon bow to a wooden pick and insert at side.

Jule-nisse is a jolly Danish goblin. Bend a 9-inch blue pipe cleaner into legs *(A)* and a 9-inch red one into arms *(B)*. Fold a 4-inch strip of blue mat stock in half and taper from 1¼ inches at fold to ⅜ inch at top. Slip legs into fold, and staple or paste arms ½ inch from top. Fold a 3-inch strip of peach gummed crepe and, with fold at bottom, cut head and ears *(C)*. Slit fold enough to slip over neck and stick together *(G)*. Add gummed dot features. Cut a beard with paste tabs at top from white mat stock. Make V-shaped cuts here and there, as shown in illustration, and stick in place. Fold 5-inch strip of brown mat stock and cut pointed hat with fold at bottom *(D)*. Slit to fit head. Bend front part forward and trim for visor *(E)*. Cut shoes from folded strip of brown gummed crepe *(F)* and stick over foot.

An English kissing ball

A Danish goblin

A charming centerpiece, with a history centuries old, is this St. Lucia's crown. Before the Middle Ages, so the legend goes, the custom of the crown was brought from Italy to Sweden; for hundreds of years girls throughout that country have worn it on their pretty heads.

Directions: To make the crown for a centerpiece, make a cone of chicken wire, which is 8 inches high and 6 inches in diameter. Cover completely with holly, fir bough, or any greenery, and allow it to skirt out a bit at the bottom edge of the wire. Stand six or eight white candles, 8″ tall, a couple of inches in from the edge, around the bottom. Scandinavians add Christmas berries and a bright gold star. Use flameproof greenery, or spray on flameproofing; even so, do not leave the centerpiece unattended even for a moment when the candles are lit. It's

a lovely and time-honored decoration, but be sure to light and enjoy it when everyone is at the table.

Danish bells are a touch of traditional decoration, and mighty pleasing to the eye as well.

Begin with a jar lid, 3¾ inches wide. Use it to trace circles on a cloth-back foil of several different colors. Cut circles in half. Knot the ends of 18-inch colored cotton string. Put two more knots in each end, 2 inches apart.

Form a half circle into a cone, keeping a knot inside the point so that the bell won't slip down on the string. Staple the edges together, then staple other bells, one above each knot, so that there are three bells on either end of the string, of different colors.

Scandinavian spirals have motion and color and shine, if you make them of foil or construc-

St. Lucia's crown, from Sweden

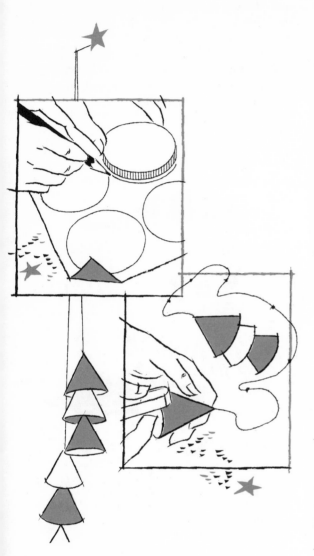

Danish bells

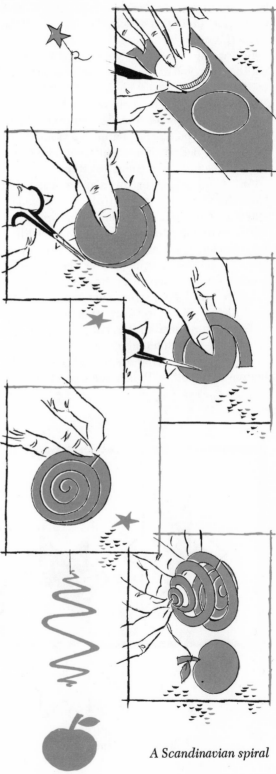

tion paper sprayed with gilt. Start by tracing 2 circles on a piece of the paper you've chosen (A). You can vary the size of your spiral by using a compass to make a circle of almost any size. Why not a very large one for an important place in the house?

Cut out the circles with small, sharp-pointed scissors.

Beginning at the very edge of each circle, draw a line that gradually widens to ⅜ inch (B).

A Scandinavian spiral

When you have cut into the circle to the ⅜-inch width, you can continue cutting a strip ⅜ inch wide until you reach the center of the circle (C).

Be careful to keep all your strips the same width while you're cutting. You can vary the width of your strips if you want variety.

The next step is to paste or staple the ends of the two spirals together as pictured (D). In this fashion, you have a continuous spiral twice as long as before. For a different effect, try fastening spirals of 2 colors together.

Any small trinket or toy can be suspended from the spiral, but to be truly Scandinavian, make a plump pig or a miniature apple from heavy cardboard or plywood. Paint with a bright color. Loop a string or thin wire (fastened to the pig or apple) over the center of a circle spiral, as shown in drawing (E).

Last of all, loop a string over the other center to hang your spiral from the tree.

To make an Austrian star, cut two six-pointed stars from two different colors of mat stock. Slash to the center from the top of one and the bottom of the other. Punch holes on either side of the top slash. Slip one star over the other and thread cord through the holes. Decorate any way you wish with gummed dots, stars, or seals.

For the United States, we have a Santa Claus mobile. Enlarge diagram 8 times. Cut hat from red mat stock; fur trimming, beard, and mustache from white mat stock.

A Santa Claus mobile

Eyes: 2 small blue Christmas balls.
Nose: Small styrofoam ball glittered with red.
Eyebrows: Short pieces of white pipe cleaner.
Pompon: Fringe 2 circles, slit, put together.
Fur band: Fringe edges of white stock.
Beard: Slash, curl on a dull knife blade.
Suspend (on black thread): eyes, eyebrows from hat; beard on thread through nose to hat; pompon to tip of hat; Santa himself from his hat. Merry, Merry Christmas mobile.

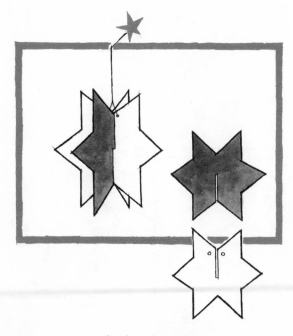

An Austrian star

Stockings for the family are decoration, too

HAVE THE FUN OF STOCKINGS

Make it a custom to hang a stocking for every member of the family, old and young; put them up several days before Christmas for the cheer they bring. Deck the mantel simply, with boughs of pine and frosty white candles. Bookshelves will serve the same purpose as a mantel.

The stockings may be made at home of felt, cut in the traditional boot shape and trimmed to the fancy of the maker or to the known tastes of the recipient. Or the stocking may be cut in a more whimsical shape, trimmed with appliqués, sequins, beads, bells, ribbon, and bow.

The lady of the household would be charmed with a stocking designed like a Gay Nineties boot. It could be made of red or green corduroy, decked with sequins, and finished off with a bit of embroidery in colored yarn and tinsel thread. *(See picture, page 114.)*

Use a simple and charming handmade stocking for distributing gifts of hard candies to large groups of children — perhaps at Sunday School. Maybe the Ladies Aid, the Girl Scouts, or the sewing class at school would undertake making them as a holiday project.

Use starched cheesecloth or tarlatan, cut to the size you have decided upon. Crochet around

A decorated stocking of felt

the edges with yarn; metallic yarn would be perfect. At the top, back corner, crochet a loop to use as a hanger. Glue sequins or other decorations on the front.

A Christmas stocking for a lady

An easy-to-make cheesecloth stocking

DECORATING THE TABLE ITSELF

The table itself can be decorated in such a way that it will light up the room for the holidays. For both the holiday dinner and for parties make a handsome Christmas tablecloth.

If you have a colorful cloth (red or green), dress it up in a happy way with little Christmas bells, sewn to its hem. Get two dozen of the little kind that tinkle; sew them on in bright thread for the great dinner. The young girl of the house can manage it simply, and everyone will be rewarded with occasional jingles at the table as they brush against the cloth.

Decorate the tablecloth with Christmas bells

Another idea for a colored Christmas tablecloth is to fringe one, and cut giant letters from heavy white paper to spell NOEL. (When the letters are removed, the cloth can be used for gala occasions the year round.) Use any bright-colored cloth that you have, or make one from linenlike, colorfast cotton, 54 inches wide, and yards of white fringe; both of these materials are inexpensive.

net, large enough to cover your own vivid table-cloth, appliqué whatever Christmas designs strike your fancy: large red felt poinsettias and holly leaves, for instance, with sequins pasted on for sparkle. The nylon net can be saved from year to year, and the cloth used without it for other occasions.

Make a bright holiday runner for a cloth of a different gay color: a red oilcloth runner on a green cloth, for instance. Edge the runner with gold rickrack and make a white rickrack tree. Packages are easy to make with squares of oilcloth in contrasting colors and rickrack string.

Fringe and lettering make a holiday cloth

Nylon net is the secret of a fascinating yet practical Christmas table. To a piece of such

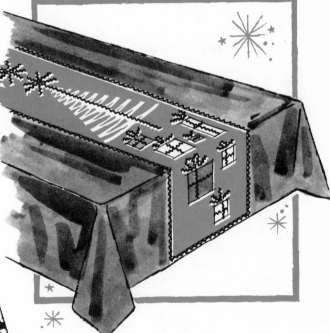

Make a decorated holiday runner

For a long, outsized table — such as the refreshment table at a Christmas party for the Sunday School — sew together two strips of 36-inch red flannel. Gold rickrack edging, pasted on, will make hemming the cloth unnecessary. Make felt cutouts in appropriate pretty designs, and attach them with snaps to the cloth, to be removed when it is laundered.

Decorated nylon net goes over your tablecloth

A huge red flannel cloth, easy to make

A tree made of three funnels

MAKE A TREE

Christmas trees have come a long way since the first one was cut down in a forest and dragged home. Today, people who live in apartments are much more likely to buy a small artificial tree scaled to the size of their dinette table. But with imagination and ingenuity one can make one's own Christmas tree with a result so unusual that it will excite comment.

A funnel tree is easy to make. Buy three funnels graduated in size, 5½, 8½ and 11½ inches long, and cover the largest and smallest with green foil wrapping paper, the middle one with red foil.

If you like, drill a few holes in all three funnels for light to flicker through when the tree is mounted over a fat, lighted candle, securely set on a decorated base. Decorate around the holes in the tree with gold lace paper doily cutouts and large sequins. Trim the edges of the funnels with fringed gold braid and small strings of multi-colored beads.

A simple, espalier-type tree may be made by wiring pine branches to a plywood or construction board mount. Then decorate the branches with colored candles, beads, small blown balls, sequinned animals, and loops of silver or gold thread.

A more elaborate espaliered tree that is striking enough to place in a picture window is the golden bell tree. The frame is dowels, the base is a wood block; the bells are paper drinking cups gilded and sprinkled with glitter, and clappered with small gold balls which are wired on. Tie the bells to the dowels with saucy red ribbons. A gold star is on top of the tree.

A little artificial tree, white or silver or pink, can become especially pretty and suitable in a young girl's feminine bedroom. It usually comes on a stand of its own. Deck it with artificial rosebuds and gauzy butterflies which can be bought at notion counters and in party departments. Trim the base with swags of red silk cord.

An espalier tree of pine branches

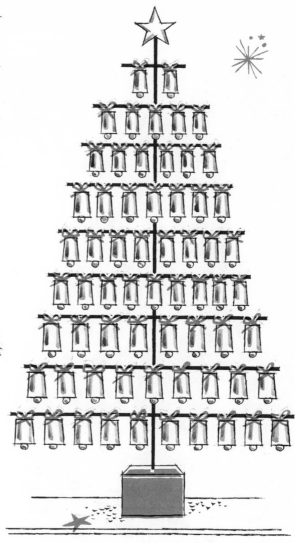

A tree of golden bells

A tree made of chicken wire will cast pretty shadows, especially when there are candles nearby. Since it's flat, and takes up little room, it might be just the thing for a buffet table.

Directions: With wire snippers, cut pieces of chicken wire and form the shapes desired. A good size for the tree is about 7 inches wide at the base and 10 inches high. With pliers, bend the raw ends of wire inward, to make a neat edge. For a standing base, bend the bottom row of wires back at least one inch; use transparent tape to secure the bottom rim of wire to the table. Paint tree with white or gold paint; be sure to cover both sides of the wire. When dry decorate to suit your whim — tiny ornaments hung in every opening are effective, as are larger ones hung in a pattern. Add other bits of sparkle, if you like. For a tree to stand at a window, you might hang bright-colored transparent ornaments, which will catch the glint of daylight in a lovely way.

What could delight children more than a Santa's boot that's good enough to eat? They can even help make it.

Young children often find that Christmas is too long in coming and too quickly gone. Decorate the kitchen beforehand, and make the waiting happier.

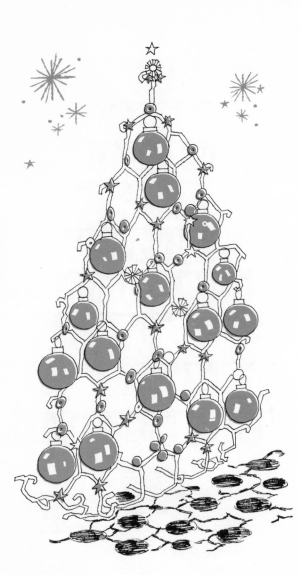

A light and charming tree for a buffet table

Children can make this candy boot and eat it later

Just take a simple bread board or wooden tray, and with paste or water-soluble glue, attach enough wrapped candy balls or peppermints to form a boot, tree, bell, star, or whatever shape you wish to create. Then prop the candy-studded board or tray in a prominent place in the breakfast nook or dinette, or mount it on the wall.

Even easier to make is a miniature tree of bow-tied evergreen twigs (they might be cuttings from the Christmas tree), set at angles into a large apple as a base. The moisture of the apple keeps the greenery fresh.

CHRISTMAS IN A CHILD'S ROOM

Have a bit of Christmas in a child's room; your youngster will wake to it in the morning

A tree made of evergreen cuttings

Christmas is for children everywhere

with pleasure and recognition all through the holidays. If there's a wide window sill, stand a tiny tree on it; decorated with icicles and little gold ornaments, it will glitter in the winter sun.

A symbol of the whole world's joy at Christmas is appropriate to a child's room. Cover the base of a world penny bank with greenery, or cotton, and stand small, snow-covered trees in a circle around it. Disguise the money slot with a red ribbon bow. Variety stores have very inexpensive banks and trees, and ornament-studded trees of place-card size.

Still another way to symbolize the holiday that comes to children everywhere is with the use of little dolls from many countries. On a pretty tray, or on cotton, place a ring of dolls, touching hands, around a festive tree. Such dolls are made in many sizes and of many materials; wood, plastic, cotton, china, and even candy. Though very young, a child will grasp the meaning of Christmas in many lands.

A toy-and-trinket tree

For a small fry party, or for the children's table throughout the holiday season, make a trinket tree that you'll use for many seasons. Children love tiny things: little dolls, animals, toys, houses, fruits, beads. Have the children make very small gift packages with one fat gumdrop inside, not to be opened until the tree is put away. Tie things on with thread, so that they swing a bit in currents of air.

Make the tree from a 1″ dowel, stuck into a square wood base. Drill 3/8″ holes in the up-right dowel for branches. Shellac and paint, if desired. Top the tree with an ornament, or two very large gold stars pasted back to back over the tip of the dowel.

Having a child decorate his own tree is a practice that might happily become a tradition in your home. Young children, who don't see the real tree being trimmed (since Santa comes so late at night!), can enjoy a felt tree, attached to a wall of their room. For a real toddler, start at the baseboard, for easy reaching. Cut out cardboard in the shape you want and cover it with green felt. Give him gummed seals, gum-med ribbon, a damp sponge, a blunt scissors, strings of tiny bead-ornaments, miniatures of all sorts, ribbon bows from last year, and a pot of paste. Let him paste away to his heart's con-tent, not necessarily all at once; he might well love to stretch the project out for days.

If you have a spot of ground to plant it in, on your child's first Christmas you might like to buy a living young evergreen tree to decorate and enjoy indoors. After the holidays take it outdoors, to grow in front of your home and be an always-green reminder of your child's first Yuletide. Since the baby will be too young for toys, decorate the tree for sheer beauty: artificial cherry blossoms, nylon butterflies, birds, and the like. Keep it in a cool place while indoors.

DECORATIONS FOR THE CHILDREN TO MAKE

Start with a couple of restless children, an-xious to get the Christmas season under way,

A child's own tree

and add construction paper, casein glue, a couple of pairs of scissors and — well, oddments.

Supply gummed strips, cellophane tape, pic-ture seals, pipe cleaners in white and colors, dots, stars, sequins, old greeting cards for cutting up, little ornaments, tiny bells, ribbon, rickrack, tin-sel — there is no end to what might be used. Some of the accompanying shapes can be dup-licated (closely enough) even if the child can-not follow directions well.

For young children you might cut out a few trains, or Christmas trees, or houses, and show them, on the first one, how much fun it is to pretty them up. Cut out a green paper tree, for instance, and trim it with four rows of white rickrack, for tinsel, and four rows of sequins, for ball ornaments. Top with a sequin or a star.

Make a train, as an example, of purple paper, white rickrack, a blue motorman's cab, and green wheels. Cut out a house of the tall, funny

Shapes the children might duplicate

Try a butterfly, or a cutout doily

kind that children love to draw, with one door, one window, and a chimney.

Let the young ones experiment freely and don't expect that there will be much perfection, or that every object will be usable. If you can convince a child he should decorate both sides, hang one of his trees up over his bed, or in the bedroom window. Or paste a village scene, with houses and trees and a church, on the kitchen window. Let the child practice and discard, but use those that he himself is proud of for a very tender, happy kind of Christmas decoration.

A butterfly is made of two identical shapes pasted over pipe-cleaner antennae, and decorated.

A lace doily can be cut out, pasted on silver paper, and stiffened with cardboard. If they were decorated on both sides, several of them could be hung free in a child's room.

A fat fish could be decorated on both sides and hung by a thread from the tree.

Paste together three paper loops, and run ribbon through slits in them, for an impressive decoration. *(See picture, page 122.)*

An ornamental bird consists of narrow strips of colored paper, all cut to the same length, then shaped to form head, neck, and tail. Use colored sequins to make the eyes and to decorate the tail feathers. For a glittery look, make the bird of colored cellophane or colored foil instead of plain paper.

Cut a gay, whirling ornament from a circle of thin cardboard in any size and color you like. Decorate both sides with dots and stars. Starting on the outside, draw a continuous line spiraling to the center. Cut on this line, and punch a hole in the center for attaching a thread to hang your spiral by.

Gumdrop stars are very easy to make and the only problem will be to keep the children from eating up the materials. The stars are nice to hang from the tree, or an archway, or perhaps from a lighting fixture in the kitchen or dinette: a colorful, and tasty, Christmas motif. To make,

A decorated fish or paper loops are easy

stick one end of a colored toothpick into a small gumdrop, the other into a styrofoam ball. Use about 20 such gumdrops-on-toothpicks, spaced haphazardly around the ball.

Almost the simplest tree decorations of all are candy canes made out of pipe cleaners. They have the added advantage, for young children, of being entirely unmessy. There's nothing to spill or stain or cut, and hardly any way for the child to come up with less than a fine-looking little cane. To make, bend chenille-type white pipe cleaners into the shape of a cane.

Try a bird of paper strips, or a whirling paper spiral

Twist red ones around the white ones to resemble stripes.

If you've a feminine little girl in your house, make, together, a lace-paper tree for her room. Fold large doilies in half, pleat them, and attach to a dowel, set in a wood block. Alternate a tier of white with a tier of gold doilies, growing smaller toward the top.

Gumdrop stars to hang from a doorway

A tree of paper doilies

White and red pipe-cleaner candy canes

Table decorations are something children love to make. A spool centerpiece is not beyond the six-year-old, if he has a little help. He takes four extra-large spools (such as empty 500- or 1000-yard spools) and paints or sprays them white, then glues a piece of red paper around the center of each. Gold letters spelling N-O-E-L are then pasted on, and tiny candles inserted. (Don't light the candles, however.)

wrapping paper, or from shelf paper, bordered with shiny gummed ribbon. Holly-decorated cellophane tape trims plates, tumblers, silver; it will not affect foods.

Children will love making a snowy scene from plastic foam balls. Use a pine cone for the tree, and let the youngsters improvise for the snowman's hat and scarf and face. Two gold stars pasted together on a toothpick will adorn the tree, and almost anything else can be added with enough ingenuity.

A spool centerpiece, easy to make

Children can also make place settings for the holiday table. Mats are cut from stiff Christmas

A snow scene from plastic foam

Even the very smallest member of the family can help make snowy soap-flake ornaments. Cut shapes from white or colored cardboard, or cover gray cardboard with bright paper. Coat with plastic starch and shake in a paper bag with soap flakes.

Spun-glass snowflakes, stars, bells and other cutouts adhere with water to mirrors and windows, and come off easily. The youngsters have a fine time sticking them up.

A nice whirligig star can be made in a few quick minutes. The brighter the colors, the better; the more decoration on it, the merrier! It's a good tree ornament (and a fine pick-up for a package).

Holiday place settings that children can make

To make, form a pattern of cardboard or brown paper before cutting out the pentagon. Each side measures 3 inches.

Select two brightly-colored papers. Place them together and cut one form from each *(A)*. Use pinking shears to make an interesting edge.

Attach the two pentagons to each other by gluing them at centers. Draw a 1¼-inch circle around the center point.

Cut from each pentagon point to the circle edge *(B)*. This will give you five triangular wedges for shaping.

Curl the left-hand point of each triangle down toward the center *(C)*. Glue these points

Ornaments with soap-flake snow

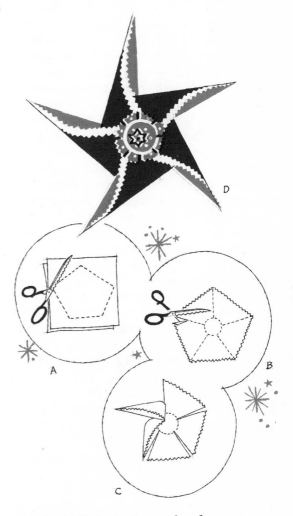

Spun-glass ornaments for the mirror

A whirligig star from colored paper

together where they meet. Now your whirligig star is formed.

To add the finishing touch, decorate the center section by gluing on circles which you have trimmed with sequins, shiny paper, and wire (D).

Adorable little angels can be made from the aluminum foil plates that frozen pies and pot pies come in. They are in several sizes, so choose whichever you wish; the height of the angel will be approximately equal to the diameter of the pie plate.

Cut off the rim of a foil plate, then mark off six sections on the circular bottom, as shown (A).

Cut along all lines with scissors; cut out the two small V-shaped sections at the top. Then draw in the head on the middle part, and cut out (B). The semicircle at the bottom forms the skirt, the two other parts make the wings (C).

Bend the lower section backward to form the skirt. Make slits in the top of the head, curl forward for hair. Cut the apron and crown from colored foil (D); curl the top of the apron, forming a ruffle. Paste the crown to the head.

Glue the apron onto the skirt; paste colored sequins onto the head for facial features (E). For variety, curl a small piece of metal pan cleaner, or yarn for the hair. Another change would be to cut the apron from a paper doily or from colored lace ribbon. Make the cap of paper lace, if you prefer.

The following are easy ornaments to make, and lots of fun for the very young ones in the family. Spaghetti and macaroni come in all sorts of odd shapes and sizes; buy as wide a variety as your biggest store supplies. Using food colors, dye them all sorts of different shades. Let the little ones string them on golden string, no matter how haphazardly, and they'll be cherished, personal, tree decorations.

Slightly older children can make more elaborate macaroni ornaments. Dip pieces of macaroni in hot water to shape them, then stick on a crinoline backing; let them dry. Natural starch holds the pieces in place. Color them with nail polish or paints.

Funny paper stockings — for decoration, not for filling — are perfect for hanging around a

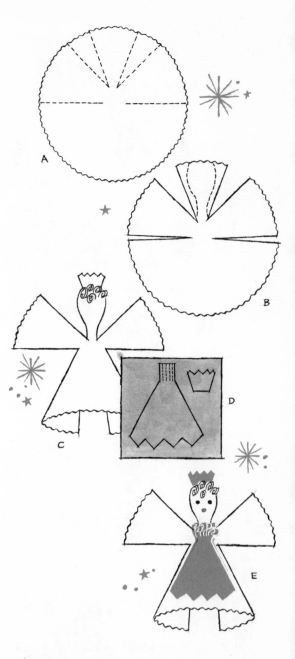

An angel from an aluminum foil pie plate

party table, or at the mantel before real stockings are hung. Cut front and back pieces from Christmas paper, and paste them together; trim with contrasting paper, ribbon, lace doilies, or anything that strikes your fancy.

Colored macaroni tree decorations

Paper stockings — for decoration, not for filling

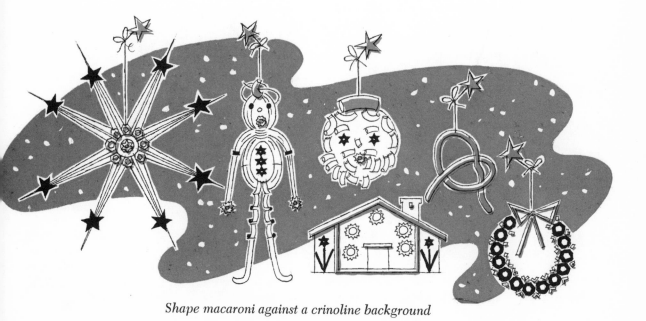

Shape macaroni against a crinoline background

For the slightly older child, who is able to trace and fold more accurately, here is the basic pattern for making angels to decorate your tree and mantel. First trace this pattern on thin paper. Then cut the tracing out, place on any heavy paper, and draw around the outline. Cut out and bend down on the lines marked A. Bend up on the lines marked B. Bend down on the lines marked C. Crimp the wings to make them stand. Make a cone of the angel's dress and paste or staple the flap D under E. Now you can begin to decorate. You can cover the dress with colored wrapping papers, tissue papers, or tinfoil, pasting it on. You can add bits of cotton or edges of lace paper napkins for trim. You can give the angel eyes, nose, and mouth, and write music notes on the sheet of music. Any number of interesting and pretty combinations can be made from this one basic pattern.

An impressive angel, from cut and folded paper

Pattern for angel

A Christmas silhouette will make the Babe in the Manger scene in your window; it will stand out boldly against the daylight, and at night the light from your room will show the Crib to those outside. Trace the accompanying figures on black paper, or use them as a model for enlarged figures. Use rubber cement, glue, or paste, to secure them to freezer wrap or cellophane. Make a cardboard frame. Hang it in your window.

A suggested grouping of the figures is shown here, but arrange them in any other pleasing way you wish.

A silhouette of the Christmas scene   *Patterns for silhouette*

A project for the nimble-fingered older child is a green and gold paper-doily tree that is inexpensive to make, handsome in effect, and useful for many years, if carefully stored.

Plastic foam 1½ inches thick is used for the base and trunk. Make the trunk 3 inches wide by 18 inches long, and taper it at the top. Fasten it with toothpicks to the base, which is 5 inches square.

Get one package each of 6-inch, 8-inch and 10-inch green lace-paper doilies. Cut all doilies in half; pleat each half; and gather all the doilies on one thread, beginning with the largest size (A). Wrap the threaded doilies around the tree trunk (B), supporting the spiral at intervals with 3 x 5-inch lengths of wire, pushed into the plastic foam trunk. Before inserting each wire, bend one end of it to form a hook for hanging a tiny gold ball (C).

Finish off the creation by hanging with balls and pinning or pasting wide gold paper ribbon around the base.

THE TREE ITSELF

Be sure that at some time in your family's experience you have an old-fashioned American tree, with popcorn, strung cranberries, cookies, and candy canes. Or at least add these things to the other ornaments for your tree. They lend a homey, family note to the Christmas tree that's deeply in keeping with the spirit of the season.

If you have very young children who feel that Santa brings the tree, intact, and who'd be disturbed to find on it popcorn that they'd popped and strung by themselves, then perhaps trim an outside tree for the birds. Or have a second little tree in the house, decorated in the old-fashioned way to commemorate the early American family who lived in a simpler time.

Never overlook the simple paper chain as decoration for the tree, or the mantel, or to festoon windows or drapes. With a kit of paper strips that are already gummed, even the youngest child can turn out long chains. Progress seems fast, and everybody's turnout can

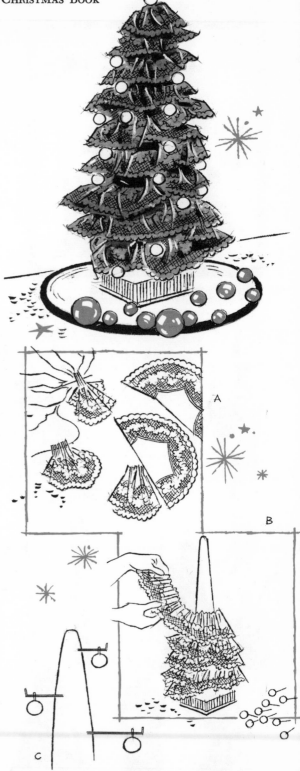

A green and gold paper tree, made of doilies

Don't forget the old-fashioned Christmas tree

Decorate paper chains with ribbon bows

be linked together and stretched all the way down the hall; output over several days can always be joined without trouble. If you'd like it to be a bit fancier for the tree, tie on ribbon bows at the high point of each swag of paper chain.

If you are truly cramped for space, yet the Day wouldn't seem like the Day with merely a little table tree, here's a solution to your problem. Cut all the branches off one side of the tree (the thinner side, of course), and back the trunk of the tree up against the wall. Half a tree, in this fashion, possesses all the majesty of a full tree, and is especially pretty when the ornaments and lights are not too large, and are more or less of the same size.

Some of the cut-off branches may come in handy to fill out bare spots on the side of the tree that faces outward. Whittle the base of the branch to fit into a hole drilled in the trunk.

Another space-saving tree, more formal and dramatic, is the espaliered tree, which takes practically no floor space at all. Make a frame of wooden dowels, and wire on a variety of evergreens for the richest, densest tree-look. For a striking, sophisticated appearance, trim the tree with fruit. *(See picture, page 132.)*

Anchor it firmly in a heavy wooden base. If possible, attach the tree tip to the wall. This applies if the tree is loaded on one side with fruit, which is heavy. Unless fastened at the top, the fruit-laden tree will be topheavy.

Do you have a picture window? Here's a brilliant way to use it, and trim both your room and all outdoors at the same time. Make an espaliered tree, with a framework of wood, up against your window; make it of commanding size. Wire hemlock twigs to both sides and decorate the tree with lights, tinsel, and glitter. Use decorations that will give the most light at night and catch the most reflected daylight during the day.

To save space, make an espaliered tree

To save space, back half a tree against the wall

A corner tree of arborvitae is another attractive tree to have in a room where space is limited or where you cannot move the furniture around conveniently. Prune the tree on three sides and brace it on a triangular stand; fit it snugly against the walls.

HOW TO TREAT A CHRISTMAS TREE

Since the Christmas tree will be the center of all our holiday activity, we should keep in mind some do's and don't's concerning it. We want it beautiful; we also want it to be safe. Every year we hear warnings about Christmas fires, but we are sometimes so occupied with more pleasant things that we hardly give them a thought. There are some important rules, however, that should be noted.

A fire extinguisher in the home is an excellent precaution at all times, but this is especially true during Christmas, when fire hazards are increased as a result of the general air of happy confusion that prevails. If you buy one, learn how to use it before Christmas. Stopping in the middle of an emergency to read directions doesn't make sense.

After you buy the tree, keep it outside until it is to be trimmed, so that it won't dry out. Natural evergreen trees cannot be fireproofed; they are always potentially dangerous. Trees can be treated with fire-retardant chemicals, but every twig and needle must be coated thoroughly. Even then, the flames will simply be slowed down. Should you wish to make your

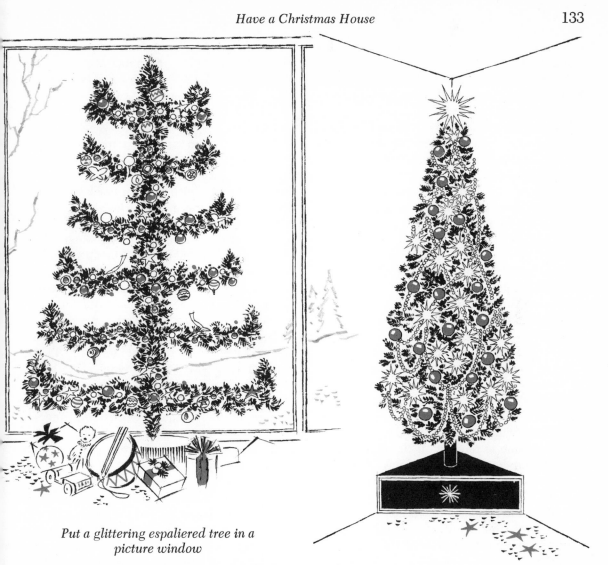

Put a glittering espaliered tree in a picture window

Fit a tree of arborvitae in a corner

tree as fire-resistant as possible, you might try doing the following: In a basin or pail mix a solution of a gallon of warm water, one cup of boric acid powder, and one and one-half cups of borax. Dip evergreen branches in the solution and wet thoroughly.

Where do you place your tree? In most rooms the best place is a corner. Don't put the tree where it may block a passage into or out of a room. Keep it away from curtains, draperies, and other flammable materials. Keep it away from fire and excess heat. Don't place it near a hot stove or radiator.

Use a base or stand which will keep the tree from being knocked over or accidentally bumped. Before putting the tree in the stand, make a diagonal cut through the bark about an inch above the end. When you put the tree in the stand, set the tree in water so that the cut is immersed. Use a container, if necessary. Be sure to check to see that there is enough water in it. If needed, add water periodically all during the time the tree is up. This will not only preserve the tree and prevent it from drying out, but will decrease fire hazards.

Place a cloth or a sheet beneath the tree before you start decorating it. This will be a big aid in keeping the tree area clean during the entire time the tree is up and while it is being dismantled.

If you use an ordinary sheet or fabric at the base of the tree, be sure that you have similarly treated it with the fire-retardant solution. It is best to use fire-resistant fabrics in the first place, however, and you can buy such fabric already treated. But remember, "fire-retardant" doesn't mean "fireproof."

If your tree is a little bare in some spots, you can pretty it up by drilling a small hole in the trunk of the tree and inserting a branch from a fuller section of the tree. It might even be wise to buy a few extra branches for just such use. To give additional support to the false branch, tie one end of a piece of colored string to the middle of the branch, the other end to the trunk of the tree. Any extremely long branches that start to droop before the season is over can also be tied back in the same way.

When you decorate the tree, it is best to have all your lights, ornaments, and toys right at hand, near the tree. Don't use lighted candles on trees — only electric lights. Don't let the lights touch limbs, twigs, or needles. Check the tree from time to time and if the needles near the lights are becoming brown, move the lights.

Before stringing the lights, check them carefully to be sure there are no frayed wires and that all of the lights are in working order. The best way to string lights is to run the extension cord up through the middle of the tree, tying it to the trunk, and then string the lights from the top downward and outward. Place lights that are close together near the top of the tree, and place large ones at the bottom because this gives the tree a more balanced appearance.

Don't place tinsel or metal foil near lights. A small piece of metal in a lamp socket can cause a short circuit. Place cords where they will not be stepped on or tripped over. Be careful that you don't overload any of the plugs. Strings of lights take little power, but they may overload the circuit.

Should you decide to use brighter lamps, such as flood lights, remember that these get very hot quickly. Keep them away from fabrics and place them where they cannot be reached by children or animals. Check the circuit for overloading.

You may want to place a tree outside, on your porch, terrace, or lawn. For such outdoor lighting use waterproof electric cords and sockets, and lamps which will not crack when they get wet. Don't use indoor strings of lights outside. Outdoor strings have rubber or synthetic rings around each lamp to keep water out of the sockets. The lamps do not break very easily and usually burn independently. If you need an extension cord use the outdoor (heavy rubber-covered) type. Tape all connections with electricians' rubber tape.

You will find in some shops three relatively new products for outdoor lighting: (1) Plastic underground wire ("direct-burial cable"). (2) A projector lamp mounted on a stake which can be driven into the ground, together with a set of glass filters of various colors. (3) An outdoor-type double outlet, also mounted on a stake; there are models for underground and surface wiring.

Keep a watchful eye on the needles of your tree. As soon as they begin to drop, it is a sign that the tree is getting too dry for safety.

There are several ways to expedite removal of the tree. If it is an overly large one, you can saw off all the branches and tie them together. In this way you will have only a bundle of branches and the trunk to remove. If the trunk is large, you may want to saw it in several sections. If the tree is not too large, just tie the branches close to the trunk so that you will have an easier time in moving it through the doorways. When you start the actual moving, it is a good idea to wrap the branches or tree in an old sheet, to save yourself the trouble of picking up hundreds of dropped needles later on.

6 Christmas Cooking

CHRISTMAS DINNER

Turkeys come in almost any size now, so that the bird can really be tailored to the size of the crowd you'll be having for Christmas. From as little as four pounds to as much as twenty-four, the turkey roasted the traditional way is tender and juicy, a mouthwatering brown.

ROAST TURKEY

Stuff turkey just before roasting. Allow ¾ to 1 cup stuffing per pound ready-to-cook weight. Stuff wishbone cavity and skewer neck skin to back. Tuck wing tips behind shoulder joints. Rub large cavity with salt. Spoon in stuffing. Shake bird to settle stuffing; do not pack. Close opening by placing skewers across it and lacing shut with cord. Tie drumsticks securely to tail. (If opening has band of skin across, push the drumsticks underneath, and you won't need to fasten opening or tie legs.)

Grease skin thoroughly. If you use a meat thermometer, insert it in the center of the inside thigh muscle adjoining the cavity. Place bird breast up on the rack (but breast down if using V-rack) in shallow roasting pan and leave in this position for entire roasting time.

Cover with loose "cap" of aluminum foil, pressing it lightly at drumstick and breast ends, but *avoid having it touch top or sides*. Roast at constant *low temperature*.

When turkey is about two-thirds done according to turkey roasting chart, cut the cord or band of skin so heat can reach inside of thighs. *(For chart, see page 136.)*

About 20 minutes before roasting time is up, test doneness by pressing thick part of drumstick between fingers (protect hand with paper towel). Meat should feel very soft. Also move drumstick up and down; it should move easily or twist out of joint. (If you use a meat thermometer, it should register 190° to 195°.) When turkey is done, remove from pan and keep warm while you make gravy from pan drippings. Let turkey stand 20 minutes before carving. Carving will be easier and slices neater.

If you need to save time, roast your king of birds in aluminum foil.

FOIL-WRAPPED ROAST TURKEY

Tie drumsticks to tail. Press wings to body so tips are flat against sides of breast. Use heavy

135

aluminum foil. Place turkey, breast up, in center of foil. (Foil should be wide enough to have 5 to 6 inches extending beyond leg and breast ends of bird; if it isn't, join 2 pieces together with drugstore or lock fold, pressing to make leakproof joining.) Bring one end of foil snugly over top of turkey; bring opposite end up, lapping over first (overlap should be 2 to 3 inches). Now fold foil down snugly at breast and legs; then press ends up (ends should be high enough to prevent drippings from running into the pan and burning).

Place foil-wrapped bird, breast up, in bottom of shallow pan (broiler pan is convenient); do not use rack. Roast at constant *high temperature.*

When turkey has cooked to within *15 to 20 minutes of total cooking time* given in the foil-wrapped turkey roasting chart, *remove from oven.* Quickly slit foil with scissors or knife and fold away from bird to edge of pan. (If you use a meat thermometer, insert it in center of inside thigh muscle adjoining cavity.) Return turkey to oven. Continue roasting till turkey is tender (test doneness in usual ways — meat thermometer should register 185° to 190°). When turkey is done, lift from foil to warm platter. Pour drippings in skillet; concentrate by simmering if you want to increase flavor and color; use in making gravy.

Thawing timetable for frozen turkeys

Ready-to-cook weight in pounds	Days in refrigerator at 40°
4 to 12	1 to 2
12 to 20	2 to 3
20 to 24	3 to 4

To speed up thawing, you can place wrapped turkey under cold running water. See label directions that come with your frozen turkey.

Turkey roasting chart

Set oven at 325°. Times are for stuffed chilled turkeys and are approximate only.

Ready-to-cook weight (before stuffing)	Time (total)
4 to 6 lbs.	3 to 3¾ hrs.
6 to 8 lbs.	3¾ to 4½ hrs.
8 to 10 lbs.	4 to 4½ hrs.
10 to 12 lbs.	4½ to 5 hrs.
12 to 14 lbs.	5 to 5¼ hrs.
14 to 16 lbs.	5¼ to 6 hrs.
16 to 18 lbs.	6 to 6½ hrs.
18 to 20 lbs.	6½ to 7½ hrs.
20 to 24 lbs.	7½ to 9 hrs.

Foil-wrapped-turkey roasting chart

Set oven at 450°. Times are for unstuffed chilled turkeys and are approximate only. For stuffed turkey, add 30 to 45 minutes to the total roasting time.

Ready-to-cook weight (before stuffing)	Time (total)
8 to 10 lbs.	2¼ to 2½ hrs.
10 to 12 lbs.	2¾ to 3 hrs.
14 to 16 lbs.	3 to 3¼ hrs.
18 to 20 lbs.	3¼ to 3½ hrs.
22 to 24 lbs.	3¼ to 3¾ hrs.

medium-dry bread, the moist from day-old or dry bread. You may use crumbs or cubes, from white, whole wheat, or corn bread.

STUFFING FOR THE HOLIDAY BIRD

Stuffing the traditional turkey is a just-before-the-roasting ritual. You can get the crumbs and seasonings ready a night ahead, but don't combine with the liquid ingredients. Use bread that is a day old or older. If the bread is fresh, first dry it out or toast it in the oven. Allow ¾ to 1 cup of stuffing per pound of the ready-to-cook weight of the bird. Some families who really

CLAM STUFFING

1 (9½-ounce) package thin corn wafers, rolled	¼ cup clam liquor
	½ cup melted butter or margarine
1 (7-ounce) can minced clams, drained	¼ teaspoon pepper
	⅛ teaspoon mace

Combine all ingredients. Toss together lightly. Use for filling neck cavity of turkey and choose another kind of stuffing for the body cavity.

love stuffing and feel they couldn't ever have enough of it demand a double recipe. Bake the extra in a greased casserole, a pan, or aluminum foil. If you like, baste the stuffing with pan drippings or giblet broth as it bakes.

There are two main types of stuffing, the moist and the fluffy. The difference is that a liquid (broth, water or milk) is added to the moist stuffing. The fluffy kind is made from

GIBLET STUFFING

- 4 cups dry bread crumbs
- 3 tablespoons chopped onion, if desired
- chopped, cooked giblets
- 1 teaspoon salt
- ¼ teaspoon pepper
- ¼ teaspoon poultry seasoning, if desired
- sage to taste
- ⅓ cup melted butter or margarine
- giblet broth to moisten

Combine bread, onion, giblets, and seasonings; add butter and sufficient liquid to moisten. Toss gently to mix. Makes 4 cups stuffing, or enough for 4- to 5-pound chicken or capon. Double recipe for 10-pound turkey.

WALNUT STUFFING

- 6 cups dry, medium bread crumbs
- ⅔ cup walnuts, whole or halved
- 2 cups diced celery
- ½ cup chopped celery leaves
- 2 teaspoons salt
- ½ teaspoon poultry seasoning
- ¼ teaspoon pepper
- 2 eggs, beaten
- ¼ cup melted butter
- 1⅓ cups water, or enough to moisten

Mix together crumbs, walnuts, celery and leaves, and seasonings. Add eggs and butter, then enough water to moisten; toss lightly. Makes enough stuffing for a 10-pound turkey.

ORANGE-PECAN STUFFING

- 56 shredded wheat wafers, finely rolled
- ¼ cup melted butter or margarine
- ¼ cup orange juice
- ¼ cup hot water
- 1 egg, lightly beaten
- ¼ cup grated orange peel
- 1½ cups finely chopped celery
- ½ cup finely chopped onion
- ½ cup chopped pecans
- 1½ teaspoons salt
- ½ teaspoon poultry seasoning

Toss crumbs lightly with melted butter or margarine. Combine orange juice and hot water. Stir into egg. Add egg mixture and remaining ingredients to crackers; blend well. Stuff body cavity of turkey. Makes 6 cups stuffing.

LIVER AND MUSHROOM STUFFING

- ¾ cup chopped celery
- ½ cup chopped onion
- ½ cup chopped green pepper
- ¼ cup butter
- 6 cups dry bread cubes
- 1 tablespoon parsley flakes
- 1 pound finely diced liver
- ¾ pound chopped mushrooms
- salt and pepper
- 3 eggs, beaten
- 1¼ cups water

Add water to bread cubes and let stand. Sauté liver, mushrooms, celery, and green pepper in butter until tender. Add this to moistened bread cubes and mix thoroughly. Add seasonings and eggs. Mix thoroughly. Makes enough stuffing for 12- to 14-pound turkey.

BASIC STUFFING GUIDE*

Poultry weight (ready to cook)	4 lbs.	6 lbs.	10 lbs.	12 lbs.	20 lbs.
Shortening	¼ cup	⅓ cup	½ cup	⅔ cup	1 cup
Chopped onion	½ cup	⅔ cup	1 cup	1⅓ cups	2 cups
Chopped celery	½ cup	⅔ cup	1 cup	1⅓ cups	2 cups
Soft bread cubes (½″ square)	6 cups	9 cups	15 cups	1⅛ gal.	1⅞ gal.
or					
Number of ⅝″ fresh bread slices	6	9	15	18	30
Salt	⅔ tsp.	1 tsp.	1½ tsps.	2 tsps.	1 tbsp.
Pepper	dash	⅛ tsp.	¼ tsp.	¼ tsp.	½ tsp.
Poultry seasoning	1⅓ tsps.	2 tsps.	1 tbsp.	1⅓ tbsps.	2 tbsps.
Water, broth or milk	⅓ cup	⅔ cup	1 cup	1⅓ cups	2 cups
Average number cups of stuffing	4	6	10	12	20

**American Institute of Baking*

GRAVY FOR THE TURKEY

A turkey dinner isn't complete without a savory brown gravy. This one is so smooth and tasty that it's a good excuse for another helping of stuffing or mashed potatoes.

After removing turkey to a warm platter, leave crusty bits in pan and pour liquid into a measuring cup. When fat comes to the top, skim it off. Then, for each cup gravy, measure 2 tablespoons of fat back into roasting pan. Add 2 tablespoons flour for each cup gravy; blend thoroughly. Cook over low heat till frothy, stirring constantly. For richer flavor and color, brown the flour to a light tan. Add 1 cup lukewarm liquid (meat juices from roasting turkey plus giblet broth, milk, or water) for each cup gravy. Cook till thick, stirring constantly and scraping bottom and sides of pan to blend in the crusty bits. Simmer about 5 minutes. Season to taste with salt and pepper. Pour into hot gravy boat.

Perhaps your family likes a rich cream gravy better — or you'd like to try it for the first time this year. Cream gravy made from the drippings of your holiday turkey can be extra special. Follow these simple directions for an easy way to make good cream gravy.

Pour fat and meat juices from the meat pan into a 2-cup measuring cup, leaving crusty particles in the pan. Fat will rise to the top of the cup, and meat juices will stay at the bottom. Skim fat off. Measure ¼ cup fat for 2 cups of gravy, and put measured fat into meat pan.

Add enough milk to the meat juices in cup to make 2 cups and pour into a jar with a screw top. Measure ¼ cup flour into the jar. Screw on lid and shake until the ingredients are well mixed.

Pour milk mixture into pan, stirring slowly to blend thoroughly. Cook over low heat, stirring constantly, until the gravy is thickened and bubbly. Simmer a few minutes. Salt and pepper to taste and serve in heated gravy boat.

Then, of course, there are those, men especially, who will hear of nothing for the bird but giblet gravy, with its wonderful meaty flavor.

Giblet gravy is made using the same method as for cream gravy, except for preparation of the giblets. To prepare giblets, cover the heart, gizzard, and liver with water and simmer in a covered saucepan until tender. Remove giblets. Save the stock and combine with meat drippings for more flavorful gravy. Dice the giblets and add to the gravy when you add the fat. Proceed as for cream gravy.

DIRECTIONS FOR CARVING A TURKEY

1. Place bird's legs to your right. Carve side away from you. To remove leg, cut down from breast to the joint. Pull to loosen leg from the socket. Cut all free tissue.

2. Hold drumstick up at right angles to plate. Cut meat to bone. Anchor thigh with knife, press leg down till joint snaps. Cut through joint. Slice thin.

3. To remove wing, stick fork in meaty part of wing. Cut at angle 1 to 1½ inches above where wing joins body. When you hit joint, run knife through cartilage.

4. Insert fork in opposite rib section or with tines astride keel bone. Cut breast in ¼ inch strips. Put tines of fork on slice before severing it, for steady hold.

MORE OF THE TURKEY

(From Mrs. Glasse *The Art of Cookery Made Plain and Easy,* 1775)

The best way to roast a Turkey is to loosen the skin on the Breast of the Turkey, and fill it with Force-Meat, made thus: Take a Quarter of a Pound of Beef Sewet, as many Crumbs of Bread, a little Lemon peel, an anchovy, some Nutmeg, Pepper, Parsley and a little Thyme.

Chop and beat them all well together, mix them with the Yolk of an Egg, and stuff up the Breast; when you have no Sewet, Butter will do; or you may make your Force-Meat thus: Spread Bread and Butter thin, and grate some Nutmeg over it; when you have enough roll it up, and stuff the Breast of the Turkey; then roast it of a fine Brown, but be sure to pin some white Paper (i.e. grease-proof) on the Breast till it is near enough. You must have a good gravy in the Dish, and Bread-Sauce, made thus: Take a good piece of Crumb, put it into a pint of Water, with a blade or two of Mace, two or three Cloves, and some Whole Pepper. Boil it up five or six times, then with a spoon take out the Spice you had before put in, and then you must pour off the Water (you may boil an Onion in it if you please) then beat up the Bread with a good Piece of Butter and a little Salt.

BUTTER BAKED TURKEY

Stuff turkey with your favorite stuffing. Truss with skewers and strong cord. Soften ½ pound butter. Spread over entire turkey, especially on tops of drumsticks, breast and wings. Place turkey on rack in shallow pan, breast side up. Cover entire turkey with a cheesecloth moistened with melted butter. Brush frequently with melted butter during roasting. Roast according to following schedule. When turkey is done, remove from roasting pan to serving platter and let stand about 15 minutes before carving.

8 to 10 pounds	325° F.	3 to 3½ hours
10 to 14 pounds	325° F.	3½ to 4 hours
14 to 18 pounds	300° F.	4½ to 5 hours
18 to 20 pounds	300° F.	5 to 6 hours
20 to 25 pounds	300° F.	6½ to 8 hours

Time and temperature chart for turkey

Festive roast duck

ROAST DUCKLING

Select a duckling, 3½ to 5 pounds ready-to-cook weight, or 5 to 7 pounds dressed weight. Clean duckling; remove wing joint and tip, leaving only meaty second joint. Rub inside with salt and stuff lightly with Orange Stuffing. Do not truss or prick the skin. Close opening with skewers and lace with cord. Place, breast side up, on rack in shallow roasting pan. Do not add water. Roast uncovered in slow oven (325°) 1½ to 2 hours for moderately done, 2 to 2½ hours for well done. Meaty part of leg should feel tender (use paper towel), and it should be easy to move leg up and down. For a pretty shine, about 30 minutes before duckling is done, brush with *Honey Glaze:* Combine 2 tablespoons honey and 1 teaspoon kitchen bouquet. Makes 3 to 4 servings.

ORANGE STUFFING FOR DUCK

¾ cup diced celery	1 tablespoon grated
½ cup boiling water	orange peel
¼ cup chopped onion	1 tablespoon finely
⅛ cup butter or	chopped parsley
margarine	4 cups toasted bread
1 teaspoon salt	cubes (measure after
1 teaspoon poultry	toasting)
seasoning	1 cup diced fresh
¼ teaspoon pepper	oranges

Cook celery in boiling water until tender. Drain. Sauté onion in butter until limp; combine with celery and remaining ingredients. Toss lightly. Spoon into body of a 4 to 5 pound duck. Close opening with skewers and string. Place duck on a rack, breast side up in a baking pan. Cook in a moderate oven (350° F.) about 2 hours or until skin is brown and crusty. Makes 4 servings.

ROAST DUCK WITH SWEDISH RAISIN STUFFING

½ cup raisins	2 tablespoons melted
2 cups cold cooked rice	butter
⅛ teaspoon ground	1 cup peeled, grated,
cardamom	raw apple
1 teaspoon grated	1 4-pound duck
orange peel	⅓ cup sifted flour
salt	2 cups water
1 tablespoon instant	parsley sprigs
minced onion	orange slices

Rinse and drain raisins. Combine raisins with rice, cardamom, orange rind, ¾ teaspoon salt, onion, butter, and apple. Mix lightly. Stuff mixture loosely into body cavity of duck; close opening with lacing pins and string. Roast duck in a moderate oven (325° F.) about 2 hours or until browned and crispy. Transfer duck to a hot platter. To make gravy, skim fat from drippings, saving ½ cup fat. Blend ½ cup fat with the flour. Add drippings from pan and water. Cook, stirring constantly, until mixture thickens. Season to taste with salt. Cut duck into quarters. Pile hot stuffing on a platter. Arrange duck pieces on top. Garnish with parsley and orange slices. Makes 4 servings.

CRANBERRY RELISH

1 pound cranberries	1 teaspoon dry musta_
2 oranges, cut up	½ teaspoon cloves
1 cup sugar	1 cup blanched
1¼ cups light corn syrup	almonds, slivered
2 teaspoons curry	⅓ cup diced candied
powder	ginger
1 teaspoon cinnamon	

Force cranberries and oranges through food chopper, using medium blade. Add remaining ingredients, and mix well. Store in refrigerator. Let stand several hours before using, to blend flavors. Makes 6 cups.

GINGER-COATED SWEET POTATO BALLS

4 large sweet potatoes	⅓ cup finely chopped
2 tablespoons butter or	nuts
margarine	15 ginger snaps, rolled
¼ cup cream	into medium crumbs
½ teaspoon salt	(1 cup)
	6 marshmallows

Cook sweet potatoes in skins in boiling water until tender, about 15 minutes. Drain and cool. Peel. Mash thoroughly. Stir in butter, cream, salt, nuts, and ¼ cup of the crumbs. Shape into balls, with a marshmallow in center of each, making sure marshmallow is well covered. Dredge balls in remaining crumbs. Bake in a very hot oven (425° F.) 10 minutes. Makes 6 servings.

SPICED APPLE AND SWEET POTATO CASSEROLE

1 (18-ounce) can sweet potatoes, sliced	½ teaspoon nutmeg
	⅓ cup pineapple juice
1 (20-ounce) can sliced apples	¼ cup butter or margarine
¾ teaspoon cinnamon	parsley flakes

Arrange sweet potato slices and apples in alternating layers in an 8-inch square baking dish, sprinkling each layer with cinnamon and nutmeg. Add pineapple juice. Dot with butter or margarine. Cover and bake in a moderately hot oven (375° F.) 15 minutes. Uncover and continue baking 20 minutes. Garnish with parsley flakes. Makes 6 servings.

Delicious apple and potato casserole

PLUM PUDDING

1 cup sifted flour	¾ cup shortening
1 teaspoon soda	1 teaspoon cinnamon
½ teaspoon salt	1 teaspoon cloves
½ cup (1 envelope) instant mashed potatoes	1 cup firmly packed brown sugar
1 cup chopped walnuts	2 eggs
⅔ cup mixed candied fruits and peels	1 cup raw grated carrots
1 cup raisins	¼ cup milk

Sift together flour, soda, and salt. Stir in potatoes, nuts, fruits, and raisins. Cream together shortening, spices, and sugar until light and fluffy. Beat in eggs. Blend in carrots and milk. Add floured fruits and mix well. Pour into a well-greased 1½-quart mold. Cover tightly. Place on a rack in a deep kettle. Add enough boiling water to reach about ⅓ the depth of the mold. Steam 2 hours. Turn out on a serving plate. Serve with rum-flavored hard sauce. Makes 12 servings.

HARD SAUCE

Cream ¾ cup butter, 3 cups sifted confectioners' sugar, 1 tablespoon cream, dash of salt, and 2 teaspoons rum extract. To serve sauce in orange shells: Cut around center of small whole oranges with sharp knife, and scoop out center. Pile sauce in shells; sprinkle with a little grated orange rind. Makes 12 to 16 servings.

CHERRY HARD SAUCE

1 egg white	dash of salt
⅓ cup butter, melted	⅛ teaspoon almond
¼ cup sour cream	extract
1½ cups confectioners'	⅔ cup canned , light
sugar	sweet cherries, pitted

Beat egg white until stiff. Fold in remaining ingredients and chill well. Serve cold over hot steamed pudding.

Holiday plum pudding

STEAMED DATE PUDDING

1¼ cups sifted flour	¼ cup shortening
2 teaspoons double	1 cup firmly packed
acting baking powder	light brown sugar
½ teaspoon salt	1 egg
1 teaspoon cinnamon	¾ cup milk
¼ teaspoon nutmeg	1 teaspoon Angostura
¼ teaspoon cloves	bitters
1 package dates, finely	
sliced	

Sift together flour, baking powder, salt, and spices. Mix ¼ cup of flour mixture with dates. Cream shortening and sugar together until light and fluffy. Beat in egg. Combine milk and bitters. Add flour mixture to sugar mixture alternately with milk, beating well after each addition. Fold in dates. Pour mixture into greased 1½-quart mold; cover tightly. Place on rack in deep kettle. Pour boiling water to half the depth of the pudding. Cover; steam 2 hours. Unmold; serve with hard sauce. Makes 8 to 10 servings.

CRANBERRY ICE

¾ cup sugar	1 cup ginger ale
2 tablespoons cornstarch	2 egg whites
1 pint cranberry juice	
cocktail	

Combine ½ cup of the sugar with cornstarch and mix thoroughly. Add to cranberry juice cocktail. Heat, stirring constantly, to boiling and cook 5 minutes. Cool; add ginger ale and freeze in ice tray until mushy. Beat egg whites until foamy. Add remaining sugar gradually and beat until stiff and glossy. Turn mushy cranberry mixture into chilled bowl. Quickly fold in egg whites. Spoon into paper baking cups in muffin pans. Freeze until firm. Serve in paper cups in a bed of ice. Makes 6 to 8 servings.

CHRISTMAS CHERRY PIE

1 envelope unflavored	⅛ teaspoon salt
gelatin	1 tablespoon lemon juice
¼ cup cold water	1 cup whipped cream
2 cans (1 pound) red ,	1 9-inch baked pie shell
sour pitted cherries	2 tablespoons cornstarch
1 cup sugar, divided	

Soak gelatin in cold water. Pour one can of cherries with liquid in a saucepan. Add ½ cup of the sugar and heat, but do not boil. Add gelatin and salt and stir until gelatin is dissolved. Add lemon juice. Chill until mixture begins to thicken. Fold in whipped cream and turn into baked pie shell. Chill about ½ hour. Drain second can of cherries. Measure liquid and add enough water to make 1 cup liquid. Combine remaining sugar and cornstarch. Stir in cherries. Cool. Spread over filling in pie shell. Chill thoroughly. Makes 6 to 8 servings.

Christmas cherry pie

MINCEMEAT PIE

2 cups sifted flour	2¾ cups prepared mince-
1 teaspoon salt	meat (28-ounce jar)
¾ cup shortening	¾ cup chopped tart
¼ cup cold water	apples

Sift together flour and salt. Cut in shortening with a pastry blender or 2 knives, until mixture is the consistency of coarse corn meal. Sprinkle water over mixture, a tablespoon at a time, tossing lightly with a fork. Shape into a ball with hands and chill for a while. Divide dough in two portions. Roll one-half out on a lightly floured board into a circle about ⅛-inch thick. Fit into a 9-inch pie plate. Trim crust about ½-inch beyond edge of plate. Combine mincemeat and apples and pour into shell. Roll out remaining dough to a diameter of about 10-inches. Cut into strips about ¾-inch wide; weave a lattice top over filling. Trim ends even with lower edge of pastry. Fold bottom edge up over strips and flute with fingers. Bake in a very hot oven (425° F.) 10 minutes, lower temperature to 350° F. and continue to bake for about 25 minutes.

Easy-to-make fruit pie

PINEAPPLE CRANBERRY PIE

1 cup sugar	¼ teaspoon salt
¾ cup water	1½ tablespoons tapioca
2½ cups crushed	red food coloring
pineapple	pastry for 2-crust pie
1½ cups raw cranberries	

Boil sugar and water together 5 minutes. Drain the crushed pineapple, adding syrup and cranberries to the boiled mixture; cover; cook till cranberries pop. Add pineapple, salt, tapioca,

and red food coloring. Cool slightly. Pour into a 9-inch unbaked crust. Finish with lattice pastry and flute edges. Bake for 10 minutes at 450° F., then at 350° F. for 20 minutes more.

Holiday chiffon pie

CRANBERRY CHIFFON PIE

1½ cups finely crushed	1 tablespoon cold water
graham cracker	24 marshmallows
crumbs	2 tablespoons orange
⅓ cup melted butter	juice
⅓ cup confectioners'	1 tablespoon grated
sugar	orange peel
1 cup evaporated milk,	1 tablespoon lemon
divided	juice
1 tablespoon unflavored	1½ cups strained
gelatin	cranberry sauce

Combine graham cracker crumbs, butter and confectioners' sugar and press into a 9-inch pie plate. Chill. Put ⅔ cup of the evaporated milk in the freezing tray of refrigerator. Freeze until ice crystals form around the edge. Soften gelatin in cold water. Combine marshmallows and remaining milk in a saucepan and melt over low heat. Add gelatin and stir until dissolved. Add orange juice and peel, and chill until mixture thickens. Pour crystallized milk into a chilled bowl. Whip with chilled beater until milk stands in peaks. Add lemon juice and whip until stiff. Fold in cranberry sauce and gelatin mixture. Turn into crumb crust and chill for several hours until set.

CRANBERRY SOUFFLÉ SALAD

1 envelope unflavored gelatin	1 teaspoon grated lemon rind
2 tablespoons sugar	1 (1-lb.) can whole cranberry sauce
¼ teaspoon salt	
1 cup very hot water	1 orange or apple, peeled and diced, or one 8½-ounce can pineapple tidbits
½ cup mayonnaise	
2 tablespoons lemon juice	
	¼ cup chopped walnuts

Mix gelatin with sugar and salt. Add hot water. Stir until dissolved. Add mayonnaise, lemon juice, and lemon rind. Blend with rotary beater. Pour into refrigerator tray and quick-chill in freezing unit 10-15 minutes, or until firm about 1 inch from edge but soft in center. Beat until fluffy. Fold in cranberry sauce, fruit, and walnuts. Pour into molds and chill until firm. Unmold on lettuce. Top with mayonnaise. Makes 6 servings.

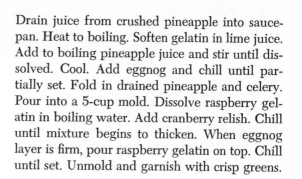

Cranberry soufflé salad

EGGNOG CHRISTMAS SALAD

1 (No. 2) can crushed pineapple	¾ cup chopped celery
1 tablespoon unflavored gelatin	1 package raspberry-flavored gelatin
3 tablespoons lime juice	2 cups boiling water
1½ cups prepared eggnog	1 (10-ounce) package frozen cranberry relish, thawed

Drain juice from crushed pineapple into saucepan. Heat to boiling. Soften gelatin in lime juice. Add to boiling pineapple juice and stir until dissolved. Cool. Add eggnog and chill until partially set. Fold in drained pineapple and celery. Pour into a 5-cup mold. Dissolve raspberry gelatin in boiling water. Add cranberry relish. Chill until mixture begins to thicken. When eggnog layer is firm, pour raspberry gelatin on top. Chill until set. Unmold and garnish with crisp greens.

PARTY CHEESE LOG

½ cup chopped walnuts	¼ teaspoon garlic salt
3 - 5 ounces Bleu or Roquefort cheese	1 tablespoon chopped green pepper
8-ounce package cream cheese	1 tablespoon pimiento

Heat oven to 350° F. Spread walnuts in a shallow pan and toast, stirring occasionally, until golden (about 8 to 10 minutes). Blend cheeses; stir in garlic salt, pimiento, and green pepper. Chill until firm; then shape into log. Roll in toasted walnuts and chill again, until serving time. Garnish with a sprig of holly, and serve with different kinds of crackers.

Party cheese log

Holiday hors d'oeuvres platter

CHRISTMAS FEAST ON FEWEST CALORIES

Traditional meal — with all the trimming — is slimming!

Our dinner for 6 is a memory-making menu that won't add weight. Planned for gourmets who want to rise to an occasion and rise from it. And the secret will be confided to the cook. Guests who diet and guests who don't will find it a savory banquet that is completely satisfying and delicious, but magically low in calories. All by way of a hostess' clever hand in the kitchen, each serving adds up to 510 calories, or 1,000 less than anyone would predict.

The merry meal begins with sea food in rosy tomatoes under a frosting of creamy cottage cheese — a fitting overture with ocean tang and holiday brilliance. A sumptuous roast turkey comes next, lording it over the dressing all spiced with thyme and rosemary and nuggeted with mushrooms and water chestnuts — but there is to be no bread! There will be cranberry-apricot sauce; there will be vegetables.

For dessert, orange crepes of a blissful flavor bide in a chafing dish. And we depart from tradition only in one way — the turkey, first broiled, then baked, comes to the table already carved. As tantalizing aromas rise, who could bear the suspense otherwise?

LOBSTER-AND-CRABMEAT COCKTAIL

Red, white and festive . . . our first course, a lobster-and-crabmeat cocktail cupped in tomato. Slice off tops of 6 small tomatoes, scoop out insides, wrap hollowed tomatoes in plastic film and chill in refrigerator. Now for the meat of tasty crustaceans. Bone 1 cup cooked crabmeat — with zeal. Add to it 1 cup cooked lobster meat, bite size. Marinate both for ½ hour in ¼ cup tarragon vinegar, then chill. Half an hour before dinner, lightly salt insides of tomatoes. Fill with sea food. We'll spoon over it *Creamy Cottage-cheese Dressing*. Combine in electric blender or put through sieve ½ cup cottage cheese, 2 tablespoons skimmed milk, 1 teaspoon grated onion, 1 teaspoon lemon juice, ¼ teaspoon salt, dash of pepper. Blend until smooth. Chill. A most refreshing dressing. And it brings calorie count up to only 71 per serving.

ROAST TURKEY WITH MUSHROOM DRESSING

Have butcher cut an 8-pound bird into 8 pieces. In shallow roasting pan, melt 2 tablespoons butter with ½ teaspoon seasoned salt, ½ teaspoon meat tenderizer, ¼ teaspoon pepper. Rub all turkey pieces with this savory seasoning, place in pan, then broil until they are bubbling and gold on both sides, about 20 minutes. Cover pan tightly with aluminum foil and bake 1 hour in moderately hot oven, 375° F. Meanwhile, the *dressing*. Cook until tender in ½ cup chicken stock 4 cups chopped fresh mushrooms, 4 cups chopped celery. Add 2 teaspoons salt, 1 teaspoon rosemary, ½ teaspoon thyme, ⅛ teaspoon pepper. Remove from heat and stir in ⅔ cup coarsely chopped water chestnuts, ¼ cup flour. Uncover the bird and put the dressing around the turkey. Re-cover and continue roasting another hour or until done. Spoon dressing into center of hot platter. Arrange turkey on top. Brush with pan juices and garnish with crisp fans of cauliflower, radish roses, and parsley. Enough here for 6-8 servings, only 224 calories per serving.

PEARL ONIONS TO BEDECK GREEN BEANS

We tell you an art here. After you peel 1 cup of the tiniest white onions, pierce the ends crisscross — it keeps them from coming apart while they cook. Simmer them gently in salted water for 10 minutes. Drain. Place 2 packages frozen cut green beans in saucepan; join the onions to their emerald companions. Cook together in boiling salted water 8-10 minutes for a courtly blend of flavors, and only 70 calories per serving.

TANGY CRANBERRY-APRICOT SAUCE

Nothing's missing — not even the noble cranberry. And here the color of the sauce is brilliant, the flavor profound. Dissolve 2 packages lemon-flavored low-calorie gelatin dessert in 1½ cups hot water. Add 6 non-caloric sweetener tablets and stir patiently until they dissolve. Open 1 medium-sized can water-packed apricots and measure 1 cup apricot juice (add water if liquid doesn't make a cup) to stir into gelatin mixture, then chill it until thick and syrupy. Meanwhile, cut apricots into medium-size pieces, grind 2 cups fresh cranberries with the coarse blade of the grinder, add 2 teaspoons lemon juice, and blend all into gelatin when it is thick enough. Stir only a bit, then chill. Each serving: 18 calories.

ORANGE CREPES SUZETTE

Our Elysian finale is going to be after-dinner pancakes fragrant with orange, luscious with strawberry, steeped in sauce set for the cockles of the heart. *The recipe:* Sift together into a bowl ¾ cup flour, 1 tablespoon sugar, 1 teaspoon baking soda, ¼ teaspoon salt. Beat together 1¼ cups buttermilk, 1 egg, grated rind of 1 orange. Stir into the dry ingredients until smooth. Bake on a hot, lightly greased griddle until golden on both sides. If you use a level measuring tablespoon to a pancake, count on 20 cakes. Cakes may be made ahead. *For the sauce,* open 1 small can mandarin orange sec-

tions. Pour the liquid into a saucepan. Add 2 tablespoons sugar and heat with strips of rind cut from 1 orange. When removing rind from orange, use a light hand — only the colored part has the flavor you want. Cook gently until liquid thickens and rind is tender. Remove rind; it has worked wonders. Add 2 teaspoons cornstarch to ¼ cup orange juice and add to the saucepan along with 1 teaspoon rum extract. Heat again until mixture thickens and add orange sections, and sliced strawberries if you wish. Stop kitchen work here if you plan to finish with a flourish at the dining room table! *Next step:* Reheat sauce, and warm pancakes in slow oven. In a chafing dish put a round of the little pancakes, heap sauce over, more pancakes, more sauce, and heat them together for 4 or 5 minutes until flavors swim together. When piping hot, serve. Servings of 3 cakes each come to only 124 calories.

With the crepes comes coffee, hot and dark, and the feast is at a fullness, the day at a peak, the compliments rise like a carol, the satisfaction is sound as a bell. Rest ye merry, everywhere, today with not an extra pound to carry into tomorrow!

CHRISTMAS BAKING

There's nothing like a day of Christmas cookie baking to establish the holiday spirit in your house. Bake on a day when the family's all at home. Let the children try to figure out how to get the most cookies out of the circle of dough, and let the decoration be inspired.

Gather the family around and let them pitch in to offer advice, help decorate as things come out of the oven, and act as official tasters. The pastry tube is handy for marking delicate lines. You'll want to tint some of the frosting with food coloring for gay holiday touches.

Fitting plastic cookie cutters on the dough is a job that the children will think is a game. Try rolling them on a rubber pastry tray with a ball-bearing rolling pin.

A flash of the rolling pin and the cookies are cut: the cutters have no handles. Lift them gently out of the dough and set them in flour to wait for the next cutting.

Ease the cookies onto the cookie sheet, to preserve their holiday shapes. If the dough seems too soft, chill it (tray and all) in the refrigerator or the freezer.

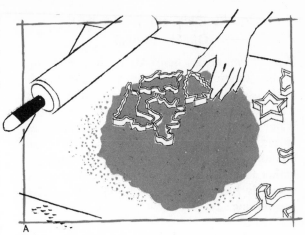

DIVINITY DROPS

2 cups sugar	¼ cup chopped seedless
½ cup water	raisins
½ cup light corn syrup	¼ cup chopped candied
⅛ teaspoon salt	cherries and citron
2 egg whites	halved candied cherries
½ teaspoon vanilla	

Combine sugar, water, and syrup in saucepan. Bring to boil, stirring until sugar is dissolved. Continue boiling, without stirring, until a little of the mixture dropped in cold water forms a hard ball (265° F. on a candy thermometer). A few minutes before syrup is ready, beat salted egg whites until stiff, but not dry. Add syrup slowly, beating constantly. Then beat until mixture becomes very stiff and loses its gloss. Add vanilla and chopped fruit; drop from tablespoon onto waxed paper. Shape; decorate with halved cherries. Makes 20.

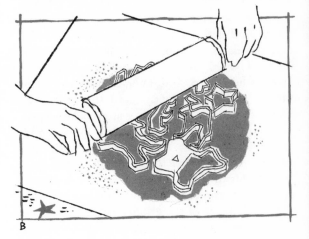

Danish Rings

DANISH RINGS

2 cups sifted flour	¾ cup soft butter
½ teaspoon salt	1 teaspoon vanilla
½ cup sugar	⅔ cup almonds, finely
1 egg	ground

Combine all ingredients; knead on lightly floured board until dough no longer clings to hands. Cut off small pieces of dough, and roll on floured board with palms of hands to size of pencil. Cut in 5-inch lengths, and form rings, crossing the ends. Bake in 350° F. oven for about 20 minutes. Makes 4 dozen.

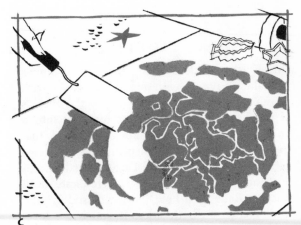

Place cutters without handles on dough and press with a rolling pin, to shape many cookies at once

GERMAN SPRITZ

2¼ cups sifted flour	1 teaspoon vanilla
¾ cup sugar	red and green candied
¼ teaspoon baking	cherries
powder	¼ cup semisweet
few grains salt	chocolate pieces
1 cup butter or	confectioners' sugar
margarine	frosting
1 egg	¼ cup chopped nuts

Sift dry ingredients. Cut in butter with pastry blender. Break egg into measuring cup. If it does not measure ¼ cup, add water to make ¼ cup. Add with vanilla to first mixture; beat well. Fill cookie press halfway. Using crown design, press onto chilled cookie sheets. Decorate crowns with cherries. Refill press. Using star design, press dough onto sheets in 2-inch strips. Bake in hot oven, 400° F., about 10 minutes. Remove at once to racks. Barely melt chocolate; spread a little on one end of cooled sticks. Spread other end with frosting; sprinkle with nuts. Makes about 5 dozen.

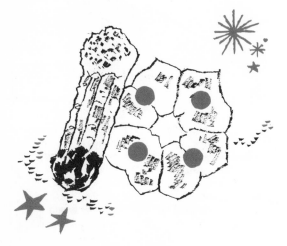

German Spritz

HOLIDAY COOKIES

2½ cups enriched all-	1 egg
purpose flour	1 teaspoon almond or
½ teaspoon baking	lemon flavoring
powder	gumdrops, candied
¼ teaspoon salt	fruit, red sugar or
1 cup shortening	multicolored deco-
¾ cup sugar	rating candy

Sift flour, measure; add baking powder and salt, sift again. Cream shortening, add sugar gradually and cream until light. Add egg and flavoring. Add flour mixture, about a third at a time; blend well. Fill cookie press with mixture and form cookies on ungreased cookie sheet about 1 inch apart. To make Christmas wreaths or candy canes, use the star plate with the press held in a slanting position instead of upright. Use the flower-forming plate for fancy round shapes and the Christmas-tree plate for the small tree shapes. Decorate cookies with small bits of gumdrop, red sugar, candied fruit or multicolored decorating candy. Bake in hot oven, 400°, for 6 to 8 minutes. Makes about 6 dozen.

NOTE: This dough may be used for refrigerator cookies. Shape dough into a roll, chill; cut in ¼ inch slices and bake as directed.

DANISH GINGER STARS

1 cup butter	1 teaspoon soda
½ cup granulated sugar	1 teaspoon salt
½ cup light brown sugar,	1 teaspoon each ginger
packed	and cinnamon
⅓ cup molasses	½ teaspoon cloves
⅔ cup light corn syrup	thin confectioners' sugar
4½ cups sifted flour	frosting

Cream butter and sugars together. Add molasses and corn syrup; mix well. Add sifted, dry ingredients; knead until smooth. Chill several hours until firm enough to roll. Roll out on lightly floured board to less than ⅛-inch thickness. Cut with floured 2-inch, star-shaped cutter. Bake on cookie sheets in moderate oven, 350° F., about 8 minutes. Cool on racks. Decorate with frosting. Makes about 12 dozen.

FRUIT COOKIES

⅓ cup strained honey	⅛ teaspoon salt
½ cup brown sugar	½ teaspoon cinnamon
1 egg	¼ teaspoon nutmeg
1½ teaspoons lemon	¼ teaspoon cloves
juice, fresh, canned,	⅓ cup seedless raisins,
or frozen	chopped
1½ cups flour, en-	¼ cup candied pine-
riched all-purpose	apple, chopped
¼ teaspoon baking	¼ cup shelled walnuts,
soda	chopped

Heat honey in small saucepan till it just comes to a boil; remove from heat, add sugar and stir until thoroughly dissolved. Beat egg in 2-quart bowl until light and fluffy; add lemon juice and honey-sugar mixture; blend well. Sift flour; measure, add soda, salt, cinnamon, nutmeg and cloves; sift into bowl containing the egg-sugar mixture; then add raisins, pineapple and walnuts; mix all together well. Chill thoroughly for 3 to 4 hours or overnight.

Roll out ¼ inch thick on lightly floured board. Cut into bars about 1 to 3 inches. Bake in moderate oven, 375°, for 12 to 15 minutes until lightly browned. Cool. If desired, frost with confectioners' frosting. Makes about 3 dozen. *To make Santa Claus cookies:* Cut dough into 3½ inch rounds with cookie cutter and place on well-greased cookie sheet about 2 inches apart. Cut 2 inch triangles and press onto rounds to form Santa's cap. Bake as directed. Cool. Frost Santa's cap with white confectioners' frosting, then sprinkle peak with red decorating sugar; add white beard of frosting, sprinkle with shredded coconut. With small bits of frosting attach raisin eyes, red gumdrop nose, strip of gumdrop for mouth. Makes about 12 Santas.

Fruit cookie dough can be used to make Santas

SWISS ALMOND DROPS

3 eggs
¼ teaspoon salt
1½ cups sugar
½ cup sifted flour
1½ cups almonds, blanched, toasted, ground
1 (6-ounce) package semisweet chocolate pieces, finely ground
1½ teaspoons vanilla

Beat eggs and salt well; gradually add sugar, and continue beating until very thick and lemon-colored. Add remaining ingredients, and mix well. Chill about 1 hour. Drop by half teaspoonfuls onto foil-covered cookie sheets. Bake in moderate oven, 325° F., about 25 minutes. Makes about 7 dozen.

Swiss almond drops

STUFFED DATE DROPS

1 pound (about 70) pitted dates
1 3-ounce package pecan or walnut halves
¼ cup shortening
¾ cup medium-brown sugar
1 egg
1¼ cups sifted enriched flour
½ teaspoon baking powder
½ teaspoon soda
¼ teaspoon salt
½ cup sour cream
1 recipe Golden Frosting

Stuff dates with nut halves. Cream shortening, sugar till light; beat in egg. Sift dry ingredients; add alternately with sour cream to creamed mixture. Stir in dates; drop onto greased cookie sheet (a date per cookie). Bake in hot oven (400°) 8 to 10 minutes. Place on rack to cool. *Top with Golden Frosting:* Lightly brown ½ cup butter or margarine; remove from heat; gradually beat in 3 cups sifted confectioners' sugar, ¾ teaspoon vanilla. Slowly add water till of spreading consistency, about 3 tablespoons. Makes 5½ dozen cookies.

CHRISTMAS COOKIES

Here are some cookies to hang on the tree, so festive and beautiful that they ought to be looked at a long time before they're gobbled up. The basic recipe is simple and standard, but the canes and three-dimensional stars that are the result will amaze the children and establish your reputation as a Christmas cook.

3 cups all-purpose flour	1 tablespoon milk
1 teaspoon baking powder	½ cup shortening
	1½ cups sugar
¾ teaspoon salt	2 eggs
	1½ teaspoons vanilla

Sift flour, measure; add baking powder and salt; sift again. Cream shortening and sugar together until light and fluffy. Add eggs one at a time, beating well each time; stir in vanilla and milk. Add dry ingredients and mix until well blended; wrap dough in waxed paper and chill about 2 hours. On lightly floured board roll dough ⅛ inch thick; cut out in your choice of shapes. Bake on greased cookie sheet in moderate oven (375°) for 8 to 10 minutes. Cool thoroughly on rack.

ORNAMENTAL FROSTING

1 egg white	1¼ cups confec-
¼ teaspoon vanilla	tioners' sugar
food coloring	

Beat 1 egg white until stiff but not dry; add 1¼ cups sifted confectioners' sugar, ¼ teaspoon vanilla; blend well. Stir in few drops water until mixture is right consistency for spreading. To pipe through decorating tube, add a little more sugar. Makes about 1 cup white frosting. *For colored frostings:* To small amounts of white frosting add a few drops of food coloring to make green wreaths, red berries, etc.

CANDY-CANE COOKIES

Make Christmas Cookie dough. Before chilling dough, divide and add about ½ teaspoon red food coloring to half of it. When chilled, pinch

off pieces of dough and roll each into ropelike strips 6 inches long and about ½ inch thick. *To make canes,* lay a red and a white strip next to each other; starting in middle, twist the two strips together to each end. Then bend one end to resemble cane; with skewer make small hole near top for hanging it up. Bake as directed for Christmas Cookies.

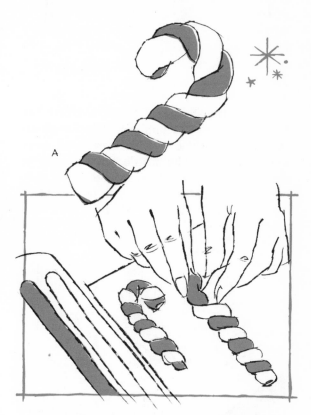

Twist strips of dough and shape into canes

3-D COOKIE STARS

Set star patterns *(Figs. A and B)* on rolled Christmas Cookie dough and cut around them with point of sharp knife, cutting half the cookies with pattern A and half with pattern B. With a skewer make small hole in the A cookies *(Fig. A)*. Bake as directed for Christmas Cookies. When cool, first string wires through holes in cookies. Then slide the 2 parts of stars together *(Fig. C)*, using a little blue ornamental

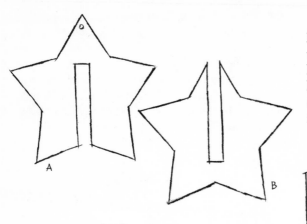

Star pattern

COOKIE SLEIGH AND REINDEER

Here are more ornamental cookies; these make up a cookie centerpiece that's just right for any kind of children's party any time during the holidays. When the party's over, every crumb can be eaten up — or taken home to treasure for as long as temptation can be resisted. The

frosting in the slits to hold stars in place. Let stand a few minutes until set, then spread all over with the blue frosting. Let stand until frosting has set. With a little white frosting in decorating tube, pipe lines around edges, then while still moist use tweezers to put on silver dragees *(Fig. D)*. Hang, by the wires, from your Christmas tree.

Sleigh pattern

outlines for sleigh and reindeer can also be traced and used for other Christmas decorations; the reindeer would make a fine start for a Christmas card for the children to make.

Prepare rolled cookie dough, using cookie

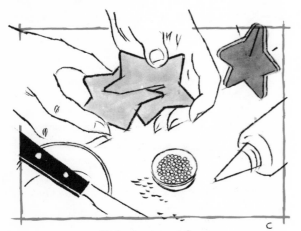

Slide stars together

Ornament star cookies to use as Christmas tree decorations

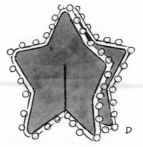

Reindeer pattern

c

Combine cookies to make a centerpiece, good for a children's party

mix or your own recipe for plain, rolled cookies or gingerbread men; roll out ⅛ to ¼ inch thick. Use cookie cutters for figures of Santa and Christmas trees. Cut out 2 cookies for Santa and 2 for each of trees. For sleigh and reindeer, make patterns by tracing outlines (*Figs. A and B*) onto cardboard; cut out. Lay cardboard patterns on cookie dough, cut around them with a sharp knife. Cut 2 pieces for sleigh, 8 reindeer. Bake cookies, placing Santas on cookie sheet so that one faces right and one left.

Prepare ornamental frosting: Beat 1 egg white until stiff; blend in 1 cup sifted confectioners' sugar; add about 1 tablespoon water until of spreading consistency. Tint 2 tablespoons of frosting red with food coloring for Santa, ¼ cup yellow for sleigh, the rest green for trees. Cover one side of each Santa and tree cookie with frosting. Frost one side of each sleigh piece, trim with red cinnamon candies; turn over and frost other side.

Prepare frosting for trim: Cream ½ cup vegetable shortening, gradually add 2 pounds sifted confectioners' sugar alternately with 6 or 8 tablespoons milk or water to give good spreading consistency.

Tint ¼ cup brown, using ¼ teaspoon instant coffee. Tint ⅛ cup green, using food coloring.

Leave rest white. Put Santas and trees together sandwich fashion with white frosting. Trim with cake decorator, using brown frosting to trim reindeer, green to outline sleigh and white on Santa. Decorate with red cinnamon candies, silver dragées, and colored sugars.

Cut base for centerpiece of heavy corrugated cardboard or plywood, 24 by 9 inches. Cover with rest of white frosting. Arrange cookie figures in frosting before it dries. For seat of sleigh, make pile of graham crackers; fill with extra cookies or candies.

SHORT-CUT BAKING

Just before the holidays, there's always more to do than there are hours on the clock. You can give yourself a head start on last-minute baking jobs by making treats that can be stored in the freezing compartment of your refrigerator. If your freezing space is limited, choose for storing the foods that save the most time. Here are hints for freezing, and some new packages that make it easy.

Bake pies in paper plates with metal rims, cool, and pack in plastic boxes with tight covers. To thaw, remove and heat 45 minutes in 350° oven. Or, they can be frozen before they are

Bake pies beforehand, and freeze in plastic boxes

baked; in this case cut vents in top crust when ready for oven, bake 15 minutes extra.

Coffeecakes, rolls, muffins or loaves keep best if baked before freezing. Cool, then wrap and seal in aluminum foil, plastic film, or other moisture-vapor-proof paper, or put in a plastic bag. To thaw, let stand at room temperature in package or heat in foil in moderate oven.

Cookies for the holidays are baked, cooled, and decorated. Put in freezer on cookie sheet for 15 minutes to set frosting, then pack in shallow plastic container, cover tightly, and

Seal breads in aluminum foil, and freeze

freeze. When ready to thaw, remove cookies and lay on flat surface, cover with waxed paper, and let stand at room temperature 15 minutes.

Have lots of cranberries during the holidays; they make all sorts of tasty things with their unusual flavor, and we tend to forget them during other seasons.

Surprise everyone with these different dishes; their color, too, couldn't be more suited to the decoration of the table.

Bake cookies, and freeze in plastic containers

CURRANT LOAF

3 cups biscuit mix	1 tablespoon grated
¾ cup sugar	orange rind
1 egg	¾ cup currants
1¼ cups orange juice	

Combine biscuit mix and sugar; add egg and orange juice and beat well. The batter will be slightly lumpy. Add grated orange rind and currants. Divide batter into three well-greased, clean tin cans (one-pound size), filling slightly more than half full. Bake, uncovered, in moderate oven (350° F.) 45-50 minutes, or until cake tester comes out clean. Cool 10 minutes; remove from cans; cool thoroughly before slicing. *Note*: Batter may also be baked in greased 9 x 5 x 3-inch loaf pan.

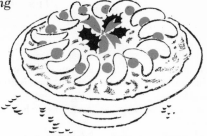

DARK FRUIT CAKE

½ cup shortening	1 cup sifted flour
⅛ teaspoon soda	¼ cup milk
¼ teaspoon salt	3 cups seedless raisins,
¾ teaspoon cinnamon	lightly chopped
¾ teaspoon nutmeg	1 cup sliced, candied
½ teaspoon allspice	cherries
¼ teaspoon cloves	1½ cups sliced, candied
⅔ cup sugar	pineapple
½ square unsweetened	1 cup thinly sliced citron
chocolate, melted	1 cup chopped pecans
½ cup molasses	1 cup sliced, blanched
3 eggs	almonds

Cream together shortening, soda, salt, and spices. Gradually blend in sugar and beat until light and fluffy. Stir in chocolate and molasses. Add eggs one at a time, and beat well after each addition. Add flour alternately with milk, and stir thoroughly after each addition. Add remaining ingredients and blend well. Line the bottom and sides of a greased 9 x 5 x 3-inch loaf pan with brown paper; grease paper well. Pour batter into pan. Bake in a very slow oven (275° F.) 3½ hours or until done. Cool cake in pan 30 minutes. Remove from pan and finish cooling. Remove paper from cake and wrap in aluminum foil to mellow. Makes one loaf cake.

SNOWBALLS WITH CRANBERRY SAUCE

Prepare white-cake mix according to package directions. Pour into 8 greased custard cups. Cover each with foil. Put on rack in large kettle, with about 1 inch of hot water, cover, and steam about 25 minutes. Turn out of cups, and serve hot with *Cranberry Sauce*: Cook 1 cup sugar with 1 cup water about 5 minutes. Add 2 cups cranberries, and cook until skins burst. Stir in 1 tablespoon cornstarch mixed with a little cold water, and bring to boil. Makes 8 servings.

CHRISTMAS WREATH RING

2 cups biscuit mix	½ cup milk
½ cup sugar	1½ cups canned cling
2 teaspoons cinnamon	peach slices
melted butter or	2 tablespoons candied
margarine	cherry halves

Combine biscuit mix, ¼ cup sugar and 1 teaspoon cinnamon. Mix ¼ cup melted butter with milk; stir into dry ingredients, mixing until barely moistened. Turn out on a lightly floured board; knead lightly 10 times. Shape into a roll about 16 inches long. Transfer to lightly greased baking sheet and join ends of roll to make a ring. Flatten roll to make a wreath about ½-inch thick. Crimp edges. Using edge of large spoon, make depressions in the dough at ½-inch intervals. Brush dough lightly with melted butter. Bake in a very hot oven (450° F.) for about 15 minutes. While wreath is baking, drain peach slices. Remove wreath from oven, sprinkle with ¼ cup sugar and 1 teaspoon cinnamon. Arrange peach slices and cherries over dough. Return to oven for 3 minutes. Brush with melted butter before serving. Makes 8 servings.

HOLIDAY NUT ROLL

2 cups brown sugar,	1 cup milk
packed	1½ cups chopped nuts
1 cup granulated sugar	¼ cup each chopped
1 tablespoon corn syrup	candied cherries,
⅛ teaspoon salt	citron

Combine sugars, corn syrup, salt, and milk in saucepan. Bring to boil, and cook, without stirring, until a small amount of the mixture dropped in cold water forms a soft ball (236° F. on a candy thermometer). Remove from heat, and let stand until lukewarm. Then beat until thick and mixture loses its gloss. Add ½ cup nuts and fruits. Shape into long roll, 2½ inches in diameter. Roll in remaining nuts; wrap in damp cloth. Makes 1¾ pounds.

STOLLEN

¼ cup milk	1 egg, beaten
¼ cup sugar	2½ cups sifted flour
2 tablespoons shortening	2 tablespoons butter
¾ teaspoon salt	¼ cup raisins
¼ cup warm, not hot, water	¼ cup finely chopped citron
1 package of cake yeast, active dry or compressed	2 tablespoons chopped, candied orange peel

Scald milk; stir in sugar, shortening and salt. Cool to lukewarm. Measure water into a large mixing bowl (warm, not hot, for active dry yeast; lukewarm for compressed yeast). Add yeast and stir until dissolved. Blend in milk mixture. Add egg and half the flour. Beat until smooth. Stir in remaining flour. Turn dough out on lightly floured board. Knead until smooth and elastic. Place in greased bowl; brush top with butter. Cover; let rise in a warm place, free from draft, about 1 hour or until doubled in bulk. Punch down and turn out on lightly floured board. Spread fruits over dough and knead to distribute them evenly. Pat the dough into an oval about 10 x 14 inches; spread with butter. Fold in half the long way. Press folded edge firmly so it won't spring open. Place on lightly greased baking sheet. Brush with butter. Let rise about 1 hour, or until doubled in bulk. Bake in a moderately hot oven (375° F.) for 40 to 45 minutes. Frost with confectioners' sugar frosting while warm.

CAKE TREES

2 cups sifted confectioners' sugar	3 cups flaked coconut
¼ cup soft butter	red cinnamon candies
¼ cup light cream	½ cup chocolate morsels
1 teaspoon rum extract	1 tablespoon vegetable shortening

Blend sugar, butter, light cream, and rum extract. Stir in coconut. Drop by teaspoonfuls onto waxed paper. Chill thoroughly, and shape into cones 1¾ inches high. Press green-tinted coconut onto sides of trees, decorate with red cinnamon candies. In a small dish, blend over hot water (not boiling), chocolate morsels and vegetable shortening. Remove from heat and dip bottoms of trees into chocolate. Chill on waxed paper.

STOCKING CAKES

A Christmas stocking cake is a real charmer for each child in the family. Make your own white cake, from a mix if you like, in a 13 x 9 x 2-inch pan. When cool, cut in half lengthwise, and place pieces 3 inches apart on a serving plate. (You need not move them, and they will make a handsome dessert centerpiece.) Measure four inches up from each lower left corner, and cut diagonally to the lower right corner to make a triangle. Move this triangle around to the opposite corner, to form the toe of the stocking. Cover thickly with frosting and decorate with candy, shredded coconut, and a name spelled out in icing. Arrange cookies at the top, to look like gifts in the stocking.

Holiday stollen

CUPCAKE FRUITCAKE

Cream 1 cup shortening and 1 cup sugar together. Add 5 eggs, one at a time; beat well after each addition. Sift together 1½ cups flour; 1 teaspoon salt and 1½ teaspoons baking powder. Add alternately with ¼ cup unsweetened pineapple juice to first mixture. Dust the following fruit with ½ cup flour: ½ cup chopped candied cherries; 1¼ cups chopped candied pineapple; ¼ pound each finely cut citron, orange and lemon peel; ½ cup each chopped pitted dates, chopped dried figs, chopped dried apricots; and ½ pound white raisins. Add fruit, ½ pound flaked coconut and 2 cups sliced blanched almonds to batter. Mix only to blend. Bake in paper baking cups in muffin pans at 275° F. for 50 minutes. Makes 32 two-inch cakes.

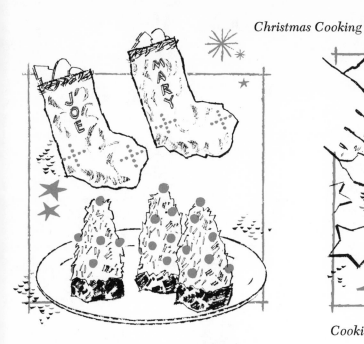

Cookie cutters come in many holiday shapes

BAKING HINTS AND GADGETS

Don't overlook the gadgets for Christmas baking that you can find in the stores. There are cake-size Christmas tree pans; a gala layer cake results with no need to cut the shape out of square layers and have snips left over. All your artistic talents can be expressed in decorating the tree.

Save time with a plastic cutout tray

Easy-to-make decorated cake tree

Decorator set

*A springerle rolling pin makes pictures
in the dough*

If you're using a recipe that makes a heavy batter (butter-cake type), in most cases the pan or mold should be filled two-thirds full.

Cookie cutters come in all sorts of holiday shapes, and perhaps some new ones have been added that you've never seen.

Plastic trays are available with holiday cut-outs, and many cookies can be stamped out in one swoop.

A rolling pin with a waffle surface gives an unusual design to cookie dough, and will cause

*As a cookie wheel rolls, it cuts shapes
in the dough*

cookie press makes many duplicates quickly

Rosette irons fashion delicious cookies

whatever sprinkles you use for decoration to fall into interesting patterns.

There's a cookie wheel that turns out shapes as you spin it over the dough. It's fascinating for children to watch, and you may find yourself making twice as many cookies just for the fun of it.

A small forest of tiny trees, or a caravan of camels, pops out of a cookie press. They're fine for the cookie jar, or for children's parties and gifts.

Rosette cookies are as pretty as they are rich and delicious. A pair of Swedish irons lets you fry them as stars and bells. Drain them on a paper towel and powder them with confectioners' sugar.

CANDIED FRUITCAKE

Sift 2 cups sifted flour, 2 teaspoons baking powder, and ½ teaspoon salt into large bowl. Add 1 pound candied pineapple, coarsely cut (2½ cups); 1 pound (2 cups) whole candied cherries; and 1¼ pounds pitted dates, coarsely cut (3½ cups). Mix well with hands to coat each piece of fruit with flour. Beat 4 eggs until frothy; gradually beat in 1 cup sugar. Add to fruit, and mix well. With hands, mix in 2 pounds (8 cups) pecan halves. Grease, and line with brown paper, two 9-inch clamp or clampless springform pans; grease paper. Divide dough into pans, and press down firmly with fingers. If necessary rearrange fruit and nuts to fill any empty spaces. Bake in slow oven, 275° F., about 1¼ hours. Let cakes stand in pans about 5 minutes. Turn out on racks, and pull off brown paper. Cool.

Candied fruitcake

French Bûche de Noel

FRENCH BÛCHE DE NOEL

5 eggs	1 tablespoon cocoa
1 cup sugar	2 teaspoons brewed
3 tablespoons cocoa	coffee
cocoa and confectioners'	1 cup heavy cream,
sugar, mixed half	whipped
and half (2 table-	¼ cup sugar
spoons of each)	melted unsweetened
⅔ cup butter or	chocolate
margarine	1 tablespoon pistachio
½ cup confectioners'	nuts, finely chopped
sugar	

Line the bottom of a jelly roll pan (11 x 7 inches) with heavily coated, greased and floured wax paper. In a bowl beat the eggs and sugar until thick and lemon-colored (about 10 minutes with electric beater). Fold in cocoa. Pour the cake mixture into pan. Bake in a moderately slow oven for 25 minutes. Place a sheet of brown paper on a rack. Coat heavily with a mixture of cocoa and confectioners' sugar. Turn cake upside-down on the coated paper. Remove waxed paper; trim edges of cake. Roll as for jelly roll, lifting the brown paper as you roll the cake. Let stand on rack until cold. Unroll carefully. It's a very thin roll at this point. Combine the butter, confectioners' sugar, cocoa, and coffee to make a mocha cream icing. Spread a thin layer on the cake. Beat the heavy cream and sugar until thick. Spread over the mocha cream. Re-roll the cake. Spread the remaining mocha cream over outside of roll. Roughen it up a bit to look like a log. Brush with melted unsweetened chocolate. Sprinkle with pistachio nuts. Refrigerate.

FRENCH ALMOND COOKIES

¾ cup butter
¼ cup granulated sugar
½ teaspoon almond
  extract
2 cups sifted flour
⅛ teaspoon salt

1 egg white, slightly
  beaten
⅛ teaspoon cinnamon
⅛ cup blanched almonds,
  finely chopped

Cream butter; add ¼ cup sugar and flavoring; beat until light. Add sifted flour and salt. Chill several hours, or until firm enough to roll. Roll to ⅛-inch thickness. Cut in 1 x 2-inch strips with pastry wheel. Put on cookie sheets. Brush with egg white. Mix 2 tablespoons sugar, cinnamon, and almonds. Sprinkle on cookies. Bake in moderate oven, 350° F., for 8 minutes. Makes about 6 dozen.

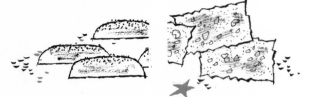

Swedish finger cookies

French almond cookies

PFEFFERNUSSE

1 cup soft butter or
  margarine
1 cup sugar
½ cup each molasses
  and dark corn syrup
3 eggs
1½ teaspoons crushed
  cardamom seed

1 teaspoon crushed
  anise seed
¼ teaspoon black
  pepper
5½ cups sifted flour
¾ teaspoon salt
½ teaspoon soda

Cream butter, sugar, molasses, and corn syrup; add eggs, and beat until light. Add flavorings and sifted flour, salt, and soda; mix well. Let stand in refrigerator overnight. Shape into rolls about ¾-inch diameter. Cut in 1-inch lengths, and put on end on cookie sheets. Bake in moderate oven, 350° F., about 20 minutes. Store 1 week before eating. Makes about 12 dozen.

Pfeffernusse

SESAME COOKIES

2½ cups sifted cake
  flour
½ teaspoon baking
  powder
⅛ teaspoon salt
1 cup sugar

1 cup soft butter
2 egg yolks
1 teaspoon vanilla
Seed such as sesame,
  anise, or caraway

Sift dry ingredients; cut in butter. Add egg yolks and vanilla; blend. Chill several hours. Roll to ⅛-inch thickness on floured board, and cut in fancy shapes. Put on cookie sheets, and sprinkle with seed. Bake in hot oven, 400° F., about 8 minutes. Makes about 8 dozen small or 4 dozen large cookies.

Sesame cookies

GERMAN LECKERLI

1 cup granulated sugar
½ cup honey
½ cup chopped, candied
  orange and lemon peel
1½ teaspoons cloves
1½ teaspoons nutmeg
1 tablespoon cinnamon

1 teaspoon soda
water
grated rind ½ lemon
1 cup unblanched
  almonds, sliced thin
2¾ cups sifted flour

Heat ½ cup sugar and honey to boiling. Remove from heat; add peel, spices, and soda dissolved in 2 tablespoons cold water. Add remaining ingredients. Knead until well blended. Roll dough to ½-inch thickness. Place on greased wax paper on cookie sheet. Bake in moderate oven, 325° F., about 25 minutes. Turn out on wire rack, and remove paper at once. Turn right side up. Cook remaining ½ cup sugar and ¼ cup water until mixture spins a thread. Spread on Leckerli. Cut in diamonds. Store airtight at least 1 week before using. Makes about 5 dozen.

German Leckerli

SWEDISH FINGER COOKIES

½ cup soft butter or margarine	1½ cups sifted cake flour
½ cup sugar	½ teaspoon salt
1 egg, separated	½ cup unblanched almonds, grated
½ teaspoon almond flavoring	12 sugar cubes, crushed

Can be frozen. Cream butter and sugar; add egg yolk, and beat until light. Add flavoring, sifted flour, and salt, and half the almonds; mix well. Chill several hours. Divide dough into fourths. Working with finger tips on lightly floured board, roll each fourth into a 12-inch strip, finger width. Cut strips crosswise into 1-inch pieces. Beat egg white slightly with fork, and brush on cookies. Dip in remaining nuts and crushed sugar cubes, mixed. Place, dipped side up, on cookie sheets. Bake in 375° F. oven, 8 to 10 minutes. Makes 4 dozen.

Snowflakes

BON BON COOKIES

½ cup soft butter	food coloring, if desired
¾ cup sifted confec- tioners' sugar	1½ cups sifted flour
1 tablespoon vanilla	⅛ teaspoon salt

Heat oven to 350° F. Mix butter, sugar, vanilla, food coloring. Blend in flour and salt thoroughly with hand. If dough is dry, add 1 to 2 table-spoons cream. Wrap level tablespoon dough around filling (cherry, date, nut, chocolate bit). Bake on ungreased baking sheet 12 to 15 minutes, until set but not brown. Cool.

Dip cookies in Icing: Mix 1 cup sifted confectioners' sugar, 2 tablespoons cream, 1 teaspoon vanilla. Add food coloring. Decorate with colorful toppings. 20 to 25 cookies.

Delicious bon bon cookies

SNOWFLAKES

⅓ cup soft shortening (part butter)	1¼ cups sifted flour
½ cup sugar	½ teaspoon baking powder
1 egg	½ teaspoon salt
¼ teaspoon lemon ex- tract or ½ teaspoon vanilla	

Mix thoroughly shortening, sugar, egg, flavoring. Sift together dry ingredients and stir in. Chill 1 hour. Heat oven to 400° F. Roll dough ⅛-inch thick on lightly floured board. Keep dough chilled, rolling only ¼ at a time. Cut with star cutter. Place on ungreased baking sheet. Bake 6 to 8 minutes until delicately brown. Decorate when cool with Shiny Glaze. Makes 4 dozen.

SHINY GLAZE

3 cups sifted confec- tioners' sugar	⅛ teaspoon salt
4 teaspoons light corn syrup	½ teaspoon lemon ex- tract or vanilla
¼ cup hot water	food coloring, if desired

Mix all ingredients until smooth and glossy. Cover. Stack cookies on rack in pairs with points of top star between points of bottom star. Place rack over pan. Pour 1 teaspoon glaze over snowflakes. While glaze is still soft, transfer cookies to wax paper and decorate as desired. Let snowflakes dry before storing.

Success Tip: Add few drops of hot water to thin glaze as necessary. Decorate before glaze dries.

WALNUT STICKS

1 recipe pastry (using 1 cup flour) or 1 stick pie crust mix	(use your favorite flavor jam)
¼ cup red jam or jelly	½ cup finely chopped walnuts

Heat oven to 450° F. Roll pastry thin, into approximately a 12-inch square. Spread half with jam and sprinkle with chopped walnuts. Fold crust over the filling, and roll lightly again. With a sharp knife, cut into strips about ¼ inch wide. Twist the strips like ribbon candy and arrange on a greased cookie sheet. Bake 7 to 10 minutes until golden brown and remove immediately to a cooling rack. This will make about two dozen 6-inch sticks, delightful both warm and cold. Shape the sticks into canes before baking.

PEPPERMINT CANDY COOKIES

1 cup butter or margarine	½ cup sifted confectioners' sugar
½ cup confectioners' sugar	2 tablespoons cream cheese
1 teaspoon vanilla	1 teaspoon milk
2½ cups sifted flour	½ cup confectioners' sugar
½ cup chopped nuts	
½ cup crushed, pink peppermint stick candy	1 drop red food coloring

Cream together butter and ½ cup confectioners' sugar until light and fluffy. Add vanilla. Gradually add flour and nuts and mix thoroughly. Chill. Combine peppermint candy and ½ cup confectioners' sugar. Reserve. Blend together cheese and milk until smooth and creamy. Gradually add ½ cup confectioners' sugar, 3 tablespoons of the peppermint stick candy mixture and food coloring and blend well. Shape cookie dough into balls, using a rounded teaspoonful for each. Make a hole in center of each and fill with about ¼ teaspoon of the filling. Seal. Place on ungreased baking sheet. Bake in a moderate oven (350° F.) 12 to 15 minutes, until set but not brown. While warm, roll in remainder of peppermint candy-sugar mixture. When cool reroll in candy mixture.

SNOWMAN BUNS

¾ cup warm water (not hot — 110 to 115° F.)	1 teaspoon salt
	2 teaspoons nutmeg
1 package active dry yeast	2 eggs
	¼ cup soft shortening
3½ cups sifted flour	currants
⅓ cup sugar	

In mixer bowl, dissolve yeast in warm water. Add half of flour, sugar, salt, nutmeg, eggs, shortening. Beat 2 minutes, medium speed on mixer or 300 vigorous strokes by hand. Scrape sides and bottom of bowl frequently. Add remaining flour and blend in with spoon until smooth. Cover with cloth and let rise in warm place until double in bulk (about 45 minutes). (If kitchen is cool, place dough on a rack over a bowl of hot water and cover completely with a towel.) Stir down by beating 25 strokes. Turn onto lightly floured board. Cut dough into 12 equal parts, one for each snowman.

TO FORM SNOWMEN:

Body: Use ½ of each piece of dough. Shape a 4-inch long oval.

Head: Use a little more than ½ of remaining dough. Shape round ball. Press currants in deeply for eyes; add tiny piece of dough for nose.

Arms: For arms, make two 2-inch pencillike rolls.

Place snowmen 3 inches apart on greased baking sheet. Let rise in warm place until double (about 45 minutes). Brush with 1 egg, beaten. Heat oven to 350° F. (moderate). Bake about 15 minutes, until brown. Makes 12.

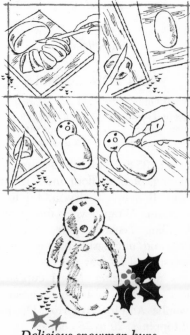

Delicious snowman buns

Appetizing candy cane rolls

CANDY CANE ROLLS

¼ cup warm water (not hot — 110 to 115°)	1 egg
1 package active dry yeast	¼ cup shortening
¾ cup lukewarm milk	3½ to 3¾ cups sifted flour
¼ cup sugar	1 cup quartered, red candied cherries, if
1 teaspoon salt	desired

In mixing bowl, dissolve yeast in water. Stir in milk, sugar, salt. Add egg, shortening, and half of flour; mix with spoon. Add rest of flour and cherries; mix with hands. Turn onto lightly floured board. Knead until smooth and blistered, about 5 minutes. Round up in greased bowl; bring greased side up. Cover with damp cloth. Let rise in warm place until double in bulk, 1½ to 2 hours. (If kitchen is cool, place dough on rack over bowl of hot water and cover with towel.) Punch down; round up. Let rise again until almost double in bulk, 30 to 40 minutes. Divide in halves. Roll each into rectangle, 12 x 7 inches. On the long side, cut twelve 1-inch strips. Twist and place 1 inch apart on greased baking sheet, shaping like canes. Press ends of canes firmly on baking sheet. Brush with melted shortening. Cover and let rise until double, about 1 hour. Heat oven to 375° F. (quick moderate). Bake about 12 minutes, or until brown. While warm, frost with a confectioners' sugar icing. Add red icing stripes after white icing is set. Makes 24 canes.

HOLIDAY WALNUT BREAD

½ cup sugar	1 egg
1¼ cups milk	3 cups biscuit mix
1½ cups chopped walnuts	

Heat oven to 350° F. Mix first 4 ingredients. Beat hard 30 seconds. Stir in crunchy walnuts. Pour into well greased loaf pan 9 x 5 x 3 inches. Bake 45 to 50 minutes, until toothpick stuck into center comes out clean. Crack in top is typical. Cool before slicing. To store, wrap in foil.

A holiday favorite

QUICK PANETTONE

1 package yeast	¾ stick (six tablespoons) soft butter
1 cup warm water	
1½ tablespoons light corn syrup	¼ cup sugar
2½ cups sifted flour	¼ teaspoon salt
1 egg	½ cup thinly sliced citron
3 egg yolks	1 cup seedless raisins

1. Soften yeast in water in the bowl of a mixer.

2. Add corn syrup and half the flour. Mix on low speed, then beat on medium speed until smooth. Add remaining flour, egg, and egg yolks; mix and then beat for three minutes. Leave beater standing in batter. Place bowl in a pan of warm water, let stand until batter has doubled in bulk, about one hour.

3. Beat batter for three minutes at medium speed. Add butter in small pieces, sugar, and salt and beat until well mixed and elastic. Remove beater.

4. Fold in citron and raisins. Turn into two greased six-cup cans or molds. Set in a warm

place to rise again until the batter reaches tops of cans, about seventy minutes.

5. Using a piece of wax paper, make a collar for each can, allowing it to extend three inches above top of can. Set a pan of water on bottom shelf of oven and preheat to 425 ° F.

6. Bake loaves on shelf with water ten minutes. Then lower heat to 350° F. and bake until panettone has browned well and shrunk slightly from sides of cans, about fifty minutes longer.

7. If a glazed top is desired, about fifteen minutes before bread is done brush tops of loaves with slightly beaten egg white mixed with a little water. Remove collars and cool on a rack. *Yield:* Two loaves.

Easy-to-make walnut bread

FOOD THAT THE CHILDREN WILL LOVE TO MAKE

Participation in Christmas activity is a fine source of holiday joy, and it can happen in the kitchen as happily as anywhere else in the house. There are lots of good things to make which are so simple and yet intriguing that the children can make them with excellent results. They're wonderful for munching and wonderful for giving; some are inexpensive enough so that the children can invite their friends in often for treats during the holidays.

PEANUT BUTTER BALLS

1 cup raisins	¼ teaspoon cinnamon
½ cup peanut butter	about 2 tablespoons
½ cup confectioners'	lemon juice
sugar	shredded coconut

Cut up a cup of raisins into small pieces. Mix with ½ cup peanut butter and ½ cup confectioners' sugar. Stir in ¼ teaspoon cinnamon and about 2 tablespoons lemon juice. Form into 30 small balls. Roll each ball in shredded coconut.

Panettone

ROLLED COOKIE FACES

3½ cups flour	1 cup sugar
1 teaspoon salt	2 eggs
1 cup butter	1 teaspoon vanilla
chocolate bits	

Sift together 3½ cups flour and 1 teaspoon salt. Beat together 1 cup butter and 1 cup sugar. When sugar and butter are fluffy, beat in 2 eggs, 1 teaspoon vanilla, and the sifted flour and salt. Wrap dough in waxed paper and chill overnight. Then roll thin and cut into 2 inch circles.

Put on an ungreased cookie sheet. Make faces with chocolate bits. Bake 10 minutes at 375°.

GUM DROP WALNUT BREAD

Make batter for Holiday Walnut bread, except use 1 cup chopped walnuts and add 1 cup chopped gum drops (except black ones). To get round loaves, bake in cans. Divide batter between three well greased 8-ounce (2 cup) cans (or No. 2 size cans), filling cans slightly more than half full. Bake, uncovered, about 45 to 50 minutes until toothpick thrust into center comes out clean.

Peanut butter balls are easy to make

EASY CHRISTMAS MINTS

3 egg whites	food coloring
6 cups confectioners' sugar	various mint extracts

In a large bowl, beat 3 egg whites until stiff. Slowly blend in 6 cups sifted confectioners' sugar. Divide candy into three bowls. Tint 1 red, 1 green, and 1 yellow. Flavor each with one of various mint extracts. Roll each mixture out between pieces of waxed paper. Cut patties

Use chocolate bits to make faces on vanilla cookies

with the mouth of an olive jar or, for tiny mints, a thimble.

Let dry overnight.

(For a fascinating way to make Christmas Mint Trees from this recipe, see page 63 in Gift Packages.)

SUGAR FROSTED APRICOTS AND PRUNES

egg white, beaten   apricots
sugar   prunes

Dip little clusters of the dried fruits in beaten egg white. Drain off the excess egg white; now, dip in confectioners' sugar. Place on paper toweling to dry, then arrange fruits on a platter.

FROSTY STUFFED FIGS

dried figs   walnuts or pecans
        confectioners' sugar

Slit side of soft whole dried figs and fill center with broken walnuts or pecans; press closed. Dip bottom of figs in sifted confectioners' sugar.

BUTTERED HONEY NUTS

Spread 6 ounces shelled, unsalted nuts on a cookie sheet. Bake in slow oven, 300° F., 15 minutes. Mix 1 tablespoon each honey and butter, and pour over nuts. Stir until nuts are completely coated with the honey mixture. Store in airtight container until ready to pack. Makes 1⅓ cups.

An olive jar will cut out Christmas mints

Frosted dried fruits

PEANUT BRITTLE

1¾ cups shelled roasted   2 cups sugar
    peanuts   1 teaspoon butter
⅛ teaspoon salt

Rub hulls from nuts; arrange on a buttered, shallow pan. Add salt to sugar, and heat in skillet until melted and caramelized, stirring constantly. Add butter; spoon mixture over peanuts, spreading to distribute syrup evenly. Let stand until cold. Break up. Makes 1¼ pounds.

*Easy-to-make peanut brittle
and buttered honey nuts*

POPCORN STARS

8 cups popped corn	¼ teaspoon salt
½ cup light corn syrup	1 tablespoon butter
¼ cup water	1 teaspoon vanilla
½ cup sugar	green food coloring

Combine sugar, corn syrup, salt, and water and
bring to a boil. Cook till a few drops form a
firm ball in cold water. Add butter, flavoring,
and green coloring and pour over corn, stirring
syrup through with two forks. Grease hands and
mold corn into star shapes or press into a kitchen
funnel for trees. Using the same method, you
can also make star shapes or wreaths with ring
or jelly molds.

*Frost ice cream cones with
instant frosting mix and
decorate with candy sprinkles
or chocolate bits*

STUFFED DATES

A tasty holiday delight for all. Split open dried dates and remove pit; stuff with peanut butter. Even children who have never liked dates will love this delicious, unusual combination.

Try stuffing dates with nuts, candied fruits, or marshmallow. Roll them in sugar or sprinkle them with shredded coconut.

A tasty treat — so good to eat!

CHRISTMAS CANDY

Candy is an institution at Christmas. People who resist it the rest of the year will eat it happily during the holidays. And those who don't make much candy, ordinarily, find themselves right in the kitchen turning out batches of sweet treats — for family, friends, and neighbors, as gifts of loving thoughtfulness.

SUGARED WALNUTS

1½ cups sugar	¼ teaspoon salt
½ cup liquid	2 to 3 cups walnuts,
(see flavors below)	halves or large pieces
1 teaspoon white corn	
syrup	

Cook first 4 ingredients to soft ball stage (236° to 240°). Remove from heat; add walnuts. Stir till creamy. Turn onto foil. Separate walnuts. *Spiced:* ½ cup water, ½ teaspoon each nutmeg, cloves, 2 teaspoons cinnamon. *Minted:* ½ cup

milk, green food coloring. ¾ teaspoon mint flavoring stirred in after cooking. *Orange Sugared:* ½ cup orange juice, 1½ teaspoons grated orange rind.

DIVINITY SNOWBALLS

3 cups sugar	½ teaspoon vanilla
½ cup light corn syrup	1 cup chopped nuts,
⅔ cup water	candied cherries,
2 egg whites	and candied ginger
⅛ teaspoon salt	1 can flaked coconut

Cook sugar, corn syrup, and water until a small amount of mixture forms an extra-hard ball when dropped in cold water (265° F. on candy thermometer). Beat egg whites and salt until stiff. Pour cooked syrup slowly into beaten egg whites, beating at high speed. Beat until mixture loses its gloss. Add vanilla, nuts, and fruit. Stir until it holds its shape. Drop by spoonfuls onto wax paper, shape into small balls. Dip your hands into a bowl of cold water before shaping, and work fast so that the candy does not cool. Roll in coconut.

*Sugared walnuts are
so easy to make*

QUICK COCONUT DROPS

1 package coconut- cream pudding mix	1 tablespoon butter grated rind of one
1½ cups sugar	orange
½ cup evaporated milk	1 can flaked coconut candied cherries

Combine all ingredients except coconut and cherries. Bring to a boil and cook, stirring constantly about 3 minutes or until a soft ball forms when a small amount is tested in cold water. Cool slightly and add coconut; beat until mixture is somewhat thick. Drop in small balls onto waxed paper, and top each with a piece of cherry.

CANDIED CRANBERRIES

Wash 2 cups large, firm cranberries; drain well, and spread in bottom of buttered baking dish. Sprinkle with 1½ cups sugar, and cover tightly. Bake in moderate oven, 350° F., 1 hour. Stir once to distribute sugar. Let cranberries cool in syrup. Lift out onto waxed paper. Sift a little sugar over berries. Let stand until dry and firm.

CANDIED GRAPEFRUIT PEEL

Cover peel of 1 large grapefruit with cold water. Bring to boil, and cook until tender, pouring off the water and adding fresh cold water several times. Drain, and with scissors, cut peel in thin strips. Boil 1 cup sugar and ½ cup water until it spins a thread. Add peel, and cook over low heat until syrup has been absorbed. Roll each strip in sugar. Let stand until cold.

FROSTED ORANGE SLICES

For each large seedless orange, thinly sliced, combine one cup sugar and ½ cup water in a large skillet and heat until sugar is dissolved; season, if you like, with whole cloves and pieces of stick cinnamon. Arrange orange slices in flat layers in the skillet. It's best to do just one or two layers at a time. Simmer gently until the oranges are well cooked; the peels will look translucent. Drain slices on a wire rack. You can reuse the syrup for the next batch, adding a little more sugar and water as needed. Dry slices overnight, then cut them in half. Mix ½ cup confectioners' sugar with enough water to thicken; heat just enough to dissolve the sugar; do not boil. Dip half slices, one by one, in frosting; drain; return to rack to dry.

PECAN PRALINES

1 cup granulated sugar	1¼ cups milk
2 cups light brown sugar, firmly packed	1 teaspoon vanilla 1½ cups unbroken
¼ cup light corn syrup	pecan halves
⅛ teaspoon salt	

Combine the sugars, corn syrup, salt, and milk in saucepan. Bring to boil, and cook without stirring, until a little of the mixture dropped into cold water forms a soft ball (236° F. on a candy thermometer). Remove from heat, and let stand until lukewarm. Add vanilla and pecans, and beat with spoon until mixture begins to thicken and loses its gloss. Drop from tablespoon onto waxed paper, and spread to form patties about 4″ in diameter. Let stand until firm. Then wrap in cellophane. Store in airtight container until ready to pack. Makes 12.

Pecan pralines — a favorite of all!

VANILLA CARAMELS

2 cups sugar	1 cup milk
1 cup light corn syrup	½ cup heavy cream
1 (14-ounce) can sweet-	¼ cup butter
ened condensed milk	2 teaspoons vanilla

1. Mix ingredients except vanilla in a heavy two-quart saucepan and cook, stirring and scraping, to 249° F. (a firm, caramel-like ball in cold water). Add vanilla.

2. Turn into an oiled 9 x 9-inch pan and cool. Cut into squares and wrap in waxed paper or use for caramel pecan rolls. Makes 2 pounds.

JELLY CANDIES

¾ cup sugar	1 package strawberry
1 cup canned apple-	or lime-flavored
sauce	gelatin
granulated sugar	⅔ cup shelled walnuts

Combine sugar and applesauce in 1-quart saucepan. Bring to boil over moderate heat and boil 3 minutes, stirring frequently. Add red or green

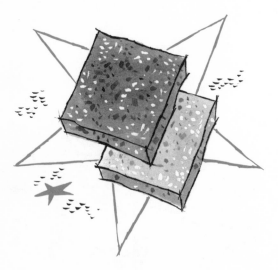

*Jelly candies can be tinted
in holiday red or green*

gelatin and stir over low heat until thoroughly dissolved. Remove from heat, add walnuts; mix well. Pour into greased 8-inch-square pan; chill until firm. Cut into 36 squares, roll in sugar, and let stand on rack at room temperature 6 to 8

hours until dry. Roll again in sugar; pack between layers of waxed paper in covered container (not airtight).

CARAMEL PECAN ROLLS

To prepare caramel pecan rolls, cool almond divinity in pan, turn it onto a board, then cut it into rectangles.

Place prepared caramel coating immediately in a pan of hot water. Drop pieces in the caramel; turn to coat.

Drop caramel-coated candy into mixed whole and chopped pecans. Toss nuts over caramels; press them into candy.

The pecan roll is best when cut into half-inch slices for serving. Leave it whole when candy is to be stored.

CARAMEL PECAN ROLLS

1 pound almond divinity	2 pounds vanilla caramel mixture
1 pound pecans	

1. Cool and cut the almond divinity into 2 x 1-inch rectangles.

2. Coarsely chop one cup of the nuts. Mix with the remaining whole pecans. Set aside.

3. Cook vanilla caramel mixture until it reaches 246° F. Stand in a pan of boiling water to prevent hardening. Add boiling water as needed to keep the caramel soft.

4. Drop a piece of the divinity into the caramel; turn with a fork to coat completely. Rub against side of the pan to remove any excess caramel and drop into the pecans.

5. Toss pecans over candy, pressing them gently into coating. Cool, cut into half-inch slices. Leftover divinity may be cut up and chocolate-coated. If any caramel remains, turn into oiled pan for plain caramel, adding pecans if desired.

Chocolate-coated divinity: Melt a six-ounce package of semi-sweet chocolate pieces and one teaspoon butter in a small saucepan over hot water. Stir until smooth. Dip tops of divinity squares into it; sprinkle with nuts.

COCONUT CREAMS

3 cups sugar	1½ cups milk
1 cup dark brown sugar	2 cups flaked coconut
	1 teaspoon vanilla

1. Cook sugars, milk and coconut to 238° F. (soft ball in cold water), stirring constantly. Cool to lukewarm.

2. Beat with wooden spoon until candy is thick and creamy and almost holds its shape when dropped from spoon. Add vanilla. Spread in an oiled 9 x 9-inch pan; cool; cut.

Yield: About two pounds.

Coconut Cherry Creams: Use one cup candied cherries and an equal amount of flaked coconut.

QUICK CANDY CREAMS

Basic recipe:

½ package (1½ ounces) cream cheese	1¼ cups sifted confectioners' sugar
dash of salt	

Let cream cheese stand at room temperature until soft in 1-quart bowl. Cream until smooth with wooden spoon; gradually stir in sugar, add salt; blend well. Shape into ball and store in tightly covered container between waxed papers.

PEPPERMINT PINWHEELS

basic recipe (above)	4 drops red food coloring
¼ teaspoon vanilla	
¼ teaspoon peppermint flavoring	3 tablespoons chopped walnuts or peanuts

Make basic recipe (above) and divide in half. Add ¼ teaspoon vanilla to one half and ¼ teaspoon peppermint flavoring and 4 drops of red food coloring to the other. Press each mixture into a ball; chill about 1 hour. Then roll vanilla mixture between 2 sheets of waxed paper into rectangle 7x5 inches. Repeat with peppermint mixture. Remove top sheet of paper from each. Turn the peppermint layer over to fit on top

Assorted Christmas candies

of the vanilla layer. Peel off paper now on top. Starting with short side roll up as for jelly roll, gently and firmly. Turn roll over in 3 tablespoons chopped walnuts or peanuts until well covered. Wrap in waxed paper; chill. Cut in ¼ inch slices when ready to use. Makes about 15 slices.

Make many candies from the same basic recipe

PISTACHIO RAISIN CONES

basic recipe (above), using 1½ cups confectioners' sugar ½ teaspoon vanilla	¼ teaspoon almond flavoring 3 drops green food coloring
¼ cup seedless raisins	

Make basic recipe, using 1½ cups confectioners' sugar; add ½ teaspoon vanilla and ¼ teaspoon almond flavoring. Stir in 3 drops of green food coloring; mix well. Blend in ¼ cup seedless raisins, chopped fine. Chill and shape into cones, using about 1½ teaspoons for each. Makes about 2 dozen.

CHOCOLATE COCONUT BALLS

basic recipe (above), using 1 cup confectioners' sugar 1 square unsweetened chocolate	½ teaspoon vanilla ¼ cup shredded coconut

Make basic recipe, but use only 1 cup of confectioners' sugar. Add 1 square unsweetened chocolate melted over hot water and ½ teaspoon vanilla. Shape into balls — about 1 level teaspoonful for each; then roll in shredded coconut (you'll need about ¼ cup). Makes about 20.

FILLED CHERRIES

basic recipe (above) candied cherries	½ teaspoon vanilla

Make up basic recipe; add ½ teaspoon vanilla. Shape into balls, using about ½ teaspoon for each. Put between candied cherries that have been cut in half. Makes about 4 dozen.

PARTY FARE

Parties and Christmas go hand in hand. Even if you're not going to give a big party this year, every visit blossoms into a small party because of the warmth of the season. Your house is decorated, radio and television are full of beloved music, everyone's eyes shine a little brighter and every house holds secrets; the stage is set and the characters are ready for fun and sharing, every time the front door opens.

CHRISTMAS CANDLE CAKE

Nothing could be more handsome for the center of the party table than a Christmas Candle Cake. It looks far more complicated and difficult to make than it really is; it's really very easy. You'll need three baking dishes of different sizes, and a custard cup, in which to bake the layers. When you're finished, you'll have a cake that is talked about as well as eaten with relish. And if anyone in your family has a birthday during the holidays, this could be exactly right as a birthday cake, if you use real lighted candles instead of candy canes.

Nut Cake

3 cups cake flour	2 egg yolks (keep
3 teaspoons baking	whites for frosting)
powder	1 cup milk or ½ cup
1 teaspoon salt	evaporated milk
1 cup shortening	and ½ cup water
1 teaspoon vanilla	1½ cups walnuts, pe-
2 cups sugar	cans or Brazil nuts,
3 eggs	finely chopped

Grease 3 baking dishes or casseroles of different sizes, an 8-cup, a 4-cup, and a 2-cup; also a custard cup; line bottoms with wax paper. Sift flour, measure; add baking powder, salt; sift again. Cream shortening, add vanilla; then add sugar gradually and continue to cream until light and fluffy (with electric mixer, use medium speed). Add eggs one at a time, then the 2 yolks, beating thoroughly with wooden spoon after each addition. Add flour mixture in 4 portions alternately with milk. Beat just enough to make smooth after each addition (or, with mixer, use low speed); fold in the nuts. Pour batter first into the custard cup and 2 smaller baking dishes, filling each a little more than half full; pour remaining batter into the 8-cup size. With spatula smooth the tops level. Bake all in moderate oven, 325°, for 35 to 55 minutes, as needed for each size.

Cakes are done when a cake tester or toothpick comes out clean when inserted in center. Cool in dishes on cake rack 15 minutes, then remove, peel off paper, and finish cooling cakes

on rack right side up. Makes 24 to 28 servings.

To Frost and Decorate: Make up 7-minute

Try a layered Christmas candle nut cake

frosting, using 2 egg whites; tint a soft green with food coloring. Place largest cake, top side up, on serving plate. Frost top and sides, keeping surface fairly smooth. Put second size on first layer; frost top and sides. Repeat with third size. Top with the cupcake, turned bottom side up; swirl on frosting to form a peak at top. Sprinkle whole cake generously with shredded coconut. To make candles (takes 24) break candy sticks into 1½ inch lengths; insert each into a yellow spice gumdrop for the flame. Insert candles in cake. If desired, add silver dragées or colored sprinkles. Attach gumdrop star with toothpick.

To serve: With wide spatula or silver pie or cake server, lift off each tier to another plate for cutting.

PARTY DRINKS

What sparks a holiday buffet more than a bright, brimming bowl of something good to drink? These punches are inviting, hospitable, and delicious.

ORANGE-CRANBERRY PUNCH

Mix one quart cranberry juice cocktail, one 6-ounce can frozen orange juice, one 28-ounce bottle ginger ale, ¼ teaspoon each salt, nutmeg, cinnamon, allspice, and cloves. Pour over ice cubes in punch bowl. Float orange slices on top. Makes 12 servings.

Floating punch is attractive and delicious

FLOATING PUNCH

1 pint vanilla ice cream, softened	⅓ cup maple syrup
¾ teaspoon rum extract	1 quart bottle chocolate milk

Combine ice cream and ¼ teaspoon rum extract. Turn into an 8-inch ring mold and pack firmly; freeze until firm. Unmold and place in punch bowl. Combine remaining ingredients; mix well and pour into punch bowl. Makes 10 to 12 servings.

CRANBERRY CREAM PUNCH

6 eggs	2 pints cranberry juice
¾ cup sugar	ground cloves
1 pint heavy cream	

Chill all liquids well, before mixing. Separate eggs, beat yolks until frothy, add ½ cup sugar and beat again until mixture is smooth. Beat whites until they shape up into soft peaks, add remaining sugar and beat again until you have a smooth, shiny meringue. Stir gently or fold yolks into whites until all patches of egg white disappear. Pour in the cream, then pour in the cranberry juice and stir thoroughly. Serve very cold with dash of ground cloves. Makes 5 pints.

QUICK PUNCH

1 (6-ounce) can frozen lemonade	⅓ cup white corn syrup
2 (6-ounce) cans frozen orange juice	1 bottle Muscatel wine
3 (6-ounce) cans frozen pineapple juice	3 quarts cold water
	2 quarts carbonated water

Combine fruit juices, corn syrup and wine, stirring well. Let stand several hours in refrigerator to blend flavors. Pour chilled liquid into a large punch bowl and add water and carbonated water. Stir just to blend. Add ice cubes and any desired fruit garnish. Makes about 6 quarts.

Quick punch

ORANGE EGGNOG

6 eggs	2 quarts orange juice
¼ cup sugar	½ cup lemon juice
¼ teaspoon cinnamon	1 quart vanilla ice
¼ teaspoon ginger	cream
¼ teaspoon cloves	1 quart ginger ale

Whip eggs until thick and light in color. Beat in sugar and spices. Stir in orange juice and lemon juice. Cut ice cream into cubes and place in punch bowl. Pour orange juice mixture over top of ice cream. Stir in ginger ale. Sprinkle with nutmeg. Makes 20 to 25 punch cups.

MORE PARTY CANDY

Here are a few chewy, holiday candies that your guests will enjoy.

PANOCHA

Put 1¼ cups brown sugar, firmly packed, a dash of salt and ¾ cup light cream into a saucepan. Cook over low heat, stirring constantly, until the sugar dissolves. Now boil rapidly until the mixture reaches the soft-ball stage when tested in cold water, or until candy thermometer registers 236° F. Remove from heat. Add 1 tablespoon butter and ½ teaspoon vanilla without stirring. Allow mixture to cool slightly. Now beat until creamy in color and texture. Add ½ cup broken pecans and fold into the mixture lightly. Pour into a well-buttered 8-inch square pan. When cool, cut into squares or funny shapes. Makes about ½ pound candy.

Fudge is easy-to-make, tempting, and tasty

JIFFY FUDGE

2 (6-ounce) packages	¾ cup sweetened con-
semi-sweet chocolate	densed milk
morsels	1 teaspoon vanilla

Melt semi-sweet chocolate morsels in top of double boiler over hot water. Remove from heat. Stir in milk and vanilla and stir until mixture is well blended. Shape into any of the following shapes. Makes 1½ pounds of fudge.

Chocolate Squares: Turn mixture into a buttered 8-inch square pan. Sprinkle with chopped nuts; press lightly. Cut into squares.

Coconut Balls: Shape into ¾-inch balls, then roll in shredded coconut.

Walnut Patties: Shape into ¾-inch balls and press a walnut half in center of each.

Pralines: Measure 1 standard tablespoon of mixture. Place on a piece of waxed paper. Use another piece of waxed paper to place on top of pralines. Press with bottom of a water glass to make a 2-inch circle. Press pecans in surface.

Chocolate Nut Roll: Add ½ cup coarsely chopped nuts to mixture. Divide mixture in half. Make two rolls about 1½-inches in diameter. Lightly press roll in chopped nuts so all area is covered. Allow to stand several hours. Slice each roll into about 16 slices.

CHINESE CHEWS

Cream ½ cup butter with 1 cup brown sugar until light and fluffy. Add 2 eggs, ½ cup chopped mixed nuts, ¼ cup cut-up dates, and 1 tablespoon each chopped raisins and coconut. Mix well. Add ¾ cup sifted flour and beat until blended. Bake in a lined 8 x 8 x 2-inch baking pan. Bake for 40 minutes or until done in a moderate oven, 350° F., and while still warm cut into squares. Makes about 16 squares.

PARTY SANDWICHES

Sandwiches are always welcome and filling at parties. For Christmas parties it's fun to make them eye-catching as well. Here are tips for a tray that will be tempting to everybody.

Make the sandwiches at least a day ahead; this gives you more time to experiment and gives you more time for other things on the day of the party.

Mix a variety of sandwich fillings at one time to meet all your party needs during the holidays.

Spread bread with softened butter or margarine before you spread on the filling so that the bread does not become soggy.

To keep sandwiches for twenty-four hours, wrap them in aluminum foil, well sealed. Or use wax paper, wrap in damp cloth, and place in the refrigerator.

If you have a home freezer, make the sandwiches as much as two weeks ahead. The best fillings to use for sandwiches that are to be frozen are: peanut butter; American cheese; sliced meat, fish, chicken, or turkey. For freezing, wrap sandwiches in foil, or other sheet packaging material, or place in a plastic box. Freeze immediately. Do not use mayonnaise, lettuce, celery, tomatoes, carrots, or egg-salad spreads.

Cut and fix party sandwiches in interesting shapes. Here are suggestions for attractive sandwiches; try your ingenuity in thinking up others.

Diamonds: Use softened pimiento cheese spread combined with chopped ripe olives, and serve as open-faced sandwiches on diamonds of whole-wheat bread. Decorate with bits of pimiento.

Rectangles: Try liverwurst combined with chopped stuffed olives and a salad dressing on rectangles of white bread. Use slices of stuffed olives to add color to top.

Crescents: Combine softened cream cheese with orange marmalade and spread generously between crescents of nut bread.

Fold-ups: Trim the crusts from sliced white bread. Spread the squares with a filling of ½ cup each of finely chopped dates and nuts plus 6 tablespoons orange juice. Bring 2 opposite corners together at center and hold with a toothpick and a sprig of water cress or parsley.

Circle Delights: Combine one 3 ounce package cream cheese, 3 finely cut uncooked prunes, ½ teaspoon sugar, ¼ teaspoon cinnamon, and 1 tablespoon chopped nuts. Spread on white bread that has been cut in circles.

Cut party sandwiches in interesting shapes

Squares: Combine 2 parts each of chopped cooked chicken or turkey and broken California walnuts with 1 part drained, crushed pineapple; moisten with salad dressing; spread on squares of whole-wheat bread. Decorate with bits of pineapple.

Open-face Crescents: Combine equal parts flaked tuna, crab meat, or lobster, and finely cut celery. Moisten with mayonnaise; spread on crescents of rye bread.

Checkerboard: Trim crusts from 2 unsliced loaves bread — 1 white, 1 dark. Slice loaves lengthwise into ½-inch-thick slices and spread Cheese Butter, alternating layers of light, dark bread. Cut lengthwise in ½-inch-thick strips; stack together alternating colors of bread. Spread outside with Cheese Butter and stack together to form checkerboard design. Wrap in waxed paper. Chill and slice crosswise to serve.

Cornucopias: These are outstanding at any party. Trim crusts from bread slices. Top with pineapple cream cheese spread. Roll into cornucopias. Petals are ripe olive slices.

Make a star cutout in the top slice of each sandwich

Use your cookie cutter for fancy little sandwiches, too. Bells and star shapes make up a handsome platter. Or make a star cutout in the top slice of the sandwich. Use thin slices cut in 2-inch squares for very dainty sandwiches, using white, wheat, rye, or a combination of breads. Pimiento olive cheese is a good filling, or any other of a color that will contrast with the top slice of bread.

Chicken salad sandwiches in holiday form

Decorate the tops of open-face sandwiches with green and red pimiento. Arrange to look like holly leaves and berries.

Spread round slices of bread with chicken salad (or turkey) and put cranberry stars on top, cut with a star cutter from jellied cranberry sauce.

Cut bread in the shape of Christmas trees, spread with cream cheese, and serve as open-faced sandwiches, with slices of pimiento-stuffed green olives placed here and there on the trees.

HINTS FOR OTHER PARTY FOODS

Whatever hot dish you decide on for the buffet supper can be trimmed to suit the holiday occasion. Make a wreath of parsley and olive slices on the top of any hot, open dish; it lends the Yuletide touch.

Open-faced Christmas tree sandwiches

Cut toast in star or snowflake shapes, for garnish

Add holiday trimmings to buffet dishes

Use toast, cut in the shape of Christmas trees, and add several to the steaming top of your favorite casserole. Swags of red pimiento slices garnish the toast trees.

Leave the top crust off meat and chicken pies and, instead of crisscrossing pastry on top, use pastry stars or bells, snowflakes, or trees, made with your cookie cutter.

Remember food coloring; use it liberally.

Rely on shapes; the tree shape, for instance, is as easy as can be and adds a holiday feeling to any dish.

Garnish serving plates with holly, parsley, spiced crabapples, flowers, Christmas balls, anything that will set the spirit of the occasion.

Think of red and green things to eat and to decorate what you eat — and use your imagination and have fun!

7 Christmas for Others

by Larry Eisenberg

F you have ever been alone, or confined, at Christmas time, you know how empty the season can be, and how grateful and happy you would have been if cheer and loving-kindness had been brought to you. Every Christmas, in every community, there are those who need such attention and would welcome and appreciate it deeply. Either as individuals or through organizations we all have almost unlimited opportunity to serve the needs of others, at this time of year. City and country alike, in any area, have some or all of the following places, where need is apparent:

Home for the Aging
School for the Blind
School for the Deaf and Hard of Hearing
Salvation Army and Volunteers of America enterprises
Hospital
Mental Hospital
Prison, Penitentiary, Prison Camp
Home for the Needy
Home for Children
Home for Crippled Children
Army Installation
Community Center

In addition to all these, there are those who live alone — shut-ins, the destitute, the aged. Sick or well, in need or not, they have in common a desperate loneliness which can, at Christmas, be relieved.

GENERAL SUGGESTIONS FOR HELPING THESE FOLK

1. Approach any of these people as having dignity, and as worthy of your respect. Don't condescend.

2. Give them personal attention. Everyone wants and enjoys personal attention; these folk usually have a special need of it. Perhaps have a name tag for everyone; this will enable you to speak to them by name as often as possible.

3. Be sure you have your signals clear with "the office," or the administration, where institutions are involved. Check with them well enough in advance for time, timing, and the suitability of the program you have planned.

4. In advance, if possible, send someone to check on the physical facilities — the availability of tables (if you are to have crafts), running water, kitchen use, lighting, everything you will need to set up, entertain, and clear away.

5. Find out how many will be involved. This

179

is of great importance. Prepare for the maximum number of persons who might attend, but do not count on this number for the success or failure of your program, since some will probably be absent or ill or occupied on the day of your visit.

6. In the case of hospitals, mental hospitals, and homes for the aging, be sure to know, in advance, which persons should not be disturbed, and how active or noisy a program is appropriate to the group. Consider carefully the handicap involved, if some are handicapped. The very best method when planning for an institution is to have someone from its staff working with you on every phase of the program.

7. Keep the plan flexible. If there are several people in your group who will lead, perform, or demonstrate, establish one of them as the leader and give him the authority to shorten the program or modify it in any way without consultation. The situation on the spot may indicate, without warning, that changes should be made.

8. Get there early. Many of these people will be almost pathetically eager for your program, and will have been anticipating it for days or weeks, during what is probably a routine, uneventful existence. Do not — by being tardy — allow the slightest alarm or confusion or anxiety to arise in the group on what should be an afternoon or evening of pure pleasure. The practical reasons for being early are obvious; your program will without question run more smoothly and successfully.

9. Be sure that your team understands thoroughly the principles you will establish during the program. Each one in your group should understand that your purpose is to create fun and good, warm feelings, and therefore, in games or participating stunts, the important thing is happiness, not skills. It doesn't matter how well a game is played or a song is sung; what does matter is that everyone has a chance to be part of the program.

10. Encourage the groups you wish to entertain to do things for themselves, if possible. Putting on a show for them has value, of course, but nothing will lift their spirits more than their own contributions to the program.

11. One of the greatest morale-builders for those in difficulty is the doing of something for others. Arrange for, and encourage, one group to work for the happiness of another group — just as *you* are arranging for *their* Christmas cheer. Some of the projects suggested below would be fine for this, and being busy at the holiday season will alleviate the loneliness of feeling unneeded.

12. When you arrive and everyone is gathered, start with something that will bring them together in spirit, such as group singing, musical games, or mixers. Then go into the rest of the program.

13. Don't let the program run too long. Some of these folk will tire easily, others may have a limited span of attention.

14. Take along a gift of some kind for each person — even if it is only a cookie apiece. This is very important, for it leaves them with a bright and cheerful remembrance of your visit.

15. Repeated visits are greatly appreciated, in most cases. If you can arrange to entertain from one year to the next, your visit becomes something to look forward to and count on.

PROJECTS AND ENTERTAINMENTS

1. *Christmas Tree Decorating Project.* Take along a Christmas tree and let the people help make the decorations. Do this considerably in advance of Christmas Eve. (In some cases, several trees might be taken and each group or department work to have a tree for themselves. However, in the case of a single family, one tree would be enough.) Let them make decorations and then decorate the tree. This can occupy the whole evening. Take along scissors and aluminum pie tins, which can be cut into beautiful shapes. *(See page 126.)* Also take aluminum milk-bottle caps, popcorn, colored popcorn, needles and string. Get colorful cellophane-wrapped candy and tie the individual pieces together with cellophane tape to make a chain of candy. Used flashbulbs coated

with paste or glue and dipped in glitter make interesting ornaments. Christmas cards unfolded and placed on branches add color to any tree. Strings of cranberries are always good. Check the suggestions on decorations which appear on pages 120 to 131, and fit them to the abilities and age groups of those you will visit.

2. *Crafts for Others.* Set up card tables, covered with newspaper. For the floor, use a painter's drop cloth. On one table, have samples of what can be done. On supply tables, have scissors, cellophane tape, paste, glue, cork, felt, feathers, seeds, buttons, pins, construction paper, toothpicks, raisins, prunes, marshmallows and the like. A good rule to follow is that all are to work at making favors, but anyone who wants to keep his may do so, if he makes a duplicate. Here is a chance for confined people to do something for others! One part of a hospital can make favors for the trays for another part, for instance.

3. *Giant Picture Christmas Card.* Get someone of skill to outline a giant card on a large piece of poster board, or even the cardboard from an outsized packing box. Have the group paint it, and send or take it to someone who will appreciate it. All can sign their names, to make it interesting. This card could be sent from a group to another group, with the names of all those to whom it is sent also written on.

4. *Christmas Friend—Mystery Friend.* Where names can be obtained and passed around, have each person in the sponsoring group "adopt" a person in the institution and send him periodic gifts and cards. Then at the final party, get the Christmas friends together.

5. *Adopt-a-Child Plan.* Many Children's Homes are happy to cooperate in allowing their children to go out into private homes to celebrate Christmas for the season (a weekend, week, even longer). The child is taken in and treated as a member of the family, and there could hardly be a more appropriate observance of the meaning of Christmas. Often adoptions take place as a result of this plan.

6. *Adopt-an-Adult Plan.* A family can make a lonely adult very happy by "adopting" him or her as an uncle or aunt or other relation for the Christmas celebration. Organizations can sponsor this idea, and homes for the aging or indigent will cooperate.

7. *Small Gift or Card Shower.* A group may meet in their regular meeting place, write cards and wrap gifts, and send them to shut-ins, people who are away from the group, those in hospitals, prisons, Children's Homes, or other institutions.

8. *White Christmas.* This is a custom of many groups. Gifts of food, toys, mittens, books, and other objects are brought to a central meeting place, wrapped in white paper. These are delivered, then, to such institutions as Children's Homes.

9. *Caroling.* Groups love to work up some Christmas carols and then go to sing to shut-ins and those otherwise confined. In some cases, it is a good idea to get some of the people in institutions to join the caroling group in singing to others.

10. *Santa's Repair Shop.* Gather broken, unpainted toys, repair them and freshen them up, and then take them to families or groups where they are needed. Or, instead of doing this at your accustomed meeting place, take selected ones of the toys to some such place as an Old Men's Home, along with materials needed, and help those who live there help someone else have a good time at Christmas.

11. *Christmas Tour.* If you'd like to help people who are able to get out, take them in cars or a bus to see the Christmas lights. If they can't get out, perhaps a good photographer can make time-exposure color slides and show them. Movies and slides on the Christmas theme can help the folks get beyond their walls.

12. *Take Color Slides of the Party, Show them Next Time.* If a return trip will be possible, take color slides with flash cameras of the activities and show them the next time you come. This always stirs interest, for we are always interested in seeing ourselves.

13. *Tape Recordings.* A tape recorder, too, is fun for all. If the group is large, more than one recorder should be used. Children, youth, adults, we all like to "hear how we sound." Have something for everyone to read or say

(such as "The Night Before Christmas") so that no one will be lost for words. Then play back what was recorded.

14. *Puppet-making.* There are several kinds of puppets that can be made and used as part of a single afternoon's or evening's entertainment, if you have chosen with some care the suitability of such a project. Divide the group into small groups of five or ten persons each. Give each one paper bags, scissors, construction paper, paste, crayons, cotton, and other materials for making paper-bag puppets. The bag should be square-bottomed, for best results, and about 5 or 6 inches wide and as deep as

To make a puppet, turn a paper bag upside down and cut holes for "arms" — thumb and fourth finger. Three middle fingers move the puppet's head.

you can find, since the depth gives the illusion of a costume.

Turn the bag upside down, so that the bottom of the bag becomes the top of the head of the puppet. Cut as shown, or in any other way that will allow the fingers to protrude, as arms, and help to animate the puppet. Then faces can be made, by pasting on eyes, nose, and mouth that have been cut from brightly colored construction paper. Faces can also be drawn or painted on. Decide which would be better for your group, or provide help with all three methods. Ears can be cut out and pasted on, or drawn or painted on. Hats, bow ties, ribbons or lace doilies can be pasted on to simulate costumes, and the part of the bag below the "arms" decorated to resemble all kinds of costumes.

Each group can be helped with puppet-making and given suggestions for putting on little shows for all the others. If this would produce too many shows, number off the groups and have number 1 put on its show for number 2, and number 2 for number 1, and so on. In this way each group *has* an audience and each group *is* an audience without taking up too much time.

Puppets can be made from fruits and vegetables, also. A hollow rubber ball, painted to resemble a head, is effective, and can be made to move realistically by cutting a round hole, where the neck would be, and inserting the middle finger. Crepe paper or cloth, gathered to the middle finger with a rubber band and with holes cut in the sides for "arms" (which are the fingers of the hand, of course) complete the illusion.

If you think it is appropriate to the age group you'll be with and your surroundings, plan and make a simple puppet stage. It can be contrived easily out of a large carton with the back cut out, and the front cut away as doors.

Children love to work on and operate puppets, even this simplest kind. But you may be surprised at how much adults like them, too, if you can overcome their inhibitions!

15. *Lumpy Stocking Idea.* This is especially good for children, but older adults might enjoy

it as well. About December 10, send each person whom you will entertain a long empty stocking. Then send a succession of gifts, each day or two, to be added unopened, by a third person, to the stocking. Have the little gifts wrapped in odd-shaped packages, so that guessing what they are will be difficult, and fun. The child may feel, rattle, or smell his lumpy stocking during the days before Christmas, but he may not look inside. On the night of the party, match up the donors with the children, and have a grand opening. It is important that each child have the undivided attention of someone as he finally gets to see his gifts. Take care with the little ones, who believe in Santa, that this stocking is not confused with the "real thing."

16. *Simulated Stained-glass Windows.* If there is time, lovely simulated stained-glass windows can be made from butcher paper on which the window designs have been drawn. Colors are kept apart by using black in the same way as lead is used in a regular window. If a light coating of raw linseed oil is applied when the "window" is finished, this makes it translucent. Mounted, it looks very much like a stained-glass window. Try this yourself at home, before you undertake it for a group, so that you will have constructive suggestions to make at the time of the party. It will be most effective if you bring along an example of the result, and show how pretty it is when the light is shining from behind it.

17. *Story-telling, or Story-reading.* Even adults like stories, and often at the climax or at the end of a program, story-telling adds the finishing touch. Try some of the stories in this book, taking care to choose one that is likely to be most effective with the age and status of the group you will read to. The readings will be especially good if done around the fire, by low light or candlelight.

18. *Hanukkah and Christmas.* In some situations, Jewish folk are involved, yet the Christmas celebration is called for, too. Then let the program recognize both Hanukkah and Christmas, giving something of the story, origin, and music of each.

19. *Finger-painting.* Any arts or crafts store can furnish the material. Children love to finger-paint, and they can be asked to make decorations in finger-painting for their rooms or for the home, the dining room, or for the sponsoring group. It is good to bring along men's old shirts for them to protect their clothing. While you are finger-painting, Christmas music or records can be played. Water-resistant table tops are needed for this; oilcloth will do the job.

A good recipe for making finger paints yourself, economically, follows. The ingredients given will make about one pint of paint; for larger groups enlarge the recipe accordingly. Remember to provide different colors. A large batch can be made and then separated into smaller quantities and tinted.

> 1 envelope of unflavored gelatin
> ½ tablespoon salt
> 2 tablespoons corn starch
> 3 tablespoons powdered coloring (artists' dry colors)
> 1 teaspoon glycerine
> 1 pint water

Dissolve gelatin in ½ cup cold water and set aside. Mix dry ingredients with remainder of water. Add glycerine to this and boil, stirring constantly. Remove from fire and stir in gelatine mixture. Pour into jar and allow to set.

20. *Performing for the Group.* Work up a Christmas play and present it. Or bring along special Christmas musicians, carolers, duets, quartets, choruses. These are always enjoyed. Or have a ceremony surrounding the lighting of the Christmas tree. Give the story of the Christmas tree. Entertainers, whether using the Christmas theme or not, are always welcome. Often radio and television personalities will join you in presenting an attractive program to needy or confined people. Older folks often appreciate watching performances more than they would enjoy trying to perform themselves. It is good to have them join you in performing only if they can, and are willing. All, however, of almost any age and inclination, can partici-

pate by making requests for the songs that are to be played or sung.

A TYPICAL PROGRAM LINEUP

When going out to groups, you may have such a plan that an actual "program" is not necessary. If you are doing a Santa's Repair Shop or Crafts, that may be enough. But let us show how a program might be arranged which would bring in several elements of variety, and give a "party" effect.

1. *Greeting, hello.* Have name tags on all of the visitors and get them on all of the "home group" too. Start with some lively songs or mixers.

2. *Report on the mystery friend.* (Who is it who has been sending those cards, presents, or the "lumps" for the "lumpy stocking"?)

3. *A game,* in small groups such as clapping out the rhythm of a Christmas song, for everyone to guess. *(See page 188.)* A good way to divide people into groups, quickly and simply, is by their birth dates. A substitute idea for this stage of the program might be for small groups to do paper-sack puppets, or some other "Christmasy" assignment. Then they will either put on acts for the whole group, one at a time, or else for each other, with group number 1 doing theirs for group number 2, and vice versa.

4. *A Christmas festival, skit or drama, presented for everyone.* The skit which follows on page 185 is the kind of performance that is very successful at this type of gathering.

5. *The giving of Christmas presents* (if that is planned).

6. *Refreshments.*

7. *Carol singing (on request), story-telling, or reading the Christmas story from Luke.*

8. *Good night, Merry Christmas!*

A VISIT FROM ST. NICK

NOTE: *This is best usable with a fairly large group. It calls for a narrator, who reads the material, and for having different people in the audience to spring to their feet and read the* *phrases capitalized, when their number is held up by the narrator. (This means that the narrator must have 27 cards to hold up at the appropriate time. If there are many more people than this, and more cards and rhymes are welcome, they can be added to, beyond 27. Have someone in your group think up interesting, funny remarks of the same nature as those that follow.)*

NARRATOR READS:

Twas the night before Christmas, when all through the house,
Not a creature was stirring . . . 1. BUT THE COOK MIXING COOKIES!
The stockings were hung by the chimney with care,
In hope that St. Nicholas . . . 2. WOULD DARN ALL THEIR HOLES!

The children were nestled all snug in their beds,
While visions of sugar plums . . . 3. MADE THEM DROOL IN THEIR PILLOWS.
And mama in her kerchief, and I in my cap,
Had just settled our brains . . . 4. BY VISITING A PSYCHIATRIST.

When out on the lawn there arose such a clatter
I sprang from the bed . . . 5. TO TELL THEM TO PIPE DOWN!
Away to the window I flew like a flash
Tore open the shutters . . . 6. AND THREW THEM ON THE DYING FIRE.

The moon, on the breast of the new-fallen snow,
Gave the luster of midday . . . 7. ON THE BICYCLE WE FORGOT TO PUT IN,
When, what to my wondering eyes should appear,
But a miniature sleigh . . . 8. WITH HYDROMATIC DRIVE.

With a little old driver, so lively and quick,
I knew in a moment it . . . 9. WAS THE FULLER BRUSH MAN.
More rapid than eagles his coursers they came,
And he whistled and shouted . . . 10. AND RAISED HIS BLOOD PRESSURE.

Now, Dasher! Now, Dancer! Now, Prancer and
Vixen!
On, Comet! On, Cupid . . . 11. ON, SAUERKRAUT
AND WIENERS!
To the top of the porch, to the top of the wall!
Now dash away! Dash away! . . . 12. AND A
DASH OF TOMATO CATCHUP.

As dry leaves that before the wild hurricane fly,
When they meet with an obstacle . . . 13. PILE
UP IN THE CORNER,
So up to the housetop the coursers they flew,
With a sleigh full of toys . . . 14. AND SOME
BUBBLE GUM TOO!

And then in a twinkling, I heard on the roof
The prancing and pawing . . . 15. OF A TELEVI-
SION REPAIRMAN.
As I drew in my head, and was turning around,
Down the chimney St. Nicholas came . . . 16.
KNOCKING SIX BRICKS LOOSE.

He was dressed all in fur, from his head to his
feet,
And his clothes were all tarnished . . . 17. AND
READY FOR THE CLEANERS.
A bundle of toys he had flung on his back,
And he looked like a peddler . . . 18. IN THE
(local) GROCERY EMPORIUM.

His eyes, how they twinkled! His dimples, how
merry!
His cheeks were like roses . . . 19. BUT NOT SO
EXPENSIVE!
His droll little mouth was drawn up like a bow
And the beard of his chin . . . 20. NEEDED TRIM-
MING A LITTLE.
The stump of a pipe he held tight in his teeth
And the smoke it encircled his head . . . 21.
LIKE A CIGARETTE AD WREATH.

He had a broad face and a round little belly,
That shook when he laughed . . . 22. LIKE A
TELEVISION PICTURE.
He was chubby and plump, a right jolly old elf,
And I laughed when I saw him . . . 23. MY
WOOL UNDERWEAR TICKLED ME.

A wink of his eye and a twist of his head
Soon gave me to know . . . 24. HE'D GOTTEN A
CINDER IN HIS EYE.
He spoke not a word, but went straight to his
work
And filled all the stockings . . . 25. BUT THE
ONES WITH HOLES IN THEM.

He sprang to his sleigh, to his team gave a
whistle,
And away they all flew . . . 26. LIKE THE DOWN
OF A THISTLE?

But I heard him exclaim, ere he drove out of
sight,
"Merry Christmas to all" . . . 27. AREN'T YOU
GLAD THIS IS OVER?

A CARD FOR CHRISTMAS
(For three boys and three girls)
By Agnes Curtis

Cast of Characters:

DIANA SNOW — *the girl who sends a Christmas card to Loretta Mills*
LORETTA MILLS — *the girl to whom Diana sends the Christmas card*
PRISCILLA HART — *the girl who wouldn't send Loretta Mills a card for anything*
HUGH HINES — *the boy who is helping at the postoffice during the Christmas rush*
GEORGE BANKS — *the boy who wouldn't send Loretta a card*
JAMES PIERCE — *the boy who thinks Loretta is a joke.*
(They all wear street clothes except Hugh. Hugh wears any home clothes.)
TIME: *The afternoon before Christmas.*
PLACE: *The postoffice at the small town of Rugby. The postoffice boxes may be easily simulated by blocking off into squares for boxes a large piece of cardboard. In the middle in the upper part of the cardboard is a postoffice window. Directly below is a slit for letters. Between the extreme left side of the cardboard and the wall is a vacant space, at the end of which a person can be so well concealed that*

he will neither be seen nor heard. At the right center is a postoffice desk. On the desk are some pens, some blotters and some ink. Above the desk is a window. An ordinary glass window will serve the purpose. The one exit is at the lower right. The curtain goes up with Diana Snow on the stage. She is standing beside the desk addressing cards. She is humming softly under her breath. Presently Priscilla enters and catches sight of Diana.

PRISCILLA: Hello, Diana!

DIANA *(turning and looking at Priscilla):* Oh, hello!

PRISCILLA *(stamping her feet and clapping her hands):* Cold, isn't it?

DIANA: I'll say so.

PRISCILLA *(her glance falling on the cards):* What? Haven't you finished your Christmas cards yet?

DIANA: Almost. Except one. I have just one left. *(Holds up card for Priscilla to see.)*

PRISCILLA *(looking at the card):* Very pretty. A nice person deserves it. Who's going to get it?

DIANA: Oh, I don't know. *(Saying the first thing that comes into her head.)* Guess I'll send it to Loretta Mills!

PRISCILLA *(staring at Diana):* Of all things! Have you gone completely mad? Whatever made you say you'd send the card to that thing!

DIANA: Don't call her a "thing," Priscilla. *(Teasingly)* Just what have you against her?

PRISCILLA *(indignantly):* Well, of course, if you want to be treated as she'll treat you when you send her that card, why just go ahead! It's your party! *(Looks in postoffice box.)* Aha! Mail for me! *(Starts to open box, but Hugh is too quick for her.)*

HUGH *(taking mail from box and holding it out the window to Priscilla):* Christmas service! One! Two! Three!

PRISCILLA *(laughing and taking the mail):* Thanks, Hugh.

HUGH *(laughing):* I always help out at Christmas! I don't know how the postmaster would make out if I didn't.

PRISCILLA: Well, Merry Christmas, Hugh! Merry Christmas, Diana!

HUGH AND DIANA *(in chorus):* Merry Christmas! *(Priscilla goes out.)*

HUGH *(sticking his head out of the office box):* Diana, what have you decided to do about that card?

DIANA *(swinging the card in her hand back and forth in an absent-minded sort of manner):* I don't know.

(At that moment George Banks enters.)

GEORGE *(in a hearty voice):* Hello there, Diana. Hello, Hugh!

HUGH: Hello.

GEORGE: My Christmas mail —

HUGH *(taking mail from box and holding it out to George):* Ready for you.

GEORGE *(taking the mail):* Whew! What service!

HUGH: It's Christmas!

GEORGE *(looking at Diana):* Diana, why are you looking at that card in that way?

DIANA: I'm getting ready to send it to Loretta Mills.

GEORGE *(in disgust):* What?

DIANA: Yes!

GEORGE *(with mock gravity):* My dear child, you surely have taken leave of your senses! Loretta Mills never sends any cards to anyone! In the first place, she's too stingy and, in the second place, she's too mean.

(Hugh is seen at the office window, listening intently.)

DIANA *(looking directly at George):* The more reason why I should send her a card, maybe.

GEORGE: Oh, don't let me keep you from doing your good deed, my child. But — beware the consequences! So long, everybody! *(Goes out.)*

HUGH *(reflectively):* Loretta's not so popular in this little town of Rugby, is she?

DIANA *(definitely):* I should say not.

(At that moment James Pierce comes in. He is carrying a package and some letters. He walks up to the postoffice window.)

JAMES: Here, Hugh. A package.

HUGH *(taking the package):* O.K.

JAMES *(dropping the letters in the mailbox):* No mail for me. Got it just fifteen minutes ago. *(Turns to Diana.)* Hi, Diana! What's on your mind these days?

DIANA (*earnestly*): I'm trying to decide whether or not I should send this card to Loretta Mills.

JAMES (*bursting into laughter*): Ha! Ha! Ha! That is a good one! Send a Christmas card to Loretta Mills! There'd be only one answer to that in my mind: "No!" What a joke! What a joke!

HUGH (*sticking his head further out the post-office window*): You don't like Loretta Mills, I take it?

JAMES (*retorting*): Like her? Who does? She's a regular old sourpuss! This is the way she goes along the street! (*Draws mouth down into the most disagreeable manner imaginable.*) Like this. (*Imitates Loretta's manner of walking which is decidedly furtive.*) Looks neither to the right nor to the left. Humph! Send her a card if you want to!

(*Both Diana and Hugh laugh.*)

DIANA: Oh, James! She's really not as bad as that! You know she isn't!

JAMES: She is, almost. Makes me think of a vinegar jug! If she'd smile once in a while! Well, I'm going now. Merry Christmas!

HUGH AND DIANA (*in chorus*): Merry Christmas! (*George goes out.*)

DIANA: Do you know, I'm rather sorry for Loretta Mills! No one has a good thing to say about her.

HUGH: Then send her the card, just for fun!

DIANA: Send her a card—for fun? Should Christmas cards be sent just — for fun? (*Happens to glance at that moment out of the window and gasps.*) Hugh! There is Loretta Mills herself, coming straight for the postoffice! I'm going to give her this card! (*Hastily scribbles address and signature on card.*) Here! (*Gives Hugh the card.*) Stamp it and let her have it when she comes in!

(*Hugh stamps card and then stands there waiting for Loretta to come in.*)

DIANA (*speaking rapidly*): I'm going to hide over here and see for myself just how Loretta will take this!

(*Runs over to left into the vacant place and crouches down at the end where she cannot be seen. A little later, Loretta enters and walks dejectedly up to the postoffice window.*)

LORETTA (*in a tired voice*): I don't suppose there's anything for me, is there?

HUGH: Yes, there is. A card for you. (*Gives Loretta the card.*)

LORETTA (*taking the card*): For me? (*Takes the card and examines it.*) A Christmas card. From — from — Diana Snow! (*Stares at the card in stunned silence.*)

HUGH: You seem surprised.

LORETTA: Surprised? Why, I never was so surprised in all my life! Nor so pleased! I had no idea Diana Snow liked me! I had no idea! I always thought she didn't like me! Most people don't. (*A long pause follows during which time Loretta continues to gaze in rapt attention at the card.*)

HUGH: It's a pretty card.

LORETTA (*still staring at the card*): Yes, it's a lovely card. I never saw a lovelier one with all these angels and their trumpets! But it's not so much that it's a pretty card. It's because a girl like Diana Snow thought of me at Christmas time! Of all people! (*Looking at Hugh.*) Do you know, Diana Snow always seemed an ideal girl to me! I've always sort of admired her, but — er — I'm afraid of her. She's beyond me, I guess. Lots of times in school when she thought I wasn't noticing, I'd look at her out of the corner of my eye and wish I could be like her. She's so popular and nice! And so pretty! (*Draws a deep sigh.*) What a wonderful thing that she sent me — me — a Christmas card! Now I am going to get a Christmas card right now and send it to Diana Snow! Right now!

(*Hurries out. Diana emerges rather sheepishly from her hiding place.*)

DIANA: Hugh, I'm ashamed of myself!

HUGH: Well, you never know what's going on in other people's minds, do you?

DIANA: No, you don't. I had no idea Loretta Mills was like that! Afraid of me! I'm going to tell the others! And from now on, every year, Loretta Mills gets a Christmas card from me!

8 Children's Christmas Parties

CHILDREN'S PARTY GAMES

PIN THE TAIL ON THE REINDEER

Convert this most favorite of all children's party games to the Christmas season; substitute a reindeer for a donkey. It takes a bit of handiwork and can be a decorative motif for the party as well as a game. Cut out a large reindeer, from white paper, and paste on a bright blue background. Spark the reindeer with glitter, and paste silver snowflakes all around in the sky. Make enough little tails, prepared with a pin, and proceed as always with this beloved game.

CLAP-A-CAROL

In a group of any number, select one person to clap out the tune of a well-known Christmas carol. The first person who recognizes the carol may then clap out his favorite, for the others to identify.

JUMBELO

Give each child a list of jumbled words, with room for him to work out their unscrambling. The one with the first correct list is the win-

ner, but set a time limit at the beginning, based on the age level of the group.

Pin a tail on a Christmas reindeer

188

A word game or word puzzle would be an excellent prize for the winner.

(Scrambled words for Christmas)

1. tassmirch (Christmas)
2. eridreen (reindeer)
3. oteltimes (mistletoe)
4. ylhol (holly)
5. rolca (carol)
6. german (manger)
7. respten (present)
8. herpsheds (shepherds)
9. etsnil (tinsel)
10. reet (tree)
11. instepoita (poinsettia)
12. Helbtheem (Bethlehem)

CARRY THE SNOWBALL

A great game for a children's party is Carry the Snowball — even if this year there's no white Christmas where you are. Prepare cotton snowballs, about 3 inches in diameter. Give each guest a snowball and a slip with a number on it. Line up everybody at one end of the room opposite a wall that you will call the North Pole. The player with the lowest number, 1, is given a tablespoon and asked to carry his snowball in it, with one hand only, as fast as he can to the North Pole. At the word *go!* he dashes. Have someone keep time and, when all the players have tried, according to their numbers, the one who does it fastest wins. If the snowball falls off, the player must pick it up and return to the starting place.

Or, you might make two teams and have relay races, with the same general procedure.

A giant popcorn snowball — or popcorn snowman — is an excellent prize for the winner.

SANTA'S STOREHOUSE

Nothing is quite so wonderful for children as a treasure hunt. Tell the children that the room they're in is Santa's storehouse, and they must gather up all sorts of goodies for the trip on Christmas eve. Give each guest a mesh stocking — or even a bright little box or bag — and have them fill it, finder's keepers. You will have hidden (each wrapped in a bit of colorful pa-

per!) all sorts of tiny gifts and treats: erasers, mints, pencils, lollipops, little metal toys, peanuts, gumdrops, pencil sharpeners, fake money, gold coins made of chocolate, just about any small inexpensive object that's easily wrapped in a twist of paper. Have enough so that even the small children can find plenty.

All together the objects might be only the sort of thing you'd want to give anyway as a tree present to take home, but in this way it makes a happy game and lends more sparkle than being handed a box at the door.

CHRISTMAS TOSS

Here is a game that's fun to play. You will need one muffin tin with 8 cups. Paint this green. Line each cup with a circle of felt or

For Christmas Toss, number the cups of a muffin tin

fabric on which you paint a number from 1 to 8. Now give each player 3 rather large coat-button "counters."

To play the game, a player must stand back about 6 feet from the tin and toss his 3 buttons, one at a time, at the muffin tin. Get each score by adding the numbers in the cups where the counters fall. The one who has the highest score after five turns is the winner.

A CHRISTMAS GIFT SCRAMBLE

Give each child a piece of paper with the following written on it:

Johnny has wrapped a Christmas present for everyone in his family. Can you unscramble the gifts?

Auntie:	whsla
Uncle:	sfignih dor
Mother:	oock oobk
Father:	lpipress
Brother:	labblsea
Big Sister:	dsaeb
Grandpa:	ecna
Grandma:	nrya

The one who unscrambles the words first is the winner.

Answers:

Shawl, fishing rod, cook book, slippers, baseball, beads, cane, yarn.

COSTUMES

We're often called on to make costumes for the children during the holidays, for parties and for plays. And of course, this is just the time of the year we are most busy with other things. It's fortunate, then, that sometimes a simple costume will suggest festivity just as much as one more difficult to make.

SANTA CLAUS CAP

For school entertainments, often a Santa Claus cap will answer the purpose as well as a complete costume.

The material you'll need for this is one fold each of white and flame-red crepe paper, and paste.

Cut a 16 inch wide, 22 inch long (or correct head size) piece of red crepe paper into a 3 inch deep fringe on one 16 inch end. Crush a 6 inch wide strip of white crepe paper. Double lengthwise and stitch the open edges to the lower edge of the red paper. Stitch seam. Gather the fringed ends to make a tassel. Double over and sew tightly to the side of the cap as

illustrated. Sew two rows of curled fringe across the back of the cap for hair.

A Santa Claus cap is easy to make

ANGEL COSTUME

For a very simple angel costume, especially good for children but useful even for adults, try this.

Stitch two 40 inch lengths of white flame-proof crepe paper together to make a piece long enough to reach from neck to floor *(Fig. A)*.

Gather one edge and sew a white ribbon along it, leaving enough at each end to tie around neck *(Fig. B)*. Cut holes for arms. Tie a sash around waist.

ANGEL WINGS

Cut wings from medium weight cardboard, following pattern. Slit as shown. Cover wings on both sides with white crepe paper icicles. Start at tips and work up, overlapping the rows like feathers. Slip lengths of white ribbon through slits to tie around neck and waist.

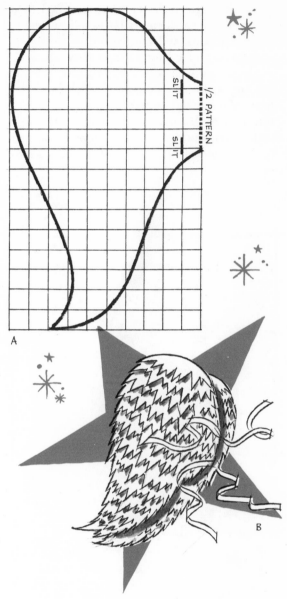

An angel's costume is easily made from white crepe paper

Wings tie on at neck and waist

CHRISTMAS GIFT

For a 14-16-year-old you will need the following material: Dennison crepe, 3 folds No. 439, grass green; 1 sheet green mat stock; 6 yards 1½ inch silver tinsel ribbon; 4 pieces each ½ inch red satin, ½ inch silver tinsel gift tying ribbon; 1½ dozen small Christmas tree balls; 1

spool No. 2 green flower wire; gummed tape; assortment of small empty boxes, gift wrapping papers, ribbons, and the like.

Make an ankle-length crepe skirt, using 3½ yards for fullness, with 6 inches turned up at the bottom for extra firmness. Stitch flat like a hem. Make a tight-fitting bodice of a double thickness of green. Add shoulder straps of 1½ inch silver ribbon. Attach wrapped packages to waistline with narrow silver ribbon. Finish

A Christmas gift costume of green crepe paper

with silver belt and corsage of silver ribbon and tree balls.

Make a cone of mat stock (F) about 14 inches high, 8 inches across opening, to fit loosely over the head. Trim with tree balls and bows of narrow silver and red ribbon fastened with spool wire thrust through the cone and twisted on the inside. Make a tight-fitting cap foundation. Paste inside cone so that it may be held firmly and comfortably on the head. The lower edge of the cone should come about 1½ inches below the bottom of the cap.

ANGEL

You will need the following material for a 6-8-year-old: Dennison crepe, 3 folds No. 400 white; 1 sheet white cardboard; 2 pieces No. 7 flower wire; 1 spool No. 1 flower wire; 2 boxes No. 5 silver gummed stars; 3 pieces ¾ inch white gift tying ribbon; 4 pieces ¾ inch silver tinsel gift tying ribbon; paste; gummed tape; muslin slip.

For the robe, seam 2-yard lengths of white crepe paper to make a floor-length skirt. Gather and sew to a slip at waistline *(Fig. A)*. Make a plain blouse with long loose sleeves, shaped as in *Fig. B*. Stitch silver ribbon to bottoms of sleeves before seaming. Make a Peter Pan collar, with ribbon trimming like that on the sleeves.

For the belt, braid 2 strands of silver ribbon and 1 strand of white to go around the waist, and allow silver ribbon ends to hang down at the front. Stick silver stars to the lower part of the skirt.

Make wings as described below.

For the halo, wrap a 36 inch piece of No. 7 wire with white crepe paper two or three times, to make about ¼ inch diameter, leaving 1½ inches at the ends unwrapped. Shape in a circle with ends about 8 inches long *(Fig. C)*. Fasten with spool wire. Wrap circle and 6 inches of extension with silver ribbon. Add silver stars, stuck back to back, around circle. Bend the 1½ inch extensions at right angles and sew to center extension of wings *(Fig. D)*. Bend circle

slightly forward into correct position over the wearer's head. Cover center section of wings with crushed crepe paper.

ANGEL WINGS

Material: Dennison crepe, 2 folds No. 400 white; 2 sheets medium-weight cardboard; 1 piece No. 7 flower wire; 4 metal paper fasteners; gummed tape; paste; 3 yards 1 inch white ribbon.

Cut cardboard foundation the desired size, following the proportions in *Fig. E*. Make each wing separately with tab extension about 3 x 4 inches. Cut out the center, leaving a rim about 1 inch wide. Overlap tabs and fasten with metal paper fasteners *(Fig. F)*. Fasten 2 pieces No. 7 wire to wings with tabs of gummed tape *(Fig. F)*.

Cover each wing smoothly on both sides with crepe paper, pasting it around the edge, and trimming surplus off closely.

Cut 4 inch wide strips of crepe paper into "feathers" 3 inches deep, ¾ inches wide *(Fig. G)*.

Beginning at the tip of the wing, paste feathers to the foundation, arranging them so that

Another angel costume, with halo attached to wings

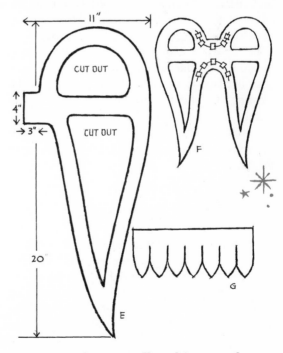

Wings have a cardboard framework

Crepe-covered, wings can be bent into position

each row overlaps the previous one about half-way and so that the feathers alternate. Cover both sides in the same way. It will usually not be necessary to paste the strips except at the edges of the wings. Sometimes a little paste is needed in the center to hold them in place.

Cover the extension with crushed crepe. Punch small holes in the four corners. Tie ribbons in place so that wings may be fastened by crossing the ribbons in front and tying them tightly in back. It may also be necessary to sew the wings to the back of the costume. Bend the wings up into correct position, as shown in the illustration.

PARTY DECORATIONS

Large-scale decorating, for a hall or stage, should be easy to make, impressive, and inexpensive. The Christmas motif can be established strikingly with large holly clusters: giant holly leaves are cut from bright green oilcloth, and red balloons blown up and affixed in the proper place. It could hardly be easier, and is very effective.

Everyone in a class or group can participate in preparing for a holiday party — with very effective results.— if you decide upon a White Christmas motif. A long strip of white wrapping paper, tacked up horizontally around the room, is a fine basis for a snowy mural; tack it at the right height and let everyone go to work with black chalk, making snow scenes. Or, individual pictures can be made the same

Red balloons are effective as giant holly berries

way if the paper is cut. Have colored chalk ready for making gold stars and red scarfs on the snowmen, or blue smoke rising from a chimney. Use icicles and angel's hair for decorating the room further, and stand up a couple of snowmen. These can be made life sized, very easily. Wad up newspaper and tape it into balls of the right size, then cover these with sheets of cotton. Use white candles on the refreshment table, and decorate it with strips of silver crepe paper and scattered silver snowflakes.

Where you need large-scale decorations, consider those materials in your area which are free and can be adapted. Greens of all kinds, of course, are the basis for Christmas beauty, but don't stop at the traditional ones. Use dried grasses or branches, sprayed green; there's an endless supply, for the taking, and the effect is pretty and appropriate. Use these same grasses and branches with gold or silver spray, for contrast; bind huge sheaves of red grasses together, for instance, and tie with green oilcloth bows.

If you have many willing hands in the weeks before Christmas, make holly garlands in the properly effective size for your hall. The instructions are given on page 93.

Streamers and fringes of crepe paper are always good and give a mass of color and movement for little expense and relatively little handiwork.

Festivals and Customs

What is the meaning of gift-giving at Christmas?

The gifts given by the Wise Men to the Infant Jesus are, of course, very probably the source of our present-day custom. We give, thus, to those we cherish, and this derivation is so direct that in many countries even today gifts are given on January 6 rather than Decem-ber 25. January 6, the Twelfth Night, is believed to be the date on which the Wise Men appeared to the Holy Family, and is so observed in Poland, Italy, Russia, Spain and the Spanish-American countries.

The belief that Saint Nicholas brings gifts stems from the legend of the generosity of Saint Nicholas, Bishop of Myra. When he died on December 6 in the year 345, he was revered for his generosity and kindness, and it became the custom to give presents to loved ones on his saint's day, the date of his death. For centuries it had been the custom for Christians to give on both Saint Nicholas' Day and Christmas Day, but in general practice the two days gradually fused into one, and Saint Nick was borrowed from his own day to be the patron saint of December 25.

Why do we give to the less fortunate especially at Christmas?

The implications of Christian charity and the general customs of giving at Christmas apply also to taking thought to the needy, "feeding the hungry, and clothing the naked." In addition, there is an ancient legend that on Christmas Eve the Christ Child wanders the earth disguised as a beggar, and seeking shelter and food. Any mercy shown a beggar was thought

to be a symbol of love of Jesus, and those who believed this would open their households to the homeless and offer their hospitality to those in need.

Where did the use of Christmas seals originate?

In 1904 a postal clerk in Denmark, named Einar Holboell, devised a plan for selling special stamps at Christmas to indicate to others that users had given charitably to some worthy cause. It seems to be a modern equivalent of ancient Christian giving to the needy, when none were turned away at the door during the Christmas season. In the United States the cause most closely associated with seals is the gathering of money for the fight against tuberculosis.

Why do children hang up a stocking on Christmas Eve?

The first Saint Nicholas, a real person who was a bishop in Asia Minor in the fourth century, is probably the source of our present Saint Nick who fills the stockings of good children on Christmas Eve. The story is that the bishop heard of a poor man who was about to sell his three daughters into slavery because he could not provide a dowry for them. Saint Nicholas saved the daughters, one by one, with gifts of gold. Each time, because he wished to remain anonymous, he threw the gift into the house rather than present it. One version of the legend is that he tossed the gold down the chimney, where it fell into a stocking that was hung there to dry. And so it is that children still hang up their stockings, and often find — in the toe — a tangerine, to represent a lump of gold.

What is the story of the Christmas tree?

The tree as a symbol of Christmas comes to us from Germany, in much the same way that we use and decorate it today. Martin Luther is said to have cut a fir tree from his garden one wintry Christmas Eve and placed it in the nursery of his home for his wife and children. He wanted to show them the great beauty of the snowy, dark night of the celebration of Jesus' birth, and he decorated the little tree with lighted candles, to represent the stars. From almost that time on, there are records of Christmas trees, and as long ago as the beginning of the seventeenth century other decorations, such as apples and colored paper, began to be added.

But the association of trees with Christmas is much, much older. In the tenth century a beautiful story spread through Europe. It is supposed to have been told by an Arabian named Georg Jacob, and it was so beautiful it was not forgotten, and became legend. On the night that Christ was born, so the story goes, all the trees in all the forests — even those in frozen countries — blossomed for one night, and bore fruit.

A thirteenth-century French legend tells of a gigantic tree lit with candles, in the forest. Some of the candles were straight and some

upside down, and at the top of the tree there was an infant with a halo around his head. The tree represented humanity, the candles were people, good and bad, and the child was the Saviour, Jesus.

And still longer ago there are stories that connect the tree with the season of Christmas. To pagan people the evergreen trees were a sign that winter would end and warmth again return to the earth, and in the feasts of the winter equinox, trees were hung with trinkets and masks. Some of our traditional Christmas-tree ornaments, such as a sun, stars and moon, and animals, are thought to descend, through the centuries, from these ancient symbols of nature. The goodness of the Creator as demonstrated in the return of spring may have been absorbed into the larger, greater celebration of the birth of His Son, Jesus.

Why do we decorate with holly?

Holly remains green throughout the winter, and is therefore a logical choice for Christmas ornamentation; its use goes far back to ancient peoples who took its greenness as a promise that the sun would again return to the earth, another year. Over the centuries many legends have surrounded it with Christian implications. The early French and English hung a piece

over the door to indicate a house in which Christ abided. The Crown of Thorns was said to have been wound with holly, whose berries turned from white to red after the Crucifixion.

A secular tale of holly states that whichever person, husband or wife, first brings the holly into the house at Christmas is the one who will rule in the new year.

How did kissing under the mistletoe originate?

Although kissing under the mistletoe is associated completely with the Christmas season, there is no reason why it should be, except for the power that custom can bestow. In a Scandinavian myth, Baldur the beautiful, god of light and spring, was troubled by dreams that his life was in danger. His mother Frigga, god-

never again be used as a weapon, and that she would place a kiss on anyone who passed under it.

Possibly the timing of Christmas-kissing comes from an old legend that at the end of a year, if a girl receives no kisses under the mistletoe, she will not marry in the new year. A berry should be removed with each kiss, and when all are gone the bough has lost its power.

How does the poinsettia come to be the flower of Christmas?

The poinsettia as a symbol of Christmas is a completely American development in the annals of the day. In 1836 it was brought to the United States when our first Minister to Mexico returned from there; his name was Dr. Joel R.

dess of love, traveled over the world asking everything from earth, air, fire, and water to promise not to hurt her son. However, she did not ask the mistletoe, a parasitic plant which attaches itself to trees and therefore does not grow from any of the four elements. Loki, god of fire, was jealous of Baldur, and finally had him slain with a dart of mistletoe. The tears of Baldur's mother became the white berries of the plant, and she decreed that mistletoe would

Poinsett and the flower was named for him. As it grew in Mexico it was a wild, small, and unimposing weed, but cultivation has produced the brilliant and flamboyant blossom we know today. Lovely legends surround the development of the flower. One such story is that a poor child who wished to give a gift to the Virgin Mary was heartbroken because she had nothing of value or beauty. As she approached the Mother of Jesus, in desperation she pulled some of the scrawny flowers at her feet, merely to make a gesture of love. As she did so, the flower was transfigured into scarlet brilliance.

What do candles in the window mean?

For centuries, the light of candles has symbolized the enlightenment that Jesus brought to the earth. From the early Christians we have a legend that the Holy Babe wanders through the

streets of the world on Christmas Eve, seeking shelter; and lighted candles in the windows will guide His steps to a house where He is welcome.

An old German belief was that the Virgin Mary and a host of angels passed over the countryside on Christmas Eve. A candle was placed in the window to guide them to a home where they might come in and eat, if they wished; and it was traditional to leave food upon the table.

Why do we burn a Yule log?

The Yule log comes to us from England before the Christian era, and burning it was orig-

inally a pagan rite. At the end of every year (based on the year's shortest day) it was thought that the sun stood still for twelve days. An enormous log was cut, large enough to burn throughout this period and burn away the evil

of the past year. Since the pagan Yule and our Christmas so nearly coincide in time, gradually the burning of the Yule log was adopted by Christians and, for hundreds and hundreds of years, has been a favorite custom.

Why are mince pie and plum pudding traditional Christmas desserts?

Mince pie has been a symbolic food of the Christmas season for as long as we have any records of the celebration. Because it is full of spices and fruits, it represents the choice and exotic treasures of the East, the home of the Wise Men. Originally it was made in the loaf shape of the manger in which Christ was laid after He was born.

Plum pudding is the other standard dessert for Christmas, and it has a history almost exactly the opposite of mince pie, which seems deliberately to have been concocted to stand for splendor and luxury. It is told that in the early days of England a king and his men were lost in the forest on Christmas Eve. Since they had intended to be at their destination for the

and then, at the stroke of twelve, a triumphant, happy pealing of the bells began. They announced the death of Satan and the birth of the Saviour.

What are the origins of carols?

One of the happiest customs of the Christmas celebration throughout the world is the singing of carols. For us in the United States it would be hard to imagine the holiday without the music that fills the air around us — the old, beloved music. Often it is a strain of melody that

celebration of the night, they had only meager provisions. The cook for the party decided to combine everything he had so that there would be one dish for all, and thus the plum pudding was first made.

Why do we ring bells at Christmas?

Ringing out the bells at Christmas is a beloved custom that is centuries old. On Christmas Eve in medieval times the bells in churches tolled, as they did for the dead, to warn the Devil of the imminent birth of Jesus, who would save the world from darkness. For an hour before midnight the ominous tolling continued

starts the season for us, before the other evidences have arrived. We hear the joyous music in our homes and in the shops and on the streets, and these are the songs we sing in soft harmony in our churches throughout the Yuletide season.

The carols that we have known and loved since childhood are part of the tradition, also, of many other countries around the world. Some of our most popular carols were written so far away and so long ago that their origins are lost in history; some are even songs of pagan origin which were adopted by early Christians and given new words.

Some were folk songs, with secular words, or shepherds' songs or lullabies. Their melodies were so easy to sing, so familiar perhaps, that long ago jubilant Christmas words were set to them. And there are other carols which are quite modern, written in recent years by Americans and set to music written in America.

Several countries have claimed to be the birthplace of caroling, but actually all that is known is that music in honor of the birth of Jesus has been part of church festivals from the very beginning of the Christian era. The word *carol* was associated with dancing until the fourteenth century, and is derived from the Italian *carolare,* a medieval ring dance accompanied by singing. Each country has developed its own ways with carols and caroling.

Probably the reason that carol-singing is done in the streets lies in the fact that early carols were not thought to be reverent enough for the inside of a church. Some of the carols seemed to emphasize the delights of the season and overlook its holy meanings, and others were set to gayer music than was thought appropriate; so, today, a group of carolers in a snowy village square on Christmas Eve has a long, long history of outdoor singing.

In England, groups of singers called "waits" continue even now with the ancient custom of making the rounds on Christmas Eve, singing outside doors and windows, and receiving gifts of goods and money from the serenaded householders.

In Wales, the carolers make their rounds at dawn on Christmas morning, and families wake from sleep to ask them in for refreshments. In France the carols are known as "noels" and are sung in the streets of cities as well as villages, and in Italy shepherds walk from house to house in the countryside singing carols to the accompaniment of bagpipes.

In Hungary and Poland carolers visit their neighbors carrying a huge lighted star, the Star of Bethlehem. This form of caroling, known as "star-singing," exists in Norway, Denmark, Germany, Austria, Holland, and Italy. Sweden's carol singers, for this reason, were known as "star-boys." They dressed in costumes to repre-

sent the Three Kings and Herod. It is pleasant to think that today, when we sing by flashlight or electric lantern, we are modern "star-singers."

Caroling was very popular in Czechoslovakia, where the boys dressed in the costumes of the Three Kings and carried a crèche, or *Jeslicky.* Processions of singers still intone the Kolyada songs in Russia, and in Rumania, where the Star of Bethlehem is decorated with frills and bells, carolers go from house to house, carrying on a pole a five-sided box with paper front and back on which there is a picture of the Virgin or some other religious subject, illuminated by a candle within.

So, in one form or another — certainly in the melodies and words of some of the carols themselves — similar caroling customs have spread to many parts of the world.

Carols, like so many other of the heart-warming traditions of Christmas, are enjoyed by so many people in so many places that they help to bring the nations of the earth closer together.

What is the history of sending Christmas cards?

It was in England that Christmas cards were first produced. People had, of course, sent private notes of good wishes to each other for uncounted Christmases, marking the birth of hope and peace and the beginning of each new

year. In addition to these notes it was customary in the first part of the nineteenth century for British students to prepare and send, at Christmas, handsome and painstaking scrolls conveying their greetings and displaying their prowess in handwriting, composition, and art work.

It was in 1843, and this date is now generally agreed upon, that Sir Henry Cole arranged to have an illustrator named John Calcott Horsley design a card especially for the day. It was printed in lithography and tinted by hand, by a professional colorer. One thousand copies were sold that first Christmas, and literally billions of cards have been sent out in the ensuing years; they bear out Sir Henry Cole's original intention to have "artistic treatment applied to 'unconsidered trifles' as well as to weightier matters."

Why are ships used so often as a motif on Christmas cards?

Many seafaring peoples have developed legends that connect ships with Christmas. The

patron saint of Greece, Saint Basil, comes each Christmastime on a ship laden with gifts, which he distributes to the people. Saint Nicholas sails to Holland from Spain, on a ship with a cargo of gifts. "I Saw Three Ships," the English carol, carries out in song the lovely idea that ships arrive on Christmas morning carrying Jesus, Mary, and Joseph. Perhaps these countries, separated as they are by water from the Holy Land, adopted the symbol of ships at Christmas to bring the great story of Jesus' birth a little closer.

Why are cattle thought blessed on Christmas Eve?

No scene of the stable is complete without the gentle cows, and from childhood we sing "the cattle are lowing" in the songs of the manger. It is in the cows' manger that the Infant Jesus was laid, and a German legend holds that at midnight on Christmas Eve cattle kneel in

adoration, and are given, for one moment, the power of speech. All over Northern and Middle Europe, cattle are given special attention on this night. In Spain, also, cows are honored, because it is thought that on the first Christmas the cow in the stable breathed on the Baby Jesus to keep Him warm.

10 Christmas on Records

(Compiled by Philip L. Miller, The New York Public Library)

CHRISTMAS PROGRAMS

All Saints Choir, Worcester, Mass.; William Self, conductor.
Christmas Carols Old and New. Classic Editions CE 1021.
The excellent church choir balances such old favorites as *Lo, How a Rose, Silent Night* and the *Wassail Song,* with some more novel and modern material.

Capilla Classica Polifónica; Enrique Ribo, conductor.
Spanish Choral Music. Angel 25257.
The program includes motets of Victoria and Morales, works of Brudieu and Vasques and folksong arrangements. Though not all Christmas music, these pieces fit well in the season. The choir, from Barcelona, exists for the

Benedictines of the Archabbey of Beuron; Pater Maurus Pfaff, conductor.
Christmas Vespers. Decca DL 7546.
The service in plain song, chanted by a choir famous for its authority.

avowed purpose of studying the works of the polyphonic masters. Perhaps some of the singing is really too intense, but the folksongs are delightful.

Concert Choir; Margaret Hillis, conductor.
Contemporary Christmas Carols. Contemporary AP 122.
The enterprising producers of this record had the happy idea of commissioning a program of new Christmas songs (as usual nowadays, the word carol is used very loosely). For the most part the results are light and attractive. The five young composers are David Kraehenbuehl, Charles Jones, Manus Sasonkind, Arthur Harris and John Gruen.

Deller, Alfred, counter tenor, and Deller Consort.
The Holly and the Ivy. Vanguard VRS 499.
Deller and his associates, with lute and recorder, sing a generous program in their customary refined and polished style. Though described as "Christmas Carols of Old England," some of the songs are not properly carols, and some are not English. Vaughan Williams' arrangement of *Wither's Rocking Hymn* is a high spot of a program including *Patapan, We Three Kings, Once in Royal David's City, In Dulci Jubilo, Wassail Song, Boar's Head Carol,* and *Adam Lay Ybounden.*

De Paur Infantry Chorus; Leonard de Paur, conductor.
Spirit of Christmas. Columbia CL 725.
This accomplished Negro choir was formed in the army but, while they may sing with military precision, their spirits are high and free. This program ranges from spirituals *(Mary, Mary, Where is Your Baby?)* and folk carols *(I Wonder as I Wander)* through such standbys as *Silent Night* and *God Rest You Merry, Gentlemen* to *White Christmas.* Another program, described in its title — *Calypso Christmas* (Columbia CL 923) — might also be mentioned.

Don Cossack Choir; Serge Jaroff, conductor.
Christmas Music and Carols. Concert Hall CHS 1191.
The titles on this program will mean little to the non-Russian, but the style of both the music and the performance has long been familiar. This is real virtuoso choral singing.

French Canadian Children's Group; Hélène Baillargeon, conductor.
Chants de Noël du Canada Français. Folkways FW 829.
Here is something genuine, even though the Canadian children include their version of *Jingle Bells* among their own Christmas songs. Most of the Noëls have their origin in France, though they have long been identified with Canada. The singing has a wonderful fresh and enthusiastic quality.

Hall Johnson Choir; Hall Johnson, conductor.
Bright, Bright Star. Era EL 20010.
The Hall Johnson Choir is, of course, an institution of long standing. Unlike the de Paur chorus listed above, it is a mixed group. This program includes *Ring Bells, Swing Bells, Shepherds and Kings,* and *Mary, Go to Egypt.*

Hayes, Roland, tenor.
Christmas Carols of the Nations. Vanguard VRS 7016.
The title here is rather free, for Hayes draws on his extensive lieder repertoire along with his spirituals and traditional songs. Hugo Wolf's *Nun Wandre,* Maria and Reger's *Mariä Wiegenlied* are thus in company with *Stille Nacht, King Herod and the Cock, O Come, All Ye Faithful* and *D'où viens-tu, Bergère?* Though approaching seventy when the record was made, Hayes remains a great artist. It might not be too inappropriate to mention here another of his discs, *The Life of Christ as Told through Aframerican Folk Song* (Vanguard VRS 462).

Janequin Chorale; Jean Périsson, conductor.
Noël-France. Concert Hall CHS 1248.
Some of the songs are familiar in this country — *Les Anges dans nos Campagnes, Il Est Né, le Divin Enfant, Un Flambeau, Jeannette, Isabelle* — others deserve to be. The choir is the Marcel Couraud Ensemble, reorganized under a new conductor. The performances are clean and unpretentious, but thoroughly professional.

King's Chapel Choir, Cambridge; Boris Ord, conductor.
A Festival of Lessons and Carols. Westminster WP 6036.
This is a Christmas Eve service, complete with boy choir, prayers and a lesson read in the beautifully cultured British voice of the senior chorister. Not all the music is originally English — *Ding, Dong, Ding* (Swedish), *Hail Blessed Mary* (Italian), *The Infant King* (Basque), *The Three Kings* (Cornelius) — but it is very well sung.

Montserrat Monastery Choir; Dom Ireneo Segarro, conductor.
Christmas Eve in 18th Century Montserrat. London LL 1617.
This service, which traditionally precedes the Midnight Mass in the famous monastery, is the composition of an eighteenth century monk named Narcise Casanovas. He may very well have studied his music in Italy, so successfully did he pick up the contemporary style. The choir, organ and orchestra give the work a spirited performance, not too much concerned with polish. Some elaborate solos are sung by a sweet-voiced boy named Buenaventura Bajet.

Niños Cantores de Morella; Romano Picutti, conductor.
In a Christmas Mood. Period SPL 1015.
A group of Spanish youngsters sing some native Christmas music with enormous and infectious gusto.

New York Pro Musica Antiqua; Noah Greenberg, conductor.
Music of the Mediaeval Court and Countryside. Decca DL 9400.
This program is subtitled *For the Christmas Season*, though some of the music is more general. Such composers as Dufay and Leonin share the honors with others less known and some anonymous. The work of this fine group has improved steadily over the years, both in the singing and the playing of old instruments. An earlier recorded program, *English Medieval Christmas Carols* (Eso-

teric ES 521), is even further from the beaten path than this one. It is recommended with less enthusiasm only because of the strides the ensemble has made in mastering the performing style.

Obernkirchen Children's Choir; Edith Möller, conductor.
Christmas Songs. Angel 65021.
The success of these children in America made such a recording as this inevitable. Their charm is irresistible. Here they sing *Adeste Fideles* in three languages, some of their own songs in German and some of ours in English, with French and Spanish thrown in. *Jingle Bells* in their quaint accent becomes a *tour de force*.

Pro Arte Motettenchor; Peter Mark, conductor.
Old World Christmas Carols. Concert Hall CHS 1232.
I know no better record to sum up the Christmas season as a person of German extraction might think of it. *O du Fröhliche, Vom Himmel hoch, O Heiland, reiss die Himmel auf, Es ist ein Ros' entsprungen, Ihr Kinderlein kommet*, and the rest are here. The choir is good, supported by the organ.

Randolph Singers; David Randolph, conductor.
Christmas Carols, Vols. 1-2. Westminster WP 6022-23.
This very popular recording pretty well covers the now standard repertory. The tonal texture is light, as this ensemble has only one voice on a part.

Royal Choral Society; Sir Malcolm Sargent, conductor.
Yuletide Hymns and Carols. Bluebird LBC 1044.
Another more or less standard selection, including a motet-anthem, in the British choir-festival tradition.

Royal Male Choir of Holland; M. Koekelkoren, conductor.
Christmas Carols. Epic LC 3074.
The internationally-minded Dutch give us English, French and German songs along with their own. Nothing strikingly novel here.

Saaby Choir; Svend Saaby, conductor.
Christmas around the World. Decca DL 8204.
Eleven countries are touched on by means
of favorite carols and songs. A group of instruments leads from one into the next with
colorful modulations. Danish, Swedish, Nor-
wegian and other selections are likely to be
unfamiliar, but all are delightful and well
presented.

St. Jordi Choir; Oriol Martorell, conductor.
Christmas in Spain. Decca DL 9800.
Here is more novelty, some eighteen Spanish
songs sung by healthy, enthusiastic young
voices.

St. Paul's Cathedral Choir; John Dykes Bower,
conductor.
*Christmas Music, Easter Music, Anthems,
Motets and Madrigals*. Angel 3516-B.
Hymns and Carols. Angel 35381.
The first listing is a rather inclusive collec-
tion, with at least a corner belonging on our
list. It was a follow-up to the good will
American tour of the famous Anglican choir
several years ago. There is an excellent per-
formance of Sweelinck's wonderful motet
Hodie Christus Natus Est and of Herbert
Howells' lovely *A Spotless Rose*.

Shaw Chorale; Robert Shaw, conductor.
Christmas Hymns and Carols, Vol. 1. RCA
Victor LM 2139. *Vol. 2*. RCA Victor LM 1711.
For some years these two selections have
been the most obvious answer for anyone
wanting good performances of our best known
Christmas carols and hymns. Most of them
are here, along with some less usual fare.
Vol. 1 has recently been reissued in what
seems to be a new recording and with the
order of the program changed. It is still probably the best buy of all the programs of this
kind, with Vol. 2 qualifying for second place.

Societas Musica Choir, Copenhagen; Jorgen
Ernsthausen, conductor.
Carols for Christmastide. Period RL 1191.
This program is apparently made in Den-
mark for the benefit of the English-speaking
world, for the carols are mostly ours and they

are sung delightfully in astonishingly clear
and correct English. But along with *Good
King Wenceslas, The Seven Joys of Mary*,
and *I Saw Three Ships* are such novelties as
People Look East and *Jesus Dressed in Garb
so Lowly*.

Summers, Andrew Rowan, tenor.
Hymns and Carols. Folkways FP 61.
Summers is one of the more musical folk
singers, with a pleasing light tenor voice and
a sense of musical line. He accompanies him-
self on the dulcimer. This recording includes
The Cherry Tree Carol and *The Babe of
Bethlehem*.

Trapp Family Choir; Franz Wasner, conductor.
*Christmas with the Trapp Family Singers,
Vols. 1-2*. Decca. DL 9553, DL 9689. *Carols*.
Camden CAL 209.
The Trapp Family was for some years an
institution of the American concert hall, especially around Christmas time. Now that
they have officially retired, the recorded leg-
acy of these singers takes on additional sentimental value. The two Decca discs are
international in scope, with each carol, motet
or hymn in its original language or dialect.
The style of singing, as always, is peaceful
and reserved. The voices were not numerous
or strong, and they kept well within their
limitations. The Camden disc is a reissue of
recordings made before the war. It is pre-
dominantly German. Another more or less
related disc is called *Sacred Music Around
the Church Year* (Concert Hall CHS 1100).

Trinity Choir, New Haven; G. Huntington Byles,
conductor.
Christmas Music from Trinity. Overtone
OVER 11.
Here are such familiars as *The Holly and the
Ivy* and *Good King Wenceslas* along with
the lesser known *Christmas in the Wood*
(Mabel Daniels) and *One Winter Night* (Reg-
inald Hunt) and Victoria's magnificent motet
O Magnum Mysterium. There is a new set-
ting of *In the Bleak Mid-Winter* by Harold
Darke, and some of the arrangements are

not the most familiar ones. A well-rounded church program well presented.

Wagner Chorale; Roger Wagner, conductor.
Joy to the World. Capitol P 8353.
This is pretty much the usual repertoire again, from the title hymn to *The Coventry Carol,* but the choir is an unusually capable one.

Welch Chorale; James B. Welch, conductor.
Music Box of Christmas Carols. Vanguard VRS 428.
The novelty here is the alternation between singing and playing. Again we have the familiar fare, but for the interludes we hear an old-fashioned Regina music box. The effect at the same time is nostalgic and festive. The Regina is from the Bornand Collection.

Westminster Abbey Choir
Carols by the Bach and Westminster Abbey Choirs. London LL 1095.
A special interest attaches to the choir of the great London abbey. The titles include *Adeste Fideles, Whence is that Goodly Fragrance,* and *Come, Rock the Cradle for Him.*

Wolff, Ernst, tenor.
German Christmas Songs. Folkways FP 947.
Dr. Wolff sings a dozen old German Christmas songs quite informally to his own accompaniment.

MUSIC BY INDIVIDUAL COMPOSERS

Bach, Johann Sebastian, 1685-1750
Cantata No. 1: *Wie schön leuchtet der Morgenstern*
Gunhild Weber, soprano; Helmut Krebs, tenor; Hermann Schey, bass; Berlin Motet Choir and Berlin Philharmonic Orchestra; Fritz Lehmann, conductor. Decca DL 9671.
Founded on one of the most beautiful and most familiar of the old chorales, this cantata is full of first-rate music. The performance recorded is acceptable without being outstanding.

Cantata No. 63: *Christen, ätzet diesen Tag*
Margit Opawsky, soprano; Hilde Rössl-Maj-

dan, contralto; Waldemar Kmentt, tenor; Harald Hermann, bass; Vienna Akademie Kammerchor and Vienna Symphony Orchestra; Michael Gielen, conductor. Bach Guild BG 518.
There is some good solo singing in this recording, especially by the contralto, though on the whole the cantata is no more than adequately performed.

Cantata No. 122; *Das neugebor'ne Kindelein*
Margit Opawsky, soprano; Hilde Rössl-Majdan, contralto; Waldemar Kmentt, tenor; Harald Hermann, bass; Vienna Akademie Kammerchor and Vienna Symphony Orchestra; Michael Gielen, conductor. Bach Guild BG 523.
Another performance that just gets by; the bass solo is obviously not easy going.

Magnificat
Friederike Sailer, soprano; Lotte Wolf-Matthaeus, mezzo-soprano; Hetty Plümacher, contralto; Johannes Feyerabend, tenor; Brüno Muller, bass; Radio Stuttgart Chorus and Pro Musica Orchestra; Rolf Reinhardt, conductor. Vox PL 8890.
Bach composed his *Magnificat* for the Christmas season in the Thomannerkirche at Leipzig. Originally he set it in the key of E-flat, adding four interpolations appropriate to Christmas, two in German and two in Latin. Though this recording follows Bach in his later transposition to D major, it includes the rarely heard extra numbers in their proper places. Thus the performance is the most complete of the several available. An English recording (Oiseau Lyre OL-50101) led by Pierre Colombo and featuring the countertenor Alfred Deller in the contralto solos is somewhat clearer and more refined in tone, but it lacks the special Christmas feature.

Weihnachts-Oratorium
Gunhild Weber, soprano; Lore Fischer, contralto; Heinz Marten, tenor; Horst Günther, bass; Detmold Academy Chorus and Orchestra; Kurt Thomas, conductor. Oiseau Lyre OL 5001-5003.

The *Christmas Oratorio,* actually a cycle of six cantatas, is one of the great masterpieces appropriate to the season. Unfortunately none of the three available recordings does it complete justice, but this one is solid in conception and certainly the best reproduced.

Berlioz, Hector, 1803-1869
L'Enfance du Christ
Florence Kopleff, contralto; Cesare Valletti, tenor; Gérard Souzay, baritone; Giorgio Tozzi, bass; New England Conservatory Chorus and Boston Symphony Orchestra; Charles Munch, conductor. RCA Victor LM 6053.
At long last this heartwarmingly simple and sincere oratorio is making its way as a regular part of our Christmas. This is the most recent of the three recordings, and easily the best. The conductor's affection for the music is at all times evident; his orchestra, one of the world's finest, realizes his every nuance, and the chorus is very good. Aside from a certain un-Frenchness in some of their work, the soloists also are excellent.

Britten, Benjamin, 1913-
A Ceremony of Carols
Copenhagen Boys' Choir; Enid Simon, harp; Benjamin Britten, conductor. London LL 1336.
Britten has given new settings to some lovely old English poems, introducing and ending the cycle with the plaintive *Hodie Christus Natus Est.* The boy choir is supported only by the harp. Under the composer's direction the Danish group is splendidly alert and musical; the English diction might serve as a model.

Saint Nicholas
Peter Pears, tenor; David Hemmings, boy soprano; Aldeburgh Festival Choir and Orchestra; Boys' and Girls' Choirs; Ralph Downes, organist; Benjamin Britten, conductor. London LL 1154.
Here is fresh and useful material for choirs with taste but modest pretentions. There is only one adult solo part. Britten introduces familiar hymns here and there for congrega-

tional singing. Here is an authentic performance to serve as a model.

Charpentier, Marc-Antoine, 1634-1704
Messe de Minuit
Ensemble Vocal de Paris; Orchestra; André Jouvé, conductor. Ducretet Thomson 93080.
This joyous and festive Mass is to be performed, of course, on Christmas Eve; it is based on several traditional carol tunes. The organist in this performance adds a few more carols by way of interludes. The music is not easy, and the singers here find some of it taxing, but the recording should not be missed. The happy coupling is Vivaldi's fine *Gloria.*

Corelli, Arcangelo, 1653-1713
Concerto Grosso, Op. 6, No. 8 ("Christmas Concerto")
Corelli Tri-Centenary String Orchestra; Dean Eckertsen, conductor. Vox PL 10500.
Vox has happily combined this classic work with similar concerti of Torelli, Manfredini and Locatelli, which is a large point in favor of this disc. As a performing group the Virtuosi di Roma (Decca DL 9649) may well be preferred.

Cornelius, Peter, 1824-1874
Weihnachtslieder
Imrgard Seefried, soprano; Erik Werba, pianoforte. Decca DL 7545.
In our age of brilliance, hurry and pretense such a simple little gem of a song cycle is apt to be forgotten. Thanks, therefore, are due Miss Seefried not only for discovering the work, but for singing it so beautifully. Among the several songs that complete the recital are Wolf's *Schlafendes Jesuskind* and Reger's *Mariä Wiegenlied.*

Distler, Hugo, 1908-1942
Die Weihnachtsgeschichte, Op. 10
Netherlands Madrigal and Motet Choir; Marinus Voorberg, conductor. Epic LC 3153.
Hugo Distler was a gifted young German composer who took his own life during the second World War. His *Christmas Story* stems directly from Schütz. It is sung unac-

companied throughout. A narrator tells the story, with other soloists impersonating the various personages in the drama. The choral parts are virtually variations on the fine old chorale *Es ist ein Ros' entsprungen*. Coupled with the Honegger *Christmas Cantata*, the recording is a real find.

Handel, George Frederic, 1685-1759
Messiah
Jennifer Vyvyan, soprano; Norma Proctor, contralto; George Maran, tenor; Owen Brannigan, bass; London Philharmonic Choir and Orchestra; Sir Adrian Boult, conductor. London LLA 19.
Of the various *Messiah* recordings this seems to be decidedly the best. Boult claims that he has returned to the "original manuscript" for his practical edition, which means simply that he has made every effort to give a performance as correct historically as is possible. At the same time he has avoided any suggestion of dry musicology. His tempi are brisk, alert and vital.

Hindemith, Paul, 1895-
Des Marienleben
Jennie Tourel, mezzo-soprano; Erich Itor Kahn, pianoforte. Columbia SL 196.
This mystical cycle, on poems of Rainer Maria Rilke, was originally composed in 1923, but realizing that he had made well-nigh impossible demands upon the singer, the composer later revised the work. The new version was introduced to New York by the present fine artists in 1949. Even as it stands now, the score is a challenge for any interpreters. Miss Tourel sings with great musicianship and style, though the tessitura is taxing for her.

Honegger, Arthur, 1892-1955
Christmas Cantata
Michel Roux, baritone; Brasseur Choir; Petits Chanteurs de Versailles; Lamoureux Orchestra; Paul Sacher, conductor. Epic LC 3153.
Honegger's Christmas message begins with darkness covering the earth and the anguish-

ed cries of humanity. The message itself comes in several languages, many people singing their own traditional carols. As the work develops, these songs weave together in counterpoint, not only of tunes but of tongues. The cantata is coupled with the fine Distler work mentioned above.

Liszt, Franz, 1811-1886
Weihnachtsbaum
Ilona Kabos, pianoforte. Bartók 910.
Of two recordings of this piano suite this is the incomplete one — Kabos plays only seven of the twelve pieces — but it is vastly superior to its rival.

Locatelli, Pietro, 1695-1764
Concerto Grosso, Op. 1, No. 8 ("Christmas Concerto")
I Musici Virtuosi; Dean Eckertsen, conductor. Vox PL 10500.
See remarks under Corelli.

Manfredini, Francesco, 1688-17—?
Christmas Concerto
I Musici Virtuosi; Dean Eckertsen, conductor. Vox PL 10500.
See remarks under Corelli.

Menotti, Gian-Carlo, 1911-
Amahl and the Night Visitors
Chet Allen, boy soprano; Rosemary Kuhlman, mezzo-soprano; etc. Chorus and Orchestra; Thomas Schippers, conductor. RCA Victor LM 1701.
Written for television, this little holiday opera found such favor that it has become a fixture in theaters as well as on the air each year. The recording preserves the original cast which, it would seem, is definitive.

Schütz, Heinrich, 1585-1672
Weihnachts Historie
Charlotte Bloecher, soprano; William Hess, tenor; Paul Matthen, bass; Cantata Singers; Arthur Mendel, conductor. REB 3.
In this wonderful work of Bach's great forerunner, the story is told by the tenor narrator, with the soprano repeating the Angel and the bass Herod. The trio of the shepherds

with obbligato by two recorders is particularly disarming. Of the various recordings that have appeared since this one (including one in Italian labeled *Nativity*) none captures the spirit quite so successfully.

Torelli, Giuseppe, 1658-1709
Concerto, Op. 8, No. 6
Reinhold Barchet, violin; Will Beh, violin; Helma Elsner, harpsichord; Pro Musica Orchestra; Rolf Reinhardt, conductor. Vox PL 10500.
Another of the group of baroque Christmas concertos now brought together on one disc.

Villa-Lobos, Heitor, 1887-
Caixinha de Boàs Festas
Rome Symphony Orchestra; J. J. Castro, conductor. RCA Victor LM 2143.
The Surprise Box is a Christmas ballet for children, written in Villa-Lobos' characteristic rhythmic and colorful style.

MISCELLANEOUS

Christmas in Europe. Choirs and organs of Europe, each in its own music. Epic LN 3315.

Christmas in France. Capitol T 10108. *Christmas in Germany.* Capitol T 10095.

Christmas in Holland. Capitol T 10096. *Christmas in Italy.* Capitol T 10093.

Christmas in Mexico. Capitol T 10092. *Christmas in Spain.* Capitol T 10094.

Christmas in Sweden. Capitol T 10079. Extended tours for those who like to travel.

Carillon for Christmas. Traditional carols played by Robert Owen. Westminster WP 6020.

Christmas Carols on the Organ. Some of the most familiar played by Virgil Fox. RCA Victor LM 1845.

Christmas Organ Music. Chorale preludes, fantasies appropriate to the season by Bach and Buxtehude, played by Fritz Heitmann. Telefunken LGX 66009.

Christmas Carols in Hi-Fi. The celebrated harpist, Carlos Salzedo, gives his version of many famous carols and songs in a brilliant recording. Mercury MG 50116.

Dickens' Christmas Carol. The famous dramatization featuring Lionel Barrymore is available on MGM E 3222.

Many Moons. Thurber's Christmas story, with Burr Tillstrom as narrator. DL 8192.

Christmas in America

THE CHRISTMAS TREE SHIP

by Harry Hansen

CHRISTMAS in Chicago, fifty years ago, was a happy, home festival in a city not yet too rich, too pretentious, to be neighborly. There was usually snow at Christmas; it lay in large heaps in the gutters and was packed solid on the streets. When snow fell it was heavy with moisture; it blocked trains and held up streetcars. The average citizen shoveled his own sidewalks clean and looked after his own fires. A few blocks beyond the Loop, where the gray wooden cottages with their scrollwork porches stretched for miles, householders would be out early in the mornings wielding their shovels, amid shouts to their neighbors, for in those days families lived long enough in one locality to become known to one another.

In the houses on the near North Side, where brick buildings abounded, the windows had little wooden blinds inside through which came the yellow rays of light from gas jets. The air in the streets outside had the close feeling of a low-ceilinged room and shouts rebounded from wall to wall. In that air bells on sleighs jingled in time a long way off and hoofbeats made a dull patter on the packed snow. As the sleigh

passed under the light of the gas lamp at the corner you could see the prancing horse, the curved dashboard, the gleam of the nickeled bars across the front, the flash of the runners. The driver would be wearing a wide fur collar and a fur cap; the woman beside him would be tucked under fur robes and look very comfortable in a brown fur neckpiece and toque.

Inside, the house was warm and a bit stuffy with dry air. The carpets had a firm surface and gay curlicues of vine leaves all over them. The hall might be dark; its walls were covered with embossed paper, stained to the color of leather, and the gaslight flickered behind a glove of pink glass ornamented with a trailing vine. You walked quickly past the parlor, which had a mantelpiece of black slate and a mirror over the fireplace and heavy chairs and settees with curved walnut legs, to the back room where all the family gathered. Here the walls were hung with photographs of young and old and there were music racks and bookshelves. If the house was heated by a furnace, the hot air flooded up through a register in the floor, but more likely a big-bellied stove, consuming

212

anthracite coal, gleamed red through mica windows in a corner. And in the bay stood the Christmas tree.

Most likely the father of the family had picked it out and carried it home. Men and women carried their own bundles in those days. Perhaps he walked down to the Clark Street bridge, a week or two before Christmas, to see if the Schuenemanns had come down from Wisconsin with a load of spruce trees. Invariably the two big, brawny lads would be there with a fishing schooner loaded with trees that they themselves had cut in the Michigan woods. They were fine, well-shaped trees and cost so little — for 75 cents you bought a full-sized tree; for $1 you had your choice of the best. Even saplings provided bright decorations for a city where people were making money, but not too much money, and where the average citizen was always fearful of hard times.

As long ago as 1887 the two Schuenemanns, Herman and August, had sailed down in a schooner from Manistique, Michigan, with a load of spruce and tied up beside the dock behind the old red-brick commission houses at the Clark Street bridge. There Chicago found them and bought their stock, and called Herman captain and remembered to look for him the following year. When snow fell on Chicago's streets in December days, the father of the family would say, "Guess I'll have to go down to the Clark Street bridge to see if the captain is in and get us a tree."

Fifty years ago the work of providing trees for Christmas was not yet the mass-production business it has become in recent times. No dealer contracted for thousands of trees as a speculation and destroyed great numbers if he had guessed wrong on the demand. No man cut down whole hillsides to satisfy the whims of people who followed a custom but didn't know how to pray. There were plenty of trees for all. The Schuenemanns went into the woods behind Manistique and Thompson, Michigan, where young trees grew on land that had been cut over to make the lumber that went into midwestern houses a generation before. They chose the trees carefully, including some tall

ones for which they had orders from churches and hotels. Sometimes they had to work in the snow and when the trees reached Chicago there was still snow on the branches. The brothers thought they had done well when they made a modest profit on a trip that occupied about six weeks of the wintry season, when it was hard to haul other cargoes.

The work was not easy, neither the cutting nor the sailing, for they always came when Lake Michigan kicked up a lot of rough sea. In 1898 August had just set sail with a load of trees when a storm arose and he and his ship were lost. Thereupon Herman determined to carry on alone. In 1899 he was back at the Clark Street dock with his boat, the *Rouse Simmons*, loaded with Christmas trees. He was a jovial man, with a very ruddy complexion and laughing wrinkles around his blue eyes, and everybody liked him.

For eleven years Herman arrived with his cargo and many people depended on him for a tree year after year. Then came the hard season of 1912, with storms and heavy seas on Lake Michigan. Late in November Herman cut his trees in the woods behind Manistique and started for Chicago in the *Rouse Simmons*, with a crew of seventeen men. There were head winds and heavy seas from the start and soon the schooner was struggling in a raging snowstorm. What took place on board we can only guess. The *Rouse Simmons* sailed into the silence that covers all the fine ships that have fallen victim to the gales of Lake Michigan, which have taken the lives of so many, from the days of La Salle's *Griffon* until now.

Long before Chicago missed the *Rouse Simmons* at its dock, reports began to come of the ship's distress. A schooner resembling it was said to have been sighted off Kewaunee, Wisconsin, flying distress signals. The steamer *George W. Orr* reported to the revenue cutter *Tuscarora* that she had seen the *Rouse Simmons* three miles offshore, but the captain later admitted that he might have been mistaken. But on December 5, 1912, fishermen off Two Rivers Point, seven miles north of Manitowoc, Wisconsin, found the tops of spruce trees entangled in their nets. Trees had been roped together on the deck of the *Rouse Simmons,* and how could they get into the lake at that point if not off a ship?

On December 13th a watcher on the beach at Sheboygan, Wisconsin, reported that he had picked up a bottle containing a message that came from the captain. It had been written on a page of the ship's log, and read:

Friday — Everybody goodbye. I guess we are all through. Sea washed over our deckload Thursday. During the night the small boat was washed over. Leaking bad. Ingvald and Steve fell overboard Thursday. God help us.

HERMAN SCHUENEMANN

The men referred to were believed to have been Steve E. Nelson, mate, and Ingvald Nylons, seaman. But if there was such a message, it never reached the captain's wife, who was eagerly waiting for scraps of news in her Manistique home. She was a valiant little woman, with a great deal of stamina. When she realized that her three little girls, Elsie and the twins, Pearl and Hazel, were now dependent wholly on her efforts, she resolved to take up her husband's task.

There was no Christmas ship at the Clark Street dock in 1912. But when 1913 came, Chicago residents who looked over the railings of the bridge beheld another schooner, loaded with trees, as in the days when Captain Herman held forth there. On board was the plucky little wife of the captain. She had gone into the woods with the woodcutters and supervised the felling of the trees. With her, too, were her girls, as well as women to weave wreaths and garlands. Chicago was to become well acquainted with the Schuenemanns. They were to come season after season for twenty-two years after the *Rouse Simmons* went down.

For years Chicago friends would ask the captain's wife whether there had been any definite report on the *Rouse Simmons,* and she could only shake her head sorrowfully. Yet the sea, which guards its secrets well, reluctantly gave up tangible evidence fourteen years after the

disaster. On April 23, 1924, the wallet of Captain Schuenemann was found at Two Rivers Point, where the spruce trees had been tangled in the fishermen's nets. It still had the original rubber band around it and the cards and clippings inside seemed to be made of plaster. Some of the clippings related to earlier voyages of the Christmas tree ship. Three years after this find, a bottle with a note signed by Charles Nelson was picked up. It read:

These lines were written at 10:30 P.M. Schooner R. S. ready to go down about 20 miles southeast Two Rivers Point between fifteen or twenty miles off shore. All hands lashed to one line. Goodbye.

Eventually the family made its last voyage to the Chicago market with Christmas trees. The mother had grown gray; the girls were handsome young women. Forty-seven years had elapsed since Herman, as an 18-year-old lad, had steered his first cargo into Chicago. The ship had become an institution.

Its fame grew. Today when the winds blow hard on the lake and the heavy surf pounds the frozen shore line watchers in the lighthouse recall the *Rouse Simmons*. Long ago it inspired a ballad. When word of its loss reached Chicago newspapers, Vincent Starrett, bibliophile and author of many books of fiction and belles-lettres, was a reporter on the *Daily News*. His editor was Henry Justin Smith. "It would make a fine ballad," said Starrett. "Why don't you write it?" replied Smith. So Starrett composed "The Ballad of the Christmas Ship," a poem of many, many quatrains, and Smith found room for it among the crowded columns of the day's news. It may never challenge the efforts of youthful orators as often as "The Wreck of the Hesperus," but the legend is just as moving and the intentions of the poet were as good as Longfellow's.

THE NIGHT WE TALKED
TO SANTA CLAUS

by Lynne Lofting

During the First World War my brother Colin and I lived with my mother in the Catskill Mountains. Our house was perched on a raised plateau, surrounded by apple trees and commanding a beautiful view of the valley and the range of mountains opposite. My mother was not with us very much; she joined the Red Cross and went overseas so that she could be near my father, who was a captain in the Irish Guards. It was at this time that we received the many illustrated letters from him about a kind, little round-faced doctor who could understand and speak to animals — letters that later became the first Doctor Dolittle book. The doctor and his animal friends were drawn on any old scraps of paper while my father was actually in the trenches.

I remembered my father only dimly. One evening he had carried me through the garden, perched on my shoulders, and had shown me the faint speck of light that was the evening star. He told me that it was "our" star and that

wherever he was when he left us, he would be looking at it and thinking of us at home.

Wars are remote to children. The months slipped past in our mountain retreat and suddenly it was just before Christmas. Our English Nanny appeared to be strangely excited. It seemed that soon, perhaps even in time for the holidays, Father and Mother would be home.

Happily forgotten in the excitement, my brother and I spent long hours in our nursery, curled up on the window seat, speculating on what we wanted most for Christmas. He was four years old and longed desperately for a real toolbox. My heart was set on a coral ring. We described these to each other in such minute detail that we had almost conjured them up before our eyes.

I can still smell the gingerbread cookies baking downstairs and taste the tang of cold air as it came in our window, blowing the curtains back suddenly to reveal the sky alive with stars. In this hushed, waiting atmosphere we stopped fighting with each other, no longer played tricks on Nanny, and became model children.

At last it was Christmas Eve. But no one had arrived and the house was oddly empty and unpromising. After supper we were allowed downstairs just long enough to hang up our stockings by the fireplace. It wasn't very gay with only ourselves and Nanny there to celebrate. Disappointed and forlorn, we dragged our feet back up the stairs, getting little staccato prods in the back as Nanny hurried us up. She tucked us in and opened the window wide; she was one who believed in plenty of good fresh air. Then she came over and gave a kiss and a hug to each of us.

"Be good children and sleep tight," she said as she left the room.

The faint smell of cookies still floated about in the hall as she opened the door to leave us, but aside from that it might have been any ordinary winter night.

For a while we stayed perfectly still, each thinking his own thoughts. Soon I was sure my brother had fallen asleep. I lay looking at the sky, where a moon the color of tin was suspended like a Christmas tree ornament. It made matters worse to feel so lonesome on such a special, beautiful night. I wished that my mother were there. My eyelids grew heavy. Despite the disappointment, sleep was overtaking me.

Then suddenly I heard the sound of bells — sharp, clear bells, coming closer all the time. No other sound had ever been so real; it could not be that I imagined them. I lay stiff as a poker with my legs straight out and my heart going like a hammer. My brother's muffled voice barely reached me. "Are you awake?" he whispered.

"Yes."

"Do you hear anything?"

"I hear bells," I said.

"So do I!" In one leap we were up on the window seat, our heads thrust out into the cold, sharp air, our toes curled under us in excitement, our trembling bodies pressed close together, as we tried to peer through the dark orchard down into the valley. Now we could hear the squeak of runners in the snow and the thud of hoofs.

Suddenly the moon came from behind a cloud and painted all the landscape silver. In the silence of that snow-covered world a deep voice shouted, "Who-oa, Prancer! Who-oa, Donder! Who-oa, Blitzen!" But no one was visible.

The sleigh finally halted somewhere behind the trees that surrounded the house. There was a brief, suspended quiet. Then there were other sounds — human footsteps in the snow, crunching, coming closer to the house. And then a fat, bouncy figure with an enormous pack on his back walked toward us beneath the branches of an apple tree.

"It's Santa!" my brother squealed, butting me in the stomach with his head. "And he'll be in our chimlee in a minute!"

"Quick! We're supposed to be in bed!" With that, my brother in a desperate effort to hide himself tried to get under his, while I hurled myself into mine and pulled the covers tightly around me like a winding sheet. In this state we waited breathlessly, while the steps, in the

house now, came closer and closer to the nursery door.

Slowly and with ceremony the door opened and then everything happened very quickly.

He came over to me first. I somehow gathered strength to put my head out from under the covers. He was near enough to touch. There were black streaks of soot about the hips and shoulders of his red suit. He put the enormous, bulging pack of toys down on the foot of my bed. Then he actually spoke to me. His great, booming voice came through a flowing beard which was white as snow and covered part of his chest.

"I hear you have been a very good little girl." He was reaching down into the pack of toys as he spoke. "So I brought you your wish." With that he handed me a tiny, beautifully wrapped package. I knew instinctively that it was my coral ring. I was so overwhelmed that my eyes swam with tears.

"Don't be afraid," he said with such love and kindness that I began to feel I knew him. "Take it — it's what you have wished for." I reached out and took it from him, unable to say a word.

Then he turned toward the other bed. My brother had covered his small face with his

hands and peered through his chubby fingers now and then, when his courage allowed him to.

"I hear that you have been very good as well, so I have a special present for you."

My brother seemed frozen but he took one hand away from his face and eyed the jolly stranger. Santa walked over and put the square, impressive box down beside him. For a second he looked as if he might be going to pick my brother up in his arms, but then he turned away. Slowly he shouldered his pack and started for the door.

"Good night," he said. "I still have a lot to do. Merry Christmas to all and to all a good night." With that he was gone.

The silence was broken by my brother who had finally found his voice:

"If he gets stuck in the chimlee, we can see him in the morning."

"He won't," I replied sharply. Two years older and wiser, I knew that such a thing could never happen.

Dazed, we moved forward again to look out the window. We heard the same steps in the snow, but this time we didn't see anyone. We heard the bells as the reindeer started up. The sleigh moved away swiftly, down, down into the dark below. Then the night was again quite empty of sound, except for our breathing. Santa might never have been there at all.

The sleep we eventually got was deep and peaceful. In the morning Nanny came in looking just as she always did. We sprang out of bed both talking at once, showing her our treasures. She received the news with just the right mixture of belief and incredulity. When she could get a word in, she said, "Well, get your clothes on now. There's a surprise downstairs for you. Your mother and your father are waiting in the living room."

We raced down the stairs. Next to Mother stood a tall man with smiling eyes which were at once sad and happy. He took us in his arms and hugged us very tight. I don't remember if he said anything to us because we were too busy telling him over and over again the story of what had happened. How, just when we

thought there would be no Christmas, Santa Claus had come, we'd seen him in our room, he'd talked to us, he'd given me my coral ring and my brother his tool chest, and then he went away because he had a lot to do and other children to visit. Then, quite out of breath, we told it all over again.

My father listened intensely, as though every detail of what we were saying was something he longed to hear. It seemed to give him so much joy that the telling of our adventure was as tinglingly alive as the experience itself.

Even when we were a great deal older, we still were telling other children that we knew there was a Santa Claus. Our conviction remained unshaken because we had seen him and spoken to him. Against any and all assaults we stood our ground.

Later, of course, we grew to know the man who had come to our room that Christmas Eve and to understand why he had made us believe in Santa Claus. We understood why, after spending three years at war, he had come back to his children at Christmas time with one purpose in his mind and heart: to keep the magic in the world alive.

That magic was the real gift he gave us on Christmas Eve so long ago. And my brother and I cherish it still.

ONCE ON CHRISTMAS

by Dorothy Thompson

It is Christmas Eve — the festival that belongs to mothers and fathers and children, all over the so-called Western world. It's not a time to talk about situations, or conditions, or reactions, or people who emerge briefly into the news. My seven-year-old son asked me this evening to tell him what Christmas was like when I was a little girl, before people came home for Christmas in airplanes, thirty odd years ago. And so I told him this:

A long, long time ago, when your mother was your age, and not nearly as tall as you, she

lived with her mother, and father, and younger
brother, and little sister, in a Methodist parsonage, in Hamburg, New York. It was a tall
wooden house, with a narrow verandah on the
side, edged with curlycues of woodwork at the
top, and it looked across a lawn at the church
where father preached every Sunday morning
and evening. In the backyard there were old
Baldwin and Greening apple trees, and a wonderful, wonderful barn. But that is another
story. The village now has turned into a sub-
urb of the neighboring city of Buffalo, and
fathers who work there go in and out every day
on the trains and buses, but then it was just a
little country town, supported by the surrounding farms.

Father preached in his main church there on
Sunday mornings but in the afternoon he had
to drive out to the neighboring village of Arm-
or where there was just a little box of church
in the middle of the farming country. For
serving both parishes, he received his house
and one thousand dollars a year. But he didn't
always get the thousand dollars. Sometimes the
crops were bad, and the farmers had no money,
and when the farmers had no money the vil-

lage people didn't have any either. Then the
farmers would come to us with quarters of
beef, or halves of pigs, or baskets of potatoes,
and make what they called a donation. My
mother hated the word, and sometimes would
protest, but my father would laugh, and say,
"Let them pay in what they can! We are all
in the same boat together."

For weeks before Christmas we were very,
very busy. Mother was busy in the kitchen,
cutting up citron and sorting out raisins and
clarifying suet for the Christmas pudding —
and shooing all of us out of the room, when
we crept in to snatch a raisin, or a bit of
kernel from the butter-nuts that my little brother was set to cracking on the woodshed floor,
with an old-fashioned flat-iron.

I would lock myself into my little bedroom,
to bend over a handkerchief that I was hem-
stitching for my mother. It is very hard to
hemstitch when you are seven years old, and
the thread would knot, and break, and then
one would have to begin again, with a little
rough place, where one had started over. I'm
afraid the border of that handkerchief was
just one succession of knots and starts.

The home-made presents were only a tiny
part of the work! There was the Christmas
tree! Mr. Heist, from my father's Armor parish,
had brought it from his farm, a magnificent
hemlock, that touched the ceiling. We were
transported with admiration, but what a tree to
trim! For there was no money to buy miles of
tinsel and boxes of colored glass balls.

But in the pantry was a huge stone jar of
popcorn. When school was over, in the afternoons, we all gathered in the back parlor, which
was the family sitting room. The front parlor
was a cold place, where portraits of John Wes-
ley and Frances Willard hung on the walls,
and their eyes, I remember, would follow a
naughty child accusingly around the room. The
sofas in that room were of walnut, with roses
and grapes carved on their backs, just where
they'd stick into your back, if you fidgeted in
them, and were covered with horse-hair which
was slippery when it was new, and tickly when
it was old. But that room was given over to

visits from the local tycoons who sometimes contributed to the church funds, and couples who came to be married.

The back parlor was quite, quite different. It had an ingrain carpet on the floor, with patterns of maple leaves, and white muslin curtains at the windows, and an assortment of chairs contributed by the Parsonage Committee. A Morris chair, I remember, and some rockers, and a fascinating cabinet which was a desk and a bookcase, and a chest of drawers, and a mirror, all in one.

In this room there was a round iron stove, a very jolly stove, a cozy stove that winked at you with its red isinglass eyes. On top of this stove was a round iron plate; it was flat, and a wonderful place to pop corn. There was a great copper kettle, used for making maple syrup, and we shook the popper on the top of the stove — first I shook, until my arm was tired, and then Willard shook, until he was tired, and even the baby shook. The corn popped, and we poured it into the kettle and emptied the kettle, and poured it full again, until there was a whole barrelful of popcorn, as white and fluffy as the snow that carpeted the lawn between the parsonage and the church.

Then we each got a darning needle, a big one, and a ball of string. We strung the popcorn into long, long ropes, to hang upon the tree. But that was only half of it! There were stars to be cut out of kindergarten paper, red and green, and silver, and gold, and walnuts to be wrapped in gold paper, or painted with gold paint out of the paintbox that I had been given for my birthday. One got the paint into one's fingernails, and it smelled like bananas. And red apples to be polished, because a shiny apple makes a brave show on a tree. And when it was all finished, it was Christmas Eve.

For Christmas Eve we all wore our best clothes. Baby in a little challis dress as blue as her eyes, and I had a new pinafore of Swiss lawn that my Aunt Margaret had sent me from England. We waited, breathless, in the front parlor while the candles were lit.

Then my mother sat at the upright piano in a rose-red cashmere dress and played, and my father sang, in his lovely, pure, gay, tenor voice:

"It came upon the midnight clear
That glorious song of old,
From angels bending near the earth
To touch their harps of gold."

And then we all marched in. It is true that we had decorated the tree ourselves, and knew intimately everything on it, but it shone in the dark room like an angel, and I could see the angels bending down, and it was so beautiful that one could hardly bear it. We all cried, "Merry Christmas!" and kissed each other.

There were bundles under the tree, most alluring bundles! But they didn't belong to Christmas Eve. They were for the morning. Before the morning came three little children would sit sleepily in the pews of their father's church and hear words drowsily, and shift impatiently, and want to go to sleep in order to wake up very, very early!

And wake up early we did! The windows were still gray, and, oh, how cold the room was! The church janitor had come over at dawn to stoke the hot air furnace in the parsonage, but at its best it only heated the rooms directly above it, and the upstairs depended on grates in the floor, and the theory that heat rises. We shuddered out of our beds, trembling with cold and excitement, and into our clothes, which, when I was a little girl, were very complicated affairs indeed. First, a long fleece-lined union suit, and then a ferris waist dripping with buttons, then the cambric drawers edged with embroidery, and a flannel petticoat handsome with scallops, and another petticoat of cambric and embroidery, just for show, and over that a gay plaid dress, and a dainty pinafore. What polishing of cheeks, and what brushing of hair and then a grand tumble down the stairs into the warm, cozy back parlor.

Presents! There was my beloved Miss Jamup with a brand new head! Miss Jam-up was once a sweet little doll, dears, who had become badly battered about the face in the course of too affectionate ministrations, and here she was again, with a new head altogether and new clothes, and eyes that open and shut. Scarfs and mittens from my mother's lively fingers. A doll house made from a wooden cracker box and odds and ends of wallpaper, with furniture cut from stiff cardboard—and that was mother's work, too. And a new woolen dress, and new pinafores!

Under the tree was a book: *The Water Babies,* by Charles Kingsley. *To my beloved daughter Dorothy.*

Books meant sheer magic. There were no automobiles — none for Methodist ministers, in those days. No moving pictures. No radio. But inside the covers of books was everything, everything that exists outside in the world today. Lovely, lovely words of poetry, that slipped like colored beads along a string; tales of rosered cities, half as old as time. All that men can imagine, and construct, and make others imagine.

One couldn't read the book now. But there it lay, the promise of a perfect afternoon. Before one could get at it, one would go into the dining room. And what a dinner! This Christmas there was Turkey — with best wishes from one of my father's parishioners. And the pudding, steaming, and with two kinds of sauce. And no one to say, "No, dear, I think one helping is enough."

We glutted ourselves, we distended ourselves, we ate ourselves into a coma, so that we all had to lie down and have a nap.

Then, lying before the stove, propped on my elbows, I opened the covers of my Christmas book.

"Once upon a time there was a little chimney sweep, and his name was Tom. He lived in a great town of the North Country . . . in England."

How well I knew that North Country, with its rows on rows of dark stone houses, its mine pits, its poor workmen. From such a town my father had come, across the ocean, to this village in upstate New York. I forgot Christmas, forgot everything, except the fate of little Tom. What a book! It wasn't just a story. There was poetry in it. The words of the poem sang in my head, so that all these years I can remember them:

When all the world is young, lad,
And all the trees are green;
And every goose, a swan, lad,
And every lass a Queen;
Then hey for boot and spur, lad,
And round the world away;
Young blood must have its course, lad,
And every dog his day.

The little girl lay and dreamed that all the world was wide and beautiful, filled only with hearts as warm and hands as tender, and spirits as generous as the only ones she had ever known . . . when she was seven years old.

I WISH YOU ALL A MERRY CHRISTMAS! I WISH US ALL A WORLD AS KIND AS A CHILD CAN IMAGINE IT!

CHRISTMAS IN MAINE

by Robert P. Tristram Coffin

If you want to have a Christmas like the one we had on Paradise Farm when I was a boy, you will have to hunt up a saltwater farm on the Maine coast, with bays on both sides of it, and a road that goes around all sorts of bays, up over Misery Hill and down, and through the fir trees so close together that they brush you and your horse on both cheeks. That is the only kind of place a Christmas like that grows. You must have a clear December night, with blue Maine stars snapping like sapphires with the cold, and the big moon flooding full over Misery, and lighting up the snowy spruce boughs like crushed diamonds. You ought to be wrapped in a buffalo robe to your nose, and be sitting in a family pung, and have your breath trailing along with you as you slide over the dry, whistling snow. You will have to sing the songs we sang, "God Rest You Merry,

Gentlemen" and "Joy to the World," and you will be able to see your songs around you in the air like blue smoke. That's the only way to come to a Paradise Christmas.

And you really should cross over at least one broad bay on the ice, and feel the tide rifts bounce you as the runners slide over them. And if the whole bay booms out, every now and then, and the sound echoes around the wooded islands for miles, you will be having the sort of ride we loved to take from town, the night before Christmas.

I won't insist on your having a father like ours to drive you home to your Christmas. One with a wide moustache full of icicles, and eyes like the stars of the morning. That would be impossible, anyway, for there has been only one of him in the world. But it is too bad, just the same. For you won't have the stories we had by the fireplace. You won't hear about Kitty Wells who died beautifully in song just as the sun came over the tops of the eastern mountains and just after her lover had named the wedding day, and you will not hear how Kitty's departure put an end to his mastering the banjo:

> *But death came in my cabin door*
> *And took from me my joy, my pride,*
> *And when they said she was no more,*
> *I laid my banjo down and cried.*

But you will be able to have the rooms of the farmhouse banked with emerald jewels clustered on bayberry boughs, clumps of everlasting roses with gold spots in the middle of them, tree evergreens, and the evergreen that runs all over the Maine woods and every so often puts up a bunch of palm leaves. And there will be rose-hips stuck in pine boughs. And caraway seeds in every crust and cookie in the place.

An aunt should be on hand, an aunt who believes in yarrow tea and the Bible as the two things needed to keep children well. She will read the Nativity story aloud to the family, hurrying over the really exciting parts that happened at the stable, and bearing down hard on what the angels had to say and the more edify-

ing points that might be supposed to improve small boys who like to lie too long abed in the mornings. She will put a moral even into Christmas greens, and she will serve well as a counter-irritant to the overeating of mince pies. She will insist on all boys washing behind their ears, and that will keep her days full to the brim.

The Christmas tree will be there, and it will have a top so high that it will have to be bent over and run along the ceiling of the sitting room. It will be the best fir tree of the Paradise forests, picked from ten thousand almost perfect ones, and every bough on it will be like old-fashioned fans wide open. You will have brought it home that very morning, on the sled, from Dragonfly Spring.

Dragonfly Spring was frozen solid to the bottom, and you could look down into it and see the rainbows where you dented it with your copper-toed boots, see whole ferns caught motionless in the crystal deeps, and a frog, too, down there, with hands just like a baby's on him. Your small sister — the one with hair like new honey laid open — in the middle of a honeycomb — had cried out, "Let's dig him up and take him home and warm his feet!" (She is the same sister who ate up all your more vivid pastel crayons when you were away at school, and then ate up all the things you had been pretty sure were toadstools in Bluejay Woods, when you were supposed to be keeping an eye on her, but were buried so deep in *Mosses from an Old Manse* that you couldn't have been dug up with horses and oxen.)

Your dog, Snoozer, who is a curious and intricate combination of many merry pugs and many mournful hound-dogs, was snuffling all the time, hot on the feather-stitching the mice had made from bush to bush while you were felling the Christmas tree. A red squirrel was taking a white-pine cone apart on a hemlock bough, and telling Snoozer what he thought of him and all other dogs, the hour or so you were there.

There will be a lot of aunts in the house besides the Biblical one. Aunts of every complexion and cut. Christmas is the one time that even the most dubious of aunts take on value. One of them can make up wreaths, another can make rock candy that puts a tremble on the heart, and still another can steer your twelve-seater bobsled — and turn it over, bottom up, with you all in just the right place for a fine spill.

There will be uncles, too, to hold one end of the molasses taffy you will pull sooner or later, yanking it out till it flashes and turns into corn-silk that almost floats in the air, tossing your end of it back and probably lassoing your uncle around his neck as you do it, and pulling out a new rope of solid honey.

The uncles will smoke, too, and that will be a help to all the younger brothers who have been smoking their acorn-pipes out in the wood-shed, and who don't want their breaths to give them away. The uncles will make themselves useful in other ways. They will rig up schooners no bigger than your thumb, with shrouds like cobwebs; they will mend the bob-sled, tie up cut fingers, and sew on buttons after you shin up to the cupola in the barn; and — if you get on the good side of them — they will saw you up so much birch wood that you won't have to lay hand to a bucksaw till after New Year's.

There will be cousins by the cart load. He-ones and she-ones. The size you can sit on, and the size that can sit on you. Enough for two armies, on Little Round Top and on Big, up in the haymow. You will play Gettysburg there till your heads are full of hay chaff that will keep six aunts busy cleaning it out. And then you will come in to the house and down a whole crock of molasses cookies — the kind that go up in peaks in the middle — which somebody was foolish enough to leave the cover off.

Every holiday that came along, in my father's house, was the gathering of an Anglo-Saxon clan. My father was built for lots of people 'round him. But Christmas was a whole assembly of the West Saxons! My father wanted people in squads. There were men with wide moustaches and men with smooth places on top of their heads, women wide and narrow. Cousins of the second and third water, even, were there. Hired men, too. They were special guests and had to be handled with kid gloves, as New England hired men must. They had to have the best of everything, and you could not find fault with them, as you could with uncles, if they smacked you for upsetting their coffee into their laps. Babies were underfoot in full cry. The older children hunted in packs. The table had to be pieced out with flour barrels and bread boards and ironing boards. It was a house's length from the head of the table, where your father sat and manufactured the roast up into slivers, to your mother dishing out the pork gravy. Whole geese disappeared on the way down. The Christmas cake, which had been left sweetly to itself for a month to age into a miracle, was a narrow isthmus when it got to Mother. But Mother always said that Christmas, to her, was watching other people eat. She was the kind of mother who claimed that the neck and the back of the chicken were the tastiest parts.

The prize goose, whom you had brought up by hand and called Oliver Cromwell, Old Iron-sides, or some such distinguished title, was duly carved. And Father found his wishbone snow-white and you all applauded, for that meant lots of snow and two more months of coasting on your sleds. There were mince pies by the legion. And if Uncle Tom were there, a whole raccoon baked just for him and girt around with browned sweet potatoes. Mother's wild strawberry jam was there on deck, winking at you like rubies from the holes in tarts that melted away like bubbles in the mouth. That dinner was three hours in Beulah Land!

Of course, there will be an apple pudding at such a season. Steamed in a lard bucket, and cut open with a string. A sauce of oranges and lemons to make an ocean around each steaming volcano of suet and russet apples as it falls crumbling from the loop of twine. It will have to be steamed in the boiler, if your Christmas is to be the size of ours, and cooked in a ten-pound lard pail. Better use a cod line instead of the twine of other holidays, to parcel it out to the members of the clan.

The whole nation of you in the house will go from one thing to another. The secret of the best Christmases is everybody doing the same things all at the same time. You will all fall to and string cranberries and popcorn for the tree, and the bright lines each of you has a hold on will radiate from the tree like ribbons on a maypole. Everybody will have needles and thread in the mouth, you will all get in each other's way, but that is the art of doing Christmas right. You will all bundle up together for a ride in the afternoon. You had better take the horse-sled, as the pung will not begin to hold you. And even then a dozen or so of assorted uncles and aunts and cousins will have to come trooping after through the deep snow, and wait for their turn on the straw in the sled. Smaller cousins will fall off the sides in great knots and never be missed, and the hullabaloo will roar on and send the rabbits flying away through the woods, showing their bobbing scuts.

Everybody will hang presents on the tree at once, when the sun has dipped down into the spruces in the west and you are back home in the sitting-room. There will be no nonsense of tiptoeing up and edging a package on when nobody is looking. Everybody knows who is giving him what. There is no mystery about it. Aunt Ella has made rag dinahs for all hands and the cook — for all under fourteen years of age — and she does not care who knows it. The dinahs are all alike, except that those for the children whose lower garments are forked, have forked red-flannel pants instead of red-flannel petticoats. They all have pearl button eyes and stocking toes for faces. There will be so many hands at work on the tree at once that the whole thing will probably go over two or three times and it will be well to make it fast with a hawser or so.

And then you will turn right around and take the presents off again, the minute you have got them all on and have lighted the candles up. There will be no waiting, with small children sitting around with aching hearts. The real candles will be a problem, in all that mass of spills. Boughs will take fire here and there. But there will be plenty of uncles around to crush out the small bonfires in their big brown hands. All the same, it would be well to have an Uncle Thomas who can take up a live coal in his thumb and finger, and light his pipe from it, cool as a cucumber. Better turn the extinguishing of the tree over to him.

There will be boughten presents, to be sure — a turtle of cardboard in a glassed, dainty box, hung on springs and swimming for dear life with all four feet, and popguns with their barrels ringed and streaked with red and yellow lines. Why popguns should be painted like broomsticks is one of the mysteries, along with the blue paint you always find on Maine cartwheels. Somebody will probably get one of those Swiss music-boxes that will eke out a ghostly "Last Rose of Summer," if tenderly cranked. There should be those little bottles of transparent candies, with real syrup in them, which I used to live for through the years. And there must be a German doll for every last girl, with mountains of yellow hair and cheeks looking as if life were a continuous blowing of bubbles. Boughten things are all right.

But if it is going to be our kind of Christmas, most of the presents will be homemade. Socks knit by the aunt who swears only by useful gifts. You have seen those socks growing up from their white toes for the last two weeks. Wristers, always red. A box of Aunt Louise's candied orange peel that she will never let on to anybody how she makes. Your father will have made a sled for every mother's son and daughter of you, with a bluebird, or robin redbreast, more real than life, painted on each one and your name underneath. You will never have another present to match that, though you grow up and become Midases. Popcorn balls, big as muskmelons, will be common ware. They will be dripping with molasses, and will stick your wristers and socks and other treasures together.

But the pith of the party is not reached until the whole nation of you sits down in rocking chairs, or lies down on their bellies in front of the six-foot gulf of the fireplace. The presents are all stowed, heaped and tucked away, stuck fast with cornballs. The last lamps are out. The firelight dances on the ceiling. It lights up the steel engraving of Major McCullock leaping from Kentucky to Ohio, with ten thousand mounted redskins yelling and reining in their steeds behind him. It lights up Daniel Boone's daughters as they lean away toward their boat's end and scream their silent screams and drop their water lilies, while Indian head after Indian head grins up at them from the river of the Dark and Bloody Ground.

All the babies will be hushed and put away. All the younger fry will be more than half asleep. The toasted cheese and red herring will go 'round. The herring, by the way — if you are worthy to wear my shoes after me — which you yourself have smoked with green oak, and have gotten your own two eyes so that they looked like two burnt holes in a blanket while doing it, and have hugely enjoyed every hour of it all.

Then you had best find a fair substitute for my father. Give him the best chair in the house — and the way to find *that* is to push the cat out of it — and let him tear! He will begin by telling you about such people as the brilliant young ladies of Philadelphia who had a piano too big to fit their house, so they put it on the porch and played on it through the open window. Then he will sit back and work his way to the Caliph of Bagdad, who had a daughter so homely that she had to wear a sack on her head when her suitors came awooing, and how she fell down a well and made herself a great fortune, and won the handsomest husband that ever wore a turban. That story, by the way, you will not find in the *Arabian Nights* even though you look for it, as I have done, till you have gray hairs in your head.

The firelight will get into your father's eyes and on his hair. He will move on from Bagdad to Big Bethel, and tell you all how the Yankee campfires looked like the high Milky Way itself, all night long before the battle; how the dew silvered every sleeping soldier's face and the stacked rifles, as the dawn came up with the new day and death. And you will hug your knees and hear the wind outside going its rounds among the snowy pines, and you will listen on till the story you are hearing becomes a part of the old winds of the world and the motion of the bright stars. And probably it will take two uncles at least to carry you to bed.

HOOFBEATS ON A BRIDGE

by Alexander Woollcott

Last December my path by chance at Christmastime crossed that of a neighbor of mine who was also far from home. Thus it befell that Katharine Cornell and I, she trouping with a play and I on a lecture tour, observed the day by dining together in a Seattle hotel. I remember that my present to her was a telephone call whereby she could send her love across the continent to a friend we both cherish — a dear friend, endowed with so many more senses than the paltry five allotted to the rest of us that I have no doubt she knew what we were up to before ever the bell rang in that Connecticut cottage of hers and the operator said, "Seattle calling Miss Helen Keller."

The year before that I had spent every waking hour of the sacred day writing (or rehearsing with the orchestra) for a broadcast that would go out on Christmas night across America and for another that would reach the British Isles at 9 P.M. on Boxing Day. And I ask no greater boon than that this Christmas will once again find me, as often in recent years, so neck-deep in work that from dawn to sundown I shall have no time to remember the Christmases that used to be.

I have said that in that Seattle hotel Miss Cornell and I were two travelers far from home. But mine was more than a mere three thousand miles away. It was three thousand miles and a quarter of a century away. And if nowadays I try to fill each Christmas Eve with the hubbub of many manufactured preoccupations, it is probably in the dread of being trapped alone in the twilight by the ghost of Christmas Past. Then, sharp but unmistakable and inexpressibly dear to me, there would be borne across the years a music that is for me more full of Christmas than sleigh bells ever were or all the carols flung down from all the belfries in the world. It is the ghost of a sound that must haunt many an old dirt road — the thud of hoofbeats on a wooden bridge. By them when I was young we could tell on the darkest night that we were nearing home.

The house where I was born was a vast, ramshackle, weather-beaten building, which had already seen better days. But not recently. A tangle of vines — trumpet vines and wistaria and white grape and crimson rambler — curtained the twelve ground-floor windows looking out toward the high road, and tactfully concealed the fact that the house had not been painted since before the Civil War. We used to speak grandly of the ballroom; but I cannot remember a time when the musicians' gallery was not taken up with stacks of old *Harper's* and other dusty, unbound magazines. In my time, at least, we could not hold a dance without sweeping the fallen plaster from the floor. But this dear old house, which had belonged to my grandfather, remained the one constant in the problem of a far-flung tribe, and back to it most of us managed to make our way at Christmastime. Often the railroad fare was hard to come by; but somehow, as long as my mother was alive, from school or college or work I

made my way home every Christmas for more than twenty years.

What ticking off of the days on the calendar as the time grew near! Then at last the arrival at the railroad station after dark on Christmas Eve, with home only five miles away. I could always find a hack — it would smell of mothballs and manure — and the driver could usually tell me how many of the cousins had got there ahead of me. A dozen or so, maybe. Then the jog trot in the deepening darkness, with one eager passenger inside — hungry for home and no longer counting the days or even the minutes. By this time I was counting the bridges. I knew them by heart. Three more. Two more. At the next, if I sat forward and peered through the window, I would see the house through the leafless trees, every window down the long front agleam with a welcoming lamp, each light a token of all the loving-kindness that dwelt under that old, shingled roof. Then the long, slow pull up the drive. Before I could get out of the hack and pay the driver, the door would be flung open, and my mother would be standing on the threshold.

Small wonder I like to be busy at Christmas. Small wonder I feel a twist at my heart whenever at any time anywhere in the world I hear the sound of a hoofbeat on a wooden bridge.

A MISERABLE, MERRY CHRISTMAS

by Lincoln Steffens

My father's business seems to have been one of slow but steady growth. He and his local partner, Llewelen Tozer, had no vices. They were devoted to their families and to "the store," which grew with the town, which, in turn, grew and changed with the State from a gambling, mining, and ranching community to one of farming, fruit-raising, and building. Immigration poured in, not gold-seekers now, but farmers, business men and home-builders, who settled, planted, reaped, and traded in the natural riches of the State, which prospered greatly, "making" the people who will tell you that they "made the State."

As the store made money and I was getting through the primary school, my father bought a lot uptown, at Sixteenth and K Streets, and built us a "big" house. It was off the line of the city's growth, but it was near a new grammar school for me and my sisters, who were coming along fast after me. This interested the family, not me. They were always talking about school; they had not had much of it themselves, and they thought they had missed something. My father used to write speeches, my mother verses, and their theory seems to have been that they had talents which a school would have brought to flower. They agreed, therefore, that their children's gifts should have all the schooling there was. My view, then, was that I had had a good deal of it already, and I was not interested at all. It interfered with my own business, with my own education.

And indeed I remember very little of the primary school. I learned to read, write, spell, and count, and reading was all right. I had a practical use for books, which I searched for ideas and parts to play with, characters to be, lives to live. The primary school was probably a good one, but I cannot remember learning anything except to read aloud "perfectly" from a teacher whom I adored and who was fond of me. She used to embrace me before the whole class and she favored me openly to the scandal of the other pupils, who called me "teacher's pet." Their scorn did not trouble me; I saw and I said that they envied me. I paid for her favor, however. When she married I had queer, unhappy feelings of resentment; I didn't want to meet her husband, and when I had to I would not speak to him. He laughed, and she kissed me — happily for her, to me offensively. I never would see her again. Through with her, I fell in love immediately with Miss Kay, another grown young woman who wore glasses and had a fine, clear skin. I did not know her, I only saw her in the street, but once I followed her, found out where she lived, and used to pass her house, hoping to see her, and yet choking with embarrassment if I did. This fascination lasted for years; it was still a sort of super-romance to me when later I was "going with" another girl nearer my own age.

What interested me in our new neighborhood was not the school, nor the room I was to have in the house all to myself, but the stable which was built back of the house. My father let me direct the making of a stall, a little smaller than the other stalls, for my pony, and I prayed and hoped and my sister Lou believed that that meant that I would get the pony, perhaps for Christmas. I pointed out to her that there were three other stalls and no horses at all. This I said in order that she should answer it. She could not. My father, sounded, said that some day we might have horses and a cow; meanwhile a stable added to the value of a house. "Some day" is a pain to a boy who lives in and knows only "now." My good little sisters, to comfort me, remarked that Christmas was coming, but Christmas was always coming and grown-ups were always talking about it, asking you what you wanted and then giving you what they wanted you to have. Though everybody knew what I wanted, I told them all again. My mother knew what I told God, too, every night. I wanted a pony, and to make sure that they understood, I declared that I wanted nothing else.

"Nothing but a pony?" my father asked.

"Nothing," I said.

"Not even a pair of high boots?"

That was hard. I did want boots, but I stuck to the pony. "No, not even boots."

"Nor candy? There ought to be something to fill your stocking with, and Santa Claus can't put a pony into a stocking."

That was true, and he couldn't lead a pony down the chimney either. But no. "All I want is a pony," I said. "If I can't have a pony, give me nothing, nothing."

Now I had been looking myself for the pony I wanted, going to sales stables, inquiring of horsemen, and I had seen several that would do. My father let me "try" them. I tried so many ponies that I was learning fast to sit a horse. I chose several, but my father always found some fault with them. I was in despair. When Christmas was at hand I had given up all hope of a pony, and on Christmas Eve I hung up my stocking along with my sisters', of whom, by the way, I now had three. I haven't mentioned them or their coming because, you understand, they were girls, and girls, young girls, counted for nothing in my manly life. They did not mind me either; they were so happy that Christmas Eve that I caught some of their merriment. I speculated on what I'd get; I hung up the

biggest stocking I had, and we all went reluctantly to bed to wait till morning. Not to sleep; not right away. We were told that we must not only sleep promptly, we must not wake up till seven-thirty the next morning — or if we did, we must not go to the fireplace for our Christmas. Impossible.

We did sleep that night, but we woke up at six A.M. We lay in our beds and debated through the open doors whether to obey till, say, half-past six. Then we bolted. I don't know who started it, but there was a rush. We all disobeyed; we raced to disobey and get first to the fireplace in the front room downstairs. And there they were, the gifts, all sorts of wonderful things, mixed-up piles of presents; only, as I disentangled the mess, I saw that my stocking was empty; it hung limp; not a thing in it; and under and around it — nothing. My sisters had knelt down, each by her pile of gifts; they were squealing with delight, till they looked up and saw me standing there in my nightgown with nothing. They left their piles to come to me and look with me at my empty place. Nothing. They felt my stocking: nothing.

I don't remember whether I cried at that moment, but my sisters did. They ran with me back to my bed, and there we all cried till I became indignant. That helped some. I got up, dressed and, driving my sisters away, I went alone out into the yard, down to the stable, and there, all by myself, I wept. My mother came out to me by and by; she found me in my pony stall, sobbing on the floor, and she tried to comfort me. But I heard my father outside; he had come part way with her, and she was having some sort of angry quarrel with him. She tried to comfort me; besought me to come to breakfast. I could not; I wanted no comfort and no breakfast. She left me and went on into the house with sharp words for my father.

I don't know what kind of breakfast the family had. My sisters said it was "awful." They were ashamed to enjoy their own toys. They came to me, and I was rude. I ran away from them. I went around to the front of the house, sat down on the steps, and, the crying over, I ached. I was wronged, I was hurt — I can feel now what I felt then, and I am sure that if one could see the wounds upon our hearts, there would be found still upon mine a scar from that terrible Christmas morning. And my father, the practical joker, he must have been hurt, too, a little. I saw him looking out of the window. He was watching me or something for an hour or two, drawing back the curtain ever so little lest I catch him, but I saw his face, and I think I can see now the anxiety upon it, the worried impatience.

After — I don't know how long — surely an hour or two — I was brought to the climax of my agony by the sight of a man riding a pony down the street, a pony and a brand-new saddle; the most beautiful saddle I ever saw, and it was a boy's saddle; the man's feet were not in the stirrups; his legs were too long. The outfit was perfect; it was the realization of all my dreams, the answer to all my prayers. A fine new bridle, with a light curb bit. And the pony! As he drew near, I saw that the pony was really a small horse, what we called an Indian pony, a bay, with black mane and tail, and one white foot and a white star on his forehead. For such a horse as that I would have given, I could have forgiven, anything.

But the man, a disheveled fellow with a blackened eye and a fresh-cut face, came along, reading the numbers on the houses, and, as my hopes — my impossible hopes — rose, he looked at our door and passed by, he and the pony, and the saddle and the bridle. Too much. I fell upon the steps, and having wept before, I broke now into such a flood of tears that I was a floating wreck when I heard a voice.

"Say, kid," it said, "do you know a boy named Lennie Steffens?"

I looked up. It was the man on the pony, back again, at our horse block.

"Yes," I spluttered through my tears. "That's me."

"Well," he said, "then this is your horse. I've been looking all over for you and your house. Why don't you put your number where it can be seen?"

"Get down," I said, running out to him.

He went on saying something about "ought to have got here at seven o'clock; told me to bring the nag here and tie him to your post and leave him for you. But, hell, I got into a drunk — and a fight — and a hospital, and —"

"Get down," I said.

He got down, and he boosted me up to the saddle. He offered to fit the stirrups to me, but I didn't want him to. I wanted to ride.

"What's the matter with you?" he said, angrily. "What you crying for? Don't you like the horse? He's a dandy, this horse. I know him of old. He's fine at cattle; he'll drive 'em alone."

I hardly heard, I could scarcely wait, but he persisted. He adjusted the stirrups, and then, finally, off I rode, slowly, at a walk, so happy, so thrilled, that I did not know what I was doing. I did not look back at the house or the man, I rode off up the street, taking note of everything — of the reins, of the pony's long mane, of the carved leather saddle. I had never seen anything so beautiful. And mine! I was going to ride up past Miss Kay's house. But I noticed on the horn of the saddle some stains like rain-drops, so I turned and trotted home, not to the house but to the stable. There was the family, father, mother, sisters, all working for me, all happy. They had been putting in place the tools of my new business; blankets, currycomb, brush, pitchfork — everything, and there was hay in the loft.

"What did you come back so soon for?" somebody asked. "Why didn't you go on riding?"

I pointed to the stains. "I wasn't going to get my new saddle rained on," I said. And my father laughed. "It isn't raining," he said. "Those are not rain-drops."

"They are tears," my mother gasped, and she gave my father a look which sent him off to the house. Worse still, my mother offered to wipe away the tears still running out of my eyes. I gave her such a look as she had given him, and she went off after my father, drying her own tears. My sisters remained and we all unsaddled the pony, put on his halter, led him to his stall, tied and fed him. It began really to rain; so all the rest of that memorable day we curried and combed that pony. The girls plaited his mane, forelock, and tail, while I pitchforked hay to him and curried and brushed, curried and brushed. For a change we brought him out to drink; we led him up and down, blanketed like a race-horse; we took turns at that. But the best, the most inexhaustible fun, was to clean him. When we went reluctantly to our midday Christmas dinner, we all smelt of horse, and my sisters had to wash their faces and hands. I was asked to, but I wouldn't, till my mother bade me look in the mirror. Then I washed up — quick. My face was caked with the muddy lines of tears that had coursed over my cheeks to my mouth. Having washed away that shame, I ate my dinner, and as I ate I grew hungrier and hungrier. It was my first meal that day, and as I filled up on the turkey and the stuffing, the cranberries and the pies, the fruit and the nuts — as I swelled, I could laugh. My mother said I still choked and sobbed now and then, but I laughed, too; I saw and enjoyed my sisters' presents till — I had to go out and attend to my pony, who was there, really and truly there, the promise, the beginning, of a happy double life. And — I went and looked to make sure — there was the saddle, too, and the bridle.

But that Christmas, which my father had planned so carefully, was it the best or the worst I ever knew? He often asked me that; I never could answer as a boy. I think now that it was both. It covered the whole distance from broken-hearted misery to bursting happiness — too fast. A grown-up could hardly have stood it.

NOW IT HAS COME

by Washington Irving

Now Christmas is come,
Let's beat up the drum,
And call all our neighbors together,
And when they appear,
Let us make them such cheer
As will keep out the wind and the weather.

WHEN CHRISTMAS
WENT OUTDOORS

by Grady Johnson

Thirty-five years ago this Christmas, ten-year-old David Jonathan Sturgeon lay in bed in Denver, doomed to die. To cheer him, his father lit a small Christmas tree in his sickroom.

Young David pointed through the window at an evergreen growing on the front lawn, exclaiming, "Oh, Daddy, please put some lights on that tree, too. It would look wonderful."

His father, David D. Sturgeon, operator of an electrical business, strung colored lights on the evergreen and David lay there smiling as he watched them sparkle like emeralds and rubies against their ermine mantle of snow.

The tree was the talk of the town. In horse-drawn carriages and chugging automobiles, people came from miles around to drive slowly past the Sturgeon home and admire the tree which Denverites proudly believe was the first lighted living Christmas tree in the land.

The Christmas after next, little David was dead. But neighbors, who had marveled at his tree, lit trees in their own yards and gardens, turning their section of town into a glittering fairyland. House by house, block by block, the idea spread; and through the years, more and more of these dazzling monuments to a dying boy's wish appeared.

Eight years later, in San Francisco, another little boy was sick at Christmastime. Because

the lad couldn't see the family tree, Clarence F. "Sandy" Pratt painted some full-size light globes and strung them on a wire around an evergreen on his lawn across the street.

Like Denver's tree, it attracted much attention. And before New Year's Eve, the sick boy was well.

This so impressed Sandy Pratt that he resolved to spend the rest of his life persuading others not only to light living trees but to plant them. He organized the Outdoor Christmas Tree Association of California, and began sending two-year-old redwood seedlings to anyone who would promise to care for them and light them at Christmastime.

For a quarter of a century, Pratt spread the gospel of the living Christmas tree via radio, the press and lectures, and dug and shipped — for mailing charges only — redwood seedlings, which grow only along a narrow coastal strip stretching from California to Oregon, to people in nearly every city of the U.S., to soldiers in the South Pacific, Europe and the Holy Land.

Today, in city parks, along highways, on dark and snow-drifted lawns alike, lighted living trees remind millions of the birth of Christ. In fact, there is probably no city or town in

the nation without its Christmas Tree Lane in one form or another. Santa Cruz County, for instance, lights 25 miles of giant redwoods along the Pacific Coast, and Orange County, to the south, stages an annual contest lighting "Forty Miles of Christmas Shrines."

While it is impossible to say exactly when and where the first outdoor tree was lit, to Sturgeon and Pratt at least must go credit for spreading the heartwarming custom. In December, 1945, NBC broadcast a tribute to Denver and to Sturgeon for originating it, with members of the family retelling the story of David's idea. At the same time, from California's Sequoia National Park, gray-haired, ruddy-faced Sandy Pratt was taking part in services broadcast from the General Sherman Redwood, the world's largest tree, which was lit every year under Pratt's sponsorship.

Until his death three years ago, at 75, Sandy could be found most any day with his shovel, buckets and wet sacks, digging, tagging and numbering his seedlings. He dug and shipped more than 14,000 and received hundreds of letters from people telling him how their trees were faring — some had grown 40 feet high. He grieved when one was reported dying, for he agreed wholeheartedly with Luther Burbank's admonition upon seeing a trainload of logs pass.

"Do not build me a monument," the great botanist told his wife in a choking voice. "Plant a tree!"

Today, there are thousands of living monuments to Sandy Pratt — and they were planted within his lifetime.

MY FIRST CHRISTMAS TREE

by Hamlin Garland

I will begin by saying that we never had a Christmas tree in our house in the Wisconsin coulée; indeed, my father never saw one in a family circle till he saw that which I set up for my own children last year. But we celebrated Christmas in those days, always, and I cannot remember a time when we did not all hang up our stockings for "Sandy Claws" to fill. As I look back upon those days it seems as if the snows were always deep, the night skies crystal clear, and the stars especially lustrous with frosty sparkles of blue and yellow fire — and probably this was so, for we lived in a Northern land where winter was usually stern and always long.

I recall one Christmas when "Sandy" brought me a sled, and a horse that stood on rollers — a wonderful tin horse which I very shortly split in two in order to see what his insides were. Father traded a cord of wood for the sled, and the horse cost twenty cents — but they made the day wonderful.

Another notable Christmas Day, as I stood in our front yard, mid-leg deep in snow, a neighbor drove by closely muffled in furs, while behind his seat his son, a lad of twelve or fifteen, stood beside a barrel of apples, and as he passed he hurled a glorious big red one at me. It missed me, but bored a deep, round hole in the soft snow. I thrill yet with the remembered joy of burrowing for that delicious bomb. Nothing will ever smell quite as good as that Wine Sap or Northern Spy or whatever it was. It was a wayward impulse on the part of the boy in the sleigh, but it warms my heart after more than forty years.

We had no chimney in our home, but the stocking-hanging was a ceremony nevertheless. My parents, and especially my mother, entered into it with the best of humor. They always put up their own stockings or permitted us to do it for them — and they always laughed next morning when they found potatoes or ears of corn in them. I can see now that my mother's laugh had a tear in it, for she loved pretty things and seldom got any during the years that we lived in the coulée.

When I was ten years old we moved to Mitchell County, an Iowa prairie land, and there we prospered in such wise that our stockings always held toys of some sort, and even my mother's stocking occasionally sagged with a simple piece of jewelry or a new comb or brush. But the thought of a family tree remained the luxury of millionaire city dwellers; indeed it was not till my fifteenth or sixteenth year that our Sunday school rose to the extravagance of a tree, and it is of this wondrous festival that I write.

The land about us was only partly cultivated at this time, and our district schoolhouse, a bare little box, was set bleakly on the prairie; but the Burr Oak schoolhouse was not only larger but it stood beneath great oaks as well and possessed the charm of a forest background through which a stream ran silently. It was our chief social center. There of a Sunday a regular preacher held "Divine service" with Sunday school as a sequence. At night — usually on Friday nights — the young people met in "lyceums," as we called them, to debate great questions or to "speak pieces" and read essays; and here it was that I saw my first Christmas tree.

I walked to that tree across four miles of moonlit snow. Snow? No, it was a floor of diamonds, a magical world, so beautiful that my heart still aches with the wonder of it and with the regret that it has all gone — gone with the keen eyes and the bounding pulses of the boy.

Our home at this time was a small frame house on the prairie almost directly west of the Burr Oak grove, and as it was too cold to take the horses out my brother and I, with our tall boots, our visored caps and our long woolen mufflers, started forth afoot, defiant of the cold. We left the gate on the trot, bound for a sight of the glittering unknown. The snow was deep and we moved side by side in the grooves made by the hoofs of the horses, setting our feet in the shine left by the broad shoes of the wood sleighs whose going had smoothed the way for us.

Our breaths rose like smoke in the still air. It must have been ten below zero, but that did not trouble us in those days, and at last we came in sight of the lights, in sound of the singing, the laughter, the bells of the feast.

It was a poor little building without tower or bell and its low walls had but three windows on a side, and yet it seemed very imposing to me that night as I crossed the threshold and faced the strange people who packed it to the door. I say "strange people," for though I had seen most of them many times they all seemed somehow alien to me that night. I was an irregular attendant at Sunday school and did not expect a present, therefore I stood against the wall and gazed with open-eyed marveling at the shining pine which stood where the pulpit was wont to be. I was made to feel the more embarrassed by reason of the remark of a boy who accused me of having forgotten to comb my hair.

This was not true, but the cap I wore always matted my hair down over my brow, and then, when I lifted it off invariably disarranged it completely. Nevertheless I felt guilty — and hot. I don't suppose my hair was artistically barbered that night — I rather guess Mother had used the shears — and I can believe that I looked the half-wild colt that I was; but there was no call for that youth to direct attention to my unavoidable shagginess.

I don't think the tree had many candles, and I don't remember that it glittered with golden apples. But it was loaded with presents, and the girls coming and going clothed in bright garments made me forget my own looks — I think they made me forget to remove my overcoat, which was a sodden thing of poor cut and worse quality. I think I must have stood agape for nearly two hours listening to the songs, noting every motion of Adoniram Burtch and Asa Walker as they directed the ceremonies and prepared the way for the great event — that is to say, for the coming of Santa Claus himself.

A furious jingling of bells, a loud voice outside, the lifting of a window, the nearer clash of bells, and the dear old Saint appeared (in the person of Stephen Bartle) clothed in a red robe, a belt of sleigh bells, and a long white beard. The children cried out, "Oh!" The girls tittered and shrieked with excitement, and the boys laughed and clapped their hands. Then "Sandy" made a little speech about being glad to see us all, but as he had many other places to visit, and as there were a great many pre-

sents to distribute, he guessed he'd have to ask some of the many pretty girls to help him. So he called upon Betty Burtch and Hattie Knapp — and I for one admired his taste, for they were the most popular maids of the school.

They came up blushing, and a little bewildered by the blaze of publicity thus blown upon them. But their native dignity asserted itself, and the distribution of the presents began. I have a notion now that the fruit upon

the tree was mostly bags of popcorn and "corny copias" of candy, but as my brother and I stood there that night and saw everybody, even the rowdiest boy, getting something we felt aggrieved and rebellious. We forgot that we had come from afar — we only knew that we were being left out.

But suddenly, in the midst of our gloom, my brother's name was called, and a lovely girl with a gentle smile handed him a bag of popcorn. My heart glowed with gratitude. Somebody had thought of us; and when she came to me, saying sweetly, "Here's something for you," I had not words to thank her. This happened nearly forty years ago, but her smile, her outstretched hand, her sympathetic eyes are vividly before me as I write. She was sorry for the shock-headed boy who stood against the wall, and her pity made the little box of candy a casket of pearls. The fact that I swallowed the jewels on the road home does not take from the reality of my adoration.

At last I had to take my final glimpse of that wondrous tree, and I well remember the walk home. My brother and I traveled in wordless companionship. The moon was sinking toward the west, and the snow crust gleamed with a million fairy lamps. The sentinel watchdogs barked from lonely farmhouses, and the wolves answered from the ridges. Now and then sleighs passed us with lovers sitting two and two, and the bells on their horses had the remote music of romance to us whose boots drummed like clogs of wood upon the icy road.

Our house was dark as we approached and entered it, but how deliciously warm it seemed after the pitiless wind! I confess we made straight for the cupboard for a mince pie, a doughnut and a bowl of milk!

As I write this there stands in my library a thick-branched, beautifully tapering fir tree covered with the gold and purple apples of Hesperides, together with crystal ice points, green and red and yellow candles, clusters of gilded grapes, wreaths of metallic frost, and glittering angels swinging in ecstasy; but I doubt if my children will ever know the keen pleasure (that is almost pain) which came to my brother and to me in those Christmas days when an orange was not a breakfast fruit, but a casket of incense and of spice, a message from the sunlands of the South.

That was our compensation — we brought to our Christmastime a keen appetite and empty hands. And the lesson of it all is, if we are seeking a lesson, that it is better to give to those who want than to those for whom "we ought to do something because they did something for us last year."

CHRISTMAS AT ORCHARD HOUSE

by Louisa May Alcott

"Christmas won't be Christmas without any presents," grumbled Jo, lying on the rug.

"It's so dreadful to be poor!" sighed Meg, looking down at her old dress.

"I don't think it's fair for some girls to have plenty of pretty things, and other girls nothing at all," added little Amy, with an injured sniff.

"We've got father and mother and each other," said Beth contentedly, from her corner.

The four young faces on which the firelight shone brightened at the cheerful words, but darkened again as Jo said sadly, —

"We haven't got father, and shall not have him for a long time." She didn't say "perhaps never," but each silently added it, thinking of father far away, where the fighting was.

Nobody spoke for a minute; then Meg said in an altered tone, "You know the reason mother proposed not having any presents this Christmas was because it is going to be a hard winter for everyone; and she thinks we ought not to spend money for pleasure, when our men are suffering so in the army. We can't do much, but we can make our little sacrifices, and ought to do it gladly. But I am afraid I don't." And Meg shook her head, as she thought regretfully of all the pretty things she wanted.

"But I don't think the little we should spend would do any good. We've each got a dollar, and the army wouldn't be much helped by our giving that. I agree not to expect anything from mother or you, but I do want to buy *Undine and Sintram* for myself; I've wanted to so long," said Jo, who was a bookworm.

"I planned to spend mine in new music," said Beth, with a little sigh, which no one heard but the hearth brush and kettle holder.

"I shall get a nice box of Faber's drawing-pencils; I really need them," said Amy decidedly.

"Mother didn't say anything about our money, and she won't wish us to give up everything. Let's each buy what we want, and have a little fun; I'm sure we work hard enough to earn it," cried Jo, examining the heels of her shoes in a gentlemanly manner.

"I know I do — teaching those tiresome children nearly all day, when I'm longing to enjoy myself at home," began Meg, in the complaining tone again.

"You don't have half such a hard time as I do," said Jo. "How would you like to be shut up for hours with a nervous, fussy old lady, who keeps you trotting, is never satisfied, and worries you till you're ready to fly out of the window or cry?"

"It's naughty to fret; but I do think washing dishes and keeping things tidy is the worst work in the world. It makes me cross; and my hands get so stiff, I can't practise well at all"; and Beth looked at her rough hands with a sigh that anyone could hear that time.

"I don't believe any of you suffer as I do," cried Amy; "for you don't have to go to school with impertinent girls, who plague you if you don't know your lessons, and laugh at your dresses, and label your father if he isn't rich, and insult you when your nose isn't nice."

"If you mean *libel*, I'd say so, and not talk about labels, as if papa was a pickle bottle," advised Jo, laughing.

"I know what I mean, and you needn't be *statirical* about it. It's proper to use good words, and improve your *vocabilary*," returned Amy, with dignity.

"Don't peck at one another, children. Don't you wish we had the money papa lost when we were little, Jo? Dear me! how happy and good we'd be, if we had no worries!" said Meg, who could remember better times.

"You said, the other day, you thought we were a deal happier than the King children, for they were fighting and fretting all the time, in spite of their money."

"So I did, Beth. Well, I think we are; for, though we do have to work, we make fun for ourselves, and are a pretty jolly set, as Jo would say."

"Jo does use such slang words!" observed Amy, with a reproving look at the long figure stretched on the rug. Jo immediately sat up, put her hands in her pockets, and began to whistle.

"Don't, Jo; it's so boyish!"

"That's why I do it."

"I detest rude, unladylike girls!"

"I hate affected, niminy-piminy chits!"

"Birds in their little nests agree," sang Beth, the peacemaker, with such a funny face that both sharp voices softened to a laugh, and the "pecking" ended for that time.

"Really, girls, you are both to be blamed," said Meg, beginning to lecture in her elder-sisterly fashion. "You are old enough to leave off boyish tricks, and to behave better, Josephine. It didn't matter so much when you were a little girl; but now you are so tall, and turn up your hair, you should remember that you are a young lady."

"I'm not! and if turning up my hair makes me one, I'll wear it in two tails till I'm twenty," cried Jo, pulling off her net, and shaking down a chestnut mane. "I hate to think I've got to grow up, and be Miss March, and wear long gowns, and look as prim as a China-aster! It's bad enough to be a girl, anyway, when I like boys' games and work and manners! I can't get over my disappointment in not being a boy; and it's worse than ever now, for I'm dying to go and fight with papa, and I can only stay at home and knit, like a poky old woman!" And Jo shook the blue army sock till the needles rattled like castanets, and her ball bounded across the room.

"Poor Jo! It's too bad, but it can't be helped; so you must try to be contented with making your name boyish, and playing brother to us girls," said Beth, stroking the rough head at her knee with a hand that all the dishwashing and dusting in the world could not make ungentle in its touch.

"As for you, Amy," continued Meg, "you are altogether too particular and prim. Your airs are funny now; but you'll grow up an affected little goose, if you don't take care. I like your nice manners and refined ways of speaking, when you don't try to be elegant; but your absurd words are as bad as Jo's slang."

"If Jo is a tomboy and Amy a goose, what

am I, please?" asked Beth, ready to share the lecture.

"You're a dear, and nothing else," answered Meg warmly; and no one contradicted her, for the "Mouse" was the pet of the family.

As young readers like to know "how people look," we will take this moment to give them a little sketch of the four sisters, who sat knitting away in the twilight, while the December snow fell quietly without, and the fire crackled cheerfully within. It was a comfortable old room, though the carpet was faded and the furniture very plain; for a good picture or two hung on the walls, books filled the recesses, chrysanthemums and Christmas roses bloomed in the windows, and a pleasant atmosphere of home-peace pervaded it.

Margaret, the eldest of the four, was sixteen, and very pretty, being plump and fair, with large eyes, plenty of soft, brown hair, a sweet mouth, and white hands, of which she was rather vain. Fifteen-year-old Jo was very tall,

thin, and brown, and reminded one of a colt; for she never seemed to know what to do with her long limbs, which were very much in her way. She had a decided mouth, a comical nose, and sharp, gray eyes, which appeared to see everything, and were by turns fierce, funny, or thoughtful. Her long, thick hair was her one beauty; but it was usually bundled into a net, to be out of her way. Round shoulders had Jo, big hands and feet, a fly-away look to her clothes, and the uncomfortable appearance of a girl who was rapidly shooting up into a woman, and didn't like it. Elizabeth — or Beth, as everyone called her — was a rosy, smooth-haired, bright-eyed girl of thirteen, with a shy manner, a timid voice, and a peaceful expression, which was seldom disturbed. Her father called her "Little Tranquillity," and the name suited her excellently; for she seemed to live in a happy world of her own, only venturing out to meet the few whom she trusted and loved. Amy, though the youngest, was a most important person — in her own opinion at least. A regular snow-maiden, with blue eyes, and yellow hair, curling on her shoulders, pale and slender, and always carrying herself like a young lady mindful of her manners. What the characters of the four sisters were we will leave to be found out.

The clock struck six; and, having swept up the hearth, Beth put a pair of slippers down to warm. Somehow the sight of the old shoes had a good effect upon the girls; for mother was coming, and everyone brightened to welcome her. Meg stopped lecturing, and lighted the lamp. Amy got out of the easy chair without being asked, and Jo forgot how tired she was as she sat up to hold the slippers nearer to the blaze.

"They are quite worn out; Marmee must have a new pair."

"I thought I'd get her some with my dollar," said Beth.

"No, I shall!" cried Amy.

"I'm the oldest," began Meg, but Jo cut in with a decided — "I'm the man of the family now papa is away, and I shall provide the slippers, for he told me to take special care of mother while he was gone."

"I'll tell you what we'll do," said Beth; "let's each get her something for Christmas, and not get anything for ourselves."

"That's like you, dear! What will we get?" exclaimed Jo.

Everyone thought soberly for a minute; then Meg announced, as if the idea was suggested by the sight of her own pretty hands, "I shall give her a nice pair of gloves."

"Army shoes, best to be had," cried Jo.

"Some handkerchiefs, all hemmed," said Beth.

"I'll get a little bottle of cologne; she likes it, and it won't cost much, so I'll have some left to buy my pencils," added Amy.

"How will we give the things?" asked Meg.

"Put them on the table, and bring her in and see her open the bundles. Don't you remember how we used to do on our birthdays?" asked Jo.

"I used to be so frightened when it was my turn to sit in the big chair with the crown on, and see you all come marching round to give the presents, with a kiss. I liked the things and the kisses, but it was dreadful to have you sit looking at me while I opened the bundles," said Beth, who was toasting her face and the bread for tea, at the same time.

"Let Marmee think we are getting things for ourselves, and then surprise her. We must go shopping tomorrow afternoon, Meg; there is so much to do about the play for Christmas night," said Jo, marching up and down, with her hands behind her back and her nose in the air.

"I don't mean to act any more after this time; I'm getting too old for such things," observed Meg, who was as much a child as ever about "dressing-up" frolics.

"You won't stop, I know, as long as you can trail round in a white gown with your hair down, and wear gold-paper jewelry. You are the best actress we've got, and there'll be an end of everything if you quit the boards," said Jo. "We ought to rehearse tonight. Come here, Amy, and do the fainting scene, for you are as stiff as a poker in that."

"I can't help it; I never saw anyone faint, and I don't choose to make myself all black and blue, tumbling flat as you do. If I can go down easily, I'll drop; if I can't, I shall fall into a chair and be graceful; I don't care if Hugo does come at me with a pistol," returned Amy, who was not gifted with dramatic power, but was chosen because she was small enough to be borne out shrieking by the villain of the piece.

"Do it this way; clasp your hands so, and stagger across the room, crying frantically, 'Roderigo! save me! save me!' " and away went Jo, with a melodramatic scream which was truly thrilling.

Amy followed, but she poked her hands out stiffly before her, and jerked herself along as if she went by machinery; and her "Ow!" was more suggestive of pins being run into her than of fear and anguish. Jo gave a despairing groan, and Meg laughed outright, while Beth let her bread burn as she watched the fun, with interest.

"It's no use! Do the best you can when the time comes, and if the audience laughs, don't blame me. Come on, Meg."

Then things went smoothly, for Don Pedro defied the world in a speech of two pages without a single break; Hagar, the witch, chanted an awful incantation over her kettleful of simmering toads, with weird effect; Roderigo rent his chains asunder manfully, and Hugo died in agonies of remorse and arsenic, with a wild "Ha! ha!"

"It's the best we've had yet," said Meg, as the dead villain sat up and rubbed his elbows.

"I don't see how you can write and act such splendid things, Jo. You're a regular Shakespeare!" exclaimed Beth, who firmly believed that her sisters were gifted with wonderful genius in all things.

"Not quite," replied Jo modestly. "I do think, 'The Witch's Curse, an Operatic Tragedy' is rather a nice thing; but I'd like to try 'Macbeth,' if we only had a trap door for Banquo. I always wanted to do the killing part. 'Is that a dagger that I see before me?' " muttered Jo, rolling her eyes and clutching at the air, as she had seen a famous tragedian do.

"No, it's the toasting fork, with mother's shoe on it instead of the bread. Beth's stage-struck!" cried Meg, and the rehearsal ended in a general burst of laughter.

Jo was the first to wake in the gray dawn of Christmas morning. No stockings hung at the fireplace, and for a moment she felt as much disappointed as she did long ago, when her little sock fell down because it was so crammed with goodies. Then she remembered her mother's promise, and, slipping her hand under her pillow, drew out a little crimson-covered book. She knew it very well, for it was that beautiful old story of the best life ever lived, and Jo felt that it was a true guidebook for any pilgrim going the long journey. She woke Meg with a "Merry Christmas," and bade her see what was under her pillow. A green-covered book appeared, with the same picture inside, and a few words written by their mother, which made their one present very precious in their eyes. Presently Beth and Amy woke, to rummage and find their little books also — one dove-colored, the other blue; and all sat looking at and talking about them, while the east grew rosy with the coming day. In spite of her small vanities, Margaret had a sweet and pious nature, which unconsciously influenced her sisters, especially Jo, who loved her very tenderly, and obeyed her because her advice was so gently given.

"Girls," said Meg seriously, looking from the tumbled head beside her to the two little night-capped ones in the room beyond, "mother wants us to read and love and mind these books, and we must begin at once. We used to be faithful about it; but since father went away, and all this war trouble unsettled us, we have neglected many things. You can do as you please; but I shall keep my book on the table here, and read a little every morning as soon as I wake, for I know it will do me good, and help me through the day."

Then she opened her new book and began to read. Jo put her arm around her, and, leaning cheek to cheek, read also, with the quiet expression so seldom seen on her restless face.

"How good Meg is! Come, Amy, let's do as they do. I'll help you with the hard words, and they'll explain things if we don't understand," whispered Beth, very much impressed by the pretty books and her sisters' example.

"I'm glad mine is blue," said Amy; and then the rooms were very still while the pages were softly turned, and the winter sunshine crept in to touch the bright heads and serious faces with a Christmas greeting.

"Where is mother?" asked Meg, as she and Jo ran down to thank her for their gifts, half an hour later.

"Goodness only knows. Some poor creeter come a-beggin', and your ma went straight off to see what was needed. There never was such a woman for givin' away vittles and drink, clothes and firin'," replied Hannah, who had lived with the family since Meg was born, and was considered by them all more as a friend than a servant.

"She will be back soon, I think; so fry your cakes, and have everything ready," said Meg, looking over the presents which were collected in a basket and kept under the sofa, ready to be produced at the proper time. "Why, where is Amy's bottle of cologne?" she added, as the little flask did not appear.

"She took it out a minute ago, and went off with it to put a ribbon on it, or some such notion," replied Jo, dancing about the room to take the first stiffness off the new army slippers.

"How nice my handkerchiefs look, don't they? Hannah washed and ironed them for me, and I marked them all myself," said Beth, looking proudly at the somewhat uneven letters which had cost her such labor.

"Bless the child! she's gone and put 'Mother' on them instead of 'M. March.' How funny!" cried Jo, taking up one.

"Isn't it right? I thought it was better to do it so, because Meg's initials are 'M.M.,' and I don't want anyone to use these but Marmee," said Beth, looking troubled.

"It's all right, dear, and a very pretty idea — quite sensible, too, for no one can ever mistake now. It will please her very much, I know," said Meg, with a frown for Jo and a smile for Beth.

"There's mother. Hide the basket, quick!" cried Jo, as a door slammed, and steps sounded in the hall.

Amy came in hastily, and looked rather abashed, when she saw her sisters all waiting for her.

"Where have you been, and what are you hiding behind you?" asked Meg, surprised to see, by her hood and cloak, that lazy Amy had been out so early.

"Don't laugh at me, Jo! I didn't mean anyone should know till the time came. I only meant to change the little bottle for a big one, and I gave all my money to get it, and I'm truly trying not to be selfish any more."

As she spoke, Amy showed the handsome flask which replaced the cheap one; and looked so earnest and humble in her little effort to forget herself that Meg hugged her on the spot, and Jo pronounced her "a trump," while Beth ran to the window, and picked her finest rose to ornament the stately bottle.

"You see I felt ashamed of my present, after reading and talking about being good this morning, so I ran round the corner and changed it the minute I was up; and I'm so glad, for mine is the handsomest now."

Another bang of the street door sent the basket under the sofa, and the girls to the table, eager for breakfast.

"Merry Christmas, Marmee! Many of them! Thank you for our books; we read some, and mean to every day," they cried, in chorus.

"Merry Christmas, little daughters! I'm glad you began at once, and hope you will keep on. But I want to say one word before we sit down. Not far away from here lies a poor woman with a little newborn baby. Six children are huddled into one bed to keep from freezing, for they have no fire. There is nothing to eat over there; and the oldest boy came to tell me they were suffering hunger and cold. My girls, will you give them your breakfast as a Christmas present?"

They were all unusually hungry, having waited nearly an hour, and for a minute no one spoke; only a minute, for Jo exclaimed impetuously, "I'm so glad you came before we began!"

"May I go and help carry the things to the poor little children?" asked Beth eagerly.

"I shall take the cream and the muffins," added Amy, heroically giving up the articles she most liked.

Meg was already covering the buckwheats, and piling the bread into one big plate.

"I thought you'd do it," said Mrs. March, smiling as if satisfied. "You shall all go and help me, and when we come back we will have bread and milk for breakfast, and make it up at dinnertime."

They were soon ready, and the procession set out. Fortunately it was early, and they went through back streets, so few people saw them, and no one laughed at the queer party.

A poor, bare, miserable room it was, with broken windows, no fire, ragged bedclothes, a sick mother, wailing baby, and a group of pale, hungry children cuddled under one old quilt, trying to keep warm.

How the big eyes stared and the blue lips smiled as the girls went in!

"Ach, mein Gott! It is good angels come to us!" said the poor woman, crying for joy.

"Funny angels in hoods and mittens," said Jo, and set them laughing.

In a few minutes it really did seem as if kind spirits had been at work there. Hannah, who had carried wood, made a fire, and stopped up the broken panes with old hats and her own cloak. Mrs. March gave the mother tea and gruel, and comforted her with promises of help, while she dressed the little baby as tenderly as if it had been her own. The girls, meantime, spread the table, set the children round the fire, and fed them like so many hungry birds — laughing, talking, and trying to understand the funny broken English.

"Das ist gut!" "Die Engel-kinder!" cried the poor things, as they ate, and warmed their purple hands at the comfortable blaze.

The girls had never been called angel children before, and thought it very agreeable, especially Jo, who had been considered a "Sancho" ever since she was born. That was a very happy breakfast, though they didn't get any of it; and when they went away, leaving comfort behind, I think there were not in all the city four merrier people than the hungry little girls who gave away their breakfasts and contented themselves with bread and milk on Christmas morning.

"That's loving our neighbor better than ourselves, and I like it," said Meg, as they set out their presents, while their mother was upstairs collecting clothes for the poor Hummels.

Not a very splendid show, but there was a great deal of love done up in the few little bundles; and the tall vase of red roses, white chrysanthemums, and trailing vines, which stood in the middle, gave quite an elegant air to the table.

"She's coming! Strike up, Beth! Open the door, Amy! Three cheers for Marmee!" cried Jo, prancing about, while Meg went to conduct mother to the seat of honor.

Beth played her gayest march, Amy threw open the door, and Meg enacted escort with great dignity. Mrs. March was both surprised and touched; and smiled with her eyes full as she examined her presents, and read the little notes which accompanied them. The slippers went on at once, a new handkerchief was slipped into her pocket, well scented with Amy's cologne, the rose was fastened in her bosom, and the nice gloves were pronounced a "perfect fit."

There was a good deal of laughing and kissing and explaining, in the simple, loving fashion which makes these home-festivals so pleasant at the time, so sweet to remember long afterward, and then all fell to work.

12 Stories for the Christmas Season

THREE YOUNG KINGS

by George Sumner Albee

THE town of Cardenas, a hundred miles to the east of Havana on the north coast of Cuba, is an old dog — a small, taffy-colored dog that is learning new tricks. Three times a week, nowadays, a ferry from Key West brings Cardenas a boatload of American tourists, and these Americans, all of whom have such white faces that they appear to have been sick, seem strange and wondrous to the people of the town. Small boys follow them on the sidewalks and, when they speak, race around in front in order to watch their lips form the mysterious, incomprehensible foreign words.

As for the small girls, they clap their hands over their mouths and giggle, for the American women often wear hats, and, as everybody knows, a hat is a garment worn solely by men. But the little girls' mothers shriek at them and snatch them indoors, for the Americans are bringing money into Cardenas and so they must be treated with the courtesy money deserves.

But this is the story of something that took place in Cardenas in the days before there were tourists or a ferry. At that time the young men sat all day on the iron rocking chairs in the park under the royal palms, talking excitedly about the day when they would go to work and make vast fortunes and buy fast automobiles. The shopkeepers opened at ten in the morning, strolled home at noon for heavy dinners of rice and black beans, took two-hour siestas and returned to their stores to play dominoes until suppertime, setting their prices sky-high so that would-be customers would not interrupt them. The women mopped their white tile floors, cooked, gossiped and, at dusk, locked themselves into the houses behind their heavy hardwood doors. And the children, when they had fathers who could pay the tuition, went to school. The boys, in white shirts and neckties of the soft blue that is the Virgin's own color, attended the *Escuela Pía*. The girls, in blue pinafores with white stripes around the hems of the skirts, went to the *Escuela de las Madres Escolapias*.

Which brings us to three boys of the *Escuela Pías:* Eduardo, Ramoncito and Lázaro.

Eduardo was sixteen, while Ramoncito and Lazaro were a few months younger. They were the oldest boys at the *colegio* and the big-

240

gest. In fact, Eduardo amounted to a giant in Cuba, where the horses are the size of large dogs and the dogs are not much larger than rabbits; his nickname was Elephant. He had a flat, snub-nosed face and a cubical skull on which his hair looked like a coat of glossy black lacquer because he soaked it daily in scented brilliantine. Ramoncito was finely made, with a headful of tight little curls and eyelashes half an inch long over eyes the color of clear green sea-water. Lázaro was the shortest of the three, but that did not keep him from being the heaviest. He was so fat that he exploded his clothes two and three times a day, popping shirt buttons and the seams of his knickerbockers or the buckles that fastened them at his plump knock-knees. Lázaro ate three huge meals a day, treated himself to custard éclairs on the way to school and fresh coconut macaroons on the way home, and devoted the recess periods to eating candy. Ramoncito's nickname was Monkey. Lázaro's was Macaroon.

The fact that they happened to be the three oldest students laid quite a few responsibilities on Eduardo, Ramoncito and Lázaro. When the school's forty-seven boys scrambled into the bus for the annual picnic at St. Michael of the Baths it was Eduardo, Ramoncito and Lázaro who served as monitors — umpiring ball games, arbitrating quarrels, seeing to it that appearances and decorum were maintained in general. And at Christmastime, because they were the oldest, it was their duty to play the parts of the Three Kings of Orient.

Jesus' birthday in Cuba is a day to. go to church, not a day for gifts. Gifts are distributed later, on the sixth of January, not by Santa Claus but by the Three Kings who carried gifts to the newborn Christ child in the manger at Bethlehem. On the second of January, therefore, Father Miguel called Eduardo, Ramoncito and Lázaro into his office.

"Seat thyselves," he directed them.

Father Miguel, who was eighty-two, was so frail that his white linen cassock appeared more often than not to be unoccupied. There was very little of him still in residence on earth. He had a small, poetically modeled head and a

voice, and that was about all. His voice, after all the years away from home, still had the lisp of his native Asturian mountains, and it too was fragile — a faint, musical buzz, like that made by a small but energetic fly in the schoolroom on a hot afternoon.

"Children," he said — for he was so aged that he could no longer perceive the difference between sixteen and six, "I have done this many times, but it is new to you, so I must explain the procedure of the Three Kings. All of the gifts your schoolmates will receive from their families and friends are upstairs in the janitor's room. The gifts for the girls are here as well; Mother Superior brought them over to me from *Madres Escolapias*. I want you here two hours before dusk on Day Five to load the mules, saddle the horses and disguise yourselves in your robes and turbans. The robes will fit; they always do. Do you ride well?"

"Yes, Father," murmured the boys. All Cuban boys ride well, using neither saddle nor bridle but only a length of rope looped at one end around the horse's muzzle.

"*Bueno;* you will be handsomely mounted. Don Alfredo de la Torre is sending me three cream-colored mares from his farm, with silver-mounted Mexican saddles and packsaddles for the mules. You will set out at dusk. It will take you three hours or so to deliver the presents; then you will return here and hand back the animals to Don Alfredo's foreman and hang away your robes. Understood?"

"Understood, Father," replied Eduardo when neither Ramoncito nor Lázaro spoke. He did not ask for leadership. It annoyed him, actually. But it was always thrust on him.

"Now go along to your homes," concluded the old priest, "and do not reveal to anyone that you are the Three Kings. We would not wish to sadden the hearts of any of the little ones."

During the next couple of days, as they discussed the roles they were to play, Ramoncito grew somewhat bitter about the "little ones." "What do we care if they find out the Kings aren't real?" he exclaimed resentfully. "We found out."

"That's no way to talk," replied Eduardo brusquely in his deep voice. "Before we knew the Kings did not exist, we thought they were marvels. We nearly went out of our heads waiting for them to come to our houses and bang the knockers. True?"

Fat little Lázaro offered no opinion one way or the other. Instead, he made a street map and planned the route they would take, so that they would be able to visit the houses on their list with the least possible amount of backtracking. Lázaro was efficient. Either that or he was lazy. Or it may be that efficiency and laziness are merely different names for the same thing.

With the school empty for the holidays, the playground seemed strange to the boys when they met there late on the afternoon of the fifth, a lonely square of red, grainy earth over which dry leaves skated. Land crabs had dug comfortable homes for themselves in the basketball court.

They loaded the four pack mules one at a time, with Eduardo carrying out the heavier toys — the tricycles and the miniature automobiles — because he was the strongest, Lázaro arranging the boxes and parcels in accordance with his map and Ramoncito, who was a passionate fisherman and good at tying knots, filling the large burlap sacks that would serve as their saddlebags and lashing them to the mahogany packsaddles. The mules, more intelligent than the horses, understood at once that they were being invited to join in some kind of game. They behaved well, neither balking nor biting. With the mules loaded, the boys saddled the three small, beautiful mares, who would have looked to an American as if they had pranced right off a merry-go-round. Then the boys put on their costumes.

The school had had the costumes for so many years that nobody remembered any longer who had made them originally — somebody's mother, probably. Whoever she was, she had used the same rich materials she would have used in embroidering an altar cloth for the church. Eduardo's robe was of turquoise satin belted with a gold cord and on his head he wore a multi-colored turban. Lázaro's robe was of heavy silver brocade and his turban was of purple velvet. Ramoncito wore a mandarinlike coat of blue silk, ornately embroidered, and a wine-colored turban. They wore their ordinary shoes, because the belled Mexican stirrups would hide them when they were on horseback and the long robes would cover them when they got down to enter the houses. Last of all, they attached their long white beards with liquid adhesive and, using an eyebrow pencil, drew the wrinkles of old age on their brown young faces.

Then, the horses ready, the mules waiting eagerly in single file on their lead ropes, the boys watched the sun go down behind the palm groves to the west. It sank, a giant illuminated peach sending up a spray of golden searchlights through the massed clouds. After it was below the horizon, the sky was filled with dazzling lime-green light, and then, with no interval, it was dusk. It had been a fruit punch of a sunset, complete with maraschino cherries and lemon sherbet, but the boys had seen it every night of their lives, and they supposed that the sun behaved as extravagantly in all countries. To them it was merely a signal that the time had come for them to start.

"Mount," ordered Eduardo, and they swung themselves into the highbacked, embossed saddles. The lead mule brayed gaily in a spirit of adventure. Off they trotted.

"The top end of Princess Street," directed Lázaro. "The Montoros live there at Number 17."

"I believe thee," replied Ramoncito, whose secret intention it was one day to marry the middle Montoro girl, Gladys.

The houses of Cardenas, like the houses in most Latin cities, are invisible. That is, you see nothing of them from the street except the front wall, which joins the front walls of the residences on either side and is plastered over with the same golden stucco. Inside the wall, from front to back, each house is divided into two long, narrow strips, side by side. One of these strips, which has no roof over it, is a tiled garden with a fountain, stone flower boxes, lime and mango and papaya trees and an array of outdoor furniture. Here the family lives three hundred days in the year. The long strip on the other side, roofed over with faded vermilion tiles, contains the formal living room with its crystal chandelier and cumbersome mahogany furniture; the bedrooms, each of which has its own door opening into the garden; the dining room, with another chandelier and a big electric refrigerator from the United States standing in a corner; and the kitchen, where the food is cooked over square cast-iron baskets of fragrant, glowing charcoal. Behind the kitchen live the servants, and all their relatives who are able to think up convincing hard-luck stories.

But there is something about the houses of Cardenas that is stranger still, and this is that the richest man in the block may live next door to the poorest. There are poor neighborhoods and rich neighborhoods, but often a banker lives in the poor one and a shrimp peddler in the rich one. For this reason, as the boys dismounted at the Montoro house they could not help but see the nine barefoot children of Emilio, the shoemaker, dressed in ragged shirts and nothing else, who stared at them hopefully as they took down the saddlebag containing the Montoro youngsters' gifts. Eduardo, whose voice was already so much deeper than many a man's, thudded on the door with the brass knocker and bellowed: "Do the good young ones of the Señores Montoro live here?"

Señor Montoro swung open the tall door, elegant in his starched white jacket of pleated linen. "Yes, sir, we have good young ones in this house," he replied. "May I ask who you are, gentlemen?"

"We are the Three Kings of Orient," boomed Eduardo.

"Enter, then. This is thy house."

The Montoro children, jabbering with excitement, accepted the presents that had their names on them as Eduardo and Ramoncito took them from the opened burlap sack. Hasty goodbyes were said, the Kings explaining that they had a great distance to travel before morning, and they mounted and rode on.

"The shoemaker's kids are all crying," said Lázaro over the clip-clop of the hooves. "I can hear them. They thought we'd leave something for them when we came out of the Montoros'."

"Maybe Jaime Montoro will give them his express wagon after he smashes it," said Ramoncito. "I'll bet there won't be a wheel left by noon tomorrow."

At the Cabrera house on Shell Street they delivered a fifty-dollar French doll to Myriam Cabrera, along with a dozen other packages. Mounting again, they turned into Anglona Street. By now it was dark, the only light on the street falling from unshaded bulbs at the intersections. They were conscious as they rode along of people, grownups as well as children, watching them from the sidewalks. Everybody was out for an evening stroll in the cool bay breeze. Now and again somebody called out "Look, the Three Kings!" and each time the voice was thrilled and reverent. There was mystery in the night. The mules felt it, pricking up their ears, and the horses, catching the murmurs of admiration, tossed their manes and lifted their forefeet higher than they really needed to, showing off. A group of men around the white pushcart of a *tamalero* cheered and waved. One of them, a farmer in high-laced boots with his sugarcane knife at his belt, ran into the street and tried to feed his tamale to Eduardo's horse.

On Saint John of God Street the horses shied at the peanut seller who was chanting, "Peanuts a little hot, peanuts a little hot," and again there were watchers in the darkness under the rustling palms. Distinctly the boys heard a little girl ask in a trembling voice: "Mama, will they come to us?" And they heard the mother's patient, desperate answer: "Who knows, soul of my soul? But if they do not come tonight you must be valiant, for surely they will come next year."

On the lead mare Eduardo, who knew a number of words which did not meet with Father Miguel's approval, muttered a particularly bad one.

"Now *she's* crying," exclaimed Lázaro, "because we've passed her house."

"If you think this is bad," said Ramoncito, "wait till we get down by the market. My brother Pepe told me when he was a King he rode through four blocks of bawling beggar kids there."

"The poor are always with us," replied Eduardo gruffly. "Jesus says so in the Bible."

"He means they are always with us to remind us to do something about them, Elephant," said Lázaro. "That's what He means."

"What do you want?" Eduardo shouted back. "Am I to blame because there are families that can't earn a living? The cane crop is poor this year."

Eduardo's anger was something to be quenched promptly; it was well known. "No, Elephant, dear, you are not to blame," said Ramoncito. "We don't say you are."

"Then shut up, the two of you!"

"I just think," said Lázaro in the clear, sweet voice that permitted him, at fifteen, still to sing in the choir, "it's a shame to take gifts to rich kids like us when it's the poor kids that need them."

"Me, too. My father is giving me a bicycle," added Ramoncito. "What do I want with a domino set and a silly card game that's supposed to teach me how to spell?"

"Father Miguel told us what to do," said Eduardo grimly, "and we're going to do it."

But not a hundred yards farther on a small boy of seven or eight, in a shirt made of secondhand cheesecloth washed white for the holiday, ran hysterically into the street crying, "Oh, Kings, Kings! We live here, señores, at Number 22!"

Eduardo reined in so sharply that he hurt his mare's dainty mouth. Leaning down from his saddle, he bellowed in a voice that frightened the boy nearly out of his senses: "What's your name? Is there light in your house so we can see? Then take us there. Monkey, gallop back and get that girl that was howling!"

In the one-room house at Number 22, where an entire family slept on the clay floor and the only light was that from the candle blinking in its ruby cup at the feet of the Virgin, they handed out half a dozen packages, Eduardo

glowering, Ramoncito scared but resolute, and Lazaro struggling to control the giggle that always assailed him at the wrong moment. The gratitude of the little boy and girl embarrassed them so terribly that they got away quickly, shutting the rickety door behind them with a slam. They gathered around the horses.

"Well, anyhow," said Eduardo, "those two won't bawl all night. But now what? You know we ought to obey the father."

"Tu eres jefe," answered Ramoncito with a shrug. "You're the boss."

"I'm not the boss," roared Eduardo. "You always make me the boss, and then I get into trouble. Do you realize the scandal it will be if we go down to the market and give all this stuff to the beggar kids?"

"Clearly it will be a scandal," responded Ramoncito. "It has never been done."

"We're wearing eleven-yard shirts now," protested Eduardo as we might say: "We're in hot water now." He turned to Lázaro. "What do you say, Macaroon?"

When a person of Spanish blood does not know what other answer to give, he answers with a proverb. "That which does not kill us," quoted Lázaro, "will make us fat." The saying did not fit the situation especially well, but it conveyed his meaning.

"All right," said Eduardo, "but you're both in this with me. Don't you forget it, either!"

"For an elephant," said Ramoncito, "you do a lot of talking."

Dramatically Lázaro crumpled his map and flung it into the gutter. They turned the horses' heads and trotted toward the market. In the street approaching it, Colonel Hangman Street, with its reek of fish heads and rotten cabbage, they drew rein. Somebody had smashed the street light with a cabbage or a pebble from a slingshot, but there was light enough from the stars to see by; the stars hung just over the rooftops like green and red Christmas tree ornaments lowered from Heaven on wires. Eduardo stood erect in his stirrups. "Hear me," he shouted. "Is this the town of Cardenas, in Cuba?" That was a fine imaginative touch. "Are there good young ones on this street who have behaved well this year? If there are, come you all to the market!"

The market, a maze of heavy stone archways, was brilliantly lighted. Curious, laughing butchers and vegetable sellers at once gathered around the Three Kings as they entered, dragging their bulky saddlebags. Even as the crowd formed a ring, dirty, barefoot children with uncombed hair and noses that badly needed wiping were pushing and wriggling and, where it was necessary, kicking their way to its center. Recklessly Eduardo, Ramoncito and Lázaro

tore away tissue paper and ribbons, so that they could see what the gifts were, and passed them out. Arguments broke out in the crowd, but not among the children. They snatched their dolls and painting sets, their toy fire engines and scooters and raced away shrieking, carrying the greatest news of their lives to brothers, sisters and deserving friends.

In twenty minutes the saddlebags were empty. Not an all-day sucker was left. Even Ramoncito's white beard was gone, for it had fallen to the concrete floor and a youngster

had snatched it in the belief that it was a toy. Streaming perspiration, and as hoarse as crows, the three boys thrust their way through the chattering, mystified, admiring crowd that jammed the sidewalk for a block, mounted and trotted back to the school under the late moon. The moon could not manage anything quite as spectacular as the sun, but it was doing its best. It turned the massed clouds over the sea into great clusters of white camellias, wrapping each cluster in shining aluminum foil.

Scientists say nothing travels more swiftly than light. This is not true; in a small town good news, bad news, any kind of news at all travels faster. By the time the boys had hung up their costumes and turned over the animals to Don Alfredo's foreman, furious, gesticulating parents were already haranguing the boys' fathers. And by morning the anger had solidified into a demand that all three of them be expelled at once from school. The movement was headed by Triunfo Anilina, who had made a large fortune out of a small drugstore by selling medicines for much more than they were worth to people too sick to argue over price.

The druggist, sending around notes to everybody's house by messenger, demanded that all parents of boys attending the *colegio* meet there and put the matter to a vote at four o'clock.

At four that afternoon the outraged parents were at the school — not two hours late, nor even one hour late, as was the custom, but on the dot. Plump fathers with cigars, plump mothers with small, exquisite feet in high-heeled, patent leather shoes, they followed Triunfo Anilina into the large, cool room in which arithmetic was taught. There they squeezed themselves into the seats behind the students' small desks while the burly druggist arrogantly preempted the mathematics teacher's desk on the dais. As for the boys themselves, without anybody's ordering them to do so, Eduardo, Ramoncito and Lázaro ranged themselves before the blackboard, standing with their backs to it. In their own minds they were guilty, convicted and ready for the firing squad.

"We are here," stated Triunfo Anilina curtly. "Let us begin."

He presented a detailed account of the crime that had been committed, using a number of large and impressive words he had picked up from his brother, a lawyer. It took him half an hour.

After this the fathers of the culprits spoke for the defense, Eduardo's father offering to repay the cost of all the gifts, Ramoncito's father pleading that boys would be boys, and Lázaro's father volunteering to pitch Triunfo and all the other male members of the Anilina family, to whom he referred as cockroaches, through the window.

But Triunfo Anilina shouted down the defense, pounding the desk with his hairy fist and upsetting the inkwell.

"The thieves must be punished!" he cried.

"Then the truth of the matter," said Eduardo's handsome father, getting once more to his feet, "is that nothing will satisfy you — not honorable apology, not repayment, nothing. What you want is revenge."

"Yes, revenge!" gasped Triunfo Anilina, his linen jacket dark with perspiration. "What a scandal! It is the first time in the history of our *colegio* that this thing has happened!"

"Ah, Anilina," came a faint, musical buzz of a voice from the rear of the room, "you have a point there."

Every head turned as Father Miguel, pausing several times to gather strength along the way, came up the aisle in his long, tallow-colored gown. All the mothers and fathers had forgotten him.

Triunfo Anilina scrambled clumsily to his feet. "Take my seat, Father," he said.

"It is not your seat," replied Father Miguel. Standing on the dais, steadying himself with one small, dry hand on the edge of the desk, his bald skull reflecting the white light from the windows, he faced the parents. "Dear friends," he whispered, "it is so. For fifty years I have sent into the town, on the eve of Three Kings' Day, the three oldest boys of the school. And always they have distributed the gifts as I bade them, because they were good boys. Not until last night have they ever disobeyed me."

Behind the desk Triunfo Anilina jerked his head sharply in agreement.

"But these three boys are good boys also, since all boys are good boys," continued Father Miguel, "so, in fairness to them, we must examine their misdeed very closely. Exactly what, we must ask ourselves, did they do? They took rich gifts, provided by the bounty of our beloved island, and carried them to babes who sleep on straw pallets, if they are lucky enough to find any straw in the streets around the market. Does the straw remind you of anything, señores and señoras? It reminds me of another Babe, swaddled in coarse cloth, who slept on straw in a manger because there was no room for Him in an inn. And with this in mind it becomes clear beyond doubt that these are not good boys. No, they are something more than ordinary good boys. In the generosity of their hearts, the sweetness of their spirit, the courage of their will they are, indeed, Three Young Kings."

At the blackboard, arms stiff at his sides, Eduardo spoke out of the corner of his mouth to fat little Lázaro. "Giggle one time," he said, "and I advise thee that it will be thy last giggle."

In the schoolroom there was silence. Then Ramoncito's mother began to cry and Lázaro's father burst into boisterous laughter.

Father Miguel raised a hand.

"Now," he said, "if you will kindly help me to my house next door, a delegation from the neighborhood of the market is waiting. They wish to thank you for your sympathy and kindliness, which have so deeply touched them. They wish also to know the identities of the three noble Kings, in order that they may kiss their hands."

AS YE SOW —

by Dorothy Canfield Fisher

Casually, not that she was especially interested, just to say something, she asked as she handed out the four o'clock pieces of bread and peanut butter, "Well, what Christmas songs are you learning in your room this year?"

There was a moment's pause. Then the three little boys, her own and the usual two of his playmates, told her soberly, first one speaking, then another. "We're not going to be let to sing." "Teacher don't want us in the Christmas entertainment." Their round, eight-year-old faces were grave.

"Well — !" said the mother. "For goodness' sakes, why not?"

Looking down at his feet, her own small David answered sadly, "Teacher says we can't sing good enough."

"Well enough," corrected his mother mechanically.

"Well enough," he repeated as mechanically. One of the others said in a low tone, "She says we can't carry a tune. She's only going to let kids sing in the entertainment that can carry a tune."

David, still hanging his head humbly, murmured, "She says we'd spoil the piece our class is going to sing."

Inwardly the mother broke into a mother's rage at a teacher. "So that's what she says, does she? What's she for, anyhow, if not to teach children what they don't know. The idea! As if she'd say she would teach arithmetic only to those who are good at it already."

The downcast children stood silent. She yearned over their shame at failing to come up to the standards of their group. "Teachers are callous, that's what they are, insensitively callous. She is deliberately planting an inferiority feeling in them. It's a shame to keep them from going up on the platform and standing in the footlights. Not to let them have their share of being applauded! It's cruel."

She drew in a deep breath, and put the loaf of bread away. Then she said quietly, "Well, lots of kids your age can't carry a tune. Not till they've learned. How'd you like to practice your song with me? I could play the air on the piano afternoons, after school. You'd get the hang of it that way."

They brightened, they bit off great chunks of their snacks, and said, thickly, that that would be swell. They did not say they would be grateful to her, or regretted being a bother to her, busy as she always was. She did not expect them to. In fact it would have startled her if they had. She was the mother of four.

So while the after-school bread-and-butter was being eaten, washed down with gulps of milk, while the November-muddy rubbers were taken off, the mother pushed to the back of the stove the interrupted rice pudding, washed her hands at the sink, looked into the dining room where her youngest, Janey, was waking her dolls up from naps taken in the dining-room chairs, and took off her apron. Together the four went into the living room to the piano.

"What song is it, your room is to sing?"

"It came upon the midnight — " said the three little boys, speaking at once.

"That's a nice one," she commented, reaching for the battered songbook on top of the piano. "This is the way it goes." She played the air, and sang the first two lines. "That'll be enough to start on," she told them. "Now — " she gave them the signal to start.

They started. She had given them food for body and heart. Refreshed, heartened, with unquestioning confidence in a grown-up's ability to achieve whatever she planned, they opened their mouths happily and sang out.

> "It came upon the midnight clear
> That glorious song of old."

They had evidently learned the words by heart from hearing them.

At the end of that phrase she stopped abruptly, and for an instant bowed her head over the keys. Her feeling about Teacher made a right-about turn. There was a pause.

But she was a mother, not a teacher. She lifted her head, turned a smiling face on the three bellowing children. "I tell you what," she said. "The way, really, to learn a tune, is just one note after another. The reason why a teacher can't get *everybody* in her room up to singing in tune, is because she'd have to teach each person separately — unless they happen to be naturally good at singing. That would take too much time, you see. A teacher has such a lot of children to see to."

They did not listen closely to this. They were not particularly interested in having justice done to Teacher, since they had not shared the mother's brief excursion into indignation. But they tolerated her with silent courtesy. They were used to parents, teachers, and other adults, and had learned how to take with patience and self-control their constantly recurring prosy explanations of things that did not matter.

"Listen," said the mother, "I'll strike just the two first notes on the piano — 'It came —' " She struck the notes, she sang them clearly. Full of good will the little boys sang with her. She stopped. Breathed hard.

"Not quite," she said, with a false smile, "prett-ty good. Close to it. But not quite, yet. I think we'd better take it one note at a time. Bill, you try it."

They had been in and out of her house all their lives, they were all used to her, none of them had reached the age of self-consciousness. Without hesitation, Bill sang, "I-i-it — " loudly.

After he had, the mother, as if fascinated, kept her eyes fixed on his still open mouth. Finally, "Try again," she said. "But first, listen." Oracularly she told them, "Half of carrying a tune is listening first."

She played the note again. And again. And again. Then, rather faintly, she said, "Peter, you sing it now."

At the note emitted by Peter, she let out her breath, as if she had been under water and just come up. "Fine!" she said. "Now we're getting somewhere! David, your turn." David was her own. "Just that one note. No, not quite. A little higher. Not quite so high." She was in a panic. What could she do? "Wait," she told David. "Try just breathing it out, not loud at all. Maybe you can get it better."

The boys had come in a little after four. It was five when the telephone rang — Bill's mother asking her to send Bill home because his Aunt Emma was there. The mother turned from the telephone to say, "Don't you boys want to go along with Bill a ways, and play around for a while outdoors? I've got to get supper ready." Cheerful, sure that she, like all adults, knew just what to do, relieved to see a door opening before them that had been slammed shut in their faces, and very tired of that one note, they put on their muddy rubbers and thudded out.

That evening when she told her husband about it, after the children had gone to bed, she ended her story with a vehement "You never heard anything like it in your life, Harry. Never. It was appalling! You can't imagine what it was!"

"Oh, yes I can too," he said over his temporarily lowered newspaper. "I've heard plenty of tone-deaf kids hollering. I know what they sound like. There are people, you know, who really can't carry a tune. You probably never could teach them. Why don't you give it up?"

Seeing, perhaps, in her face, the mulish mother-stubbornness, he said, with a little exasperation, "What's the use of trying to do what you can't do?"

That was reasonable, after all, thought the mother. Yes, that was the sensible thing to do. She would be sensible, for once, and give it up. With everything she had to do, she would just be reasonable and sensible about this.

So the next morning, when she was downtown doing her marketing, she turned in at the public library and asked for books about teaching music to children. Rather young children, about eight years old, she explained.

The librarian, enchanted with someone who did not ask for a light, easy-reading novel, brought her two books, which she took away with her.

At lunch she told her husband (There were just the two of them with little Janey; the older children had their lunch at school.), "Musical experts say there really is no such thing as a tone-deaf person. If anybody seems so, it is only because he has not had a chance to be carefully enough trained."

Her husband looked at her quickly. "Oh, all right," he said, "all right! Have it your own way." But he leaned to pat her hand. "You're swell," he told her. "I don't see how you ever keep it up as you do. Gosh, it's one o'clock already."

During the weeks between then and the Christmas entertainment, she saw no more than he how she could ever keep it up. The little boys had no difficulty in keeping it up. They had nothing else to do at four o'clock. They were in the indestructible age, between the frailness of infancy and the taut nervous tensions of adolescence. Wherever she led they followed her cheerfully. In that period of incessant pushing against barriers which did not give way, she was the one whose flag hung limp.

Assiduous reading of those two reference books on teaching music taught her that there were other approaches than a frontal attack on the tune they wanted to sing. She tried out ear-experiments with them, of which she would never have dreamed, without her library books. She discovered to her dismay that sure enough, just as the authors of the books said, the little boys were musically so far below scratch that, without seeing which piano keys she struck, they had no idea whether a note was higher or lower than the one before it. She adapted and invented musical "games" to train their ear for this. The boys standing in a row, their backs to the piano, listening to hear whether the second note was "up hill or down hill" from the first note, thought it as good a game as any other, rather funnier than most because so new to them. They laughed raucously over each other's mistakes, kidded and joshed each other, ran a contest to see who came out best, while the mother, aproned for cooking, her eye on the clock, got up and down for hurried forays into the kitchen where she was trying to get supper.

David's older brother and sister had naturally good ears for music. That was one reason why the mother had not dreamed that David had none. When the two older children came in from school, they listened incredulously, laughed scoffingly, and went off to skate, or to rehearse a play. Little Janey, absorbed in her family of dolls, paid no attention to these male creatures of an age so far from hers that they were as negligible as grown-ups. The mother toiled alone, in a vacuum, with nobody's sympathy to help her, her great stone rolling down hill as fast as she toilsomely pushed it up.

Not quite in a vacuum. Not even in a vacuum. Occasionally the others made a comment, "Gee, Mom, those kids are fierce. You can't do anything with them." "Say, Helen, an insurance man is coming to the house this afternoon. For heaven's sake keep those boys from screeching while he is here. A person can't hear himself think."

So, she thought, with silent resentment, her task was not only to give up her own work, to invent and adapt methods of instruction in an hour she could not spare, but also to avoid bothering the rest. After all, the home was for the whole family. They had the right to have it the background of what they wanted to do, needed to do. Only not she. Not the mother. Of course.

She faltered. Many times. She saw the ironing heaped high, or Janey was in bed with a cold, and as four o'clock drew near, she said to herself, "Now today I'll just tell the boys that I can *not* go on with this. We're not getting anywhere, anyhow."

So when they came storming in, hungry and cheerful and full of unquestioning certainty that she would not close that door she had half-opened for them, she laid everything aside and went to the piano.

As a matter of fact, they were getting somewhere. She had been so beaten down that she was genuinely surprised at the success of the exercises ingeniously devised by the authors of those books. Even with their backs to the piano, the boys could now tell, infallibly, whether a second note was above or below the first one. Sure. They even thought it distinctly queer that they had not been able to, at first. "Never paid any attention to it, before," was their own accurate surmise as to the reason.

They paid attention now, their interest aroused by their first success, by the incessant practicing of the others in their classroom, by the Christmas-entertainment thrill which filled the schoolhouse with suspense. Although they were allowed no part in it, they also paid close attention to the drill given the others, and sitting in their seats, exiled from the happy throng of singers, they watched how to march along the aisle of the Assembly Hall, decorously, not too fast, not too slow, and when the great moment came for climbing to the platform how not to knock their toes against the steps. They fully expected — wasn't a grown-up teaching them? — to climb those steps to the platform with the others, come the evening of the entertainment.

It was now not on the clock that the mother kept her eye during those daily sessions at the piano, it was on the calendar. She nervously intensified her drill, but she remembered carefully not to yell at them when they went wrong, not to screw her face into the grimace which she felt, not to clap her hands over her ears and scream, "Oh, horrible! *Why* can't you get it right!" She reminded herself that if they knew how to get it right, they would of course sing it that way. She knew (she had been a mother for sixteen years) that she must keep them cheerful and hopeful, or the tenuous thread of their interest and attention would snap. She smiled. She did not allow herself even once to assume the blighting look of patience.

Just in time, along about the second week of December, they did begin to get somewhere. They could all sound — if they remembered to sing softly and to "listen to themselves" — a note, any note, within their range, she struck on the piano. Little Peter turned out, to his surprise and hers, to have a sweet clear soprano. The others were — well, all right, good enough.

They started again, very cautiously, to sing that tune, to begin with "It ca-ame — " having drawn a deep breath, and letting it out carefully. It was right. They were singing true.

She clapped her hands like a girl. They did not share her overjoyed surprise. That was where they had been going all the time. They had got there, that was all. What was there to be surprised about?

After that it went fast; the practicing of the air, their repeating it for the first skeptical, and then thoroughly astonished Teacher, their triumphant report at home, "She says we can sing it good enough. She says we can sing with the others. We practiced going up on the platform this afternoon."

Then the Christmas entertainment. The tramping of class after class up the aisle to the moment of foot-lighted glory; the big eighth graders' Christmas pantomime, the first graders' wavering performance of a Christmas dance as fairies — or were they snowflakes? Or perhaps angels? It was not clear. They were tremendously applauded, whatever they were. The swelling hearts of their parents burst into wild hand-clapping as the first grade began to file down the steps from the platform. Little Janey, sitting on her mother's lap, beat her hands together too, excited by the thought that next year she would be draped in white cheesecloth, would wear a tinsel crown and wave a star-tipped wand.

Then it was the turn of the third grade, the eight- and nine-year-olds, the boys clumping up the aisle, the girls switching their short skirts proudly. The careful tiptoeing up the steps to the platform, remembering not to knock their toes on the stair-treads, the two lines of round faces facing the audience, bland and blank in their ignorance of — oh, of everything! thought David's mother, her hand clutching her handbag tensely.

The crash from the piano giving them the tone, all the mouths open,

"It came upo-on the midnight clear
That glorious song of old."

The thin pregnant woman sitting in front of the mother, leaned to the shabbily dressed man next to her, with a long breath of relief. "They do real *good*, don't they?" she whispered proudly.

They did do real good. Teacher's long drill and hers had been successful. It was not howling, it was singing. It had cost the heart's blood, thought the mother, of two women, but it was

singing. It would never again be howling, not from those children.

It was even singing with expression — some. There were swelling crescendos, and at the lines

"The world in solemn stillness lay
To hear the angels sing."

the child-voices were hushed in a diminuendo. Part of the mother's very life had been spent in securing her part of that diminuendo. She ached at the thought of the effort that had gone into teaching that hushed tone, of the patience and self-control and endlessly repeated persistence in molding into something shapely the boys' puppy-like inability to think of anything but aimless play. It had taken hours out of her life, crammed as it was far beyond what was possible with work that must be done. Done for other people. Not for her. Not for the mother.

This had been one of the things that must be done. And she had done it. There he stood, her little David, a fully accredited part of his corner of society, as good as anybody, the threat of the inferiority-feeling averted for this time, ready to face the future with enough self-con-

fidence to cope with what would come next. The door had been slammed in his face. She had pushed it open, and he had gone through.

The hymn ended. The burst of parental applause began clamorously. Little Janey, carried away by the festival excitement, clapped with all her might — "learning the customs of her corner of society," thought her mother, smiling tenderly at the petal-soft noiselessness of the tiny hands.

The third grade filed down the steps from the platform and began to march back along the aisle. For a moment, the mother forgot that she was no longer a girl, who expected recognition when she had done something creditable. David's class clumped down the aisle. Surely, she thought, David would turn his head to where she sat and thank her with a look. Just this once.

He did turn his head as he filed by. He looked full at his family, at his father, his mother, his kid sister, his big brother and sister from high school. He gave them a formal, small nod to show that he knew they were there, to acknowledge publicly that they were his family. He even smiled, a very little, stiffly, fleetingly. But his look was not for her. It was just as much for those of his family who had been bored and impatient spectators of her struggle to help him, as for her who had given part of her life to roll that stone up hill, a part of her life she never could get back.

She shifted Janey's weight a little on her knees. Of course. Did mothers ever expect to be thanked? They were to accept what they received, without bitterness, without resentment. After all, that was what mothers worked for — not for thanks, but to do their job. The sharp chisel of life, driven home by experience, flaked off expertly another flint-hard chip from her blithe, selfish girlhood. It fell away from the woman she was growing to be, and dropped soundlessly into the abyss of time.

After all, she thought, hearing vaguely the seventh-graders now on the platform (none of her four was in the seventh grade), David was only eight. At that age they were, in personality, completely cocoons, as in their babyhood they had been physical cocoons. The time had not come yet for the inner spirit to stir, to waken, to give a sign that it lived.

It certainly did not stir in young David that winter. There was no sign that it lived. The snowy weeks came and went. He rose, ravenously hungry, ate an enormous breakfast with the family, and clumped off to school with his own third-graders. The usual three stormed back after school, flinging around a cloud of overshoes, caps, mittens, windbreakers. For their own good, for the sake of their wives-to-be, for the sake of the homes which would be dependent on them, they must be called back with the hard-won, equable reasonableness of the mother, and reminded to pick up and put away. David's special two friends came to his house at four to eat her cookies, or went to each other's houses to eat other cookies. They giggled, laughed raucously, kidded and joshed each other, pushed each other around. They made snow-forts in their front yards, they skated with awkward energy on the place where the brook overflowed the meadow, took their sleds out to Hingham Hill for coasting, made plans for a shack in the woods next summer.

In the evening, if the homework had been finished in time, they were allowed to visit each other for an hour, to make things with Meccano, things which were a source of enormous pride to the eight-year-olds, things which the next morning fell over, at the lightest touch of the mother's broom.

At that age, thought the mother, their souls, if any, were certainly no more than seeds, deep inside their hard, muscular, little-boy flesh. How do souls develop, she wondered occasionally, as she washed dishes, made beds, selected carrots at the market, answered the telephone. How do souls develop out of those rough-and-ready little males? If they do develop?

David and Peter, living close to each other, shared the evening play-hour more often than the third boy who lived across the tracks. They were allowed to go by themselves, to each other's house, even though it was winter-black

at seven o'clock. Peter lived on the street above theirs, up the hill. There was a short-cut down across a vacant lot, which was in sight of one or the other house, all the way. It was safe enough, even for youngsters, even at night. The little boys loved that downhill short-cut. Its steep slope invited their feet to fury. Never using the path, they raced down in a spray of snow kicked up by their flying overshoes, arriving at the house, their cheeks flaming, flinging themselves like cannonballs against the kitchen door, tasting a little the heady physical fascination of speed, on which later, as ski-runners, they would become wildly drunken.

"Sh! *David!* Not so *loud!*" his mother often said, springing up from her mending at the crash of the banged-open door. "Father's trying to do some accounts," or "Sister has company in the living room."

Incessant acrobatic feat — to keep five people of different ages and personalities, all living under the same roof, from stepping on each other's feet. Talk about keeping five balls in the air at the same time! That was nothing compared to keeping five people satisfied to live with each other, to provide each one with approximately what he needed and wanted without taking away something needed by one of the others. (Arithmetically considered, there were of course six people living under that roof. But she did not count. She was the mother. She took what she got, what was left. . . .)

That winter, as the orbits of the older children lay more outside the house, she found herself acquiring a new psychological skill that was almost eerie. She could be in places where she was not, at all. She had an astral body which could go anywhere. Anywhere, that is, where one of her five was. She was with her honey-sweet big daughter in the living room, playing games with high-school friends (was there butter enough, she suddenly asked herself, for the popcorn the young people would inevitably want, later?). She was upstairs where her husband sat, leaning over the desk, frowning in attentiveness at a page of figures — that desk-light was not strong enough. Better put the flood-light up there tomorrow. She was in the sun-porch of the neighbor's house, where her little son was bolting Meccano-strips together with his square, strong, not-very-clean hands — his soul, if any, dormant far within his sturdy body. She floated above the scrimmage in the high-school gym, where her firstborn played basketball with ferocity, pouring out through that channel the rage of maleness constantly gathering in his big frame which grew that year with such fantastic rapidity that he seemed taller at breakfast than he had been when he went to bed. She sent her astral body upstairs to where her little daughter, her baby, her darling, slept with one doll in her arms, and three others on the pillow beside her. That blanket was not warm enough for Janey. When she went to bed, she would put on another one.

She was all of them. First one, then another. When was she herself? When did her soul have time to stretch its wings?

One evening this question tried to push itself into her mind, but was swept aside by her suddenly knowing, as definitely as if she had heard a clock strike, or the doorbell ring, that the time had passed for David's return from his evening play-hour with Peter. She looked at her watch. But she did not need to. A sixth sense told her heart, as with a blow, that he should before this have come pelting down the hill, plowing the deep snow aside in clouds, hurling himself against the kitchen door. He was late. Her astral self, annihilating time and space, fled out to look for him. He must have left the other house some time ago. Peter's mother always sent him home promptly.

She laid down the stocking she was darning, stepped into the dark kitchen, and put her face close to the window to look out. It was a cloudless cold night. Every detail of the backyard world was visible, almost transparent, in the pale radiance that fell from the stars. Not a breath of wind. She could see everything: the garbage pail at the woodshed door, the trampled snow of the driveway, the clothes she had washed that morning and left on the line, the deep unbroken snow beyond the yard, the path leading up the hill.

Then she saw David. He was standing half way down, as still as the frozen night around him.

But David never stood still.

Knee-deep in the snow he stood, looking all around him. She saw him slowly turn his head to one side, to the other. He lifted his face toward the sky. It was almost frightening to see *David* stand so still. What could he be looking at? What was there he could be seeing? Or hearing? For as she watched him, the notion crossed her mind that he seemed to be listening. But there was nothing to hear. Nothing.

She did not know what was happening to her little son. Nor what to do. So she did nothing. She stood as still as he, her face at the window, lost in wonder.

She saw him, finally, stir and start slowly, slowly down the path. But David never moved slowly. Had he perhaps had a quarrel with Peter? Had Peter's mother been unkind to him?

It could do no harm now to go to meet him, she thought, and by that time, she could not, anxious as she was, not go to meet him. She opened the kitchen door and stepped out into the dark, under the stars.

He saw her, he came quickly to her, he put his arms around her waist. With every fiber of her body which had borne his, she felt a difference in him.

She did not know what to say, so she said nothing.

It was her son who spoke. "It's so still," he said quietly in a hushed voice, a voice she had never heard before. "It's so still!"

He pressed his cheek against her breast as he tipped his head back to look up. "All those stars," he murmured dreamily, "they shine so. But they don't make a sound. They — they're *nice*, aren't they?"

He stood a little away from her to look up into her face. "Do you remember — in the song — 'the world in solemn stillness lay'?" he asked her, but he knew she remembered.

The starlight showed him clear, his honest, little-boy eyes wide, fixed trustingly on his mother's. He was deeply moved. But calm. This had come to him while he was still so young that he could be calmed by his mother's being with him. He had not known that he had an inner sanctuary. Now he stood in it, awe-struck at his first sight of beauty. And opened the door to his mother.

As naturally as he breathed, he put into his mother's hands the pure rounded pearl of a shared joy. "I thought I heard them singing — sort of," he told her.

THE FESTIVAL OF SAINT NICHOLAS

by Mary Mapes Dodge

We all know how, before the Christmas tree began to flourish in the home life of our country, a certain "right jolly old elf," with "eight tiny reindeer," used to drive his sleigh-load of toys up to our housetops, and then bound down the chimney to fill the stockings so hopefully hung by the fireplace. His friends called him Santa Claus; and those who were most intimate ventured to say, "Old Nick." It was said that he originally came from Holland. Doubtless he did; but, if so, he certainly, like many other foreigners, changed his ways very much after landing upon our shores. In Holland, Saint Nicholas is a veritable saint, and often appears in full costume, with his embroidered robes glittering with gems and gold, his mitre, his crosier, and his jewelled gloves. *Here* Santa Claus comes rollicking along on the 25th of December, our holy Christmas morn; but in Holland, Saint Nicholas visits earth on the 5th, a time especially appropriated to him. Early on the morning of the 6th, he distributes his candies, toys, and treasures, and then vanishes for a year.

Christmas Day is devoted by the Hollanders to church-rites and pleasant family visiting. It is on Saint Nicholas Eve that their young people become half wild with joy and expectation. To some of them it is a sorry time; for the saint is very candid, and, if any of them have been bad during the past year, he is quite sure to tell them so. Sometimes he carries a birch-rod under his arm, and advises the parents to give them scoldings in place of confections, and floggings instead of toys.

It was well that the boys hastened to their abodes on that bright winter evening; for, in less than an hour afterwards, the saint made his appearance in half the homes of Holland. He visited the king's palace, and in the selfsame moment appeared in Annie Bouman's comfortable home. Probably one of our silver half-dollars would have purchased all that his saint-ship left at the peasant Bouman's. But a half-dollar's worth will sometimes do for the poor what hundreds of dollars may fail to do for the rich: it makes them happy and grateful, fills them with new peace and love.

Hilda van Gleck's little brothers and sisters were in a high state of excitement that night. They had been admitted into the grand parlor: they were dressed in their best, and had been given two cakes apiece at supper. Hilda was as joyous as any. Why not? Saint Nicholas would never cross a girl of fourteen from his list, just because she was tall and looked almost like a woman. On the contrary, he would probably exert himself to do honor to such an august-looking damsel. Who could tell? So she sported and laughed and danced as gayly as the youngest, and was the soul of all their merry games. Father, mother, and grandmother looked on approvingly; so did grandfather, before he spread his large red handkerchief over his face, leaving only the top of his skullcap visible. This kerchief was his ensign of sleep.

Earlier in the evening, all had joined in the fun. In the general hilarity, there had seemed to be a difference only in bulk between grandfather and the baby. Indeed, a shade of solemn expectation, now and then flitting across the faces of the younger members, had made them seem rather more thoughtful than their elders.

Now the spirit of fun reigned supreme. The very flames danced and capered in the polished grate. A pair of prim candles, that had been staring at the astral lamp, began to wink at other candles far away in the mirrors. There was a long bell-rope suspended from the ceiling in the corner, made of glass beads, netted over a cord nearly as thick as your wrist. It generally hung in the shadow, and made no sign; but tonight it twinkled from end to end. Its handle of crimson glass sent reckless dashes of red at the papered wall, turning its dainty blue stripes into purple. Passers-by halted to catch the merry laughter floating through curtain and sash into the street, then skipped on their way with the startled consciousness that the village was wide awake. At last matters grew so uproarious that the grandsire's red kerchief came down from his face with a jerk. What decent old gentleman could sleep in such a racket! Mynheer van Gleck regarded his children with astonishment. The baby even showed symptoms of hysterics. It was high time to attend to business. Madame suggested that, if they wished to see the good Saint Nicholas, they should sing the same loving invitation that had brought him the year before.

The baby stared, and thrust his fist into his mouth, as Mynheer put him down upon the floor. Soon he sat erect, and looked with a sweet scowl at the company. With his lace and embroideries, and his crown of blue ribbon and whalebone (for he was not quite past the tumbling age), he looked like the king of the babies.

The other children, each holding a pretty willow basket, formed at once in a ring, and moved slowly around the little fellow, lifting their eyes meanwhile; for the saint to whom they were about to address themselves was yet in mysterious quarters.

Madame commenced playing softly upon the piano; soon the voices rose — gentle, youthful voices, rendered all the sweeter for their tremor —

"Welcome, friend! Saint Nicholas, welcome!
Bring no rod for us tonight!
While our voices bid thee welcome,
Every heart with joy is light.

"Tell us every fault and failing;
We will hear thy keenest railing
So we sing, so we sing:
Thou shalt tell us everything!

"Welcome, friend! Saint Nicholas, welcome!
Welcome to this merry band!
Happy children greet thee, welcome!
Thou are gladdening all the land.

"Fill each empty hand and basket;
'Tis thy little ones who ask it.
So we sing, so we sing:
Thou wilt bring us everything!"

During the chorus, sundry glances, half in eagerness, half in dread, had been cast towards the polished folding-doors. Now a loud knocking was heard. The circle was broken in an instant. Some of the little ones, with a strange mixture of fear and delight, pressed against their mother's knee. Grandfather bent forward, with his chin resting upon his hand; grandmother lifted her spectacles; Mynheer van Gleck, seated by the fireplace, slowly drew his meerschaum from his mouth; while Hilda and the other children settled themselves beside him in an expectant group.

The knocking was heard again.

"Come in," said Madame, softly.

The door slowly opened; and Saint Nicholas, in full array, stood before them. You could have heard a pin drop. Soon he spoke. What a mysterious majesty in his voice! What kindliness in his tones!

"Karel van Gleck, I am pleased to greet thee, and thy honored *vrouw*, Kathrine, and thy son, and his good *vrouw*, Annie.

"Children, I greet ye all — Hendrick, Hilda, Broom, Katy, Huygens, and Lucretia. And thy cousins — Wolfert, Diedrich, Mayken, Voost, and Katrina. Good children ye have been, in the main, since I last accosted ye. Diedrich was rude at the Haarlem fair last fall; but he has tried to atone for it since. Mayken has failed, of late, in her lessons; and too many sweets and trifles have gone to her lips, and too few stivers to her charity-box. Diedrich, I trust, will be a polite, manly boy for the future; and Mayken will endeavor to shine as a student. Let her remember, too, that economy and thrift are needed in the foundation of a worthy and generous life. Little Katy has been cruel to the cat more than once. Saint Nicholas can hear the cat cry when its tail is pulled. I will forgive her, if she will remember from this hour that the smallest dumb creatures have feeling, and must not be abused."

As Katy burst into a frightened cry, the saint graciously remained silent until she was soothed.

"Master Broom," he resumed, "I warn thee that boys who are in the habit of putting snuff upon the foot-stove of the school-mistress may one day be discovered, and receive a flogging—"

(Master Broom colored, and stared in great astonishment.)

"But, thou art such an excellent scholar, I shall make thee no further reproof.

"Thou, Hendrick, didst distinguish thyself in the archery match last Spring, and hit the bulls-eye, though the bird was swung before it to unsteady thine eye. I give thee credit for excelling in manly sport and exercise — though I must not unduly countenance thy boat-racing since it leaves thee too little time for thy proper studies.

"Lucretia and Hilda shall have a blessed sleep tonight. The consciousness of kindness to the poor, devotion in their souls, and cheerful, hearty obedience to household rule will render them happy.

"With one and all I avow myself well content. Goodness, industry, benevolence and thrift have prevailed in your midst. Therefore, my blessing upon you — and may the New Year find all treading the paths of obedience, wisdom and love. Tomorrow you shall find more substantial proofs that I have been in your midst. Farewell!"

With these words came a great shower of sugar-plums, upon a linen sheet spread out in front of the doors. A general scramble followed. The children fairly tumbled over each other in their eagerness to fill their baskets. Madame cautiously held the baby down in their midst, till the chubby little fists were filled. Then the bravest of the youngsters sprang up and burst open the closed doors — in vain they peered into the mysterious apartment — Saint Nicholas was nowhere to be seen.

Soon there was a general rush to another room, where stood a table, covered with the finest and whitest of linen damask. Each child, in a flutter of excitement, laid a shoe upon it. The door was then carefully locked, and its key hidden in the mother's bedroom. Next followed good-night kisses, a grand family-procession to the upper floor, merry farewells at bedroom doors — and silence, at last, reigned in the Van Gleck mansion.

Early the next morning the door was solemnly unlocked and opened in the presence of the assembled household, when lo! a sight appeared proving Saint Nicholas to be a saint of his word!

Every shoe was filled to overflowing, and beside each stood many a colored pile. The table was heavy with its load of presents — candies, toys, trinkets, books and other articles. Everyone had gifts, from grandfather down to the baby.

Little Katy clapped her hands with glee, and vowed, inwardly, that the cat should never know another moment's grief.

Hendrick capered about the room, flourishing a superb bow and arrows over his head. Hilda laughed with delight as she opened a crimson box and drew forth its glittering contents. The rest chuckled and said "Oh!" and "Ah!" over their treasures, very much as we did here in America on last Christmas day.

THE MOUSE THAT DIDN'T BELIEVE IN SANTA CLAUS

by Eugene Field

The clock stood, of course, in the corner; a moonbeam floated idly on the floor, and a little mauve mouse came from the hole in the chimney corner and frisked and scampered in the light of the moonbeam upon the floor. The little mauve mouse was particularly merry; sometimes she danced upon two legs and sometimes upon four legs, but always very daintily and always very merrily.

"Ah, me," sighed the old clock, "how different mice are nowadays from the mice we used to have in the old times! Now there was your grandma, Mistress Velvetpaw, and there was your grandpa, Master Sniffwhisker — how grave and dignified they were! Many a night have I seen them dancing upon the carpet below me, but always that stately minuet and never that crazy frisking which you are executing now, to my surprise — yes, and to my horror, too!"

"But why shouldn't I be merry?" asked the little mauve mouse. "Tomorrow is Christmas, and this is Christmas Eve."

"So it is," said the old clock. "I had really forgotten all about it. But, tell me, what is Christmas to you, little Miss Mauve Mouse?"

"A great deal to me!" cried the little mauve mouse. "I have been very good for a very long time; I have not used any bad words, nor have I gnawed any holes, nor have I stolen any canary seed, nor have I worried my mother by running behind the flour barrel where that horrid trap is set. In fact, I have been so good that I'm very sure Santa Claus will bring me something very pretty."

This seemed to amuse the old clock mightily; in fact, the old clock fell to laughing so heartily that in an unguarded moment she struck twelve instead of ten, which was exceedingly careless.

"Why, you silly little mauve mouse," said the old clock, "you don't believe in Santa Claus, do you?"

"Of course I do," answered the mauve mouse. "Believe in Santa Claus? Why shouldn't I? Didn't Santa Claus bring me a beautiful butter cracker last Christmas, and a lovely gingersnap, and a delicious rind of cheese, and — lots of things? I should be very ungrateful if I did *not* believe in Santa Claus, and I certainly shall not disbelieve in him at the very moment when I am expecting him to arrive with a bundle of goodies for me.

"I once had a little sister," continued the little mauve mouse, "who did not believe in Santa Claus, and the very thought of the fate that befell her makes my blood run cold and my whiskers stand on end. She died before I was born, but my mother has told me all about her. Her name was Squeaknibble, and she was in stature one of those long, low, rangy mice that are seldom found in well-stocked pantries. Mother says that Squeaknibble took after our ancestors who came from New England, and seemed to inherit many ancestral traits, the most conspicuous of which was a disposition to sneer at some of the most respected dogmas in mousedom. From her very infancy she doubted, for example, the widely accepted theory that the moon was composed of green cheese; and this heresy was the first intimation her parents had of her sceptical turn of mind. Of course, her parents were vastly annoyed, for they saw that this youthful scepticism would lead to serious, if not fatal, consequences. Yet all in vain did they reason and plead with their headstrong and heretical child.

"For a long time Squeaknibble would not believe that there was any such archfiend as a cat; but she came to be convinced one memorable night, on which occasion she lost two inches of her beautiful tail, and received so terrible a fright that for fully an hour afterward her little heart beat so violently as to lift her off her feet and bump her head against the top of our domestic hole. The cat that deprived

my sister of so large a percentage of her tail was the same ogress that nowadays steals into this room, crouches treacherously behind the sofa, and feigns to be asleep, hoping, forsooth, that some of us, heedless of her hated presence, will venture within reach of her claws. So enraged was this ferocious monster at the escape of my sister that she ground her fangs viciously together, and vowed to take no pleasure in life until she held in her devouring jaws the innocent little mouse which belonged to the mangled bit of tail she even then clutched in her remorseless claws."

"Yes," said the old clock, "now that you recall the incident, I recollect it well. I was here then, and I remember that I laughed at the cat and chided her for her awkwardness. My reproaches irritated her; she told me that a clock's duty was to run itself down, *not* to be depreciating the merits of others! Yes, I recall the time; that cat's tongue is fully as sharp as her claws."

"Be that as it may," said the little mauve mouse, "it is a matter of history, and therefore beyond dispute, that from that very moment the cat pined for Squeaknibble's life; it seemed as if that one little two-inch taste of Squeak-

nibble's tail had filled that cat with a consuming appetite for the rest of Squeaknibble. So the cat waited and watched and hunted and schemed and devised and did everything possible for a cat — a cruel cat — to do in order to gain her murderous ends.

"One night — one fatal Christmas Eve — our mother had undressed the children for bed, and was urging them all to go to sleep earlier than usual, since she fully expected that Santa Claus would bring each of them something very nice before morning. Thereupon the little dears whisked their cunning tails, pricked up their beautiful ears, and began telling one another what they hoped Santa Claus would bring. One asked for a slice of Roquefort, another for Swiss, another for Brick, and a fourth for Edam; one expressed a preference for Cream cheese, while another hoped for Camembert. There were fourteen little ones then, and consequently there were diverse opinions as to the kind of gift which Santa Claus should best bring; still there was, as you can readily understand, an enthusiastic agreement upon this point, namely, that the gift should be cheese of some brand or other.

" 'My dears,' said our mother, 'we should be content with whatsoever Santa Claus bestows, so long as it is cheese, disjoined from all traps whatsoever, unmixed with Paris green, and free from glass, strychnine, and other harmful ingredients. As for myself, I shall be satisfied with a cut of nice, fresh American cheese. So run away to your dreams now, that Santa may find you sleeping.'

"The children obeyed — all but Squeaknibble. 'Let the others think what they please,' said she, 'but I don't believe in Santa Claus. I'm not going to bed, either. I'm going to creep out of this dark hole and have a quiet romp, all by myself, in the moonlight.' Oh, what a vain, foolish, wicked little mouse was Squeaknibble! But I will not reproach the dead; her punishment came all too swiftly. Now listen: who do you suppose overheard her talking so disrespectfully of Santa Claus?"

"Why, Santa Claus himself," said the old clock.

"Oh, no," answered the little mauve mouse. "It was that wicked, murderous cat! Just as Satan lurks and lies in wait for bad children, so does the cruel cat lurk and lie in wait for naughty little mice. And you can depend upon it that, when that awful cat heard Squeaknibble speak so disrespectfully of Santa Claus, her wicked eyes glowed with joy, her sharp teeth watered, and her bristling fur emitted electric sparks as big as peas. Then what did that bloody monster do but scuttle as fast as she could into Dear-my-Soul's room, leap up into Dear-my-Soul's crib, and walk off with the pretty little white muff which Dear-my-Soul used to wear when she went for a visit to the little girl in the next block! What upon earth did the horrid old cat want with Dear-my-Soul's pretty little white muff? Ah, the ingenuity of that cat! Listen.

"In the first place," resumed the little mauve mouse, after a pause that showed the depth of her emotion, "in the first place, that wretched cat dressed herself up in that pretty little white muff, by which you are to understand that she crawled through the muff just so far as to leave her four cruel legs at liberty."

"Yes, I understand," said the old clock.

"Then she put on the boy doll's cap," said the little mauve mouse, "and when she was arrayed in the boy doll's fur cap and Dear-my-Soul's pretty little white muff, of course she didn't look like a cruel cat at all. But whom did she look like?"

"Like the boy doll," suggested the old clock.

"No, no!" cried the little mauve mouse.

"Like Dear-my-Soul?" asked the old clock.

"How stupid you are!" exclaimed the little mauve mouse. "Why, she looked like Santa Claus, of course!"

"Oh, yes; I see," said the old clock. "Now I begin to be interested; go on."

"Alas!" sighed the little mauve mouse, "not much remains to be told; but there is more of my story left than there was of Squeaknibble when that horrid cat crawled out of that miserable disguise. You are to understand that, contrary to her mother's warning, Squeaknibble issued from the friendly hole in the chimney corner, and gamboled about over this very carpet, and, I dare say, in this very moonlight.

"Right merrily was Squeaknibble gamboling," continued the little mauve mouse, "and she had just turned a double somersault without the use of what remained of her tail, when, all of a sudden, she beheld, looming up like a monster ghost, a figure all in white fur! Oh, how frightened she was, and how her little heart did beat! 'Purr, purr-r-r,' said the ghost in white fur. 'Oh, please don't hurt me!' pleaded Squeaknibble. 'No, I'll not hurt you,' said the ghost in white fur; 'I'm Santa Claus, and I've brought you a beautiful piece of savory old cheese, you dear little mousie, you.' Poor Squeaknibble was deceived; a sceptic all her life, she was at last befooled by the most fatal of frauds. 'How good of you!' said Squeaknibble. 'I didn't believe there was a Santa Claus, and —' but before she could say more she was seized by two sharp, cruel claws that conveyed her crushed body to the murderous mouth of the cat. I can dwell no longer upon this harrowing scene. Before the morrow's sun rose upon the spot where that tragedy had been enacted, poor Squeaknibble passed to that bourne to which two inches of her beautiful tail had preceded her by the space of three weeks to a day. As for Santa Claus, when he came that Christmas Eve, bringing cheese and goodies for the other little mice, he heard with sorrow of Squeaknibble's fate; and ere he departed he said that in all his experience he had never known of a mouse or a child that had prospered after once saying he didn't believe in Santa Claus."

DO YOU BELIEVE IN MIRACLES?

by Lois T. Henderson

The Reverend Paul Edwards stood at the back of the auditorium of the church and looked at the Christmas decorations. The decorating committee had just gone home, and he was alone in the dim sanctuary, alone with the glittering tree and the fragile silver star that hung above the altar.

But, for all the beauty, he was not stirred or moved, and a minister ought not to feel like that, he knew, not when he was only thirty and fairly new to the ministry. He ought to be filled with a fire. Especially when it was Christmas Eve.

But that was the whole trouble. He couldn't get excited about Christmas. He only knew he was tired and let down and maybe even a little disillusioned. He remembered Christmases when he was a theological student, and it had seemed as though all the air were filled with a sense of the miraculous. But now the air was just air, and misery engulfed him to think that it was so.

He sat in one of the pews and slid down on the end of his spine to stare at the artificial star against the darkened windows. That's just it, he thought, everything is artificial. The decorations, the very hearts of people. And mine too.

Suddenly he was frightened. He didn't want to feel the weariness, the artificiality. He wanted to feel as he had once felt, that miracles did happen on Christmas Eve, that animals could talk at midnight, that flowers did bloom out of the snow as gifts for the Christ child. He wanted the feeling so badly that it was like an aching in him.

I'll go home, he decided. Jeannie will cheer me up. He thought of his wife, small and merry and wise, and some of the panic dissolved in him. Jeannie will know what to say, he thought again, and pulled on his coat to go out into the night.

The darkness and the wind struck at him as he opened the church door. The snow drifted against his face to melt into little spots of wetness on his cheeks and lips. Boyishly, he stuck out his tongue to the snow, and it tasted cool and wet. The street lights made little pools of yellow in the dark, and the snow seemed to swirl in miniature whirlwinds under each light.

It looks like Christmas, he admitted to himself, but it doesn't feel like Christmas. And for a minister, it has to. It absolutely has to.

He walked swiftly to his house and came in out of the night and the cold to find light and fragrance and warmth. Jeannie met him in the hall, and her kiss was sweeter than usual.

"Cookie dough," she explained, and rubbed at her mouth.

Her eyes were soft and shining. She gets more beautiful every day, Paul felt, especially with the baby on the way. Her body was large and awkward with the weight of the child she carried but her face was tender and lovely.

As he looked at her standing there, he knew he couldn't tell her. Not on Christmas Eve. He couldn't tell her he was tired and frightened and not so sure of miracles any more. He couldn't transmit his fear to her. She believed in all the magic of Christmas — you could see it in her eyes — and he just couldn't spoil it for her.

So he attempted lightness instead. "How's the little mother?" he asked. "Not you. You're only making promises so far. I mean the *real* one."

Jeannie laughed with indulgent scorn. "That Hildy!" she said. "You'd think she was the only dog in all the world who ever had puppies. Honestly, she *polishes* them."

"It's her German heritage," Paul pronounced. "All dachshunds are abnormally clean."

"She's just fussy," Jeannie said, starting for

the kitchen. "I hope I'll be a little more casual with our baby."

She leaned over heavily to take a tray of cookies from the oven.

"You're not baking cookies again?" he said. "Not at the last minute?"

She looked apologetic. "Not many. Just some gingerbread men. And these are the scraps. I remembered about six o'clock that I hadn't fixed a single thing for Penny Ellis, and I just *had* to do something."

Paul thought of Penny with sorrow. Poor little six-year-old Penny who had been desperately ill from polio in the summer and who was just now home from the hospital, facing the long difficult time of learning to walk again — if she ever did.

"Maybe we could have bought her something," he said.

"No, she'll get plenty of dolls and fancy things. But I thought she'd love a gingerbread boy. With lots of icing."

"You!" he said. "You always think of the right things. Every single time."

"I did when I picked you," she said.

And he wondered what she would say if she knew of the thoughts that had tormented him lately. Not doubt — it wasn't that. He still believed in God and in God's plan for him. It wasn't that at all. It was just that all the shine had worn off and he had begun to wonder if even the ministry, which he had thought would always be a thing of wonder and glory, had gotten drab and had lost much of its meaning. He wondered if cynicism, the greatest thief of all, had come into his life and heart.

"You take them over to her," Jeannie said, interrupting his thoughts. "She'll be extra thrilled if the minister comes on Christmas Eve."

"I don't think her Dad will be very thrilled," Paul said.

"Poor Guy," Jeannie murmured. "I feel so sorry for him."

"I feel sorrier for Penny," Paul said.

"No, because Penny still has faith in life. Guy doesn't. He's so bitter and resentful. Can't you help him, Paul?"

Paul's heart cried: How can I help him when I'm so mixed up myself! "I don't know," he answered guardedly. "He's pretty touchy right now, isn't much interested in preaching."

Jeannie laughed. "Oh, heavens, I don't mean preach at him. I mean just show him somehow, some way — you'll know how, Paul — that life is still wonderful. I think he thinks God has a special, personal grudge against him."

"He isn't the only man whose child ever had to suffer," Paul said.

"But he feels Penny's suffering so intensely," Jeannie answered. "And I'm afraid his bitterness will hurt her. I'm afraid it'll break down her confidence. Aren't you?"

"Yes, I am," Paul admitted. "Well, I'll get along. Want to go along?"

"I'd love to, but I'm going to clean up the kitchen and then lie down on the couch for an hour or two so I'll be rested for the midnight service. This son of yours has been pretty active today," she said smugly.

"Daughter, you mean," Paul corrected her.

He took her in his arms. It seemed he had never loved her more than now. Her face still bore a faint trace of cookie dough, there was flour on her cheek, and her mouth looked tired. He held her gently, sensing the movements of their unborn child. Jeannie, he thought silently, pray for me, help me regain what I've lost.

"I love you," he said, kissing her.

"I love you too," she answered. "Come on now and take the cookies. I don't want you to be out too late."

He took the cookies wrapped in bright paper and went out again in the snow and the wind. In his present frame of mind, he really dreaded going to the Ellises'. He loved Penny, and his heart ached for her, but it seemed to him that he almost bruised himself on the bitterness of Guy Ellis. It was really more than bitterness with Guy, Paul felt; it was lack of belief and faith and hope. It was a sullen sort of despair.

In a few minutes Paul knocked at the door of the Ellis home, and Nancy, Penny's mother, came to let him in.

"Why, Reverend Edwards," she cried. "How nice to see you. Guy, here's Reverend Edwards."

Guy Ellis came to greet the young minister, and his handclasp was cordial enough. Only his eyes showed the defeat and the despair.

"Merry Christmas," Paul said smiling. "I came to see Penny."

Nancy looked pleased. "She's not asleep yet. I was just going to read her a story. She'll be so tickled to see you."

Paul followed Nancy down the hall to the bedroom that had the high plain hospital bed in the center of it. Lying on the bed was a very thin little girl with quick-moving hands and too-still legs. Her light hair was pulled into braids, and her eyes were large from recent suffering.

"Reverend Edwards," she said, and the small pointed face grew bright. "I was just thinking about you."

"Were you?" Paul said. "And I was thinking about you."

"I'll let you talk to Penny," Nancy said, "and I'll go and tend to some secrets."

She winked at Paul and he marveled at her courage in the face of such odds.

"I'm glad she's gone," Penny confided as soon as her mother had left. "I was just layin' here wishin' you'd come, and you did. So now I know the other thing will happen, too."

Paul felt a faint prickle at the nape of his neck. "How — just wishing I'd come?" he said cautiously.

Penny smiled. "I just said a while ago — in a little whisper, you know, so nobody'd hear — I just said, 'Dear God, please let Reverend Edwards come to see me 'cause I just have to tell somebody my secret.' And you came."

Paul's lips felt a little dry. Coincidence, said the cynical part of his heart, and he listened to it.

"So you have a secret?" he said and he tried to sound gay.

But she was very serious. "This is a very important secret," she said. "Very terrible important. I wasn't going to tell anybody. Just God, you know. But then I felt the secret would just bust out of me if I didn't tell someone."

She put her thin little hands on her chest as though the secret were lodged there.

"Then I thought about you," she went on, "and how well you know God, so I knew it would be all right to tell you."

Paul stared at the child. "How well I know God?" he asked, shaken.

She nodded. "You talk to Him in church like — well, kind of like He lived next door to you."

Paul couldn't say anything. There were just no words to say to the child.

"The secret's something I asked God for," Penny said. "For Christmas. Lean down so I can whisper."

Paul felt an agony in him. She has asked God to make her walk, he thought. And she believes it will happen, like a miracle. And I can't stand to see her hurt.

"What did you ask for?" he whispered and bent close to her.

He was so amazed when her soft answer came that for a second he only looked at her blankly. "What?"

"A dog," she repeated. And Paul's heart soared. I have it in *my* power to work a miracle for her, he exulted to himself. I can bring over one of Hildy's pups and the prayer will be answered.

But then Penny went on solemnly, "A little gold-colored dog with long curly ears. And I'll call him Star. Wouldn't it be beautiful to get a real live golden Star on Christmas?"

Paul stared at the child, feeling utterly cast down. Hildy's pups would never do, for who could possibly explain to Penny that God could make a mistake and send a dark red-brown sleek little dachshund when a gold fluffy-eared cocker spaniel had been requested. No, I won't be able to work a miracle, after all, he thought. It was foolish to believe I could.

"Did you tell your Mommy?" he asked. "Or your Daddy?"

She shook her head against the pillow. "No, just God. And now you. But I know God will give me the dog."

There was such confidence and faith in her eyes that Paul thought he could not bear it. Because where would such a dog come from if her parents didn't know she wanted one? Why hadn't she written it in a letter to Santa like other kids did and then her father could have read the letter? Why had she prayed about it? And in secret? And then, suddenly, Paul knew as plainly as though someone had told him. Penny was testing God. That was it. She was testing the strength and power of God. If He could get her this dog for Christmas, He could make her walk again. Paul felt sick at the pit of his stomach.

Penny smiled placidly. "I feel better now I've told you," she said. "Secrets get too big sometimes, don't they?"

"Yes," he said, "they do." And his mind was filled with whirling thoughts. Where could you get a gold-colored dog with curly ears that could be called Star, especially at nine o'clock on Christmas Eve?

He got up and tried to smile at Penny. "I'm glad you told me," he said. "But I'm going to have to leave, Penny, I've got so much to do. Merry Christmas, sweetheart."

"Merry Christmas," she answered, and her voice sounded relaxed and sleepy.

Paul hurried from the room and went to the living room. Guy and Nancy Ellis looked up from the packages they were wrapping.

"Finished talking so soon?" Nancy said.

Paul nodded. "I've got to talk to you," he whispered, "where Penny won't hear."

Guy regarded him with something like suspicion and Nancy spoke quickly.

"I'll just run in and cover her up," she said. "Then we can go into the kitchen to talk where she can't hear."

Paul and Guy waited without speaking until Nancy came back, and then they went together down the hall to the kitchen.

"Is something wrong?" Nancy asked.

"I'll say something is wrong," Paul said. "That poor little kid has got her heart completely set on something for Christmas that she hasn't told either one of you about."

"Oh, no!" Nancy's hand went to her mouth.

"What is it?" Guy asked. "I'll get her anything. She's had enough of a rotten deal. What is it?"

"She prayed about it," Paul explained. "She

asked God to give it to her. It's a dog she wants — and from the description I'd say she wants a gold cocker spaniel and she wants to name it Star because it came on Christmas."

Nancy and Guy stared at him without speaking. He knew they were thinking, as he had, that it would be impossible to find a dog like that now, at this hour, on Christmas Eve.

"Why didn't she tell me?" Guy said, and his voice was savage. "Why did she have to pray about it?"

Paul felt sure the other man's thoughts were bitter ones, that he was thinking he could give to his child the things God would not or could not give. Paul tried to speak gently. "I think she's sort of testing God," he said. "I think she feels if He can get her a dog, He can do anything." He paused. "Even make her walk," he said.

There were tears on Nancy's face.

"The doctors say she might walk," she whispered. "But she'll have to believe it herself."

"How can she believe it when I don't believe it?" Guy said, and the hopelessness was evident in his voice. "She'll never walk again. Never."

Nancy turned on him. "If it weren't for you," she said, but she kept her voice pitched low, "Penny wouldn't have felt it necessary to try God out. It's *your* lack of faith that has made her afraid."

Guy stared at his wife, and Paul's heart ached for both of them.

"I can't help it," Guy said. "I just can't help it."

"You don't try," Nancy sobbed. "You don't even try. And now, what's going to happen to her? We can't get the dog. You know we can't."

"We can try," Paul interposed. "Come on, Guy. I've got two hours till church service. Let's get going."

While Guy went for his wraps, Paul spoke to Nancy. "Did you know Penny prayed much?" he asked. "I mean, had she ever told you?"

Nancy wiped at tears with her hands. "Yes," she said shakily. "Sometimes I go in and her eyes are shut and her lips are moving, and when I speak to her she looks very reproachful and says she's talking to God. I thought it was all right."

"It *is* all right," Paul said. "You know it is." In the midst of all his troubled thoughts he remembered Jeannie's voice saying, "I remembered about six o'clock I hadn't fixed a thing for Penny Ellis."

I'm being foolish, Paul thought, this is crazy. But he stilled the cynicism and forced himself to ask the question. "Nancy," he said, "did you notice Penny praying tonight?"

She thought for a minute. "Why, yes," she answered, "when I took in her supper, about six o'clock. Why?"

"Nothing," Paul said, but he felt a great stirring in his heart, a great trembling.

"Where'll we start?" Guy said.

"My house," Paul decided. "We can use the phone without Penny hearing. We'll call the owner of every pet store we can find."

"There's only two," Guy reminded him. "It isn't as if we were in a big city."

"We'll call the police," Paul went on. "Maybe they've picked up a stray."

"I don't think it'll do any good," Guy said.

Paul felt a touch of impatience. "Well, at least we can try before we give up."

Guy hunched his chin into his collar. "I guess it's pretty easy for a preacher to have faith," he said, and his voice was filled with mockery, "when he's never had trouble or sorrow."

Paul's impatience died away. "No," he said. "It's not even easy then."

Guy's face jerked toward the minister. "You mean *you* have doubts, too?"

"I think everyone has doubts," Paul said, "only some of mine are going away." And, on sudden impulse, he told Guy of Penny's praying for him to come to her and of Jeannie's decision to make the gingerbread boy.

"Coincidence," Guy said. "You know it if you're an educated man."

"Maybe," said Paul, because part of him felt that Guy was right and he was weary from the warring in his soul.

An hour and a half later, Guy and Paul were riding hopelessly and almost aimlessly through the snow-filled streets. They had spent half an hour on the telephone and an hour driving around in the cold, but they had been completely unsuccessful.

"Now talk about prayer," Guy said bitterly. "Or haven't you prayed about this dog? Is that too little a thing to bother God about?"

"Of course I've prayed," Paul said. "Because it isn't little. Because I think if Penny could get this dog it would give her all the faith she'd need to walk again."

"I believe that too," Guy admitted, and his words sounded ragged. "Only there isn't any dog."

"Maybe if you prayed too?" Paul suggested, and he knew that Jeannie and Nancy were adding their prayers to his.

"Me?" Guy said. "Why should I? Do you think a God who would let a little kid get crippled would help us find a dog?"

Paul realized the man was crying and he thought, I wish I knew what to say. I wish I had confidence to give him. I wish I could say that it's bound to happen just because it's Christmas. But I can't say that.

The motor coughed and Paul glanced swiftly at the dashboard. He was out of gas, and at this hour! But when he glanced up again, he saw that he was within a block of a gas station and the owner, Dick Hayson, who lived next door to the station, was one of his parishioners. I'm in luck, Paul thought, and let the car drift coughing to the driveway of the station. He stopped by one of the tanks and went to ask Hayson for some gas.

Hayson was obliging and, while he filled the tank, Paul looked at his watch. Only 25 minutes until he had to be in church for the midnight service. And no dog for Penny. And no comfort or peace to offer to the unhappy man in his car. Paul silently pounded one clenched fist into the other hand.

At that moment a sound came through the night, a soft hesitant sound. The whimper of a small dog. Paul looked up, dazed and unbelieving, to see a gold cocker spaniel come toward him across the snow-covered drive. The puppy stopped in front of Paul, and, staring down at the dog, Paul felt himself possessed of the urge to shout with exultation. And at the same instant, he felt a great compulsion to stand in silence and reverence as though this were a holy place.

Dick Hayson looked up to see the dog at Paul's feet. "Well, I'll be darned," he said. "How'd that pup get out? He must have squeezed out right past my feet."

It was almost too much for Paul. His hopes had soared and fallen too many times, and he felt battered from it all.

He wet his lips with his tongue and managed to speak at last. "You mean it's yours?" And what did you think, a tired, bitter voice said in his heart — that God would fashion a cocker puppy out of snow?

Hayson smiled. "Got it for my boy for Christmas. Cute, isn't he?"

Paul nodded humbly. He wanted to weep but he managed to say courteously, "Yes! I hope it will be a happy surprise for your boy."

Hayson laughed, and his laughter had a rueful sound. "It'll be a surprise all right — but I don't know how happy. He wants another kind of dog altogether."

Paul stood very still but he felt a trembling in his body. Again he licked his lips and when he spoke his voice came in a husky whisper. "What kind of a dog?" he asked, but he knew what the answer would be.

"A dachshund. But we couldn't find one anywhere."

The night was suddenly starred with serenity. This was *right*, Paul knew, not an ethereal, impossible-to-understand miracle, but a practical thing. Coincidence? questioned his heart once more, but his faith was stronger, all at once, than any questioning. This wasn't coincidence, but a Plan conceived in love and executed with mercy.

In a few brief words, he explained the situation to Hayson and promised to come back immediately after the midnight service with a dachshund puppy if he could take the gold cocker spaniel to Penny. Hayson was delighted, handed the little dog to Paul, and went back to his house shaking his head in wonderment at his "luck."

Paul walked to the car, and when Guy Ellis looked up and saw the dog, his face seemed to sag. "Whose is it?" he managed to ask.

"Penny's," Paul said.

"But where'd it come from?"

Paul looked into the other man's eyes. "I think God sent it," he said.

"I don't see — it couldn't — can you explain —" Guy began, stammering.

Paul put the dog into the other man's arms and explained what had happened as he drove along the snowy street.

"It's a coincidence," Guy said at last, but his voice was not steady.

"But a God-given coincidence," Paul said.

"But God didn't just send him through the air," Guy insisted. "If we had just stayed home praying, the dog wouldn't have come floating through a window."

"Probably not. Maybe we have to help miracles happen." And it was a moment of discovery for Paul, too. "But God did answer Penny's prayer, Guy. Somehow, He did."

"Maybe — I guess you're right," Guy said at last, and Paul heard the faint warmth of hope in Guy's voice. Maybe with hope would come faith, the young minister exulted silently, all the faith Penny would need in the days ahead.

After he delivered Guy and the dog, he hurried home to get Jeannie. He was filled with a recurring sense of wonder as he told her about the dog, and she accepted the news with gladness, but he knew somehow that she had never doubted it would happen.

They walked together to the church, and just before they reached the door, Paul turned to Jeannie.

"I didn't believe it would happen," he confessed. "I needed the — the miracle too, Jeannie. Why can't my faith stay strong?"

She smiled and squeezed his hand. "Peter had to have the walking on the water," she said. "Everyone needs something like that once in a while to help him."

"But not you," he protested.

"I have a miracle growing in me," she said. "And I have you. That's all I need."

They walked into the church together, and

the night was bright with candles and the sound of the organ and the glimmering of the fragile star above the altar. Paul looked at it and thought of the light that would be in Penny's eyes when she saw her golden Christmas Star the next morning.

A great happiness filled him and his eyes clung to Jeannie's face as he sang with his people, "Joy to the World, the Lord Is Come."

WHEN FATHER CHRISTMAS WAS YOUNG

by Coningsby Dawson

Someone had hinted that there wasn't a Santa Claus. If there wasn't, who brought Christmas presents? For weeks, when Mac had been put to bed and was supposed to be asleep, he had lain awake puzzling. He had reached the point at which suspense ached like a guilty conscience. He simply had to share his secret with a wiser person.

He had postponed and postponed till at last it was Christmas Eve. All day Daddy had been finishing a story. Daddy could be so inconvenient. When he was finishing a story, he turned the key in his lock and everybody went on tiptoe.

Mac had returned from his afternoon's walk with Nannie. Streets and stores had been gay with excited preparations. To make things perfect, snow was falling. Mac had prayed for snow. He'd set himself a task, which was nothing less than to prove that Santa Claus existed. If there was snow on housetops, it would be impossible for old Santa to tether his reindeer to chimneys without leaving tracks.

And now to take Daddy into his confidence. Having escaped from the nursery, he twisted the handle of the study door. It wasn't locked. An instant later a jolly voice invited him to enter. Across the threshold he halted, his fat legs astride, a worried expression on his cherubic countenance.

"I've been thinking, Daddy."

"You don't say, old son! Climb on my knee and tell me."

The red lacquer room with the fire shining afforded a friendly setting. Yet Mac couldn't blurt out the wicked heresy he had overheard. Instead he cuddled against the smoky jacket and asked:

"Who was Santa when he was young? He's terribly old now, but he must have been little as me once. Who taught him to be fond of reindeer and to come down chimbleys and to leave presents? Was he the first to do things like that or did he have a mummy and daddy who did them before him?"

His father filled and lit a pipe. He was playing for time. He hated to disappoint his son; he hated still more to deceive him. He said:

"I'm afraid you'll consider me a most ignorant parent. I don't know the answer to a single one of your questions. I ought to. I've no excuse. With your help, I propose to educate myself. Do you see all those books — the tall ones? They're books of reference, which means that they can answer anything. All you have to do is to open them and turn to the word 'potato,' for instance; every fact about a potato is recorded. Let's make a game of it and go on a hunt. . . . What shall we look for?" Daddy prompted.

"Santa Claus."

Daddy ran his eyes along the shelves.

"'Who's Who in America.' We shan't find him mentioned there; he's international. Let's try the encyclopedia."

But the encyclopedia proved stodgy. As soon as you'd hit on what you thought you wanted, it referred you to another volume. Having looked up Santa Claus, you were at once informed that you ought to have looked up Saint Nicholas. When you looked up Saint Nicholas you were told that he had lived in a funny place called Myra in Lycia. In fact he'd been a bishop who had been tortured to death. He had gained the reputation of being fond of children. In England alone four hundred churches had been dedicated to his memory, each of them containing a stained-glass window representing him pulling three little boys out of a tub.

"That's silly, Daddy. Why a tub?"

"Goodness knows. But listen, Doodles; this is interesting. He's the Russian Santa Claus and the greatest saint in Russia; that brings him close to reindeer. Reindeer live up north in Lapland. And here's something else; after he'd been dead for hundreds of years, some people from another city stole his bones, made a huge procession and built an enormous church over him. After which all the world started to make pilgrimages to his sepulcher. He worked miracles, especially for children."

"Go on, Daddy. Read more."

"It ends there." Daddy frowned. "Darn the idiots; they always dry up when you're hoping to learn something. Tell you what — the last volume is an index; we'll look up Christmas."

The items recorded about Christmas were even more confusing. The origin of the yule log was traced and the prerogatives of the Lord of Misrule. In olden days, it appeared, the Lord of Misrule — a sort of clown — was appointed to direct the Christmas festivities. He was king for a day, who did whatever he pleased while the season lasted. In still older days he'd been the king of the Roman Saturnalia and had been killed at the end of the revels for having made himself a nuisance.

"Very enlightening!" Daddy banged the volume back on its shelf. "That helps a lot."

Taking down another volume he struck luck and grew good-humored. He had run across the name Befana.

"By Jove, that's a new one!"

The little boy peered above his shoulder. The words were too long for him to spell.

"Is it about reindeer, Daddy?"

"It isn't. It's about stockings. According to what's printed here, this Befana was a fairy. The Three Wise Men on their journey to Bethlehem passed by her cottage. She was too busy or too disagreeable to look out of her window — said she'd see them when they came back. Of course they didn't come back, on account of Herod. Her punishment was to gaze in vain from her window for them always."

"Is she still gazing, Dad?"

"I expect so. But that's not all. She was given a second punishment; on the anniversary of the night when she'd been too busy to see the Wise Men pass, she was ordered to fill children's stockings. But the angel who ordered her punishment was careless. What he'd meant was that she must fill children's stockings with presents. He didn't say with presents; he forgot. As she was spiteful, what do you suppose she did? She filled the children's stockings with ashes."

"She doesn't now. I never found no ashes in my stocking," Mac objected.

"Neither did I," Daddy agreed. "Something that these stupid books don't relate must have happened."

"Then look up stockings," Mac suggested. "We'll find the rest of the story."

"Afraid not." Daddy shoved the books back on the shelves disgustedly. "The trouble with the fellows who write all this learned rot is that they aren't poets. If we're going to discover the truth about when Father Christmas was young, we'll have to make it up."

"Are we poets?" The little boy blushed at the compliment.

"You bet — at least you are. All children are poets — they're much wiser than these encyclopedia fellows. We believe in Santa Claus, you and I, Doodles; they don't and didn't. They were like Befana, who might have ridden with the Wise Men to Bethlehem if only she hadn't been too busy to have faith."

"Can't one be busy if one has faith?" the little boy inquired.

"Not often. Being busy kills faith, as a rule. I've been busy lately — too busy. That's why I'm appealing to you. You're not busy because you're young. That's the reason you ought to believe in almost everything. If you try, I'm certain you can tell me about Santa's boyhood."

They shifted the lamp, so that it spilled a pool of illumination over the deep armchair. Minutes ticked by. They sat as though merged into one.

"I'm waiting," Daddy urged.

"Don't know where to start."

"That's obvious — with Befana. She lived in a forest so dark that she hardly ever saw the sun. A highroad ran through it along which camels plodded with their tinkling bells. You see, even I know that."

"I know more." Mac wagged a finger, imitating one of his father's gestures.

"Then, for the love of Mike, prove it."

"Befana was like you, Daddy, when you're finishing a story; she was cross, but she wasn't bad."

"Is that so?" Daddy chuckled. "Thanks for your frankness."

"Yes, that's so, Daddy. If she wasn't finishing something, she was hurrying to begin something."

"What sort of things, Doodles?"

"Don't 'zactly know. But yet, I do," Mac corrected himself. "She was a writer of fairy stories. She lived in the dark forest 'cause she simply had to be quiet, same as you lock your door. She never could find time to do her housework, so she was very glad one morning when she opened her door and saw Santa on her step."

"What on earth was he doing there?"

"He wasn't doing nuffing; he'd been left. Someone passing with the camels had dropped him. He was as tiny as a doll. He couldn't even talk and the bottle beside him was empty. Befana took him in and stared. She twiddled his toes, and he laughed. She thought, 'He's an orphling. I can keep him. I'll learn him to do my housework.'"

"Teach, Mackie — not learn."

"All right, teach," Mac conceded, "but it don't make no difference. Not till evening, when she was putting him to bed, did she learn what he was called. A piece of paper had been pinned to his frock with 'Nick' written on it. That was what he was called first; the Santa name came after."

"Did he have a beard?" Daddy questioned.

"Course not; nor no hair. He was a baby." Mac cuddled closer. "Befana washed his bottles and pushed his pram through the forest. She was sorry for him, but he was an awful bother."

"I'm surprised to hear that she was sorry for him," Daddy attempted to guide the story. "A fairy who could be so cruel as to put ashes into children's stockings — "

"But listen," Mac seized his father's chin. "She wasn't married. She didn't know about chillen; she spoiled him and upset his stomick. She let him sit up late, the way you let me on Christmas. She did it every night and she gave him candies before breakfast."

"Extremely foolish!" Daddy looked shocked. "Why did she?"

"To keep him quiet so she could do her fairy stories. As he growed bigger, he learned to talk. She couldn't write when people talked. To get rid of him, she ordered him to do all the housework, which was hard for a little boy. And he cooked the meals and he swept and dusted."

"Befana must have been a great lazy lump," Daddy interrupted. "Didn't she help him?"

"She was always writing. Jack-and-the-Beanstalk was one of hers. So was Cinderella. Oh, almost all of them."

"I believe you are inventing." Daddy squinted down his nose.

"Trufe and honor I'm not," Mac asserted. "Her fingers was inky. Nick would call to her to come and play. She would shake her head. He was most awful lonely. When he'd dusted the cottage, he'd go out and sit by the road to watch the camels pass. He would wonder where the camels were going and wish he could follow them. Sometimes he'd wonder whether they was driven by people what had dropped him. He was about as big as me, when one day coming terrible fast —"

"How fast would you say, Mackie?"

"As fast as when we ride in a taxi. They was three racing camels, each with a man sitting on him. The men wore crowns and was all dressed up. He knowed they must be kings. A great white star floated over them just above the branches. It made the forest, which was always dark, quite bright. Nacherly he guessed something wonderful was going to happen."

"Naturally," Daddy nodded.

"Well, little Nick, who was no bigger than me, thought they were going to rush past him. But they saw him in time and they pulled up.

"'Little boy,' one of them asked, 'where is Bethlehem?'"

"He said more than that." Daddy wished to

be helpful. "He said, 'Where is He that is born King of the Jews? For we have seen his star in the East and are come to worship Him.'"

"P'raps he did," Mac grudgingly agreed. "Nick was so little he'd never heard of Bethlehem. He asked the Wise Men to wait a minute while he runned in and asked Aunt Befana. He was breathless with climbing the stairs to her study. The door was locked. When he tapped, she didn't answer. Then he started to explain, the way I do to you, Daddy, through the keyhole.

"'Go 'way,' she grunted.

"The Wise Men was in a hurry, so Nick didn't dare stop longer. He had to go back and say that Aunt Befana was too busy even to answer their question.

"They rode away very sad, the star sailing over them. Soon the forest growed dark, like it always was.

"That night at supper Nick told Aunt Befana how they'd rode on racing camels, wearing crowns, so that he was sure they was kings.

"'Kings don't wear crowns when they ride camels. You're fibbing,' she said.

"She didn't want to believe that he was telling the trufe, so she spanked him.

"Next day she couldn't write fairy tales for fancying what she'd missed. She'd never seen three kings all together. She made Nick come to her study and promised not to spank him if he'd tell her over again what had happened."

"But you're forgetting, Mackie." Daddy caressed the bare knees. "I didn't halt you before because I hoped you might remember. Two of the kings were old; but the third was young. The young one had told Nick why they were in such a hurry to reach Bethlehem. A baby was to be born who would be King of all the world. When He grew up He would be King, especially of children. He would take them in His arms and play with them. Nick had never been properly loved and he'd never been played with at all. He wished he'd been born later, so he could have played with the King of children. As it was, he'd be a man by the time the King was grown up, so he'd be too big for the King to take him in His arms. Most of this he said to Befana. The more he talked about the

Wise Men, the more sorry she became that she hadn't taken the time off to see them.

"'But I haven't missed much,' she pretended; 'they'll be coming back.'

"As you know, Doodles, they didn't."

"'Cause of Herod."

"Precisely. They were warned in a dream that Herod would seek the child to slay Him, so they went back to the East secretly by a different route."

"But Befana didn't know they'd been warned." Mac seized the telling of the story. "Every day she sat by her study window watching. She hid behind her curtains ashamed, so Nick wouldn't see her and would think she was writing. And, Daddy, I forgot to tell you. She kept the table spread for five instead of two. You see why, don't you?"

"So as to be ready to invite the Three Kings to eat a meal with her, whatever hour they returned," Daddy conjectured. "Do you know that's very interesting? People still do it in Russia. They bake King's Cake and put it outside the door on Christmas Eve to let the Three Kings know they're welcome."

"Befana did the same," Mac nodded like a turtle. "She called it King's Cake, too. But don't

you think, Daddy, that you could tell a little of the story?"

"With pleasure," Daddy stroked the narrow shoulders. "As the news began to spread about the wonder-child who had been born at Bethlehem she regretted everything most dreadfully. One day when she was watching the road she saw a man who looked like a man yet wasn't, approaching through the forest. She saw him stop little Nick to pat his head, the next moment he was tapping at her cottage."

"He wore wings, didn't he, Daddy?"

"He may have."

"But if he wore wings, Daddy, even though his coat was over them, they'd be humpy."

"I expect they were; but the humps aren't important. The important thing is that he'd been sent to punish her. Long after the angel had gone away, she stayed locked up in her study. When she came down to supper, little Nick could see by the redness of her eyes that she'd been crying. Of course you and I know what the angel had told her: that she must watch forever for the Wise Men and that once a year she must fill children's stockings."

"But why had she been crying, Daddy?"

"Because as long as she lived she'd never have time to write any more fairy stories. Don't forget, Mackie, that till now she'd been a most distinguished authoress. Little Nick didn't know why she'd been crying and he didn't dare ask. The first hint he got was next morning. Having swept out the fireplace, he was throwing away the ashes.

"'Don't do that,' she snapped. 'Take them back. We're going to save them.'

"Overnight she'd been thinking hard with what she was to fill the children's stockings; she'd decided on ashes. According to you, when first she saw Nick on her doorstep she was rather sorry for him. She wasn't any longer. She grew crankier and crankier. Because of her punishment, she grew to hate children. Little Nick was the child who came handiest; she was perfectly horrid to him. She kept him always working at dirty jobs. She complained of the meals he prepared for her, and, because he was dirty, refused to sit down with him."

"As it came near Christmas," Mac took up the running, "she growed nervouser and nervouser. She'd been counting her ashes and was certain there wasn't enough to fill all the stockings. So what did she do? She thought of soot. There wasn't much difference between soot and ashes. She made poor Nick climb her chimbley to shake the soot down."

"You're probably correct," Daddy said, "but it doesn't sound sensible."

"It wasn't." Mac clapped his hands gleefully. "It wasn't his fault. Befana made him. That was how he learned the habit. When he was young he climbed up them; now he's old he climbs down them."

"I see," Daddy smiled, "at what you're driving."

"When the first Christmas Eve came round after the Wise Men had passed," Mac continued, "Nick was awful tired. All day he'd been tying up ashes in sacks. About four o'clock in the afternoon Befana surprised him. She said she'd be gone for the whole night and he must hang up his stocking. He asked why his stocking; she told him that next morning if he looked in it, he'd find something. So he went to bed early and closed his eyes tight. He was so 'cited he wanted morning to come quicker. He thought his Aunt Befana had gone to town to buy a wonderful present."

"And instead, when he woke and looked in his stocking, Doodles, we know what he found. It was cruel of her."

"And there she was back for breakfast, as though nothing had happened, Daddy, and all the sacks was disappeared."

"How had she carried them?"

"She was a fairy. By magic. Every Christmas after that she always did the same and Nick was always hoping that instead of ashes he'd find a present."

"He never did, of course?"

Mac shook his head dolefully.

"That's why he's kind to boys and girls. He remembers how sad he was. When he growed up, he ran away from Befana and became a saint for chillen. He washed them."

Again his father was astounded.

"Washed them! Who told you that?"

"Those tall books, they said there was hundreds of churches with picture windows, showing Santa pulling three little boys out of a tub. He was washing them, 'cause when he was young, he'd hated to be dirty. That was how he got killed and became a saint, 'cause people was so angry with him for washing their chillen. He never asked if he might; he just did it."

"Perhaps there's another mystery you can clear up," Daddy rubbed his chin thoughtfully. "Being a saint through having been martyred, he went straight to Heaven. On earth for many years he was forgotten. Then the people from another town stole his body, honored him by building a huge church over him and were rewarded by finding that his tomb worked miracles. According to the encyclopedia, the miracles started pilgrimages. Sick little children were brought to touch his tomb and were instantly cured. Now, as everybody knows, the sickness children usually have is the tummy-ache. Why should he have been so good at curing that?"

The reply came promptly.

" 'Cause he'd always had a tummy-ache himself. He sat up too late — I've told you that — and Befana, knowing nuffin' about chillen, allowed him to eat candy before breakfast."

"Your explanation sounds reasonable, Doodles. But for the life of me I don't see how our story goes on."

"It's only begun, Daddy. Santa wasn't happy in Heaven. 'Cause why? 'Cause he kept on thinking how Befana was still filling chillen's stockings with ashes. He went to God and told him how miser'ble he'd been every Christmas morning when he'd been little. He said:' 'Tisn't right to be miser'ble Christmas morning. Chillen will always be miser'ble so long as they find ashes. If no one else wants to do it, I'm going to give them presents.' "

"And God thought the idea splendid." Daddy's tone was delighted. "In order that Santa might get to all the stockings before Befana filled them with ashes, he lent him the Three Wise Men's camels. They were racing camels."

"But he uses reindeer, Daddy."

"So he does." Daddy hung his head.

"You're right." The little boy took compassion on his father. "At first he did use camels. On earth he'd lived in hot countries. Everyone did in those days. It was nacheral for him to choose camels. But presently the world growed larger. People went to live in cold places like Russia. The camels weren't so good on snow."

"Excuse my interrupting." Daddy's recent blunder had made him humble. "It's a fact this that you're telling me. Russian children still believe that Christmas presents are brought on camels. They believe that the Three Wise Men ride out from the East every Christmas Eve just as they did when they sought the Christ child —"

"They don't now," the little boy broke in hurriedly. "Santa doesn't deliver presents that way any longer. Camels wasn't quick on ice. One Christmas in Lapland he got stuck. 'Never again,' he said, and changed to reindeer."

"I think he was very wise," Daddy nodded gravely. "A camel's such a big animal to go prancing over roofs and chimneys."

"And that was why, too, Daddy. So now we know, don't we?"

"You know everything, Doodles. Poets do. You're a poet."

Suddenly Mackie hugged his father, crushing his face against the smoky jacket.

"Somebody told me," he almost sobbed; "somebody said there wasn't no Santa Claus."

"But there is. That's ridiculous. If there isn't a Santa Claus, how did he get into the encyclopedia? Encyclopedias print nothing but facts. They do really, I assure you, Doodles. Everything we've found out about Santa Claus' boyhood is set down there in those large volumes. All about Befana. All about the ashes in stockings. All about —"

A tear-stained face glanced up.

"Then tomorrow let's prove it. Promise?"

"If you know how to prove it, Doodles, I promise."

A tap fell on the study door. Nannie's voice was heard announcing that Mac's bath was ready.

"Don't come in. One minute," Daddy implored. He bent over his little boy. "I promise. But how to prove it?"

The child's voice sank to a whisper.

"It's snowing. Tomorrow we'll go on the roof. If Santa truly is, we'll find marks of reindeer and sleigh runners."

Daddy had promised — and a promise is a promise.

Next morning after breakfast — Christmas morning — having evaded Mummy and Nannie, father and son climbed the stairs to the attic, placed a ladder against the trap door solemnly and peered out. Not a sign of a reindeer's hoof or a sleigh runner.

"But he's been, 'cause he's left the presents," Mackie whispered. For a moment he looked worried; then his expression cleared. "How silly of us, Daddy! They wouldn't be here. We'll have to wait till next Christmas. A new lot of snow has fallen."

So it had. Even in the many streets, which could be seen from so high up, there was scarcely a track noticeable.

Mummy's voice calling:

"What on earth are you two lunatics doing, catching cold up there?"

Daddy closed the trap hurriedly. As they scuttled down the ladder he whispered, "You're right again, Doodles. The new snow has fooled us. If you're still a poet, we'll try again next Christmas."

THE STATE VERSUS SANTA CLAUS

by Arthur Stringer

The shy old man in Turkey red trimmed with rabbit skin began to look worried. He wasn't used to crowds. And the courtroom was warm. And he didn't like the way people kept staring at him. It made him feel a good deal like a polar bear in a zoo.

He was almost glad when he heard a crack-voiced court attendant shout: "Everybody rise!" For that meant, of course, that the Judge was coming out of his chamber and seating himself in the big black chair under the solemn crossed flags.

But the prisoner at the bar, as he mopped a broad red face with his foolish rabbit-fringed sleeve, was a trifle disappointed about the Judge, whom the Prosecutor addressed as Father Time. For that Judge seemed a bit too old for his job. He looked as though he hadn't known a good meal or cracked a smile for half a century. His glance, it's true, was as sharp as a weasel's, but his shoulders sagged and his face looked tired, as though he had heard too many cases and reviewed too many crimes and seen too many prisoners pass out the side door with the iron grille and never come back.

Nor did the portly figure in Turkey red altogether like the appearance of the Prosecuting Attorney. He too was an old man, hard-eyed and gaunt and lean, with a nutcracker profile and an eye that told you he'd be as quick and merciless as a steel trap. His narrow face, in fact, had worn an acid smile of contempt as he glanced about at the rubicund old figure in red, a smile which said as plain as day: "Well, Old Boy, it won't take me long to finish *you* up!"

Santa Claus, as he shifted in his seat, wished there had been a few children about. He seemed to get along better with children. His earlier suspicion that he wasn't among friends even deepened to a conviction as he turned and studied the Jury. He had really hoped for a different sort of Jury, one that could give a chuckle now and then and whisper behind their hands and nudge neighboring ribs and perhaps make a spitball or two and wonder how you would build up Exhibit A on the Prosecutor's table and whether the red paint on Exhibit B actually had the adorable painty smell that all Noah's arks ought to have. But the twelve good men and true on *this* Jury impressed him as twelve dried-up old prunes who wouldn't know anything more about putting a toy airplane together than they'd know about spinning a musical top. And it wasn't only their age he objected to. It was no crime, after all, being old. What he didn't like was the enmity in their rheumy old eyes when they blinked down at the Christmas Tree, marked Exhibit X, on the Prosecutor's table. And Santa Claus wasn't used to enmity. He didn't thrive on it. Those twelve old Jurors, in fact, looked so much like twelve old owls blinking solemnly down on a blighted world that he was glad to turn away and let his eyes rest on the Counsel who'd been assigned to defend him.

But even then the prisoner didn't perceptibly brighten. That lawyer, the Big Policeman downstairs had said, was just the man for him. He'd never lost a case. On the other hand, he'd never won a case, for the simple reason that he always got them so mixed up they never came to an end. He was invariably addressed as "Mr. Folly," being a senior member of the old and established firm of Folly & Youth. But he, too, was plainly too old for his job. When the prisoner had pointed out that they were giving him a decrepit octogenarian in his second childhood, the Big Policeman had sagely wagged his head up and down and said: "That's why you're getting him!" And this thought began to disturb Santa Claus. It disturbed him almost as much as did an inspection of his learned Counsel, who, instead of paying attention to the court procedure, occupied himself by counting his waistcoat buttons and drawing little pictures on his brief case and trying to balance three pencils at once on the inkwell.

And those court proceedings obviously ought to be paid some attention to, the rotund prisoner suddenly realized, for the Prosecuting Attorney was already on his feet. He was not only on his feet but he was talking about the prisoner, and talking about him in a way which very promptly gave that prisoner gooseflesh. And that prisoner's lawyer, as the tirade went on, merely sat back laughing at the way the Prosecutor's Adam's-apple went up and down with a three-inch plunge as he discoursed. It was no wonder Santa Claus's face lost a little of its ruddiness. Things certainly weren't looking any too well for him. And cases certainly weren't won by laughing at your adversary's Adam's-apple.

"This prisoner," the Prosecutor was proclaiming, "is an impostor. He's more than an impostor; he's an absurdity. And for the good of

the People I want him abolished. I want him done away with, just as we did away with Fairy Tales in this state last year, just as we did away with Music the year before. I speak, sir, for Science and Truth. And before we can progress into perfect statehood we must abolish these foolish old myths that are an affront to reason and a confusion to the mind of youth."

"Objection," casually announced the prisoner's attorney as he succeeded in balancing his third pencil on the inkwell cover.

"Objection denied," barked back the stooping old graybeard on the bench.

"This old scoundrel," proceeded the Prose-

cutor, directing a long and bony finger towards the cowering Santa Claus, "has not only outlived his usefulness — if he ever had any — but has also blocked the highway of progress. He is pagan in ancestry and pagan in spirit. We know, gentlemen, that in this enlightened age we never get anything for nothing. We know that life is struggle and combat, and that to the strong belong the spoils. Yet this old deceiver claims to give us things for nothing. He seeks to delude our children and our children's children with the contention that for one day in the year the ironclad laws of commerce and competition can be dispensed with. He keeps youth credulous and soft-hearted when they should be practical-minded and satisfied with an eye for an eye and a tooth for a tooth. On that one irrational and irresponsible day in a year of reason, he says, the laws of give-and-take can be abrogated and things can come to us unearned. He claims, in other words, that miracles can still be brought about in this workaday world of ours. That claim is not only fraudulent, but this ruddy prisoner is fraudulent in the way in which he presents it. Even his place of abode is fraudulent. He contended, I understand, that his home was in the once conveniently vague neighborhood of the North Pole. But that Pole has now been found and explored, and those explorations have failed to disclose any such home. This is an age of steel and stone, of skyscrapers and towering cities. Yet today, in this age of elevators and steam-heated apartments, this old impostor claims to travel by sled and reindeer and —"

"Objection," said the attorney for the defense, looking up from a locomotive he was drawing on a brief back.

"Objection noted," proclaimed the Bench, rousing himself from what looked suspiciously like forty winks.

"And even here," pursued the blandly smiling Prosecutor, "I shall not only anticipate but I shall elucidate my opponent's objection. Why that sled and reindeer, I ask? Simply because, in the medieval era of his origin, sled and reindeer stood for the fastest means of locomotion known to semicivilized man. But we live in a new age, an age of progress. And any self-appointed peddler of unsolicited charities who can't today travel one-tenth as fast as one of our mail planes is no longer entitled to his job!"

The Prosecutor, on ending that peroration, took a drink of ice water and smiled icily at the murmur of approval that swept through the courtroom. Then he once more directed a lean and accusatory finger at the prisoner.

"There's something else that this old impostor lays claim to. He contends that while on his brief but incredibly active annual pilgrimage of debauching and pauperizing our rising generation he enters their midnight homes by way of the chimney. By the chimney, mark you, by the chimney and under cover of darkness. And that, gentlemen, is as far as I need to go. We may not be versed in Norse mythology; but we all know modern architecture. So I merely ask you, gentlemen of the jury, to take one good look at this old impostor. Study him closely, gentlemen. Note his ample proportions, his potbelly, his obesity doubtlessly due to a life of overindulgence. All I ask of you, gentlemen, is to give him the once-over and then decide for yourselves whether or not a figure of those dimensions could get down a modern chimney flue!"

Again the Prosecutor took a drink of ice water, a murmur of approval swept through the courtroom, and a far-from-happy prisoner mopped his forehead with the rabbit-fringed tail of his Turkey-red surtout.

"But that, gentlemen, is not all," resumed the gaunt and grim-eyed Prosecutor. "This crafty old impostor not only succeeds in deluding youth, he triumphs as well in depraving parenthood itself. He beguiles careless-minded mothers and fathers into a communion of deception. He makes them passive agents in his nefarious enterprises. He prompts them to perpetuate a tradition that is a blot on this nation of truth lovers. And above and before everything, we must have Truth!"

"That's right," suddenly cackled our Juror Number Nine. "Sixty-eight years ago I lied to my step-mother about shovelin' the snow off our well platform, and all I got that Christmas was a stockin' full o' coal. And I've hated Christmas ever since."

It was the infirm Mr. Folly who at this juncture restored the picture puzzle he'd been working over to the table of exhibits and rose blandly to his feet.

"If Your Honor will permit me," he casually observed, "I am prompted to move for a mistrial."

The Judge who looked so disconcertingly like Father Time sat back on the bench, blinking at a window which a court attendant had opened to cool off the overheated room.

"On what grounds?" he finally demanded.

"On the grounds," said Mr. Folly with an unexpectedly stern glance toward the jury box, "that my client is not being tried before a body of his peers."

"That looks like a pretty intelligent jury to *me*," ventured the Judge, "even though Number Nine didn't know enough to keep his mouth shut."

"I'm not attacking their intelligence," pursued the quiet-toned Mr. Folly. "What I'm criticizing is their age."

"Fiddlesticks," retorted the Judge, "every man in this courtroom is an old man, and you know it, sir!"

"All except one, Your Honor," contended the unabashed Mr. Folly.

"What one?" demanded the Bench.

"My client, Your Honor," replied the wizened counsel for the man in red, whose color deepened as the eyes of the courtroom were once more directed on his uncomfortable person.

"I can't say that he looks much like a spring chicken," said the Man on the Bench, with a throaty cackle that was unctuously re-echoed by the crowd.

"Appearances, Your Honor, are sometimes deceptive," said Mr. Folly.

"How about those white whiskers?" demanded the irate Prosecutor.

"Your Honor," said Mr. Folly, hobbling closer to the Judge's bench, "I wouldn't care to have it generally known, but this client of mine is a trifle off in the upper story. He's quite child-minded, in fact. And those whiskers are only a disguise. Under them, he's merely a child, a child who refused to grow up. For the foolish old fellow still has a forlorn craving for happiness. He keeps on believing in good-will and kindliness and all that sort of thing. It's a very sad case. And instead of cluttering up the Calendar this way, he really ought to be handed over to the care of his friends."

"Has he any friends?" demanded the Judge.

"Not here," said the astute Mr. Folly.

"Then how are we to know he has any?"

Mr. Folly scratched his bald head in perplexity. "That's not an easy question to answer, Your Honor. But I'd suggest, in the circumstances, that we let the children decide it."

"But there are no children about," demurred the Court.

"Then we might take a ballot," suggested Mr. Folly.

"A ballot? What kind of ballot?" demanded the Judge. But that question remained unanswered. For the woebegone prisoner himself, who had got unsteadily up from his chair, was crossing to the open window. Through that open window he thrust his two fat arms encased in Turkey red. And a tear ran down his plump but wrinkled cheek as he stared out at the wintry sky that had darkened as the afternoon wore away.

"Children," he cried in a voice tremulous with emotion. *"Children, do you want me?"*

A hush fell over the courtroom. And in that hush three hundred straining ears heard only the sighing of the wind. But as that wind increased in force two objects of white fluttered down and rested on the outstretched and unsteady hands of the wistful old figure in Turkey red. Some people said they were slips of paper; and some people always claimed that they were only especially large snowflakes. But they came in a stream, and then in a cloud. They came so thick the Big Policeman had to pull down the window to keep them from covering the courtroom floor. But even then they flattened themselves against the panes, and piled up about the outside walls, and grew deeper and deeper, until the room darkened and the hushed watchers looked at one another with childish wonder in their eyes.

"Dear me," said the decrepit old court attendant as he turned on the lights, "if it isn't one of those old-fashioned blizzards again!"

"Looks to me," observed the Big Policeman, blinking up at the gray oblong that had once been a window, "like it's goin' to be worse than that blizzard of 1888!"

WHY SANTA CLAUS CHOSE THE REINDEER

by Estella Hitchcock Lane

This is a story about the very first Christmas Eve that Santa Claus ever made his trip around the world. He was quite a young man then, and he had found it rather dreary at the North Pole, with nothing to do but slide down icebergs and play with the Polar Bears. One day, some of the Snow Birds that come north for the summer told him about many children living in the rest of the world, who were sad because they had no toys. That gave Santa Claus an idea. He built a great big work shop and called together the Elves and Brownies and Fairies, who were his good friends. All the year long, they worked together, making dolls and sleds and games and books.

The animals wanted to help. They, too, were Santa Claus' friends. He let them into the shop, but it just didn't work very well. The Polar Bears, who insisted on playing with the dolls, were so clumsy they were always dropping and breaking them. The Seals *would* stand up on their tails and dance to the tunes of the music boxes, and were in everybody's way. The Arctic Dogs just couldn't resist shaking up all the stuffed cats and bunnies. The Reindeer suddenly became quite frivolous when they saw all the gay balloons. They tossed them into the air with their noses, but the balloons caught on their antlers and broke with a bang.

Santa Claus finally just had to put out the animals and lock the door. They stood in the snow, looked longingly into the windows, and felt hurt because Santa Claus didn't come out to play with them any more. In fact, they grumbled a good deal.

Finally, the toys were all completed. The shop was overflowing.

Santa Claus drew a long breath and sat down to rest, while all the Elves and Brownies and Fairies curled up and went to sleep, they were so tired.

"Now," said Santa Claus, "the next question is how to get all these things to the children! Here are the toys and there is my sleigh waiting to take them, but who will pull it?"

"We will," cried the Polar Bears, delighted at a chance to have a share in things again.

"We will!" cried the Reindeer.

"Oh, please let us!" exclaimed the Seals, flopping up to Santa and crowding around him.

"The idea!" cried the Dogs. "The very idea of Seals drawing a sleigh! They're so slow they wouldn't get there for a year. We are the ones to do it, of course."

This hurt the Seals' feelings. They were very sensitive about being slow on land. When Santa Claus saw big tears rolling down from their eyes and dropping onto their flippers, he just couldn't stand it, for he was very tender-hearted.

"Of course the Seals shall do it," he said. "What if they are a little slow? If they keep at it, they'll get there all right."

He hitched the Seals up to the sleigh, and away they went, flopping along over the ice. It was a little slow, but Santa Claus was very patient. When, however, they were about 15 degrees from the North Pole and Santa Claus told them to head first for Alaska, one Seal said:

"Oh, no! Let's go to Greenland first. I have a third cousin who lives in Greenland, and I've always wanted to see that country. This is a great chance!" And he set out for Greenland.

"I should say not!" said the second Seal. "I've always heard that the fish in the waters of Australia are the most delicious in the world. We'll go to Australia first." And he set out for Australia.

Each Seal wanted to go in a different direction. Santa Claus tried to reason with them.

"But the main thing is to get these gifts to the children. We can see every one of these countries in the end, if only you will all pull together and follow my directions."

But the Seals were very stubborn; and Santa Claus had to give up and go back to the North Pole.

"I'll let the Dogs do it," he said to himself. "After all, they are the ones best fitted to draw the sleigh."

He hitched up the Dogs and set out again.

But before they had reached Alaska the Dogs began to quarrel with each other.

"You've got to pull your share of the load or I won't pull mine," said the first Dog.

"I *am* pulling my share. You're the one that's holding back," snarled the second Dog.

"I think you're all leaving most of it to me!" whined another Dog.

"Come! Come!" said Santa, "this is no way to do. Let's stop trying to see who's not doing his share. Let's all try to pull as hard as we can ourselves and never mind what the other Dog does. After all, the main thing is to get these gifts to the children, isn't it?"

The Dogs agreed that it was. They all wanted to get the gifts to the children, but each one was so afraid he was doing more than his share.

Finally, the first Dog stopped short. That stopped the rest of them. It stopped Santa Claus and the sleigh, too.

"I'm not going any further unless the rest will do their share," said the first Dog.

Then Santa Claus almost lost his patience.

"If you can't all forget yourselves and work together, we'll never get there," he said, and he took them back to the North Pole.

Both the Reindeer and the Polar Bears wanted very much to help, but the Reindeer, being always unselfish, gave in to the Polar Bears, and off they went.

"Now we'll surely get there," said Santa Claus to himself, for the Polar Bears were always very good natured and obliging. They trotted along merrily, Santa Claus singing lustily as they went, until they came down to the timber line.

"Oh, just wait a minute while I go and climb that tree!" said the first Polar Bear, and before Santa Claus could stop him, he was off, taking most of the team with him.

"No! No!" shouted the second Bear, "I want to explore that cave." And he set out in the other direction.

"Oh, dear!" exclaimed Santa Claus, very much discouraged. "I had forgotten how curious these Bears always are. We'll never get this job done, if they have to investigate everything they see."

He got out of the sleigh and made them all sit down in the snow, while he talked to them very seriously.

"Don't you see," he said, "that the main thing is to get these gifts to the children? We must do that whether or not we do all these other things."

The Polar Bears agreed, and promised to be good, and they went on again. But every time they came to something new, they forgot all about the children and the toys and started to investigate.

Santa Claus was pretty discouraged, when he had to turn back for the third time. As he finally set out with the Reindeer harnessed to the sleigh, he wondered if he'd have to give up the whole thing.

Before they went far, the first Reindeer said to the others, "Remember, we all want one thing more than anything else — to get these gifts to the children. So let's forget everything else we might like to do and all pull together until the job is done." And away they went like the wind.

The other animals were very cross. The Seals went and banged their heads against an iceberg. The Dogs crowded into a corner of the work shop and sulked. The Polar Bears spent their time teasing the Brownies. They tickled the Fairies and woke them up.

But because they forgot themselves and all pulled together the Reindeer carried Santa's sleigh safely and swiftly around the world. And that's why they have been doing it ever since.

CHRISTMAS WITH MR. PICKWICK

by Charles Dickens

It was a very pleasant thing to see Mr. Pickwick in the centre of the group, now pulled this way, and then that, and first kissed on the chin and then on the nose, and then on the spectacles, and to hear the peals of laughter which were raised on every side; but it was a still more pleasant thing to see Mr. Pickwick blinded shortly afterwards with a silk-handkerchief, falling up against the wall, and scrambling into corners, and going through all the mysteries of blind-man's buff, with the utmost relish for the game, until at last he caught one of the poor relations; and then had to evade the blindman himself, which he did with a nimbleness and agility that elicited the admiration and ap-

plause of all beholders. The poor relations caught just the people whom they thought would like it; and when the game flagged, got caught themselves. When they were all tired of blindman's buff, there was a great game at snap-dragon, and when fingers enough were burned with that, and the raisins gone, they sat down by the huge fire of blazing logs to a substantial supper, and a mighty bowl of wassail, something smaller than an ordinary wash-house copper, in which the hot apples were hissing and bubbling with a rich look, and a jolly sound, that were perfectly irresistible. . . . Up flew the bright sparks in myriads as the logs were stirred, and the deep red blaze sent forth a rich glow, that penetrated into the furthest corner of the room, and cast its cheerful tint on every face.

A CHRISTMAS CAROL*

by Charles Dickens

IN FOUR STAVES

*(EDITOR'S NOTE: This is the shortened version of the Carol, made by Dickens himself for use in his public readings.)

Stave One: Marley's Ghost

Marley was dead, to begin with. There is no doubt whatever about that. The register of his burial was signed by the clergyman, the clerk, the undertaker, and the chief mourner. Scrooge signed it. And Scrooge's name was good upon 'Change for anything he chose to put his hand to.

Old Marley was as dead as a door-nail.

Scrooge knew he was dead? Of course he did. How could it be otherwise? Scrooge and he were partners for I don't know how many years. Scrooge was his sole executor, his sole administrator, his sole assign, his sole residuary legatee, his sole friend, his sole mourner.

Scrooge never painted out old Marley's name, however. There it yet stood, years afterwards, above the warehouse door — Scrooge and Marley. The firm was known as Scrooge and Marley. Sometimes people new to the business called Scrooge Scrooge, and sometimes Marley. He answered to both names. It was all the same to him.

Oh! But he was a tight-fisted hand at the grindstone, was Scrooge! a squeezing, wrenching, grasping, scraping, clutching, covetous old sinner! External heat and cold had little influence on him. No warmth could warm, no cold could chill him. No wind that blew was bitterer than he, no falling snow was more intent upon its purpose, no pelting rain less open to entreaty. Foul weather didn't know where to have him. The heaviest rain and snow and hail and sleet could boast of the advantage over him in only one respect — they often "came down" handsomely, and Scrooge never did.

Nobody ever stopped him in the street to say, with gladsome looks, "My dear Scrooge, how are you? When will you come to see me?" No beggars implored him to bestow a trifle, no children asked him what it was o'clock, no man or woman ever once in all his life inquired the way to such and such a place, of Scrooge. Even the blind men's dogs appeared to know him, and when they saw him coming on, would tug their owners into doorways and up courts; and then would wag their tails as though they said, "No eyes at all is better than an evil eye, dark master!"

But what did Scrooge care! It was the very thing he liked. To edge his way along the crowded paths of life, warning all human sympathy to keep its distance, was what the knowing ones call "nuts" to Scrooge.

Once upon a time — of all the good days in the year, upon a Christmas eve — old Scrooge sat busy in his counting house. It was cold, bleak, biting, foggy weather; and the city clocks had only just gone three, but it was quite dark already.

The door of Scrooge's counting-house was open, that he might keep his eye upon his clerk, who, in a dismal little cell beyond, a sort of tank, was copying letters. Scrooge had a very small fire, but the clerk's fire was so very much smaller that it looked like one coal. But he couldn't replenish it, for Scrooge kept the coal-box in his own room; and so surely as the clerk came in with the shovel, the master predicted that it would be necessary for them to part. Wherefore the clerk put on his white comforter, and tried to warm himself at the candle; in which effort, not being a man of a strong imagination, he failed.

"Merry Christmas, uncle! God save you!" cried a cheerful voice. It was the voice of Scrooge's nephew, who came upon him so quickly that this was the first intimation Scrooge had of his approach.

"Bah!" said Scrooge; "humbug!"

"Christmas a humbug, uncle! You don't mean that, I am sure?"

"I do. Out upon Merry Christmas! What's Christmas time to you but a time for paying bills without money; a time for finding yourself a year older, and not an hour richer; a time for balancing your books and having every item in 'em through a round dozen of months presented dead against you? If I had my will, every idiot who goes about with 'Merry Christmas' on his lips should be boiled with his own pudding, and buried with a stake of holly through his heart. He should!"

"Uncle!"

"Nephew, keep Christmas in your own way, and let me keep it in mine."

"Keep it! But you don't keep it."

"Let me leave it alone, then. Much good may it do you! Much good it has ever done you!"

"There are many things from which I might have derived good, by which I have not profited, I dare say, Christmas among the rest. But I am sure I have always thought of Christmas time, when it has come around — apart from the veneration due to its sacred origin, if anything belonging to it can be apart from that — as a good time; a kind, forgiving, charitable, pleasant time; the only time I know of in the long calendar of the year, when men and women seem by one consent to open their shut-up hearts freely, and to think of people below them as if they really were fellow-travelers to the grave, and not another race of creatures bound on other journeys. And therefore, uncle, though it has never put a scrap of gold or silver in my pocket, I believe that it has done me good, and will do me good; and I say, God bless it!"

The clerk in the tank involuntarily applauded.

"Let me hear another sound from you," said Scrooge, "and you'll keep your Christmas by losing your situation! You're quite a powerful speaker, sir," he added, turning to his nephew. "I wonder you don't go into Parliament."

"Don't be angry, uncle. Come! Dine with us tomorrow."

Scrooge said that he would see him — yes, indeed he did. He went the whole length of the expression, and said that he would see him in that extremity first.

"But why?" cried Scrooge's nephew. "Why?"

"Why did you get married?"

"Because I fell in love."

"Because you fell in love!" growled Scrooge, as if that were the only one thing in the world more ridiculous than a merry Christmas. "Good afternoon!"

"Nay, uncle, but you never came to see me before that happened. Why give it as a reason for not coming now?"

"Good afternoon."

"I want nothing from you; I ask nothing of you; why cannot we be friends?"

"Good afternoon."

"I am sorry, with all my heart, to find you so resolute. We have never had any quarrel, to which I have been a party. But I have made the trial in homage to Christmas, and I'll keep my Christmas humour to the last. So A Merry Christmas, uncle!"

"Good afternoon!"

"And A Happy New-Year!"

"Good afternoon!"

His nephew left the room without an angry word, notwithstanding. The clerk, in letting Scrooge's nephew out, had let two other people in. They were portly gentlemen, pleasant to behold, and now stood, with their hats off, in Scrooge's office. They had books and papers in their hands, and bowed to him.

"Scrooge and Marley's, I believe," said one of the gentlemen, referring to his list. "Have I the pleasure of addressing Mr. Scrooge or Mr. Marley?"

"Mr. Marley has been dead these seven years. He died seven years ago, this very night."

"At this festive season of the year, Mr. Scrooge," said the gentleman, taking up a pen, "it is more than usually desirable that we should make some slight provision for the poor and destitute, who suffer greatly at the present time. Many thousands are in want of common necessaries; hundreds of thousands are in want of common comforts, sir."

"Are there no prisons?"

"Plenty of prisons. But under the impression that they scarcely furnish Christian cheer of mind or body to the unoffending multitude, a few of us are endeavouring to raise a fund to buy the poor some meat and drink, and means of warmth. We choose this time, because it is a time, of all others, when Want is keenly felt, and Abundance rejoices. What shall I put you down for?"

"Nothing!"

"You wish to be anonymous?"

"I wish to be left alone. Since you ask me what I wish, gentlemen, that is my answer. I don't make merry myself at Christmas, and I can't afford to make idle people merry. I help to support the prisons and the workhouses — they cost enough — and those who are badly off must go there."

"Many can't go there; and many would rather die."

"If they would rather die, they had better do it, and decrease the surplus population."

At length the hour of shutting up the counting-house arrived. With an ill-will Scrooge, dismounting from his stool, tacitly admitted the fact to the expectant clerk in the tank, who instantly snuffed his candle out, and put on his hat.

"You want all day to-morrow, I suppose?"

"If quite convenient, sir."

"It's not convenient, and it's not fair. If I was to stop half a crown for it, you'd think yourself mightily ill-used, I'll be bound?"

"Yes, sir."

"And yet you don't think me ill-used, when I pay a day's wages for no work."

"It's only once a year, sir."

"A poor excuse for picking a man's pocket every twenty-fifth of December! But I suppose you must have the whole day. Be here all the earlier next morning."

The clerk promised that he would, and Scrooge walked out with a growl. The office was closed in a twinkling, and the clerk, with the long ends of his white comforter dangling below his waist (for he boasted no great-coat), went down a slide, at the end of a lane of boys, twenty times, in honour of its being Christmas eve, and then ran home as hard as he could pelt, to play at blindman's buff.

Scrooge took his melancholy dinner in his usual melancholy tavern; and having read all the newspapers, and beguiled the rest of the evening with his banker's book, went home to bed. He lived in chambers which had once belonged to his deceased partner. They were a gloomy suite of rooms, in a lowering pile of building up a yard. The building was old enough now, and dreary enough, for nobody lived in it but Scrooge, the other rooms being all let out as offices.

Now it is a fact, that there was nothing at all particular about the knocker on the door of the house, except that it was very large; also, that Scrooge had seen it, night and morning, during his whole residence in that place; also, that Scrooge had as little of what is called fancy about him as any man in the city of London. And yet Scrooge, having his key in the lock of the door, saw in the knocker, without its undergoing any intermediate process of change, not a knocker, but Marley's face.

Marley's face, with a dismal light about it, like a bad lobster in a dark cellar. It was not angry or ferocious, but it looked at Scrooge as Marley used to look — ghostly spectacles turned up upon its ghostly forehead.

As Scrooge looked fixedly at this phenomenon, it was a knocker again. He said, "Pooh, pooh!" and closed the door with a bang.

The sound resounded through the house like thunder. Every room above, and every cask in the wine-merchant's cellars below, appeared to have a separate peal of echoes of its own. Scrooge was not a man to be frightened by echoes. He fastened the door, and walked across the hall, and up the stairs. Slowly too, trimming his candle as he went.

Up Scrooge went, not caring a button for its being very dark. Darkness is cheap, and Scrooge liked it. But before he shut his heavy door, he walked through his rooms to see that all was right. He had just enough recollection of the face to desire to do that.

Sitting-room, bedroom, lumber-room, all as they should be. Nobody under the table, nobody under the sofa; a small fire in the grate; spoon and basin ready; and the little saucepan of gruel (Scrooge had a cold in his head) upon the hob. Nobody under the bed; nobody in the closet; nobody in the dressing-gown, which was hanging up in a suspicious attitude against the wall. Lumber-room as usual. Old fire-guards, old shoes, two fish-baskets, washing-stand on three legs, and a poker.

Quite satisfied, he closed his door, and locked himself in; double-locked himself in, which was not his custom. Thus secured against surprise, he took off his cravat, put on his dressing-gown and slippers and his nightcap, and sat down before the very low fire to take his gruel.

As he threw his head back in the chair, his glance happened to rest upon a bell, a disused bell, that hung in the room, and communicated, for some purpose now forgotten, with a chamber in the highest story of the building. It was with great astonishment, and with a strange, inexplicable dread, that, as he looked, he saw this bell begin to swing. Soon it rang out loudly, and so did every bell in the house.

This was succeeded by a clanking noise, deep down below as if some person were dragging a heavy chain over the casks in the wine-merchant's cellar.

Then he heard the noise much louder, on the floors below; then coming up the stairs; then coming straight towards his door.

It came on through the heavy door, and a spectre passed into the room before his eyes. And upon its coming in, the dying flame leaped up, as though it cried, "I know him! Marley's ghost!"

The same face, the very same. Marley in his pigtail, usual waistcoat, tights, and boots. His body was transparent; so that Scrooge, observing him, and looking through his waistcoat, could see the two buttons on his coat behind.

Scrooge had often heard it said that Marley had no bowels, but he had never believed it until now.

No, nor did he believe it even now. Though he looked the phantom through and through, and saw it standing before him, — though he felt the chilling influence of its death-cold eyes, and noticed the very texture of the folded kerchief bound about its head and chin, — he was still incredulous.

"How now!" said Scrooge, caustic and cold as ever. "What do you want with me?"

"Much!" — Marley's voice, no doubt about it.

"Who are you?"

"Ask me who I *was*."

"Who *were* you then?"

"In life I was your partner, Jacob Marley."

"Can you — can you sit down?"

"I can."

"Do it, then."

Scrooge asked the question, because he didn't know whether a ghost so transparent might find himself in a condition to take a chair; and felt that, in the event of its being impossible, it might involve the necessity of an embarrassing explanation. But the ghost sat down on the opposite side of the fireplace, as if he were quite used to it.

"You don't believe in me."

"I don't."

"What evidence would you have of my reality beyond that of your senses?"

"I don't know."

"Why do you doubt your senses?"

"Because a little thing affects them. A slight disorder of the stomach makes them cheats. You may be an undigested bit of beef, a blot of mustard, a crumb of cheese, a fragment of an underdone potato. There's more of gravy than of grave about you, whatever you are!"

Scrooge was not much in the habit of cracking jokes, nor did he feel in his heart by any means waggish then. The truth is, that he tried to be smart, as a means of distracting his own attention, and keeping down his horror.

But how much greater was his horror when, the phantom taking off the bandage round its head, as if it were too warm to wear indoors, its lower jaw dropped down upon its breast!

"Mercy! Dreadful apparition, why do you trouble me? Why do spirits walk the earth, and why do they come to me?"

"It is required of every man that the spirit within him should walk abroad among his fellow-men, and travel far and wide; and if that spirit goes not forth in life, it is condemned to do so after death. I cannot tell you all I would. A very little more is permitted to me. I cannot rest, I cannot stay, I cannot linger anywhere. My spirit never walked beyond our counting-house — mark me! — in life my spirit never roved beyond the narrow limits of our money-changing hole; and weary journeys lie before me!"

"Seven years dead. And travelling all the time? You travel fast?"

"On the wings of the wind."

"You might have got over a great quantity of ground in seven years."

"O blind man, blind man! not to know that ages of incessant labour by immortal creatures for this earth must pass into eternity before the good of which it is susceptible is all developed. Not to know that any Christian spirit working kindly in its little sphere, whatever it may be, will find its mortal life too short for its vast means of usefulness. Not to know that no space of regret can make amends for one life's opportunities misused! Yet I was like this man; I once was like this man!"

"But you were always a good man of business, Jacob," faltered Scrooge, who now began to apply this to himself.

"Business!" cried the Ghost, wringing its hands again. "Mankind was my business. The common welfare was my business; charity, mercy, forbearance, benevolence, were all my business. The dealings of my trade were but a drop of water in the comprehensive ocean of my business!"

Scrooge was very much dismayed to hear the spectre going on at this rate, and began to quake exceedingly.

"Hear me! My time is nearly gone."

"I will. But don't be hard upon me! Don't be flowery, Jacob! Pray!"

"I am here tonight to warn you that you have yet a chance and hope of escaping my fate. A chance and hope of my procuring, Ebenezer."

"You were always a good friend to me. Thank'ee!"

"You will be haunted by Three Spirits."

"Is that the chance and hope you mentioned, Jacob? I — I think I'd rather not."

"Without their visits, you cannot hope to shun the path I tread. Expect the first tomorrow night, when the bell tolls One. Expect the second on the next night at the same hour. The third, upon the next night, when the last stroke of Twelve has ceased to vibrate. Look to see me no more; and look that, for your own sake, you remember what has passed between us!"

It walked backward from him; and at every step it took, the window raised itself a little, so that, when the apparition reached it, it was wide open.

Scrooge closed the window, and examined the door by which the Ghost had entered. It was double-locked, as he had locked it with his own hands, and the bolts were undisturbed. Scrooge tried to say, "Humbug!" but stopped at the first syllable. And being, from the emotion he had undergone, or the fatigues of the day, or his glimpse of the invisible world, or the dull conversation of the Ghost, or the lateness of the hour, much in need of repose, he went straight to bed, without undressing, and fell asleep on the instant.

Stave Two: The First of the Three Spirits

When Scrooge awoke, it was so dark, that, looking out of bed, he could scarcely distinguish the transparent window from the opaque walls of his chamber, until suddenly the church clock tolled a deep, dull, hollow, melancholy ONE.

Light flashed up in the room upon the instant, and the curtains of his bed were drawn aside by a strange figure, — like a child; yet not so like a child as like an old man, viewed through some supernatural medium, which gave him the appearance of having receded from the view, and being diminished to a child's proportions. Its hair, which hung about its neck and down its back, was white as if with age; and yet the face had not a wrinkle in it, and the tenderest bloom was on the skin. It held a branch of fresh green holly in its hand; and, in singular contradiction of that wintry emblem, had its dress trimmed with summer flowers. But the strangest thing about it was, that from the crown of its head there sprung a bright clear jet of light, by which all this was visible; and which was doubtless the occasion of its using, in its duller moments, a great extinguisher for a cap, which it now held under its arm.

"Are you the Spirit, sir, whose coming was foretold to me?"

"I am!"

"Who and what are you?"

"I am the Ghost of Christmas Past."

"Long Past?"

"No. Your past. The things that you will see with me are shadows of the things that have been; they will have no consciousness of us."

Scrooge then made bold to inquire what business brought him there.

"Your welfare. Rise and walk with me!"

It would have been in vain for Scrooge to plead that the weather and the hour were not adapted to pedestrian purposes; that bed was warm, and the thermometer a long way below freezing; that he was clad but lightly in his slippers, dressing-gown, and nightcap; and that he had a cold upon him at that time. The grasp, though gentle as a woman's hand, was not to be resisted. He rose; but finding that the Spirit made towards the window, clasped its robe in supplication.

"I am a mortal, and liable to fall."

"Bear but a touch of my hand *there*," said the Spirit, laying it upon his heart, "and you shall be upheld in more than this!"

As the words were spoken, they passed through the wall, and stood in the busy thoroughfares of a city. It was made plain enough by the dressing of the shops that here, too, it was Christmas time. The Ghost stopped at a certain warehouse door, and asked Scrooge if he knew it.

"Know it! I was apprenticed here!"

They went in. At sight of an old gentleman in a Welsh wig, sitting behind such a high desk that, if he had been two inches taller, he must have knocked his head against the ceiling, Scrooge cried in great excitement: "Why, it's old Fezziwig! Bless his heart, it's Fezziwig, alive again!"

Old Fezziwig laid down his pen, and looked up at the clock, which pointed to the hour of seven. He rubbed his hands; adjusted his capacious waistcoat; laughed all over himself, from his shoes to his organ of benevolence; and called out in a comfortable, oily, rich, fat, jovial voice: "Yo ho, there! Ebenezer! Dick!"

A living and moving picture of Scrooge's former self, a young man, came briskly in, accompanied by his fellow-apprentice.

"Dick Wilkins, to be sure!" said Scrooge to the Ghost. "My old fellow-prentice, bless me, yes. There he is. He was very much attached to me, was Dick. Poor Dick! Dear, dear!"

"Yo ho, my boys!" said Fezziwig. "No more work to-night. Christmas eve, Dick. Christmas, Ebenezer! Let's have the shutters up, before a man can say Jack Robinson! Clear away, my lads, and let's have lots of room here!"

Clear away! There was nothing they wouldn't have cleared away, or couldn't have cleared away, with old Fezziwig looking on. It was done in a minute. Every movable was packed off, as if it were dismissed from public life for evermore; the floor was swept and watered, the lamps were trimmed, fuel was heaped upon the fire; and the warehouse was as snug and warm and dry and bright a ballroom as you would desire to see on a winter's night.

In came a fiddler with a music-book, and went up to the lofty desk, and made an orchestra of it, and tuned like fifty stomach-aches. In came Mrs. Fezziwig, one vast substantial smile. In came the three Miss Fezziwigs, beaming and lovable. In came the six young followers whose hearts they broke. In came all the young men and women employed in the business. In came the housemaid, with her cousin the baker. In came the cook, with her brother's particular friend the milkman. In they all came one after another; some shyly, some boldly, some gracefully, some awkwardly, some pushing, some pulling; in they all came, anyhow and everyhow. Away they all went, twenty couples at once; hands half round and back again the other way; down the middle and up again; round and round in various stages of affectionate grouping; old top couple always turning up in the wrong place; new top couple starting off again, as soon as they got there; all top couples at last, and not a bottom one to help them. When this result was brought about, old Fezziwig, clapping his hands to stop the dance, cried out, "Well done"; and the fiddler plunged his hot face into a pot of porter especially provided for that purpose.

There were more dances, and there were forfeits, and more dances, and there was cake, and there was negus, and there was a great piece of Cold Roast, and there was a great piece of Cold Boiled, and there were mince-pies, and plenty of beer. But the great effect of the evening came after the Roast and Boiled, when the fiddler struck up "Sir Roger de Coverley." Then old Fezziwig stood out to dance with Mrs. Fezziwig. Top couple, too; with a good stiff piece of work cut out for them; three or four and twenty pair of partners; people who were not to be trifled with; people who *would* dance, and had no notion of walking.

But if they had been twice as many — four times — old Fezziwig would have been a match for them, and so would Mrs. Fezziwig. As to *her*, she was worthy to be his partner in every sense of the term. A positive light appeared to issue from Fezziwig's calves. They shone in every part of the dance. You couldn't have predicted, at any given time, what would become of 'em next. And when old Fezziwig and Mrs. Fezziwig had gone all through the dance, — advance and retire, turn your partner, bow and courtesy, corkscrew, thread the needle, and back again to your place, — Fezziwig "cut," — cut so deftly, that he appeared to wink with his legs.

When the clock struck eleven this domestic ball broke up. Mr. and Mrs. Fezziwig took their stations, one on either side the door, and, shaking hands with every person individually as he or she went out, wished him or her a Merry Christmas. When everybody had retired but the two 'prentices, they did the same to them; and thus the cheerful voices died away, and the lads were left to their beds, which were under a counter in the back shop.

"A small matter," said the Ghost, "to make these silly folks so full of gratitude. He has spent but a few pounds of your mortal money, — three or four perhaps. Is that so much that he deserves this praise?"

"It isn't that," said Scrooge, heated by the remark, and speaking unconsciously like his former, not his latter self, — "it isn't that, Spirit. He has the power to render us happy or unhappy; to make our service light or burdensome; a pleasure or a toil. Say that his power lies in words and looks; in things so slight and insignificant that it is impossible to add and count 'em up: what then? The happiness he gives is quite as great as if it cost a fortune."

He felt the Spirit's glance, and stopped.

"What is the matter?"

"Nothing particular."

"Something, I think?"

"No, no. I should like to be able to say a word or two to my clerk just now. That's all."

"My time grows short," observed the Spirit. "Quick!"

This was not addressed to Scrooge, or to any one whom he could see, but it produced an immediate effect. For again he saw himself. He was older now; a man in the prime of life.

He was not alone, but sat by the side of a fair young girl in a black dress, in whose eyes there were tears.

"It matters little," she said softly to Scrooge's former self. "To you very little. Another idol has displaced me; and if it can comfort you in time to come, as I would have tried to do, I have no just cause to grieve."

"What idol has displaced you?"

"A golden one. You fear the world too much. I have seen your nobler aspirations fall off one by one, until the master-passion, Gain, engrosses you. Have I not?"

"What then? Even if I have grown so much wiser, what then? I am not changed towards you. Have I ever sought release from our engagement?"

"In words, no. Never."

"In what, then?"

"In a changed nature; in an altered spirit; in another atmosphere of life; another Hope as its great end. If you were free today, tomorrow, yesterday, can even I believe that you would choose a dowerless girl; or, choosing her, do I not know that your repentance and regret would surely follow? I do; and I release you. With a full heart, for the love of him you once were."

"Spirit! Remove me from this place."

"I told you these were shadows of the things that have been," said the Ghost. "That they are what they are, do not blame me!"

"Remove me!" Scrooge exclaimed. "I cannot bear it! Leave me! Take me back. Haunt me no longer!"

As he struggled with the Spirit he was conscious of being exhausted, and overcome by an irresistible drowsiness; and, further, of being in his own bedroom. He had barely time to reel to bed before he sank into a heavy sleep.

Stave Three: The Second of the Three Spirits

Scrooge awoke in his own bedroom. There was no doubt about that. But it and his own adjoining sitting-room, into which he shuffled in his slippers, attracted by a great light there, had undergone a surprising transformation. The walls and ceiling were so hung with living green, that it looked a perfect grove. The leaves of holly, mistletoe, and ivy reflected back the light, as if so many little mirrors had been scattered there; and such a mighty blaze went roaring up the chimney, as that petrifaction of a hearth had never known in Scrooge's time, or Marley's, or for many and many a winter season gone. Heaped upon the floor, to form a kind of throne, were turkeys, geese, game, brawn, great joints of meat, sucking pigs, long wreaths of sausages, mince-pies, plum-puddings, barrels of oysters, red-hot chestnuts, cherry-cheeked apples, juicy oranges, luscious pears, immense twelfth-cakes, and great bowls of punch. In easy state upon this couch there sat a Giant glorious to see; who bore a glowing torch, in shape not unlike Plenty's horn, and who raised it high to shed its light on Scrooge, as he came peeping round the door.

"Come in, — come in! and know me better, man! I am the Ghost of Christmas Present. Look upon me! You have never seen the like of me before."

"Never."

"Have never walked forth with the younger members of my family; meaning (for I am very young) my elder brothers born in these later years?" pursued the Phantom.

"I don't think I have, I am afraid I have not. Have you had many brothers, Spirit?"

"More than eighteen hundred."

"A tremendous family to provide for! Spirit, conduct me where you will. I went forth last night on compulsion, and I learnt a lesson which is working now. Tonight, if you have aught to teach me, let me profit by it."

"Touch my robe!"

Scrooge did as he was told, and held it fast.

The room and its contents all vanished instantly, and they stood in the city streets upon a snowy Christmas morning.

Scrooge and the Ghost passed on, invisible, straight to Scrooge's clerk's; and on the threshold of the door the Spirit smiled, and stopped to bless Bob Cratchit's dwelling with the sprinklings of his torch. Think of that! Bob had but fifteen "bob" a week himself; he pocketed on Saturdays but fifteen copies of his Christian name; and yet the Ghost of Christmas Present blessed his four-roomed house!

Then up rose Mrs. Cratchit, Cratchit's wife, dressed out but poorly in a twice-turned gown, but brave in ribbons, which are cheap and make a goodly show for sixpence; and she laid the cloth, assisted by Belinda Cratchit, second

of her daughters, also brave in ribbons; while Master Peter Cratchit plunged a fork into the saucepan of potatoes, and getting the corners of his monstrous shirt-collar (Bob's private property, conferred upon his son and heir in honour of the day) into his mouth, rejoiced to find himself so gallantly attired, and yearned to show his linen in the fashionable Parks. And now two smaller Cratchits, boy and girl, came tearing in, screaming that outside the baker's they had smelt the goose, and known it for their own; and, basking in luxurious thoughts of sage and onion, these young Cratchits danced about the table, and exalted Master Peter Cratchit to the skies, while he (not proud, although his collars nearly choked him) blew the fire, until the slow potatoes, bubbling up, knocked loudly at the saucepan-lid to be let out and peeled.

"What has ever got your precious father then?" said Mrs. Cratchit. "And your brother Tiny Tim! And Martha warn't as late last Christmas day by half an hour!"

"Here's Martha, mother!" said a girl, appearing as she spoke.

"Here's Martha, mother!" cried the two young Cratchits. "Hurrah! There's such a goose, Martha!"

"Why, bless your heart alive, my dear, how late you are!" said Mrs. Cratchit, kissing her a dozen times, and taking off her shawl and bonnet for her.

"We'd a deal of work to finish up last night," replied the girl, "and had to clear away this morning, mother!"

"Well! Never mind so long as you are come," said Mrs. Cratchit. "Sit ye down before the fire, my dear, and have a warm, Lord bless ye!"

"No, no! There's father coming," cried the two young Cratchits, who were everywhere at once. "Hide, Martha, hide!"

So Martha hid herself, and in came little Bob, the father, with at least three feet of comforter, exclusive of the fringe, hanging down before him; and his threadbare clothes darned up and brushed, to look seasonable; and Tiny Tim upon his shoulder. Alas for Tiny Tim, he bore a little crutch, and had his limbs supported by an iron frame!

"Why, where's our Martha?" cried Bob Cratchit, looking around.

"Not coming," said Mrs. Cratchit.

"Not coming!" said Bob, with a sudden declension in his high spirits; for he had been Tim's blood-horse all the way from church, and had come home rampant, — "not coming upon Christmas day!"

Martha didn't like to see him disappointed, if it were only in joke; so she came out prematurely from behind the closet door, and ran into his arms, while the two young Cratchits hustled Tiny Tim, and bore him off into the wash-house, that he might hear the pudding singing in the copper.

"And how did little Tim behave?" asked Mrs. Cratchit, when she had rallied Bob on his credulity, and Bob had hugged his daughter to his heart's content.

"As good as gold," said Bob, "and better. Somehow he gets thoughtful, sitting by himself so much, and thinks the strangest things you ever heard. He told me, coming home, that he hoped the people saw him in the church, because he was a cripple, and it might be pleasant to them to remember, upon Christmas day, who made lame beggars walk and blind men see."

Bob's voice was tremulous when he told them this, and trembled more when he said that Tiny Tim was growing strong and hearty.

His active little crutch was heard upon the floor, and back came Tiny Tim before another word was spoken, escorted by his brother and sister to his stool beside the fire; and while Bob, turning up his cuffs, — as if, poor fellow, they were capable of being made more shabby, — compounded some hot mixture in a jug with gin and lemons, and stirred it round and round, and put it on the hob to simmer, Master Peter and the two ubiquitous young Cratchits went to fetch the goose, with which they soon returned in high procession.

Mrs. Cratchit made the gravy (ready beforehand in a little saucepan) hissing hot; Master Peter mashed the potatoes with incredible vigour; Miss Belinda sweetened up the apple-sauce; Martha dusted the hot plates; Bob took Tiny Tim beside him in a tiny corner at the table; the two young Cratchits set chairs for everybody, not forgetting themselves, and mounting guard upon their posts, crammed spoons into their mouths, lest they should shriek for goose before their turn came to be helped. At last the dishes were set on, and grace was said. It was succeeded by a breathless pause, as Mrs. Cratchit, looking slowly all along the carving-knife, prepared to plunge it in the breast; but when she did, and when the long-expected gush of stuffing issued forth, one murmur of delight arose all round the board, and even Tiny Tim, excited by the two young Cratchits, beat on the table with the handle of his knife, and feebly cried, Hurrah!

There never was such a goose. Bob said he didn't believe there ever was such a goose cooked. Its tenderness and flavour, size and cheapness, were the themes of universal admiration. Eked out by apple-sauce and mashed potatoes, it was a sufficient dinner for the whole family; indeed, as Mrs. Cratchit said with great delight (surveying one small atom of a bone upon the dish) they hadn't ate it all at last! Yet

every one had had enough, and the youngest Cratchits in particular were steeped in sage and onion to the eyebrows! But now, the plates being changed by Miss Belinda, Mrs. Cratchit left the room alone, — too nervous to bear witnesses, — to take the pudding up, and bring it in.

Suppose it should not be done enough! Suppose it should break in turning out! Suppose somebody should have got over the wall of the back yard, and stolen it, while they were merry with the goose, — a supposition at which the two young Cratchits became livid! All sorts of horrors were supposed.

Hallo! A great deal of steam! The pudding was out of the copper. A smell like a washing-day! That was the cloth. A smell like an eating-house and a pastry-cook's next door to each other, with a laundress's next door to that! That was the pudding! In half a minute Mrs. Cratchit entered, — flushed but smiling proudly, — with the pudding, like a speckled cannon-ball, so hard and firm, blazing in half of half a quartern of ignited brandy, and bedight with Christmas holly stuck into the top.

Oh, a wonderful pudding! Bob Cratchit said, and calmly too, that he regarded it as the greatest success achieved by Mrs. Cratchit since their marriage. Mrs. Cratchit said that now the weight was off her mind, she would confess she had had her doubts about the quantity of flour. Everybody had something to say about it, but nobody said or thought it was at all a small pudding for a large family. Any Cratchit would have blushed to hint at such a thing.

At last the dinner was all done, the cloth was cleared, the hearth swept, and the fire made up. The compound in the jug being tasted, and considered perfect, apples and oranges were put upon the table, and a shovelful of chestnuts on the fire.

Then all the Cratchit family drew round the hearth, in what Bob Cratchit called a circle, and at Bob Cratchit's elbow stood the family display of glass, — two tumblers and a custard-cup without a handle.

These held the hot stuff from the jug, however, as well as golden goblets would have

done; and Bob served it out with beaming looks, while the chestnuts on the fire spluttered and crackled noisily. Then Bob proposed: —

"A Merry Christmas to us all, my dears. God bless us!"

Which all the family re-echoed.

"God bless us every one!" said Tiny Tim, the last of all.

He sat very close to his father's side, upon his little stool. Bob held his withered little hand in his, as if he loved the child, and wished to keep him by his side, and dreaded that he might be taken from him.

Scrooge raised his head speedily, on hearing his own name.

"Mr. Scrooge!" said Bob; "I'll give you Mr. Scrooge, the Founder of the Feast!"

"The Founder of the Feast indeed!" cried Mrs. Cratchit, reddening. "I wish I had him here. I'd give him a piece of my mind to feast upon, and I hope he'd have a good appetite for it."

"My dear," said Bob, "the children! Christmas day."

"It should be Christmas day, I am sure," said she, "on which one drinks the health of such an odious, stingy, hard, unfeeling man as Mr. Scrooge. You know he is, Robert! Nobody knows it better than you do, poor fellow!"

"My dear," was Bob's mild answer, "Christmas day."

"I'll drink his health for your sake and the day's," said Mrs. Cratchit, "not for his. Long life to him! A merry Christmas and a happy New Year! He'll be very merry and very happy, I have no doubt!"

The children drank the toast after her. It was the first of their proceedings which had no heartiness in it. Tiny Tim drank it last of all, but he didn't care twopence for it. Scrooge was the Ogre of the family. The mention of his name cast a dark shadow on the party, which was not dispelled for full five minutes.

After it had passed away, they were ten times merrier than before, from the mere relief of Scrooge the Baleful being done with. Bob Cratchit told them how he had a situation in his eye for Master Peter, which would bring him, if obtained, full five and sixpence weekly. The two young Cratchits laughed tremendously at the idea of Peter's being a man of business; and Peter himself looked thoughtfully at the fire from between his collars, as if he were deliberating what particular investments he should favour when he came into the receipt of that bewildering income. Martha, who was a poor apprentice at a milliner's, then told them what kind of work she had to do, and how many hours she worked at a stretch, and how she meant to be abed to-morrow morning for a good long rest; to-morrow being a holiday she passed at home. Also how she had seen a countess and a lord some days before, and how the lord "was much about as tall as Peter;" at which Peter pulled up his collars so high that you couldn't have seen his head if you had been there. All this time the chestnuts and the jug went round and round, and by and by they had a song, about a lost child travelling in the snow, from Tiny Tim, who had a plaintive little voice, and sang it very well indeed.

There was nothing of high mark in this. They were not a handsome family; they were not well dressed; their shoes were far from being waterproof; their clothes were scanty; and Peter might have known, and very likely did, the inside of a pawnbroker's. But they were happy, grateful, pleased with one another, and contented with the time; and when they faded, and looked happier yet in the bright sprinklings of the Spirit's torch at parting, Scrooge had his eye upon them, and especially on Tiny Tim, until the last.

It was a great surprise to Scrooge, as this scene vanished, to hear a hearty laugh. It was a much greater surprise to Scrooge to recognize it as his own nephew's, and to find himself in a bright, dry, gleaming room, with the Spirit standing smiling by his side, and looking at that same nephew.

It is a fair, even-handed, noble adjustment of things, that while there is infection in disease and sorrow, there is nothing in the world so irresistibly contagious as laughter and good-humour. When Scrooge's nephew laughed, Scrooge's niece by marriage laughed as heartily as he. And their assembled friends, being not a bit behind-hand, laughed out lustily.

"He said that Christmas was a humbug, as I live!" cried Scrooge's nephew. "He believed it too!"

"More shame for him, Fred!" said Scrooge's niece, indignantly. Bless those women! they never do anything by halves. They are always in earnest.

She was very pretty; exceedingly pretty. With a dimpled, surprised-looking, capital face; a ripe little mouth that seemed made to be kissed, — as no doubt it was, all kinds of good little dots about her chin, that melted into one another when she laughed; and the sunniest pair of eyes you ever saw in any little creature's head. Altogether she was what you would have called provoking, but satisfactory, too. Oh, perfectly satisfactory.

"He's a comical old fellow," said Scrooge's nephew, "that's the truth; and not so pleasant as he might be. However, his offences carry their own punishment, and I have nothing to say against him. Who suffers by his ill whims? Himself, always. Here he takes it into his head to dislike us, and he won't come and dine with us. What's the consequence? He don't lose much of a dinner."

"Indeed, I think he loses a very good dinner," interrupted Scrooge's niece. Everybody else said the same, and they must be allowed to have been competent judges, because they had just had dinner; and, with the dessert upon the table, were clustered round the fire, by lamplight.

"Well, I am very glad to hear it," said Scrooge's nephew, "because I haven't any great faith in these young housekeepers. What do you say, Topper?"

Topper clearly had his eye on one of Scrooge's niece's sisters, for he answered that a bachelor was a wretched outcast, who had no right to express an opinion on the subject. Whereat Scrooge's niece's sister — the plump one with the lace tucker; not the one with the roses — blushed.

After tea they had some music. For they were a musical family, and knew what they were about, when they sung a Glee or Catch, I can assure you,—especially Topper, who could growl away in the bass like a good one, and never swell the large veins in his forehead, or get red in the face over it.

But they didn't devote the whole evening to music. After a while they played at forfeits; for it is good to be children sometimes, and never better than at Christmas, when its mighty Founder was a child himself. There was first a game at blindman's buff though. And I no more believe Topper was really blinded than I believe he had eyes in his boots. Because the way in which he went after that plump sister in the lace tucker was an outrage on the credulity of human nature. Knocking down the fire-irons, tumbling over the chairs, bumping up against the piano, smothering himself among the curtains, wherever she went there went he! He always knew where the plump sister was. He wouldn't catch anybody else. If you had fallen up against him, as some of them did, and stood there, he would have made a feint of endeavouring to seize you, which would have been an affront to your understanding, and would instantly have sidled off in the direction of the plump sister.

"Here is a new game," said Scrooge. "One half-hour, Spirit, only one!"

It was a Game called Yes and No, where Scrooge's nephew had to think of something, and the rest must find out what; he only answering to their questions yes or no, as the case was. The fire of questioning to which he was exposed elicited from him that he was thinking of an animal, a live animal, rather a disagreeable animal, a savage animal, an animal that growled and grunted sometimes, and talked sometimes, and lived in London, and walked about the streets, and wasn't made a show of, and wasn't led by anybody, and didn't live in a menagerie, and was never killed in a market, and was not a horse, or an ass, or a cow, or a bull, or a tiger, or a dog, or a pig, or a cat, or a bear. At every new question put to him, this nephew burst into a fresh roar of laughter; and was so inexpressibly tickled, that he was obliged

to get up off the sofa and stamp. At last the plump sister cried out: —

"I have found it out! I know what it is, Fred! I know what it is!"

"What is it?" cried Fred.

"It's your uncle Scro-o-o-oge!"

Which it certainly was. Admiration was the universal sentiment, though some objected that the reply to "Is it a bear?" ought to have been "Yes."

Uncle Scrooge had imperceptibly become so gay and light of heart, that he would have drank to the unconscious company in an inaudible speech. But the whole scene passed off in the breath of the last word spoken by his nephew; and he and the Spirit were again upon their travels.

Much they saw, and far they went, and many homes they visited, but always with a happy end. The Spirit stood beside sick-beds, and they were cheerful; on foreign lands, and they were close at home; by struggling men, and they were patient in their greater hope; by poverty, and it was rich. In almshouse, hospital, and jail, in misery's every refuge, where vain man in his little brief authority had not made fast the door, and barred the Spirit out, he left his blessing, and taught Scrooge his precepts. Suddenly, as they stood together in an open place, the bell struck twelve.

Scrooge looked about him for the Ghost, and saw it no more. As the last stroke ceased to vibrate, he remembered the prediction of old Jacob Marley, and, lifting up his eyes, beheld a solemn Phantom, draped and hooded, coming like a mist along the ground towards him.

Stave Four: The Last of the Spirits

The Phantom slowly, gravely, silently approached. When it came near him, Scrooge bent down upon his knee; for in the air through which this Spirit moved it seemed to scatter gloom and mystery.

It was shrouded in a deep black garment, which concealed its head, its face, its form, and left nothing of it visible save one outstretched hand. He knew no more, for the Spirit neither spoke nor moved.

"I am in the presence of the Ghost of Christmas Yet to Come? Ghost of the Future! I fear you more than any spectre I have seen. But as I know your purpose is to do me good, and as I hope to live to be another man from what I was, I am prepared to bear you company, and do it with a thankful heart. Will you not speak to me?"

It gave him no reply. The hand was pointed straight before them.

"Lead on! Lead on! The night is waning fast, and it is precious time to me, I know. Lead on, Spirit!"

They scarcely seemed to enter the city; for the city rather seemed to spring up about them. But there they were in the heart of it; on 'Change, amongst the merchants.

The Spirit stopped beside one little knot of business men. Observing that the hand was pointed to them, Scrooge advanced to listen to their talk.

"No," said a great fat man with a monstrous chin. "I don't know much about it either way. I only know he's dead."

"When did he die?" inquired another.

"Last night, I believe."

"Why, what was the matter with him? I thought he'd never die."

"God knows," said the first, with a yawn.

"What has he done with his money?" asked a red-faced gentleman.

"I haven't heard," said the man with the large chin. "Company, perhaps. He hasn't left it to me. That's all I know. By, by."

Scrooge was at first inclined to be surprised that the Spirit should attach importance to conversation apparently so trivial; but feeling assured that it must have some hidden purpose, he set himself to consider what it was likely to be. It could scarcely be supposed to have any bearing on the death of Jacob, his old partner, for that was Past, and this Ghost's province was the Future.

He looked about in that very place for his own image; but another man stood in his accustomed corner, and though the clock pointed to his usual time of day for being there, he saw no likeness of himself amongst the multitudes that poured in through the Porch. It gave him little surprise, however; for he had been revolving in his mind a change of life, and he thought and hoped he saw his newborn resolutions carried out in this.

They left this busy scene, and went into an obscure part of the town, to a low shop where iron, old rags, bottles, bones, and greasy offal were bought. A grey-haired rascal, of great age, sat smoking his pipe. Scrooge and the Phantom came into the presence of this man, just as a woman with a heavy bundle slunk into the shop. But she had scarcely entered, when another woman, similarly laden, came in too; and she was closely followed by a man in faded black. After a short period of blank astonishment, in which the old man with the pipe had joined them, they all three burst into a laugh.

"Let the charwoman alone to be the first!" cried she who had entered first. "Let the laundress alone to be the second; and let the undertaker's man alone to be the third. Look here, old Joe, here's a chance! If we haven't all three met here without meaning it!"

"You couldn't have met in a better place. You were made free of it long ago, you know; and the other two ain't strangers. What have you got to sell? What have you got to sell?"

"Half a minute's patience, Joe, and you shall see."

"What odds then! What odds, Mrs. Dilber?" said the woman. "Every person has a right to take care of themselves. *He* always did! Who's the worse for the loss of a few things like these? Not a dead man, I suppose."

Mrs. Dilber, whose manner was remarkable for general propitiation, said, "No, indeed, ma'am."

"If he wanted to keep 'em after he was dead, a wicked old screw, why wasn't he natural in his lifetime? If he had been, he'd have had somebody to look after him when he was struck with Death, instead of lying gasping out his last there, alone by himself."

"It's the truest word that ever was spoke, it's a judgment on him."

"I wish it was a little heavier judgment, and it should have been, you may depend upon it, if I could have laid my hands on anything else. Open that bundle, old Joe, and let me know the value of it. Speak out plain. I'm not afraid to be the first nor afraid for them to see it."

Joe went down on his knees for the greater convenience of opening the bundle, and dragged out a large and heavy roll of some dark stuff.

"What do you call this? Bed-curtains!"

"Ah! Bed-curtains! Don't drop that oil upon the blankets, now."

"*His* blankets?"

"Whose else's do you think? He isn't likely to take cold without 'em, I dare say. Ah! You may look through that shirt till your eyes ache; but you won't find a hole in it, nor a threadbare place. It's the best he had, and a fine one too. They'd have wasted it by dressing him up in it, if it hadn't been for me."

Scrooge listened to this dialogue in horror.

"Spirit! I see, I see. The case of this unhappy man might be my own. My life tends that way, now. Merciful Heaven, what is this!"

The scene had changed, and now he almost touched a bare, uncurtained bed. A pale light, rising in the outer air, fell straight upon this bed; and on it, unwatched, unwept, uncared for, was the body of this plundered unknown man.

"Spirit, let me see some tenderness connected with a death, or this dark chamber, Spirit, will be for ever present to me."

The Ghost conducted him to poor Bob Cratchit's house, — the dwelling he had visited before, — and found the mother and the children seated round the fire.

Quiet. Very quiet. The noisy little Cratchits were as still as statues in one corner, and sat looking up at Peter, who had a book before him. The mother and her daughters were engaged in needlework. But surely they were very quiet!

"'And he took a child, and set him in the midst of them.'"

Where had Scrooge heard those words? He had not dreamed them. The boy must have read them out, as he and the Spirit crossed the threshold. Why did he not go on?

The mother laid her work upon the table, and put her hand up to her face. "The colour hurts my eyes," she said.

The colour? Ah, poor Tiny Tim!

"They're better now again. It makes them weak by candlelight; and I wouldn't show weak eyes to your father when he comes home, for the world. It must be near his time."

"Past it rather," Peter answered, shutting up his book. "But I think he has walked a little slower than he used, these few last evenings, mother."

"I have known him walk with — I have known him walk with Tiny Tim upon his shoulder, very fast indeed."

"And so have I," cried Peter. "Often."

"And so have I," exclaimed another. So had all.

"But he was very light to carry, and his father loved him so, that it was no trouble, — no trouble. And there is your father at the door!"

She hurried out to meet him; and little Bob in his comforter — he had need of it, poor fellow — came in. His tea was ready for him on the hob, and they all tried who should help him to it most. Then the two young Cratchits got upon his knees and laid, each child, a little cheek against his face, as if they said, "Don't mind it, father. Don't be grieved!"

Bob was very cheerful with them, and spoke pleasantly to all the family. He looked at the work upon the table, and praised the industry and speed of Mrs. Cratchit and the girls. They would be done long before Sunday, he said.

"Sunday! You went to-day, then, Robert?"

"Yes, my dear," returned Bob. "I wish you could have gone. It would have done you good to see how green a place it is. But you'll see it often. I promised him that I would walk there on a Sunday. My little, little child! My little child!"

He broke down all at once. He couldn't help it. If he could have helped it, he and his child would have been farther apart, perhaps, than they were.

"Spectre," said Scrooge, "something informs me that our parting moment is at hand. I know it, but I know not how. Tell me what man that was, with the covered face, whom we saw lying dead?"

The Ghost of Christmas Yet to Come conveyed him to a dismal, wretched, ruinous churchyard.

The Spirit stood amongst the graves, and pointed down to One.

"Before I draw nearer to that stone to which you point, answer me one question. Are these the shadows of the things that Will be, or are they shadows of the things that May be only?"

Still the Ghost pointed downward to the grave by which it stood.

"Men's courses will foreshadow certain ends, to which, if persevered in, they must lead. But if the courses be departed from, the ends will change. Say it is thus with what you show me!"

The Spirit was immovable as ever.

Scrooge crept towards it, trembling as he went; and, following the finger, read upon the stone of the neglected grave his own name — EBENEZER SCROOGE.

"Am *I* that man who lay upon the bed? No, Spirit! Oh no, no! Spirit! hear me! I am not the man I was. I will not be the man I must have been but for this intercourse. Why show me this, if I am past all hope? Assure me that I yet may change these shadows you have shown me by an altered life."

For the first time the kind hand faltered.

"I will honour Christmas in my heart, and try to keep it all the year. I will live in the Past, the Present, and the Future. The Spirits of all three shall strive within me. I will not shut out the lessons that they teach. Oh, tell me I may sponge away the writing on this stone!"

Holding up his hands in one last prayer to have his fate reversed, he saw an alteration in the Phantom's hood and dress. It shrunk, collapsed, and dwindled down into a bedpost.

Yes, and the bedpost was his own. The bed was his own, the room was his own. Best and happiest of all, the Time before him was his own, to make amends in!

He was checked in his transports by the churches ringing out the lustiest peals he had ever heard.

Running to the window, he opened it, and put out his head. No fog, no mist, no night; clear, bright, stirring, golden day.

"What's to-day?" cried Scrooge, calling downward to a boy in Sunday clothes, who perhaps had loitered in to look about him.

"Eh?"

"What's to-day, my fine fellow?"

"To-day! Why *Christmas day.*"

"It's Christmas day! I haven't missed it. Hallo, my fine fellow!"

"Hallo!"

"Do you know the Poulterer's, in the next street but one, at the corner?"

"I should hope I did."

"An intelligent boy! A remarkable boy! Do you know whether they've sold the prize Turkey that was hanging up there? Not the little prize Turkey, — the big one?"

"What, the one as big as me?"

"What a delightful boy! It's a pleasure to talk to him. Yes, my buck!"

"It's hanging there now."

"Is it? Go and buy it."

"Walk-*er!*" exclaimed the boy.

"No, no, I am in earnest. Go and buy it, and tell 'em to bring it here, that I may give them the direction where to take it. Come back with the man, and I'll give you a shilling. Come back with him in less than five minutes, and I'll give you half a crown!"

The boy was off like a shot.

"I'll send it to Bob Cratchit's! He sha'n't know who sends it. It's twice the size of Tiny Tim. Joe Miller never made such a joke as sending it to Bob's will be!"

The hand in which he wrote the address was not a steady one, but write it he did, somehow, and went down stairs to open the street door, ready for the coming of the poulterer's man.

It was a Turkey! He never could have stood upon his legs, that bird. He would have snapped 'em short off in a minute, like sticks of sealing-wax.

Scrooge dressed himself "all in his best," and at last got out into the streets. The people were by this time pouring forth, as he had seen them with the Ghost of Christmas Present; and, walking with his hands behind him, Scrooge regarded every one with a delighted smile. He looked so irresistibly pleasant, in a word, that three or four good-humoured fellows said, "Good morning, sir! A merry Christmas to you!" And Scrooge said often afterwards, that, of all the blithe sounds he had ever heard, those were the blithest in his ears.

In the afternoon, he turned his steps towards his nephew's house.

He passed the door a dozen times, before he had the courage to go up and knock. But he made a dash, and did it.

"Is your master at home, my dear?" said Scrooge to the girl. Nice girl! Very.

"Yes, sir."

"Where is he, my love?"

"He's in the dining-room, sir, along with mistress."

"He knows me," said Scrooge, with his hand already on the dining-room lock. "I'll go in here, my dear."

"Fred!"

"Why, bless my soul!" cried Fred, "who's that?"

"It's I. Your uncle Scrooge. I have come to dinner. Will you let me in, Fred?"

Let him in! It is a mercy he didn't shake his arm off. He was at home in five minutes. Nothing could be heartier. His niece looked just the same. So did Topper when *he* came. So did the plump sister when *she* came. So did every one when *they* came. Wonderful party, wonderful games, wonderful unanimity, won-derful happiness!

But he was early at the office next morning. Oh, he was early there. If he could only be there first, and catch Bob Cratchit coming late! That was the thing he had set his heart upon.

And he did it. The clock struck nine. No Bob. A quarter past. No Bob. Bob was full eighteen minutes and a half behind his time. Scrooge sat with his door wide open, that he might see him come into the tank.

Bob's hat was off before he opened the door; his comforter too. He was on his stool in a jiffy; driving away with his pen, as if he were trying to overtake nine o'clock.

"Hallo!" growled Scrooge, in his accustomed voice, as near as he could feign it. "What do you mean by coming here at this time of day?"

"I am very sorry, sir. I *am* behind my time."

"You are? Yes. I think you are. Step this way if you please."

"It's only once a year, sir. It shall not be repeated. I was making rather merry yesterday, sir."

"Now, I'll tell you what, my friend. I am not going to stand this sort of thing any longer. And therefore," Scrooge continued, leaping from his stool, and giving Bob such a dig in the waistcoat that he staggered back into the tank again, — "and therefore I am about to raise your salary!"

Bob trembled, and got a little nearer to the ruler.

"A merry Christmas, Bob!" said Scrooge, with an earnestness that could not be mistaken, as he clapped him on the back. "A merrier Christmas, Bob, my good fellow, than I have given you for many a year! I'll raise your salary, and endeavour to assist your struggling family, and we will discuss your affairs this very afternoon, over a Christmas bowl of smoking bishop, Bob! Make up the fires, and buy a second coal-scuttle before you dot another *i*, Bob Cratchit!"

Scrooge was better than his word. He did it all, and infinitely more; and to Tiny Tim, who did *not* die, he was a second father. He became as good a friend, as good a master, and as good a man as the good old city knew, or any other good old city, town, or borough in the good old world. Some people laughed to see the alteration in him; but his own heart laughed, and that was quite enough for him.

He had no further intercourse with Spirits, but lived in that respect upon the Total Abstinence Principle ever afterwards; and it was always said of him that he knew how to keep Christmas well, if any man alive possessed the knowledge. May that be truly said of us, and all of us! And so, as Tiny Tim observed, God Bless Us, Every One!

A MERRY, SCARY CHRISTMAS

by Dick Ashbaugh

To those ingenious gentlemen, the American toy manufacturers, I bow low. Their crusade for realism has been relentless, unflagging and mildly terrifying. They have given us dolls that walk, talk and cry, and mechanical cowboys that shoot from the hip.

Still, I do not think the toy designers have gone far enough. In training the little ones for future parenthood, I believe a number of other realities could be scaled down to tot-size. The following list is tentative, but I believe it has possibilities.

FOR JUNIOR:

The Little Family Man. A kit of toy unpaid bills just like daddy's. Printed on sturdy bond paper, these bills are the last word in realism. Several are marked: "Final Notice." The kit also includes toy bankbook showing balance of $4.61.

Young Handy Man. Set of two full-scale leaky faucets plus repair parts. Parts are machined slightly out of line so faucets continue to leak after hours of work. A provocative toy for the junior mechanic.

The Little Soldier. Highly colored plastic set containing mailbox with toy draft card, bite-sized samples of Army food and complete equipment for permanent rank of master sergeant. (Officer material slightly higher.)

The Young Statesman. Toy convention stage with fireproof bunting in full color. Scale-model Senate Chamber includes harmless, electrically operated filibuster. AC or DC. Specify party.

FOR SISTER:

Toy Baking Failure. Exact model of three-layer cake. Falls in middle when placed in oven. Ideal for the young hostess.

Dinner Party. Complete equipment for party of eight. Includes tough steak from butcher, and instructions for borrowing extra silver from the neighbors. Choice of underdone vegetables. Plastic and inedible for protection of smaller guests.

Budget-wise. The thrifty young mother will love this miniature play budget. Handsomely bound, it shows a deficit at the end of the month. Just like mummy's.

Joy Baby. The perfect doll for the Little Mother. A simple control causes doll to cry for bottle at three A.M. Nineteen inches high, with a gorgeous permanent that uncurls in damp weather.

LET NOTHING YOU DISMAY

by Ruth Harnden

She had spent the afternoon trimming the tree. She had trimmed it after the fashion of her native land, with bright red polished apples hanging, for balance and for beauty, under each pure-white candle. The old customs, her distant youth, were sharp to her memory. Sometimes they were sharper than the events of her present life in this New England village where she had come so many years ago and raised her American family. Sometimes, and more often of late, she would find herself forgetting things that had happened only the week before. She would make confusing mistakes, answer letters she had answered already, or else forget to answer them at all. It surprised her very much. She could remember so brilliantly every tree in her mother's garden, every street in the small Swedish town where she had grown up, every face and name of her early playmates and neighbors. It was very puzzling.

She sat now in the dark room, in the fragrance from the balsam tree, and watched the year's first snow falling beyond the window. She would not light the candles yet. She was saving them for the children. If the snow kept up, she knew, it would make the walking bad. But she hoped that it would keep up. She found it beautiful — and more than that. She had never lost, or perhaps she had found again, a childlike sense of magic in the presence of the first snowfall.

How strange it must be, she thought, to live where there is always snow. There was Hilda in the mountains of Oregon — Hilda who had cooked for her so faithfully until she married that crazy miner and went to live in some shack in the wilds. *So cold,* she would write in her letters. *Always so cold it is, I think I never be warm again.*

Rocking gently in the warm room, smelling the Christmas tree, watching the quick, feathered air outside, she thought with satisfaction of the socks she had knit for Hilda. Six pairs, extra heavy. Hilda's feet, at least, would be warm.

She had mailed them in plenty of time. Last week, wasn't it? And there was still a week to go before Christmas. But then, she asked herself abruptly, what was it that she had mailed this morning? Something to Hilda, she was sure. She remembered thinking of her at the post office this morning, and she had written on the wide, flat box — But that was impossible! That was the box from Martins. That was the nightie for Janie who was getting married right after Christmas.

Her granddaughter getting married! Only think. It was hard to realize. And it was the loveliest nightie she could find, the color of honeysuckle and trimmed with real lace. "Extravagant," she told herself dutifully now, but it didn't prevent her from smiling. It was so beautiful, and so was Janie — and she was getting married. Nineteen. Janie was nineteen. It

didn't seem possible. And she had sent the nightie this morning to . . .

She stopped the gently rocking chair and sat straighter, trying to stop her thoughts until she could straighten them.

She had stood at the table in the post office, under the placard listing the states and their mailing dates — For Florida, For Oregon — and she had thought of Hilda. "Oh, dear!" she said aloud, because now she could remember very clearly writing Mrs. Hilda Borge, writing the Oregon address. "And the socks?" she asked herself. Had she sent the socks to Janie in Florida? But she could write to Janie. She could explain. It was of Hilda that she needed to think.

For a moment she was seeing the plain and practical Hilda with an awful clarity, because she was seeing her in relation to the bridal nightie, the gleaming satin, the cobweb lace. It was a picture so incongruous as to be almost indecent. And no one would be quicker to know that than Hilda herself. How she scorned all softness, all luxury and beauty, out of the protective shell she had built around her own

poverty and plainness. "Such nonsense!" she could hear Hilda saying. "When so many are hungry, and cold." But it was really the beauty that Hilda feared, as though she had to deny its existence or she would have to admit her own deprivation — her small, middle-aged, shapeless body, her homely work-scarred hands, the hopeless plainness of her face. She was unredeemed by a single beauty, and the only wonder was that even the thickheaded, bowlegged miner had wanted to marry her.

Would Hilda ever understand that it was only an old woman's fumbling mistake and not an insult, not a mockery to send that exquisite gossamer nightie into her poor stark shack where, in all likelihood, she slept in her long woolen underwear? Or would it break her heart with its terrible contrast to her own ugliness, its terrible reminder of all the luxury and loveliness that had no place in her own life? "How could I?" she asked herself. "And for Christmas, too?" The happiest time of the year, the time for remembering old friends with love and with loving gifts. Even now in the distance, but still distinctly, she could hear the carol singers lifting their voices on the sharp and snow-filled air. "God rest you merry, gentlemen, let nothing you dismay..." How ironic the words seemed to her now, like a rebuke to her shameful stupidity, her cruel blunder.

It was only the day after Christmas that she had Janie's wire from Miami — Janie who was so young and impatient, and too busy with her wedding plans to sit down and write a letter. *Marvelous ski socks,* the wire read. *How did you guess where we were spending our honeymoon?* So that, at least, was all right, even though she had forgotten, after all, to write an explanation to Janie. Now she was glad that she hadn't written. Ski socks, indeed! It made her think of her own youth in Sweden, and it was a number of minutes before her mind returned to the present. But then she *had* sent the nightie to Hilda! For a little while, for a few happy Christmas days she had forgotten.

It was another week before Hilda's letter came. *Old Hilda,* it began (in the middle of her own thought, after the habit of her simplic-

ity). For a second she thought her worst fears had been realized and her heart shook. But her eyes moved rapidly on. *Old Hilda, they think, there is only to keep her warm. So they send the sweaters, the mittens, the socks. What could make her pretty, such a one, eh? But you, my lovely friend, you have the other heart, the other eyes, and I am beautiful now! I open up the tight-air stove so the room is full of heat, and I put on my so beautiful dress made for dancing, and what you think? I dance! Old Hilda dance, can you think of it? And my Tim he come and dance with me. Ha, I think my Tim he fall in love with me all over again.*

THE GIFT OF THE MAGI, *first published in 1907, is probably the most famous story that O. Henry ever wrote. When we consider that at the time it was written $20 a week was thought to be a decent salary, this tender story becomes all the more touching.*

THE GIFT OF THE MAGI

by O. Henry

One dollar and eighty-seven cents. That was all. And sixty cents of it was in pennies. Pennies saved one and two at a time by bulldozing the grocer and the vegetable man and the butcher until one's cheeks burned with the silent imputation of parsimony that such close dealing implied. Three times Della counted it. One dollar and eighty-seven cents. And the next day would be Christmas.

There was clearly nothing to do but flop down on the shabby little couch and howl. So Della did it. Which instigates the moral reflection that life is made up of sobs, sniffles, and smiles, with sniffles predominating.

While the mistress of the home is gradually subsiding from the first stage to the second, take a look at the home. A furnished flat at $8 per week. It did not exactly beggar description, but it certainly had that word on the lookout for the mendicancy squad.

In the vestibule below was a letter-box into which no letter would go, and an electric button from which no mortal finger could coax a ring. Also appertaining thereunto was a card bearing the name "Mr. James Dillingham Young."

The "Dillingham" had been flung to the breeze during a former period of prosperity when its possessor was being paid $30 per week. Now, when the income was shrunk to $20, the letters of "Dillingham" looked blurred, as though they were thinking seriously of contracting to a modest and unassuming D. But whenever Mr. James Dillingham Young came home and reached his flat above he was called "Jim" and greatly hugged by Mrs. James Dillingham Young, already introduced to you as Della. Which is all very good.

Della finished her cry and attended to her cheeks with the powder rag. She stood by the window and looked out dully at a gray cat walking a gray fence in a gray backyard. To-morrow would be Christmas Day, and she had only $1.87 with which to buy Jim a present. She had been saving every penny she could for months, with this result. Twenty dollars a week doesn't go far. Expenses had been greater than she had calculated. They always are. Only $1.87 to buy a present for Jim. Her Jim. Many a happy hour she had spent planning for something nice for him. Something fine and rare and sterling — something just a little bit near to being worthy of the honor of being owned by Jim.

There was a pier-glass between the windows of the room. Perhaps you have seen a pier-glass in an $8 flat. A very thin and very agile person may, by observing his reflection in a rapid sequence of longitudinal strips, obtain a fairly accurate conception of his looks. Della, being slender, had mastered the art.

Suddenly she whirled from the window and stood before the glass. Her eyes were shining brilliantly, but her face had lost its color within twenty seconds. Rapidly she pulled down her hair and let it fall to its full length.

Now, there were two possessions of the James Dillingham Youngs, in which they both took a mighty pride. One was Jim's gold watch that had been his father's and his grandfather's. The other was Della's hair. Had the Queen of Sheba lived in the flat across the airshaft, Della would have let her hair hang out the window some day to dry just to depreciate Her Majesty's jewels and gifts. Had King Solomon been the janitor, with all his treasures piled up in the basement, Jim would have pulled out his watch every time he passed, just to see him pluck at his beard from envy.

So now Della's beautiful hair fell about her rippling and shining like a cascade of brown waters. It reached below her knee and made itself almost a garment for her. And then she did it up again nervously and quickly. Once she faltered for a minute and stood still while a tear or two splashed on the worn red carpet.

On went her old brown jacket; on went her old brown hat. With a whirl of skirts and with the brilliant sparkle still in her eyes, she fluttered out the door and down the stairs to the street.

Where she stopped the sign read: "Mme. Sofronie. Hair Goods of All Kinds." One flight up Della ran, and collected herself, panting. Madame, large, too white, chilly, hardly looked the "Sofronie."

"Will you buy my hair?" asked Della.

"I buy hair," said Madame. "Take yer hat off and let's have a sight at the looks of it."

Down rippled the brown cascade.

"Twenty dollars," said Madame, lifting the mass with a practised hand.

"Give it to me quick," said Della.

Oh, and the next two hours tripped by on rosy wings. Forget the hashed metaphor. She was ransacking the stores for Jim's present.

She found it at last. It surely had been made for Jim and no one else. There was no other like it in any of the stores, and she had turned all of them inside out. It was a platinum fob chain simple and chaste in design, properly proclaiming its value by substance alone and not by meretricious ornamentation — as all good things should do. It was even worthy of The

Watch. As soon as she saw it she knew that it must be Jim's. It was like him. Quietness and value — the description applied to both. Twenty-one dollars they took from her for it, and she hurried home with the 87 cents. With that chain on his watch Jim might be properly anxious about the time in any company. Grand as the watch was, he sometimes looked at it on the sly on account of the old leather strap that he used in place of a chain.

When Della reached home her intoxication gave way a little to prudence and reason. She got out her curling irons and lighted the gas and went to work repairing the ravages made by generosity added to love. Which is always a tremendous task, dear friends — a mammoth task.

Within forty minutes her head was covered with tiny, close-lying curls that made her look wonderfully like a truant schoolboy. She looked at her reflection in the mirror long, carefully, and critically.

"If Jim doesn't kill me," she said to herself, "before he takes a second look at me, he'll say I look like a Coney Island chorus girl. But what could I do — oh! what could I do with a dollar and eighty-seven cents?"

At 7 o'clock the coffee was made and the frying-pan was on the back of the stove hot and ready to cook the chops.

Jim was never late. Della doubled the fob chain in her hand and sat on the corner of the table near the door that he always entered. Then she heard his step on the stair way down on the first flight, and she turned white for just a moment. She had a habit of saying little silent prayers about the simplest everyday things, and now she whispered: "Please God, make him think I am still pretty."

The door opened and Jim stepped in and closed it. He looked thin and very serious. Poor fellow, he was only twenty-two — and to be burdened with a family! He needed a new overcoat and he was without gloves.

Jim stopped inside the door, as immovable as a setter at the scent of quail. His eyes were fixed upon Della, and there was an expression in them that she could not read, and it terrified her. It was not anger, nor surprise, nor disapproval, nor horror, nor any of the sentiments that she had been prepared for. He simply stared at her fixedly with that peculiar expression on his face.

Della wriggled off the table and went for him.

"Jim, darling," she cried, "don't look at me that way. I had my hair cut off and sold it because I couldn't have lived through Christmas without giving you a present. It'll grow out again — you won't mind, will you? I just had to do it. My hair grows awfully fast. Say 'Merry Christmas,' Jim, and let's be happy. You don't know what a nice — what a beautiful, nice gift I've got for you."

"You've cut off your hair?" asked Jim, laboriously, as if he had not arrived at that patent fact yet even after the hardest mental labor.

"Cut it off and sold it," said Della. "Don't you like me just as well, anyhow? I'm me without my hair, ain't I?"

Jim looked about the room curiously.

"You say your hair is gone?" he said, with an air almost of idiocy.

"You needn't look for it," said Della. "It's sold, I tell you — sold and gone, too. It's Christmas Eve, boy. Be good to me, for it went for you. Maybe the hairs of my head were numbered," she went on with a sudden serious sweetness, "but nobody could ever count my love for you. Shall I put the chops on, Jim?"

Out of his trance Jim seemed quickly to wake. He enfolded his Della. For ten seconds let us regard with discreet scrutiny some inconsequential object in the other direction. Eight dollars a week or a million a year — what is the difference? A mathematician or a wit would give you the wrong answer. The magi brought valuable gifts, but that was not among them. This dark assertion will be illuminated later on.

Jim drew a package from his overcoat pocket and threw it upon the table.

"Don't make any mistake, Dell," he said, "about me. I don't think there's anything in the way of a haircut or a shave or a shampoo that could make me like my girl any less. But if you'll unwrap that package you may see why you had me going a while at first."

White fingers and nimble tore at the string and paper. And then an ecstatic scream of joy; and then, alas! a quick feminine change to hysterical tears and wails, necessitating the immediate employment of all the comforting power of the lord of the flat.

For there lay The Combs — the set of combs, side and back, that Della had worshipped for long in a Broadway window. Beautiful combs, pure tortoise shell, with jewelled rims — just the shade to wear in the beautiful vanished hair. They were expensive combs, she knew, and her heart had simply craved and yearned over them without the least hope of possession. And now, they were hers, but the tresses that should have adorned the coveted adornments were gone.

But she hugged them to her bosom, and at length she was able to look up with dim eyes and a smile and say: "My hair grows so fast, Jim!"

And then Della leaped up like a little singed cat and cried, "Oh, oh!"

Jim had not yet seen his beautiful present. She held it out to him eagerly upon her open palm. The dull precious metal seemed to flash with a reflection of her bright and ardent spirit.

"Isn't it a dandy, Jim? I hunted all over town to find it. You'll have to look at the time a hundred times a day now. Give me your watch. I want to see how it looks on it."

Instead of obeying, Jim tumbled down on the couch and put his hands under the back of his head and smiled.

"Dell," said he, "let's put our Christmas presents away and keep 'em a while. They're too nice to use just at present. I sold the watch to get the money to buy your combs. And now suppose you put the chops on."

The magi, as you know, were wise men — wonderfully wise men — who brought gifts to the Babe in the manger. They invented the art of giving Christmas presents. Being wise, their gifts were no doubt wise ones, possibly bearing the privilege of exchange in case of duplication. And here I have lamely related to you the uneventful chronicle of two foolish children in a flat who most unwisely sacrificed for each other the greatest treasures of their house. But in a last word to the wise of these days let it be said that of all who give gifts these two were the wisest. Of all who give and receive gifts, such as they are wisest. Everywhere they are wisest. They are the magi.

CHRISTMAS EVERY DAY

by W. D. Howells

The little girl came into her papa's study, as she always did Saturday morning before breakfast, and asked for a story. He tried to beg off that morning, for he was very busy, but she would not let him. So he began:

"Well, once there was a little pig — "

She put her hand over his mouth and stopped him at the word. She said she had heard little pig stories till she was perfectly sick of them.

"Well, what kind of story *shall* I tell, then?"

"About Christmas. It's getting to be the season. It's past Thanksgiving already."

"It seems to me," argued her papa, "that I've told as often about Christmas as I have about little pigs."

"No difference! Christmas is more interesting."

"Well!" Her papa roused himself from his writing by a great effort. "Well, then, I'll tell you about the little girl that wanted it Christmas every day in the year. How would you like that?"

"First-rate!" said the little girl; and she nestled into comfortable shape in his lap, ready for listening.

"Very well, then, this little pig — Oh, what are you pounding me for?"

"Because you said little pig instead of little girl."

"I should like to know what's the difference between a little pig and a little girl that wanted it Christmas every day!"

"Papa," said the little girl, warningly, "if you don't go on, I'll *give* it to you!" And at this her papa darted off like lightning, and began to tell the story as fast as he could.

Well, once there was a little girl who liked Christmas so much that she wanted it to be Christmas every day in the year; and as soon as Thanksgiving was over she began to send postal cards to the old Christmas Fairy to ask if she mightn't have it. But the old Fairy never answered any of the postals; and, after a while, the little girl found out that the Fairy was pretty particular, and wouldn't notice anything but letters, not even correspondence cards in envelopes; but real letters on sheets of paper, and sealed outside with a monogram — or your initial, any way. So, then, she began to send her letters; and in about three weeks — or just the day before Christmas, it was — she got a letter from the Fairy, saying she might have it Christmas every day for a year, and then they would see about having it longer.

The little girl was a good deal excited already, preparing for the old-fashioned, once-a-year Christmas that was coming the next day, and perhaps the Fairy's promise didn't make such an impression on her as it would have made at some other time. She just resolved to keep it to herself, and surprise everybody with it as it kept coming true; and then it slipped out of her mind altogether.

She had a splendid Christmas. She went to bed early, so as to let Santa Claus have a chance at the stockings, and in the morning she was up the first of anybody and went and felt them, and found hers all lumpy with packages of candy, and oranges and grapes and pocket-books and rubber balls and all kinds of small presents and her big brother's with nothing but the tongs in them, and her young lady sister's with a new silk umbrella, and her papa's and mamma's with potatoes and pieces of coal wrapped up in tissue paper, just as they always had every Christmas. Then she waited around till the rest of the family were up, and she was the first to burst into the library, when the doors were opened, and look at the large presents laid out on the library-table — books, and portfolios and boxes of stationery, and breast-pins, and dolls, and little stoves and dozens of handkerchiefs, and ink-stands, and skates, and snow-shovels, and photograph-frames, and little easels, and boxes of water-colors, and Turkish paste, and nougat, and candied cherries, and dolls' houses, and waterproofs — and the big Christmas-tree, lighted and standing in a waste-basket in the middle.

She had a splendid Christmas all day. She ate so much candy that she did not want any breakfast; and the whole forenoon the presents kept pouring in that the expressman had not had time to deliver the night before; and she went 'round giving the presents she had got for other people, and came home and ate turkey and cranberry for dinner, and plum-pudding and nuts and raisins and oranges and more candy, and then went out and coasted and came in with a stomach-ache, crying; and her papa said he would see if his house was turned into that sort of fool's paradise another year; and they had a light supper, and pretty early everybody went to bed cross.

Here the little girl pounded her papa in the back, again.

"Well, what now? Did I say pigs?"

"You made them *act* like pigs."

"Well, didn't they?"

"No matter; you oughtn't to put it into a story."

"Very well, then, I'll take it all out."

Her father went on:

The little girl slept very heavily, and she slept very late, but she was wakened at last by the other children dancing 'round her bed with their stockings full of presents in their hands.

"What is it?" said the little girl, and she rubbed her eyes and tried to rise up in bed.

"Christmas! Christmas! Christmas!" they all shouted, and waved their stockings.

"Nonsense! It was Christmas yesterday."

Her brothers and sisters just laughed. "We don't know about that. It's Christmas to-day, any way. You come into the library and see."

Then all at once it flashed on the little girl that the Fairy was keeping her promise, and her year of Christmases was beginning. She was dreadfully sleepy, but she sprang up like a lark — a lark that had overeaten itself and gone to bed cross — and darted into the library. There it was again! Books, and portfolios, and boxes of stationery, and breast-pins —

"You needn't go over it all, Papa; I guess I can remember just what was there," said the little girl.

Well, and there was the Christmas-tree blazing away, and the family picking out their presents, but looking pretty sleepy, and her father perfectly puzzled, and her mother ready to cry. "I'm sure I don't see how I'm to dispose of all these things," said her mother, and her father said it seemed to him they had had something just like it the day before, but he supposed he must have dreamed it. This struck the little girl as a kind of a joke; and so she ate so much candy she didn't want any breakfast, and went 'round carrying presents, and had turkey and cranberry for dinner, and then went out and coasted, and came in with a —

"Papa!"

"Well, what now?"

"What did you promise, you forgetful thing?"

"Oh! oh, yes!"

Well, the next day, it was just the same thing over again, but everybody getting crosser; and at the end of a week's time so many people had lost their tempers that you could pick up lost tempers everywhere; they perfectly strewed the ground. Even when people tried to recover their tempers they usually got somebody else's, and it made the most dreadful mix.

The little girl began to get frightened, keeping the secret all to herself; she wanted to tell her mother, but she didn't dare to; and she was ashamed to ask the Fairy to take back her gift, it seemed ungrateful and ill-bred, and she thought she would try to stand it, but she hardly knew how she could, for a whole year. So it went on and on, and it was Christmas on St. Valentine's Day, and Washington's Birthday just the same as any day, and it didn't skip even the First of April, though everything was counterfeit that day, and that was some *little* relief.

After a while, coal and potatoes began to be awfully scarce, so many had been wrapped up in tissue paper to fool papas and mammas with. Turkeys got to be a thousand dollars apiece —

"Papa!"

"Well, what?"

"You're beginning to fib."

"Well, *two* thousand, then."

And they got to passing off almost anything for turkeys, — half-grown humming-birds, and even rocs out of the *Arabian Nights* — the real turkeys were so scarce. And cranberries — well, they asked a diamond apiece for cranberries. All the woods and orchards were cut down for Christmas-trees, and where the woods and orchards used to be, it looked just like a stubble-field, with the stumps. After a while they had to make Christmas-trees out of rags, and stuff them with bran, like old-fashioned dolls; but there were plenty of rags, because people got so poor, buying presents for one another, that they couldn't get any new clothes, and they just wore their old ones to tatters. They got so poor that everybody had to go to the poor-house, except the confectioners, and the fancy storekeepers, and the picture-booksellers, and the expressmen; and *they* all got so rich and proud that they would hardly wait upon a person when he came to buy; it was perfectly shameful!

Well, after it had gone on about three or four months, the little girl, whenever she came into the room in the morning and saw those great ugly lumpy stockings dangling at the fire-place, and the disgusting presents around everywhere, used to just sit down and burst out crying. In six months she was perfectly exhausted; she couldn't even cry any more; she just lay on the lounge and rolled her eyes and panted. About the beginning of October she took to sitting down on dolls, wherever she found them — French dolls, or any kind — she hated the sight of them so; and by Thanksgiving she was crazy, and just slammed her presents across the room.

By that time people didn't carry presents around nicely any more. They flung them over the fence, or through the window, or anything; and, instead of running their tongues out and taking great pains to write "For dear Papa," or "Mamma," or "Brother," or "Sister," or "Susie," or "Sammie," or "Billie," or "Bobby," or "Jim-mie," or "Jennie," or whoever it was, and troubl-ing to get the spelling right, and then signing their names, and "Xmas, 188 ——," they used to write in the gift-books, "Take it, you horrid old thing!" and then go and bang it against the front door. Nearly everybody had built barns to hold their presents, but pretty soon the barns

overflowed, and then they used to let them lie out in the rain, or anywhere. Sometimes the police used to come and tell them to shovel their presents off the sidewalk, or they would arrest them.

"I thought you said everybody had gone to the poor-house," interrupted the little girl.

"They did go, at first," said her papa; "but after a while the poor-houses got so full that they had to send the people back to their own houses. They tried to cry, when they got back, but they couldn't make the least sound."

"Why couldn't they?"

"Because they had lost their voices, saying 'Merry Christmas' so much. Did I tell you how it was on the Fourth of July?"

"No; how was it?" And the little girl nestled closer, in expectation of something uncommon.

Well, the night before, the boys stayed up to celebrate, as they always do, and fell asleep before twelve o'clock, as usual, expecting to be wakened by the bells and cannon. But it was nearly eight o'clock before the first boy in the United States woke up, and then he found out what the trouble was. As soon as he could get his clothes on, he ran out of the house and smashed a big cannon-torpedo down on the pavement; but it didn't make any more noise than a damp wad of paper, and, after he tried about twenty or thirty more, he began to pick them up and look at them. Every single torpedo was a big raisin! Then he just streaked it up-stairs, and examined his fire-crackers and toy-pistol and two-dollar collection of fireworks, and found that they were nothing but sugar and candy painted up to look like fireworks! Before ten o'clock, every boy in the United States found out that his Fourth of July things had turned into Christmas things; and then they just sat down and cried — they were so mad. There are about twenty million boys in the United States, and so you can imagine what a noise they made. Some men got together before night, with a little powder that hadn't turned into purple sugar yet, and they said they would fire off *one* cannon, any way. But the cannon burst into a thousand pieces, for it was nothing but rock-candy, and some of the men nearly got killed. The Fourth of July orations all turned into Christmas carols, and when anybody tried to read the Declaration, instead of saying, "When in the course of human events it becomes necessary," he was sure to sing, "God rest you merry, gentlemen." It was perfectly awful.

The little girl drew a deep sigh of satisfaction.

"And how was it at Thanksgiving?" she asked.

Her papa hesitated. "Well, I'm almost afraid to tell you. I'm afraid you'll think it's wicked."

"Well, tell any way," said the little girl.

Well, before it came Thanksgiving, it had leaked out who had caused all these Christmases. The little girl had suffered so much that she had talked about it in her sleep; and after that, hardly anybody would play with her. People just perfectly despised her, because if it had not been for her greediness, it wouldn't have happened, and now, when it came Thanksgiving, and she wanted them to go to church, and have a squash pie and turkey, and show their gratitude, they said that all the turkeys had been eaten up for her old Christmas dinners, and if she would stop the Christmases, they would see about the gratitude. Wasn't it dreadful? And the very next day the little girl began to send letters to the Christmas Fairy, and then telegrams, to stop it. But it didn't do any good; and then she got to calling at the Fairy's house, but the girl that came to the door always said "Not at home," or "Engaged," or "At dinner," or something like that; and so it went on till it came to the old once-a-year Christmas Eve. The little girl fell asleep, and when she woke up in the morning —

"She found it was all nothing but a dream," suggested the little girl.

"No, indeed!" said her papa. "It was all every bit true!"

"Well, what did she find out then?"

"Why, that it wasn't Christmas at last, and wasn't ever going to be, any more. Now it's time for breakfast."

The little girl held her papa fast around the neck.

"You shan't go if you're going to leave it so!"

"How do you want it left?"

"Christmas once a year."

"All right," said her papa; and he went on again.

Well, there was the greatest rejoicing all over the country, and it extended clear up into Canada. The people met together everywhere, and kissed and cried for joy. The city carts went around and gathered up all the candy and raisins and nuts, and dumped them into the river; and it made the fish perfectly sick; and the whole United States, as far out as Alaska, was one blaze of bonfires, where the children were burning up their gift-books and presents of all kinds. They had the greatest *time!*

The little girl went to thank the old Fairy because she had stopped its being Christmas, and she said she hoped she would keep her promise, and see that Christmas never, never came again. Then the Fairy frowned, and asked her if she was sure she knew what she meant; and the little girl asked her, why not? and the old Fairy said that now she was behaving just as greedily as ever, and she'd better look out. This made the little girl think it all over carefully again, and she said she would be willing to have it Christmas about once in a thousand years; and then she said a hundred, and then she said ten, and at last she got down to one. Then the Fairy said that was the good old way that had pleased people ever since Christmas began, and she was agreed. Then the little girl said, "What're your shoes made of?" And the Fairy said, "Leather." And the little girl said, "Bargain's done forever," and skipped off, and hippity-hopped the whole way home, she was so glad.

"How will that do?" asked the papa.

"First-rate!" said the little girl; but she hated to have the story stop, and was rather sober. However, her mamma put her head in at the door, and asked her papa:

"Are you never coming to breakfast? What have you been telling that child?"

"Oh, just a moral tale."

The little girl caught him around the neck again.

"*We* know! Don't you tell *what*, Papa! Don't you tell *what!*"

PERFUME IS A MAN'S BEST FRIEND

by Harrison Kinney

The Christmas season, which seems to arrive every three months in our household, found me this year without a profitable idea regarding an "original" gift for my wife. Then a short newspaper article, describing perfume as "a blending of art and chemistry," caught my eye and sent my thoughts galloping off in that direction. "Many stores," the article read, "report far more perfume sales to men than to women, perfume being a suggestive and *telling* gift."

It was all the encouragement I needed and the next day found me nudging up to the perfume bar of a Fifth Avenue department store trying to look as if I didn't mean to stay more than a minute. An alert-looking blonde woman behind the counter raised her head and nailed me to the spot with an inquiring look.

"I understand," I said foolishly, "that perfume is a clever blending of art and chemistry."

The salesgirl looked alarmed and seemed about to call a floor manager when I quickly added, "I'd like some perfume for my wife."

Her face at once dissolved into the most winning of smiles. "Of course," she purred. "And may I ask what your wife is like?"

I hesitated. "Well," I began, "she tends to be a little grouchy in the morning before she's had her coffee, but generally speaking . . ."

"No, no, no, no, no!" said the girl in exasperation. "I mean, is she conservative, sophisticated or the simple . . ."

"Complicated," I replied at once. I gathered from the scowl on the girl's face that that was another wrong answer. We didn't seem to be getting along at all, and I began to wonder if maybe I shouldn't get my wife another wool scarf with matching mittens.

"Perfume," said the girl in the tone of voice I use with my two-year-old child, "is an intimate gift. It should either reflect the woman's actual personality or her desired personality. A woman of any sensibility can be very unhappy with the wrong scent."

She stopped to get an assortment of perfume bottles from beneath the counter and I was immediately jostled aside by a well-dressed, middle-aged woman who quickly seized a sample bottle of cologne water equipped with an atomizer, doused her neck and bosom with it, replaced the bottle on the counter and departed. The salesgirl looked after the woman sadly, "We lose gallons that way," she said.

I sniffed the lingering cologne scent and raised my eyebrows quizzically at the salesgirl. "You wouldn't want that for your wife," she assured me at once. "That's one of our oriental blends.

"I just mean," the girl said, "it isn't your wife's *type*."

"What type is it for?" I persisted, continuing to sniff the scented air.

The girl leaned across the counter top in a confidential pose. "The sultry type," she whispered. "Now don't tell me your wife is the kind who lies about on leopard-skin rugs!"

I felt the woman was being much too arbitrary. "Maybe lying on leopard-skin rugs is part of my wife's desired personality," I said defiantly.

"Still," said the girl just as defiantly, "I would urge, in your case, that we just shop among the bouquets and fruity blends."

In no time at all I was sniffing at bottle stoppers, atomizer nozzles and scented spots the girl sprayed on her arms. To my consternation I decided that I liked them all, although I still found the suggestiveness and secret hints implicit in the sultry perfume somewhat irresistible.

"Of course," the girl said uneasily, as I returned again to the forbidden bottle, "perhaps your wife . . ."

It was too late. I was intoxicated with the sense of power that comes from knowing one is in a position to condition, in some little way, his wife's personality. "I want this," I said giddily, holding the sultry perfume aloft. "I'll take my chances."

A mustached gentleman, wearing a Homburg, stepped into the cloud of perfumed mist that by now enshrouded our immediate vicinity, and sneezed. He looked contemptuously at the litter of perfume bottles before me and crisply ordered another perfume I had sniffed in a spirit of adventurousness. The choice seemed to me reckless and ill-considered.

"Pardon me," I said, "how can you be so definite in your choice?"

He widened his eyes at me. "It's for my wife," he said shortly. "I like it and she likes it."

"In that order?" I continued. For although I had purchased from selfish and power-mad motives, it saddened me to see a fellow human being follow along the same path of ruthless gift-giving. "We men should remember that perfume is a personal thing," I told him. "It should reflect either the woman's actual personality or her desired personality."

His response was reassuring enough to brighten my holiday season. "Relax, Buster," he said, writing a check. "It's my experience that women are glad to get *any* kind of perfume."

HOW I SPENT MY MILLION

by Edgar J. Park

I rubbed my eyes and looked at the letter a second time. Yes, I was not asleep, the thing had happened. There was my cup of coffee and the half-eaten doughnut just as I had left them when I went to the door for the mail. There was the other letter that had come, still unopened, and here was this one from a firm of lawyers I had never heard of before. And the sum and substance of it was this: — my old neighbor, John Doby, whose funeral I had just attended two days before, had made me the sole legatee of his entire estate, which, to quote the letter before me, "runs considerably over one million dollars."

My first act was to pour the whole pitcher of cream — half of which I intended keeping for supper — into my coffee, what did it matter? — I was a millionaire.

"Well," I said to myself, "I can have anything I want now. I'm a millionaire." Then I thought to myself: "What in the world were those things I wanted so much? I remember thinking of them lately and wishing I could have them but knowing I couldn't have them. I shall be able to have them now. What in the world were they?" One by one they began to come back to me: — I had wished many a time that Mary's, my old housekeeper's nose, might be about an eighth of an inch shorter than it was. Perhaps that was the thing that had irritated me most in life. Then the other thing was the way my brother's wife was always praising up her children and the way she used the phrase, "though I say it as shouldn't," when she was relating some particularly extravagant judgment upon the miraculous endowments of her progeny. Oh, yes, I remember another thing I had often said to myself I desired more than anything else in the world. That was that my sister Jane might have a sense of humor. The way she always tried to explain my jokes to the rest of the company had always been one of my most exacting crosses.

Well, I was a millionaire now and could have anything I wanted so, of course, I would have these things attended to right off. Suddenly it struck me with a cold shock that after all, I was no better off than I was before. Even a million would not go any way at all towards reducing Mary's nose or changing the vulgar trait in

Maria, or giving Jane a sense of humor — no nor in winning the other thing which, if the truth be told, I desired more than any of these — no, I sadly thought, even the possession of a million would not make me appear a whit more attractive or desirable in the eyes of someone who seemed to regard me now, as far as I could ascertain, as a mere object in her landscape. The fact was the million did not seem to help me to get the things I wanted most after all. Money tends to cushion you up among things and it was people I was most interested in. I took a drink of water to get the taste of the coffee out of my mouth. There had been too much cream in it. After all what did I want with a million?

One thing was clear. I'd give that million away and get done with it the first opportunity I could get. I said this to myself as I took up and opened the second letter which was lying unopened beside my plate.

"Ah, yes," I said, as I read it over quickly, "here is a chance right off to do some good with it." This was the other letter:

National Society for the Redemption of
Christmas
23 Wail Street, New York

Dear Sir:

A number of public-spirited citizens have banded together for the purpose of redeeming Christmas from the many wasteful and useless features which cluster around it and of transforming it into an annual event which will be of real economic and moral value to the community. In the past the untrue legend of Santa Claus has made many young children liars; the destruction of thousands of young trees has robbed the future of many hundred dollars' worth of white pine and spruce lumber, a great amount of money is expended on absolutely useless illuminated cards, Christmas tree ornaments, candles, fancy wrapping paper, ribbon and house decorations, holly, mistletoe and other such extravagant and useless vanities.

If the money which runs to waste in these useless channels were only saved and put in the savings bank we calculate that every man, wo-man and child in the United States would have 53½ cents to his name in his bank book on January first.

Still more serious is this matter when we regard it from the point of view of what this money would do in providing strictly useful gifts for those who need them this year. It has actually been calculated that the amount thus wasted on fal-de-ral would purchase one warm, winter, flannel petticoat, two mittens and a chest protector for every worthy widow in the United States, and enough would be left over to provide 1¾ pairs of stout boots for each orphan in public institutions throughout the country.

In view of these facts we ask you to sign and send to us the enclosed pledge that you will spend this year an entirely rational and utilitarian Christmas, spending money only on useful and rational objects. We also ask you to enclose ten dollars as a membership fee to pay salary of secretary, treasurer, office expenses, etc., of this new organization. Larger donations are requested from those interested.

(signed) Bartimaeus Tintoes,
President

"What wonderful luck!" I said to myself, "to get a million and directions for the most useful method of spending it both in the same mail."

The street door bell rang, and in a moment Mary's nose appeared at the door, followed after the lapse of a moment by Mary to say Miss Helene Gracie wished to see me just for a moment. What a morning I was having! All the best things in the world were pouring in upon me: — money, directions for spending it, and now — the very beatific vision herself, who although the reader may not be aware of it has already been referred to in this narrative, was at my door to see me.

She came in and sat down in the brown plush armchair by the fire. She had never been to see me before, but somehow as she sat there I remembered having seen her in that very chair thousands of times in my daydreams.

"Won't you have a doughnut?" I said, handing her the plate.

She took one, saying she was quite hungry, as she had been out skating for an hour since an early breakfast.

"Take a lot," said I; "take two! Don't mind the expense. I'm a millionaire."

"I'm so glad to hear that," she said, "because I have called to ask you for a subscription."

Immediately I assumed that stony, abstracted appearance so necessary a part of a rich man's defense against suggestion of attack by humanitarian bandits.

"I am sorry," I said, "but you could not have struck me at a worse time. I refer not merely to the shrinkage in my holdings which makes me feel rather poor this morning but also I have just arranged to give liberally to this cause," and I handed her the letter of Mr. Bartimaeus Tintoes.

"Oh, I am sorry," she said, as she took it, "I wanted you to give a half a dollar to help us buy old Mrs. Gulpins a dicky-bird and a cage."

I gasped in amazement, but said nothing till she read the letter through. She read it without a word or sign, folded it carefully up into a very small size and then suddenly leaning forward stuck it into the reddest part of the fire, where it was burned in a moment.

"Oh, I have the address on the envelope all right," I said. "You're mad because you know it's perfectly true.

"Mrs. Gulpins — a dicky-bird — " I said in derision. "You know perfectly she has not enough to eat. She needs potatoes and mittens, instead of a dicky-bird. Now, it is quite true, Miss Gracie, what you took for a joke. Mr. Doby has made me his heir," and I handed her the lawyer's letter.

She read that through and returned it to me with these cabalistic words: "Well, that spoils you! No, I won't ask you even for fifty cents. You can't afford it, you poor man. They've robbed you of all the riches of life and given you instead another man's cast-off clothes." She rose to go. "It's all nonsense," she said. "It's all nonsense, this practical business. Mrs. Gulpins wants a dicky-bird in a gold cage. She has been dreaming of having one in her sunny bay window for the last forty years. You and I think

she ought to have potatoes and mittens. Well, perhaps she ought to have them. If so, we ought to see she gets them some other time. But not at Christmas. For all the potatoes and mittens in the world would not make her one-millionth time so happy as this canary she has set her heart upon. Christmas is the time for giving people happiness, instead of giving them the things you think they need. Look at my small brother Tommy. Now, what I think he needs most of all is a sound spanking, but Christmas is not the time for giving him that. I'm going to give him the most useless toy telescope you ever saw because he wants it."

I sighed deeply, a safe-deposit vault sigh, and saw her into the hall. At the street door I said:

"Miss Gracie, I made two vows just before you came in this morning. One was to get rid of this entire million before Christmas Day, so as to be able to enjoy myself then. And the second was to spend it all on things that may be as frivolous and useless as they like, provided they give real pleasure to the people who get them. I want to blow it all in into a great bacchanalia of joy to other folk of the most unexpected and yet longed-for luxuries and happinesses, and I want you and your mother to help me to plan the whole thing out. Will you help me if I come round this evening?"

"Show me you are in earnest," she said, "by giving me that fifty cents."

I handed it to her, saying, "Now I have only $999,999.50 to spend, the burden is lightening."

"You have more sense than I thought," said she. "Come this evening."

In the evening I rang the bell at Mrs. Gracie's door. I found them both sitting at the dining-room table, which had been cleared. Each of them had a blank sheet of paper in front of her, and a pencil in her hand. As I came into the room the face of each was as blank as the paper. Miss Helene looked up as I entered. "Oh, I had no idea it was going to be such work," she said. "Mother and I sat down here after dinner gaily to spend your million for you as foolishly as we could and we can't think of a single useless way to make away with it that won't do more harm than good. Before I had one — I mean before you had one — to dispose of I knew lots of ways to spend it, but now I can't think of one."

We all sat round the table, appalled at the situation, blank paper, blank faces, hearts beating regularly, blank, blank, blank —

Sadly I began to be convinced of the impossibility of doing any real good with my million. I could take away the self-respect of the students at the State University by paying their fees for them or I could increase the bricks and mortar of a score of schools, but what those schools needed was more inspirational person-

alities in the teaching chairs and more ambitious students in the learners' desks, and that my money was powerless to give. I wanted something that would give at least a moment of glorious life to people that had never had the chance to feel that way before.

At last Helene broke the silence. "This won't do," she said. "Who are the people who most deserve to have the fun out of this million? We must all have the answer to that question on our papers before the clock strikes nine."

I looked up and saw it was five minutes to. The wheels in my brain began to buzz. Some-

thing must be thought, and thought immediately. Helene had her hands over her eyes, and the room seemed darkened thereby. Her mother's head was on the table. Three minutes, four minutes passed, and just as the clock gave that whir, its warning that it was just getting up steam to strike, we all simultaneously took up our pencils and wrote something on our papers.

Now, you may believe in magic or not, as you please, but the fact remains that the word each of us had written was the same. The word we had all written down was this, the word "Mothers." At last we had something to start on. We were all agreed that the mothers of the world were those who denied themselves the things they wanted in order that they should give to others the things those others thought they needed.

"I have the whole scheme ready now," she said in a minute. "You get in touch with the teachers of the schools in the East Side wards and have them set this subject for a theme, that all the children are to write and bring this coming Monday, 'What Would Mother Like for Christmas.' You make the regulations, explain that it is not what Mother needs, but what Mother would like, and that it is not what Mother would like others to have, but what she would like for herself; and have it explained in each school that there are chances that a certain Santa Claus will do his best to help the child who writes the simplest and sincerest theme to give Mother just what she wants for Christmas."

"And," said I, "let's appoint ourselves the judges."

It seemed only a few days before we gathered together around the same table with a pile of themes in front of us, several hundred in number. In addition, there was a list of several thousand articles costing less than one hundred dollars each, of none of which Mr. Bartimaeus Tintoes would have approved, but which the larger board of judges thought would bring genuine joy to the mothers whose children had suggested them.

Miss Helene had been granted a week's leave of absence from the school where she taught in order to go over the returns thoroughly. What a wonderful study they had been! First, there were a great many rejected suggestions in which our fallen human nature had played a great part, of which this is a specimen:

"I think the thing which would give my mother the greatest pleasure would be to see me riding round on one of those little cycles which are in the window of Tontine's store. She has often said that she would enjoy that more than anything else."

Some had to be rejected because they suggested things that no money could buy: that little children who had gone to the better land might come back into the mother's empty arms if it were only for a moment; that coarse, cruel, dissolute husbands might be transformed into the Sir Galahads they once seemed in the eyes of loving maidens — Oh, the pathos of that suggestion! — "the thing my mother would like most would be that my father should be the way he used to be."

The list of articles suggested included very many pieces of jewelry, and silk dresses, new hats, "stylish" baby carriages, pictures of all kinds, chiefly enlarged family photographs, rocking chairs for the parlor. One mother wanted enough to print a little book of poems she had written that she might give copies of it to her friends. Another wanted to be able to pay for prayers for the rest of the soul of her dead son. Another's longing was for a rosebud paper with ribbons on the parlor wall. Several dreamed of a season ticket to the winter's series of concerts; and for a great many the idea of being able to have some big yellow chrysanthemums on the table once in a while was perfectly intoxicating. Furs of various forms and shapes attracted many and Helene, who knew some of them, said they were those whom you would least expect to care for such finery. I chuckled as I thought how enraged Mr. Bartimaeus Tintoes would be to see me writing an order for a set of expensive furs for an Italian woman who supported her family by washing floors. But that was what little Angelina Maria said her mother wanted most of all, and I calculated it would give Mrs. Ferrari more of pleasure

than anything anyone could dream of giving the wife of the man upon whose kitchen floor she worked Tuesday and Saturday. She probably would put them in a box and keep them there till the moths ate them, but in the meantime every morning she woke up she would feel the beatitude of the possession of those furs as a kind of glory in the back of her mind, and maybe take a glance at them in their box before she slipped out in the dark to wash floors till it grew dark again. It was great fun going over the pile of themes upon the table. "My mother would like most of all to see her old home in Sweden again and her old mother, who lives there still, but she cannot get anyone to look after us children when she's away." Helene knew how that could be arranged and I wrote out an order for the Swedish trip.

Gold-rimmed eyeglasses instead of steel spectacles attracted the soul of one Mrs. Moriarty, and a "piano to put ornaments on" was provided for Mrs. Stevaniski. Forty-two mothers were given orders for holidays at various longed-for summer resorts from Atlantic City to Coney Island, with free passes to all the shows, and provisions made for a trained helper to look after their homes in the meantime. The way one of these suggestions was worded was very realistic. "Mother says what she would like most of all would be to get away from the sound of a baby or any of us children for about a week, so as she could sleep mornings and sit down once in a while daytimes."

We really spent a series of most delightful evenings together till at last the week before Christmas I began, with the aid of some experts, to total up just how much I had spent. Hard to spend a million? Why, it was the easiest thing in the world. How the figures did mount up! We were in the tens of thousands almost before we had started, and when you have spent $450,000 on the little things, with all the larger trips to Europe and such things before you, well, you begin to appreciate how small a sum of money a million really is.

Another happy afternoon we spent together, Helene, her mother and I, sorting out the labels which the children had written to accompany the presents. On the evening of the day before Christmas they were all distributed.

Never since the day when the voice was heard in Rama of Rachel weeping for her children was there ever heard so great a swelling of the voices of mothers, this time weeping for joy, singing for gladness, but most of all lost in transport at the thought that it was their little Alfredo, that it was their little Michael, that it was their own little Mary or Priscilla who had brought to them by their own skill at school these great gifts.

Early on that Christmas eve, Helene and I went out to bring Mrs. Gulpins the bird and cage she had contented herself to expect in heaven. As we walked home, house after house was illuminated and the sounds of greatest joy came often out of the smallest houses. "Things taste so much better and seem so much more heavenly in little houses," said Helene, as we stood outside one and heard the screams of delight and enraptured huggings and kissings of some little mortal who was crying out at the top of her shrill voice, "I knew it all the time. It's a present from Me. Mamma, it's from Me."

There were tears in both our eyes and we went on down street after street — we could hardly tear ourselves away. "Well," I said, "I don't think a million ever gave such pleasure before, do you?"

"No," she said, "it has given at least one moment of crowded glorious life to the very mothers who thought their life was doomed to be drab for the rest of time, drabber every year. Only one thing I regret," she said; "you've gone and spent $50 more than your million and you haven't bought yourself a thing out of it. I wish I'd asked Mary, your housekeeper, what useless luxury you'd have liked and I could easily have slipped it into the accounts somehow without your knowing."

"I'll tell you exactly what I do want," I said, "it comes into our contract perfectly, because it is something absolutely useless and ornamental only."

We were coming in under the shade of the trees that fronted on her house and I took my life in my hand and told her just exactly what it was I wanted more than anything else in the world.

The clock struck nine as I came to her door and began to say good night; at ten-thirty she rang the bell in spite of me.

"Mother," she cried, as we got into the hall, "we forgot that you were a mother, too, and have come to ask you what you wanted for Christmas."

Her mother looked at us both, then, kissing me, she said, "My little girl told you, didn't she? that I wanted a son more than anything else in the world."

"No," I said, "I told her."

"A merry Christmas!" she said, kissing us both again.

MERRY CHRISTMAS IN TEN PIECES

by Robert M. Yoder

Yes, Virginia, there is a Santa Claus, and he has a home near the North Pole, where it is colder than a bathroom floor. But don't believe that story about his having a lot of little dwarfs who put toys together for him, singing as they hammer. Nobody puts toys together, until Christmas Eve. Toys come in sixteen pieces, with one missing, and are put together by a large band of Involuntary Elves who call ourselves Santa's Press-Gang Helpers. We don't exactly sing, either, although a certain low, ominous murmur can be heard rising from a million homes on Christmas Eve. Put it this way, kid: That ain't no dwarf; that's your old man, beaten down. The luckless peon bought the toys; now he is learning that he has to finish manufacturing them, too, and by one A. M. his mood will make Scrooge seem like Sunny Ebenezer.

The first thing your frightened eye lights on, in the store, is a nice little red wagon, and you think, in your fatuous adult way, that this is just the thing to brighten the young heart. If you weren't partially paralyzed by the fear that you are shopping too late, you would realize that if the kid wants a wagon at all, it isn't this chaste little model. He would want one twice this size, with demountable tires, a ram-jet engine, electric lights, an overdrive and a windshield wiper, at $79.75. The kid next door has had one like that for two years and uses it only to haul his good toys in. Then you see the rocket-firing antiaircraft gun and realize that this is the answer. While it will not do bodily harm, and is therefore a partial bust to start with, it is a realistic-looking little number, and you buy it, at an exceedingly realistic price.

About the hour on Christmas Eve when you are in mild shock for fear the thing won't arrive, the delivery man stumbles in with a large package that can't be anything else. Will you put it under the tree that way? Or will you have it out in the open, so the child may see this splendid sight first thing in the morning? Full of Christmas sentiment, you decide to expose the gun to full, gladsome view. So you tear off the wrapping. Here is a dial, here is a leg, here is a muzzle. You thought it would look like the model in the store, did you? Well, Santa has a little surprise for you. It's in pieces, and you are going to have to put it together. Merry Christmas, in at least ten pieces.

There is a sheet or folder of directions which could not get under your skin worse if they were in Spanish. They are written in the special language of directions, a mechanical gobbledegook achieved by writing the directions first in Ruthenian and then allowing the translation to curdle. A stop sign from the same mumbling pen would take 200 words. In the language of directions, "close the door" would read like this: "Grasp door-opening device with right knob-grasper and exert pressure outward until Panel A fills Aperture B. If scream is heard, other hand may be caught in opening." Along with being as turgid as possible, the directions are printed in a miniature type face known as Myopia Old Style, which is two sizes smaller than pearl and is otherwise used only to print the Declaration of Independence on souvenir pennies.

Well, lying there in pieces, the gun looks like nothing at all; it's got to be assembled. The first line you encounter in the directions says: "Using ring grasper from Assembly Kit, grasp collector ring near tube spar tightening guide rod" . . . but, thank heaven, that goes with some other toy. Your own directions start out more simply: "Connect round opening at end of Feeder Spring A with hooked end of trigger lock restraining bar by placing round opening over hook and pressing." What'd he think you'd do — spot-weld it? (The answer, unfortunately, is that he expects more than that, but not just yet.) Now the guy begins getting esoteric.

"If retaining mechanism fails to admit trigger, horizontal opening of drum impeding stopper should be widened horizontally." He means if the damned trigger won't go into the guard, you got to cut more room, and sure enough, it won't. This is going to be the only gun in the neighborhood with a demountable (falling out) trigger, unless you fix it. If retaining mechanism fails to admit what it's supposed to retain, then it should never have left the factory, but it's too late for that kind of recrimination now. Getting a hammer from the basement, a good paring knife and a screwdriver, you manage to make the trigger go where it should, with one very bad moment when you think you've split the thing.

Well, the barrel, H, slides into place nicely; maybe things are beginning to go your way. The next step is to fit Firing Platform Z on Tripod, the Tripod being made by inserting Metal-tipped Ends of Legs into Sockets, which is child's play. Now all it takes is two bolts, L and M, which you slip into place with great efficiency. They must be firmly in place, the directions say, or gun will not swivel on Platform Z; you might say, it won't swivel on any platform. A neat little bag contained the bolts, and in it you find the nut for Bolt L. But half an hour later you are still rummaging through wrapping paper in a grim search for the other nut, the crucial nut, the nut without which, as the Latins say, nothing. You may have 128 nuts of assorted sizes in a jar in the basement, but you will not have one that fits Bolt M. That is a freak size used nowhere else in the whole panoply of American industry. It is part of a shipment the toy manufacturer bought up from the Uruguayan War Assets Administration.

It is 11:45 by the time you manage to make the bolt hold with a piece of wire wrapped around it, and if the kid looks at that part, he will feel sure this toy is something the fireman repainted for the poor. Meanwhile the house has grown cold, three of the Christmas-tree lights have winked at you by burning out, and your cigarette has fallen out of the ash tray and burned a six-dollar hole in the carpet. But the gun is starting to look like a weapon, and there can't be much more — only a couple of odd-looking metal pieces are left and a cardboard circle marked "Cosmic Ray Computer Dial."

One of the pieces of metal is easy enough to use. It's the missing plug, for lack of which the barrel has had that tendency to point to the floor like the tail of a whipped hound. The other is the crank with which the young gunner moves the barrel to keep on his target. You tackle the easiest job first — the computer is nothing more than two sections of light cardboard. "Bending Tabs A, C, E and G," the directions say, "fit them into Slots B, D, F and H." The cardboard is a special kind which is as stiff as metal for a minute and then relaxes completely as you push, so that in twenty minutes you have four dog-eared tabs holding one crumpled dial marked with a little blood from the finger you cut trying to enlarge the slots.

Now you reach the part of the directions that tell you to fix on the telescopic sight. The diagram shows a handsome metal gadget coming to a square end, fitted into a ring fastened neatly around the end of the barrel. The only piece of metal you have left, outside of the crank, is a cotter pin. Even if you had missing part R, you still would have nothing like missing part Q which fits into it. You ransack the wrapping paper again, in what the novelists call cold fury, but with no luck. Finally, with great self-control you smooth the wrinkled directions and read that jargon over again out loud. It is then that you come across Step 2. "In assembling Model A-100 Junior, our second-rate cheaper model for piker, Step 1 may be disregarded," the directions say. "No sight

comes with this model. There is, however, a cotter pin. You can stick it on the barrel with adhesive tape and play like it's a sight. It ain't much, but neither are you."

There is one final step — mounting the crank. "Slip Directional Crank 16 through Arm Y into Slot EE," the directions say. "When in position, give crank one quarter turn counterclockwise. Trigger should then fall sharply back into firing position." This is simplicity itself, and the only trouble is that if the crank goes through Arm Y, it misses Slot EE by a good quarter of an inch. The bitter thoughts that arise on Christmas Eve about the sleepwalker who bored that slot must visibly affect the temperature.

But the direction writer thought about this impasse, forehanded soul that he is. "It may be necessary, for best results" — meaning, to make the thing work at all — " to enlarge aperture in Arm Y. This can be done quickly and easily by using a 16.3 metal file without tang, a 13-oz. dinging hammer, and some Australian-canoe-builders' flux." This is equipment the ordinary household would be just as likely to have as a Javanese blowgun and a guroo bird, and you know, as your thoughts profane the early Christmas air, that the only 16.3 file in the world is one resting in the manufacturer's plant 850.3 miles away across the snowy landscape. So you gouge out a new Slot EE four times the proper size, the crank falls into place, wobbling foolishly, and the task is done. If it holds together until Christmas afternoon, you will be agreeably surprised, and a glance at the clock tells you that won't be long.

Yes, Virginia, there is a Santa Claus. If there weren't, ugly mobs of maddened parents would rove the streets Christmas Day armed with bolts, pins, wheels and axles, and some toy manufacturer would end up assembled on Movable Rail A wearing Feathers B and Tar C, after a slight going-over with No. 16 emery paper and a common hydraulic half-knurled center punch.

THE LITTLE MATCH GIRL

by Hans Christian Andersen

It was late on a bitterly cold, snowy, New Year's Eve. A poor little girl was wandering in the dark cold streets; she was bareheaded and barefooted. She certainly had had shoes on when she left home, but they were not much good, for they were so huge. They had last been worn by her mother, and they fell off the poor little girl's feet when she was running across the street to avoid two carriages that were rolling rapidly by. One of the shoes could not be found at all; and the other was picked up by a boy, who ran off with it, saying that it would do for a cradle when he had children of his own. So the poor little girl had to go on with her little bare feet, which were blue with the cold. She carried a quantity of matches in her old apron, and held a packet of them in her hand. Nobody had bought any from her during all the long day; nobody had even given her a copper.

The poor little creature was hungry and perishing with cold, and she looked the picture of misery. The snowflakes fell upon her long yellow hair, which curled so prettily round her face, but she paid no attention to that. Lights were shining from every window, and there was a most delicious odour of roast goose in the streets, for it was New Year's Eve — she could not forget that. She found a protected place where one house projected a little beyond the next one, and here she crouched, drawing up her feet under her, but she was colder than ever. She did not dare to go home, for she had not sold any matches and had not earned a single penny. Her father would beat her; besides, it was almost as cold at home as it was here. They lived in a house where the wind whistled through every crack, although they tried to stuff up the biggest ones with rags and straw. Her tiny hands were almost paralyzed with cold. Oh, if she could only find some way to warm them! Dared she pull one match out of the bundle and strike it on the wall to warm her fingers? She pulled one out. "Ritsch!" How it spluttered, how it blazed! It burnt with a bright clear flame, just like a little candle when she held her hand round it. It was a very curious candle, too. The little girl fancied that she was sitting in front of a big stove with polished brass feet and handles. There was a splendid fire blazing in it and warming her so beautifully, but — what happened? Just as she was stretching out her feet to warm them, the blaze went out, the stove vanished, and she was left sitting with the end of the burnt-out match in her hand. She struck a new one, it burnt, it blazed up, and where the light fell upon the wall against which she lay, it became transparent like gauze, and she could see right through it into the room inside. There was a table spread with a snowy cloth and pretty china; a roast goose stuffed with apples and prunes was steaming on it. And what was even better, the goose hopped from the dish with the carving knife and fork sticking in his back, and it waddled across the floor. It came right up to the poor child, and then — the match went out and there was nothing to be seen but the thick black wall.

She lit another match. This time she was sitting under a lovely Christmas tree. It was much bigger and more beautifully decorated than the one she had seen when she had peeped through the glass doors at the rich merchant's house this Christmas day. Thousands of lighted candles gleamed upon its branches, and coloured pictures such as she had seen in the shop windows looked down upon her. The little girl stretched out both her hands towards them — then out went the match. All the Christmas candles rose higher and higher, till she saw that they were only the twinkling stars. One of them fell and made a bright streak of light across the sky. "Some one is dying," thought the little girl; for her old grandmother, the only person who had ever been kind to her, used to say, "When a star falls a soul is going up to God."

Now she struck another match against the wall, and this time it was her grandmother who appeared in the circle of flame. She saw her quite clearly and distinctly, looking so gentle and happy.

"Grandmother!" cried the little creature. "Oh, do take me with you! I know you will vanish when the match goes out; you will vanish like the warm stove, the delicious goose, and the beautiful Christmas tree!"

She hastily struck a whole bundle of matches,

because she did so want to keep her grandmother with her. The light of the matches made it as bright as day. Grandmother had never before looked so big or so beautiful. She lifted the little girl up in her arms, and they soared in a halo of light and joy, far, far above the earth, where there was no more cold, no hunger, no pain, for they were with God.

THE FIR TREE

by Hans Christian Andersen

Out in the forest stood a pretty little Fir Tree. It had a good place; it could have sunlight, air there was in plenty, and all around grew many larger comrades — pines as well as firs. But the little Fir Tree wished ardently to become greater. It did not care for the warm sun and the fresh air; it took no notice of the peasant children, who went about talking together, when they had come out to look for strawberries and raspberries. Often they came with a whole potful, or had strung berries on a straw; then they would sit down by the little Fir Tree and say, "How pretty and small that one is!" and the Fir Tree did not like to hear that at all.

Next year he had grown a great joint, and the following year he was longer still, for in fir trees one can always tell by the number of rings they have how many years they have been growing.

"Oh, if I were only as great a tree as the others!" sighed the little Fir, "then I would spread my branches far around and look out from my crown into the wide world. The birds would then build nests in my boughs, and when the wind blew I could nod just as grandly as the others yonder."

He took no pleasure in the sunshine, in the birds, and in the red clouds that went sailing over him morning and evening.

When it was winter, the snow lay all around, white and sparkling, a hare would often come jumping along, and spring right over the little Fir Tree. Oh! this made him so angry. But two winters went by, and when the third came the little Tree had grown so tall that the hare was obliged to run around it.

"Oh! to grow, to grow, and become old; that's the only fine thing in the world," thought the Tree.

In the autumn woodcutters always came and felled a few of the largest trees; that was done this year too, and the little Fir Tree, that was now quite well grown, shuddered with fear, for the great stately trees fell to the ground with a crash, and their branches were cut off, so that the trees looked quite naked, long, and slender — they could hardly be recognized. But then they were laid upon wagons, and horses dragged them away out of the wood. Where were they going? What destiny awaited them?

In the spring when the Swallows and the Stork came, the tree asked them, "Do you know where they were taken? Did you not meet them?"

The Swallows knew nothing about it, but the Stork looked thoughtful, nodded his head, and said:

"Yes, I think so. I met many new ships when I flew out of Egypt; on the ships were stately masts; I fancy these were the trees. They smelled like fir. I can assure you they're stately — very stately."

"Oh that I were only big enough to go over the sea! What kind of thing is this sea, and how does it look?"

"It would take too long to explain all that," said the Stork, and he went away.

"Rejoice in thy youth," said the Sunbeams; "rejoice in thy fresh growth, and in the young life that is within thee."

And the wind kissed the Tree, and the dew wept tears upon it; but the Fir Tree did not understand about that.

When Christmas time approached, quite young trees were felled, sometimes trees which were neither so old nor so large as this Fir Tree, that never rested, but always wanted to go away. These young trees, which were always the most beautiful, kept all their branches; they were put upon wagons, and the horses dragged them away out of the wood.

"Where are they all going?" asked the Fir Tree. "They are not greater than I — indeed, one of them was much smaller. Why do they keep all their branches? Whither are they taken?"

"We know that! We know that!" chirped the Sparrows. "Yonder in the town we looked in at the windows. We know where they go. Oh! they are dressed up in the greatest pomp and splendor that can be imagined. We have looked in at the windows, and have perceived that they are planted in the middle of a warm room, and adorned with the most beautiful things — gilt apples, honey cakes, playthings, and many hundreds of candles."

"And then?" asked the Fir Tree, and trembled through all its branches. "And then? What happens then?"

"Why, we have not seen anything more. But it is incomparable."

"Perhaps I may be destined to tread this glorious path one day!" cried the Fir Tree, rejoicingly. "That is even better than traveling across the sea. How painfully I long for it! If it were only Christmas now! Now I am great and grown up, like the rest who were led away last year. Oh, if I were only on the carriage! If I were only in the warm room, among all the pomp and splendor! And then? Yes, then something even better will come, something far more charming, or else why should they adorn me so? There must be something grander, something greater still to come; but what? Oh! I'm suffering. I'm longing! I don't know myself what is the matter with me!"

"Rejoice in us," said the Air and Sunshine. "Rejoice in thy fresh youth here in the woodland."

But the Fir tree did not rejoice at all, but it grew and grew; winter and summer it stood there, green, dark green. The people who saw it said, "That's a handsome tree!" and at Christmas time it was felled before any of the others. The ax cut deep into its marrow, and the tree fell to the ground with a sigh; it felt a pain, a sensation of faintness, and could not think at all of happiness, for it was sad at parting from its home, from the place where it had grown up;

it knew that it should never again see the dear old companions, the little bushes and flowers all around — perhaps not even the birds. The parting was not at all agreeable.

The Tree only came to itself when it was unloaded in a yard, with other trees, and heard a man say:

"This one is famous; we want only this one!"

Now two servants came in gay liveries, and carried the Fir Tree into a large, beautiful salon. All around the walls hung pictures, and by the great stove stood large Chinese vases with lions on the covers; there were rocking-chairs, silken sofas, great tables covered with picture-books, and toys worth a hundred times a hundred dollars, at least the children said so. And the Fir Tree was put into a great tub filled with sand; but no one could see that it was a tub, for it was hung round with green cloth, and stood on a large, many-colored carpet. Oh, how the Tree trembled! What was to happen now? The servants, and the young ladies also, decked it out. On one branch they hung little nets, cut out of colored paper; every net was filled with sweetmeats; golden apples and walnuts hung down, as if they grew there, and more than a hundred

little candles, red, white, and blue, were fastened to the different boughs. Dolls that looked exactly like real people — the tree had never seen such before — swung among the foliage, and high on the summit of the Tree was fixed a tinsel star. It was splendid, particularly splendid.

"This evening," said all, "this evening it will shine."

"Oh," thought the Tree, "that it were evening already! Oh, that the lights may soon be lit up! When may that be done? Will the sparrows fly against the panes? Shall I grow fast here, and stand adorned in summer and winter?"

Yes, he did not guess badly. But he had a complete backache from mere longing, and backache is just as bad for a tree as a headache for a person.

At last the candles were lighted. What a brilliance, what a splendor! The Tree trembled so in all its branches that one of the candles set fire to a green twig, and it was scorched.

"Heaven preserve us!" cried the young ladies; and they hastily put the fire out.

Now the Tree might not even tremble. Oh, that was terrible! It was so afraid of setting fire to some of its ornaments, and it was quite bewildered with all the brilliance. And now the folding doors were thrown wide open, and a number of children rushed in as if they would have overturned the whole Tree; the older people followed more deliberately. The little ones stood quite silent, but only for a minute; then they shouted till the room rang; they danced gleefully round the Tree, and one present after another was plucked from it.

"What are they about?" thought the Tree. "What's going to be done?"

And the candles burned down to the twigs, and as they burned down they were extinguished, and then the children received permission to plunder the Tree. Oh! they rushed in upon it, so that every branch cracked again: if it had not been fastened by the top and by the golden star to the ceiling, it would have fallen down.

The children danced about with their pretty toys. No one looked at the Tree except one old man, who came up and peeped among the branches, but only to see if a fig or an apple had not been forgotten.

"A story! A story!" shouted the children; and they drew a little fat man toward the tree; and he sat down just beneath it — "for then we shall be in the green wood," said he, "and the tree may have the advantage of listening to my tale. But I can only tell one. Will you hear the story of Ivede-Avede, or of Klumpey-Dumpey, who fell downstairs, and still was raised up to honor and married the Princess?"

"Ivede-Avede!" cried some, "Klumpey-Dumpey!" cried others, and there was a great crying and shouting. Only the Fir Tree was quite silent, and thought, "Shall I not be in it? Shall I have nothing to do in it?" But he had been in the evening's amusement, and had done what was required of him.

And the fat man told about Klumpey-Dumpey who fell downstairs and yet was raised to honor and married a Princess. And the children clapped their hands and cried, "Tell another! tell another!" and they wanted to hear about Ivede-Avede; but they only got the story of Klumpey-Dumpey. The Fir Tree stood quite silent and thoughtful; never had the birds in the wood told such a story as that. Klumpey-Dumpey fell downstairs, and yet came to honor and married a Princess!

"Yes, so it happens in the world!" thought the Fir Tree, and believed it must be true, because that was such a nice man who told it. "Well, who can know? Perhaps I shall fall downstairs, too, and marry a Princess!" And it looked forward with pleasure to being adorned again, the next evening, with candles and toys, gold and fruit. "Tomorrow I shall not tremble," it thought.

"I shall rejoice in all my splendor. Tomorrow I shall hear the story of Klumpey-Dumpey again, and perhaps that of Ivede-Avede, too."

And the Tree stood all night quiet and thoughtful.

In the morning the servants and the chambermaid came in.

"Now my splendor will begin afresh," thought the Tree. But they dragged him out of the room, and upstairs to the garret, and here they put

him in a dark corner where no daylight shone.

"What's the meaning of this?" thought the Tree. "What am I to do here? What is to happen?"

And he leaned against the wall, and thought, and thought. And he had time enough, for days and nights went by, and nobody came up; and when at length some one came, it was only to put some great boxes in a corner. Now the Tree stood quite hidden away, and the supposition is that it was quite forgotten.

"Now it's winter outside," thought the Tree. "The earth is hard and covered with snow, and people cannot plant me; therefore I suppose I'm to be sheltered here until Spring comes. How considerate that is! How good people are! If it were only not so dark here, and so terribly solitary! — not even a little hare? That was pretty out there in the wood, when the snow lay thick and the hare sprang past; yes, even when he jumped over me; but then I did not like it. It is terribly lonely up here!"

"Piep! piep!" said a little Mouse, and crept forward, and then came another little one. They smelled at the Fir Tree, and then slipped among the branches.

"It's horribly cold," said the two little Mice, "or else it would be comfortable here. Don't you think so, old Fir Tree?"

"I'm not old at all," said the Fir Tree. "There are many much older than I."

"Where do you come from?" asked the Mice. "And what do you know?" They were dreadfully inquisitive. "Tell us about the most beautiful spot on earth. Have you been there? Have you been in the storeroom, where cheeses lie on the shelves, and hams hang from the ceiling, where one dances on tallow candles, and goes in thin and comes out fat?"

"I don't know that," replied the Tree; "but I know the wood, where the sun shines and the birds sing."

And then it told all about its youth.

And the little Mice had never heard anything of the kind; and they listened and said:

"What a number of things you have seen! How happy you must have been!"

"I?" replied the Fir Tree; and it thought

about what it had told. "Yes, those were really quite happy times." But then he told of the Christmas Eve, when he had been hung with sweetmeats and candles.

"Oh!" said the little Mice, "how happy you have been, you old Fir Tree!"

"I'm not old at all," said the Tree. "I only came out of the wood this winter. I'm only rather backward in my growth."

"What splendid stories you can tell!" said the little Mice.

And the next night they came with four other little Mice, to hear what the Tree had to relate; and the more it said, the more clearly did it remember everything, and thought. "Those were quite merry days! But they may come again. Klumpey-Dumpey fell downstairs, and yet he married a Princess. Perhaps I shall marry a Princess, too!" And the Fir Tree thought of a pretty little Birch Tree that grew out in the forest; for the Fir Tree, that Birch was a real Princess.

"Who's Klumpey-Dumpey?" asked the little Mice.

And then the Fir Tree told the whole story. It could remember every single word; and the little Mice were ready to leap to the very top of the Tree with pleasure. Next night a great many more Mice came, and on Sunday two Rats even appeared; but these thought the story was not pretty, and the little Mice were sorry for that, for now they also did not like it so much as before.

"Do you know only one story?" asked the Rats.

"Only that one," replied the Tree. "I heard that on the happiest evening of my life; I did not think then how happy I was."

"That's a very miserable story. Don't you know any about bacon and tallow candles — a storeroom story?"

"No," said the Tree.

"Then we'd rather not hear you," said the Rats.

And they went back to their own people. The little Mice at last stayed away also; and then the Tree sighed and said:

"It was very nice when they sat round me, the merry little Mice, and listened when I spoke to them. Now that's past too. But I shall remember to be pleased when they take me out."

But when did that happen? Why, it was one morning that people came and rummaged in the garret; the boxes were put away, and the Tree brought out; they certainly threw him rather roughly on the floor, but a servant dragged him away at once to the stairs, where the daylight shone.

"Now life is beginning again!" thought the Tree.

It felt the fresh air and the first sunbeam, and now it was out in the courtyard. Everything passed so quickly that the Tree quite forgot to look at itself, there was so much to look at all round. The courtyard was close to a garden, and here everything was blooming; the roses hung fresh over the paling, the linden trees were in blossom, and the swallows cried, "Quinze-wit! quinze-wit! my husband's come!" But it was not the Fir Tree they meant.

"Now I shall live!" said the Tree, rejoicingly, and spread its branches far out; but, alas! they were all withered and yellow; and it lay in the corner among nettles and weeds. The tinsel star was still upon it, and shone in the bright sunshine.

In the courtyard a couple of the merry children were playing who had danced round the tree at Christmas time, and had rejoiced over it. One of the youngest ran up and tore off the golden star.

"Look what is sticking to the ugly old fir tree!" said the child, and he trod upon the branches till they cracked again under his boots.

And the Tree looked at all the blooming flowers and the splendor of the garden, and then looked at itself, and wished it had remained in the dark corner of the garret; it thought of its fresh youth in the wood, of the merry Christmas Eve, and of the little Mice which had listened so pleasantly to the story of Klumpey-Dumpey.

"Past! past!" said the old Tree. "Had I but rejoiced when I could have done so! Past! past!"

And the servant came and chopped the Tree into little pieces; a whole bundle lay there; it blazed brightly under the great brewing copper, and it sighed deeply, and each sigh was like a little shot; and the children who were at play there ran up and seated themselves at the fire, looked into it, and cried "Puff! puff!" But at each explosion, which was a deep sigh, the Tree thought of a summer day in the woods, or of a winter night there, when the stars beamed; he thought of Christmas Eve and of Klumpey-Dumpey, the only story he had ever heard or knew how to tell; and then the Tree was burned.

The boys played in the garden, and the youngest had on his breast a golden star, which the Tree had worn on its happiest evening. Now that was past, and the Tree's life was past, and the story is past too: past! past! — and that's the way with all stories.

13 Christmas in the Future

THE CHRISTMAS OF THE FUTURE

by Frank Sullivan

THERE is every reason to believe that the old haphazard and unscientific methods of celebrating Christmas are slowly dying out and that the Christmas of the future will be observed with a maximum of efficiency and a minimum loss of energy.

In the past, Christmas as a holiday has often been fraught with danger to life and limb, but science is making rapid strides in the direction of making the Yuletide safe for democracy. An example of this: I heard only the other day of the admirable work a prominent inventor is doing to combat the holly menace. There are few of us who at one time or another have not received flesh wounds — not serious, to be sure, but none the less painful — as a result of sitting unawares on barbed holly left in chairs by frenzied Christmas-tree trimmers. Such lesions will soon be a thing of the past. I am not authorized to give details but I understand that within the year this inventor I speak of will have a serviceable and cheap rubber holly on the market, guaranteed not to puncture.

Other time-honoured Christmas features seem to have outlived their day. You no longer find Christmas trees festooned with ropes of pop-corn. Those of us who are in our forties can remember when days were spent popping corn and stringing it into yards of trimming for the Christmas tree. By the time the tree was taken down at Twelfth Night the popcorn had hung long enough to acquire an attractively gamey tang, with a flavour of tinsel dust, lint, and dried evergreen needles. It was considered quite a delicacy by the small fry of those times. For years hot buttered popcorn seemed quite tame to me by comparison. This eating of mummified popcorn and the wholesale consumption by tots of Christmas-tree candles were probably, with the recent depression, the main factors in producing the dyspepsia which is so marked a characteristic of the generation of the present writer. Popcorn and wax candles have joined the dodo and the Yule log. The children of today must find some other means of acquiring acute indigestion. They are resourceful and ingenious, and will no doubt have little trouble doing so.

Another Christmas reform impends. I am told that within a year or two science will have stripped the kiss under the mistletoe of its terrors. For some time past experiments have been

321

proceeding with a new automatic antiseptic mistletoe. The leaves are of sterilized green satin and the berries are made of indurated milk. It will function on the principle of the automatic sprinkler, in this manner: Two kissers approach the mistletoe in a spirit of holiday lust. As they square off under the mistletoe the heat generated by their fondness for each other releases hundreds of tiny sprinklers concealed in the mistletoe "berries" and a spray of healing formaldehyde sifts gently down upon them like a benison, destroying all coryza, grippe, influenza, pneumonia, or tetanus germs that may be lurking about the kissers' kissers.

Of course, the antiseptic mistletoe is only a temporary measure. Eventually the kiss under the mistletoe must go, bag and baggage. It is unhygienic, sloppy, and sentimental; and it breeds unscientific thinking. It has no place in our modern life.

The Christmas of the future will be a triumph of science over waste. Energy now frittered away in futile holiday pursuits will be conserved for more constructive purposes. For one thing, Christmas will be made to end immediately after dinner on Christmas Day, thus eliminating the demoralizing Christmas afternoon, the most depressing few hours in the Christian calendar. I refer to the period from about three o'clock on, when reaction from the hysteria of trimming the tree and opening the presents has set in and all the world seems dark and dreary; when the fruit cake is irrevocably inside the celebrant and has made unmistakably clear its determination not to merge with the port wine, walnuts, oyster stuffing, cranberry sauce, and the rest of the Christmas viands. It is the time when the kiddies begin to do battle for the possession of the few toys that remain unbroken; and it is the time when daddy, called upon to fix the electric train, trips over the track — or the baby — and plunges headlong into the Christmas tree, ripping off the electrical trimmings and causing a short circuit. Christmas afternoon must go.

In the Christmas of the future the gift problem, with its associated problems of shopping, mailing, wrapping, exchanging, etc., will cease

to be the *bête noire* it is today. Every one will co-operate. Christmas cards will be mailed earlier and earlier until the bulk of them will have been delivered about the time the second income-tax instalments begin to clog the mails. Parcels will be wrapped more and more securely as the years go by until he will be a fast worker indeed who gets his presents all unwrapped by the second Sunday after Epiphany.

Shopping will not be the bedlam it is today. It will be controlled. The energies of women will be harnessed. There will be national leagues of shoppers. Teams from stores will compete with each other in shopping bouts under the rules now governing wrestling. It will be no time at all before controlled Christmas shopping has developed a hardy, buxom race of women shoppers which might well serve as a first line of national defense in case of emergency. Perhaps it may eventually be said of the democratic countries that our victories were won on the counters of Wanamaker's or Selfridge's.

One of the worst psychological effects of Christmas on people is the rage that follows when a person gives a friend a gift and the friend fails to reciprocate. This will be eliminated in the Christmas of the future by the Declaration of Gift. This will simply be a public notice of every citizen's Christmas intentions. Early in the fall every one will be required by law to file a list with the Collector of Internal Revenue of the persons to whom he proposes to give Christmas presents, with the nature and the planned cost of each gift.

These lists will be tacked up at the post office and department stores of each city for public scrutiny. Each person can examine the lists, find out what his friends are doing, and act accordingly. If I have you on my list for a necktie or a compact and I find from the public list that you have not put me down for anything, I can just cross you off my list. Or, if a citizen thinks he has a right to expect a present from a friend who has failed to declare to that effect, the injured party shall have the legal right to apply to the courts for a writ of mandamus compelling the defendant, or recalcitrant donor, to show cause why the aforesaid present should not be given to the plaintiff, or piqued donee.

Two people who find that they are giving each other presents of equal value can pair off like senators voting at Washington and cancel both gifts, taking the will for the deed. This practice will be called phantom giving.

As Christmas becomes more and more scientific and less encumbered with sentimental flubdub children will play less and less part in its celebration. The heaviest burden of the Christmas celebration has always fallen on the tots, for it is the season of the year when parents have to be coddled and humoured more than at any other time. The child has to simulate an unfelt curiosity in mysterious packages that arrive during December and are whisked furtively to the attic. Children have to compose letters to Santa Claus to placate Christmas-crazed parents, and they are hauled off to department stores, where they are expected to display glee at the sight of a Santa Claus in palpably fake whiskers.

All this is too much of a strain on their little libidos. It fills their subconsciousnesses with impressions that pop out twenty or thirty years later in the most blood-curdling manifestations. In the future it is probable that Santa Claus will be required to be clean-shaven and that only disciples of Dr. Freud will be allowed to continue wearing a beard.

So it will go. As we progress scientifically we shall slough off the antiquated customs and leave off saying "Merry Christmas" or drinking wassail (of slight nutritive value and totally lacking in the essential vitamins). The celebration of Christmas will become more and more efficient until it will at last be so efficient that it will become unnecessary to keep Christmas at all.

THE YEAR THERE WAS NO CHRISTMAS

by Samuel Grafton

There had been signs for a long time that it was coming, but 1984 was actually the year in which the whole country almost forgot to celebrate Christmas altogether.

As I look back, I can see that it happened rather naturally and nobody was really to blame.

After all, we'd become kind of used to having the government do everything, and Christmas is — well, it's sort of private enterprise. Bit by bit, in those middle years of the century, Christmas began to slip out of our minds. You remember that time, or at least you've read about it: everything upset, the world in turmoil. It was very hard to buy anything with which to make a Christmas. We were building up our defenses then, and you need about the same materials to celebrate Christmas as you need for national security. A Christmas tree uses a lot of electric equipment when you get right down to it, and toys had become more and more electric, and every nursery in the country was competing with the Air Force, and it became kind of rugged.

That was when the government set up the Bureau of Christmas Economics. The government had discovered that Christmas was becoming awfully important. About a quarter of the year's department-store sales were keyed to Christmas, in one way or another, and government statisticians found that Christmas ranked right up there with the meat industry in our economy. It clearly needed the attention of a new bureau.

The BCE, as the new bureau was known, didn't set out deliberately to extinguish Christmas, but tried to steer the holiday celebration into paths that wouldn't bother the defense effort. We were urged to give presents made only of plastics or paper. But then, in '77, the plastics shortage hit, and the next few years were paper Christmases.

It became rather foolish to keep harping on only so many shopping days left to Christmas when all you could give anybody was a memo book or a book of matches, and the usual warning notices began to drop out of the newspapers. TV and radio announcers stopped mentioning Christmas too, because they found it made people sad to be reminded of the good times they had had. It became polite not to talk about Christmas.

All these trends apparently came to a head in 1984. The microfiles of the newspapers of the period show that there was no editorial mention of Christmas that year at all. The world was in so much trouble that even to talk about gay, good holidays carried a kind of unpatriotic implication.

And so December 20 came around, and then the twenty-first and the twenty-second, and nobody had mentioned Christmas and there was no decoration in any window. It was truly a terrible year.

People would look at the calendar — December 23 — and then they'd walk by store windows that were showing nothing except utility suits for men (all paper except for the seats and knees) and seam pencils, with which women

drew lines on the back of their legs to make it look as if they were wearing nylons.

Somewhere inside of everybody, of course, the pressure must have been building up. The historians have written many accounts of the event that finally took place on the night of December 24-25. Since I was an eyewitness, and since my family was involved, I feel I ought to add my own version.

You see, the hero was my father. I don't mind writing about it now. I guess I was pretty ashamed of him for a long time, though. He had spent six or seven years in the Federal Attitudes Hospital, and we used to go visit him every week. There was nothing really wrong with him except that — well, he became pretty excited sometimes.

Around the end of October he would begin to talk about bobbing for apples in a washtub. Nobody had done that for years, not with apples being used as a prime raw material for the mastics that were being substituted everywhere for plastics. And on the night of the last day of the year, he would jump onto a chair and wave a glass of water and holler "Whoopee!" until they got him down and gave him a sedative.

He had lost contact with reality, they said. It was a common-enough type of psychological disorder: He was living in the past. They would try gently to bring him up to the present by talking to him about current events and taking him on tours around town. But about five o'clock he would start talking about going into a quiet place and having a couple of quick ones, and they'd have to take him back to the hospital. It had been more than twenty years since the government had permitted people to sit around in bars and drink up good aviation fuel.

He was sweet and gentle most of the time. I saw him badly upset only once. We'd gone to visit him, early in July, and we found him bursting paper bags to make a popping noise, and crying. He was always bad, they told us, near the beginning of July. September was troublesome too. He always wanted to take a long automobile drive on the first Monday in September; and when they told him he had to have a certificate of necessity for a long automobile drive, he would go to his bed and lie in it all day.

How he escaped on December 24, 1984, isn't clear. He had begun to talk rationally a few days before. One morning he mentioned to his doctor that he was glad people didn't celebrate Christmas any more, because it was a waste of material and energy. They thought he was improving wonderfully, and they gave him the run of the hospital. I suppose he just walked out the front door December 24 and came home.

He was carrying a lot of cardboard boxes. We saw him coming across the front lawn and were scared, but Mother told us not to say anything to upset him. He came in the door with the biggest smile you ever saw, and he gave each of us one of the boxes.

There was a seam pencil in the one he gave Mother, and a kind of white leather ball with red stitching on it in the one he gave me. It looked pretty old and it had the name "Babe Ruth" written on it in ink. Sis' box had some ribbons in it, made of real paper.

Mother looked worried, but we children thought it was an interesting game, being given boxes with different things in them. We got down on the floor to play with our things, and I remember Father saying to Mother, "They're looking for the tree," which seemed an odd thing to say. How could there be a tree inside the house?

He went upstairs to the attic, and Mother shushed us and phoned the hospital.

When he came down, he looked weird. He had found a kind of red suit with white trimming on it and put it on. He had stuck a lot of white cotton to his chin, and he had on a red pointed hat, and he walked around the room laughing.

We were scared, I can tell you, watching him do that. Then all of a sudden he waved to us and walked out the front door, and Mother became real panicky.

"Go after him," she told me.

He was walking slow, smiling at everybody, and waving. I didn't want anybody to know he was my father, so I hung back a good deal,

just keeping him in sight. People began to follow him, as I guess they would in that getup, and they were all laughing too.

A man would glance out of a window and see him, look kind of scared, and then break into a big grin and come out on the street laughing. Pretty soon I guess there were a hundred people following Father.

Somewhere he'd got a bell, and he was ringing it as he walked along. Every time he'd ring

it the people behind him would laugh, and more people would come out, and they were all laughing and clapping each other on the back.

They arrested him, of course, when he got to the Avenue. One policeman held his arm while another one phoned for the wagon with his walkie-lookie; and when the wagon came, they pushed him inside and took him away, leaving all those people on the sidewalk.

They weren't laughing any more. They looked kind of strange; they had expressions like they were angry. Scared too, but more angry than scared.

I knew the police would take him to the city home for the maladjusted, Stay-a-While House, where people who couldn't get along with society were kept, so I walked across town to it.

It was getting dark, and what struck me funny was that a lot of other people were walking toward the same place. Some of them would stop in at almost every building we passed, and pretty soon they'd come out again with more people, and before you knew it, all the streets leading to the place were crowded.

It was nighttime when I got to the building. There was no moon; it was real dark. But stars were out and shining, and although you could see your breath cloud into fog in front of you, it wasn't too cold. And there were so many people around me on all sides, crowding into the square, that it felt kind of warm.

They looked up at the building with the bars on the windows, and I heard the people wondering out loud which room Father was in, and then suddenly they started to sing.

You could hear the song start up at one corner of the square and kind of move across, getting picked up and becoming louder and louder. People sang loud, but there was a kind of something about the song that wasn't loud. It was like each man and woman in the crowd was singing to himself. "'Silent night,'" they sang, "'holy night,'" and you could hear it roll across the square.

When they finished that one, they started on another — "Good King Wenceslas," I now know it was.

Some men came out in front of the building; they set up a public-address system, and a man made a speech. He told everybody to go home, that my father would be given the best of care and the most expert medical attention, and that there was no need for concern.

Nobody went home, so far as I could see. The crowd just went on singing.

Along about eleven o'clock at night the news-reel trucks came and floodlighted the square for pictures; then the mobile television cameras moved in, inching their way through the crowd.

I guess that was the biggest mistake the police made, letting the television cameras pick up that singing crowd.

I had thought practically all the people in town were there already, but now they really began to come in. Every street leading into the square was packed, and these new people were all carrying lighted candles.

They passed candles down into the crowd that was in the square already, and everybody on all sides of me started lighting them and holding them up high, and it was like a wonderful floating fire of pinpoint lights, and over it you could hear that song they seemed to like the best rolling up against the building: "Silent night, holy night . . . "

The clock in the tower tolled twelve for midnight as they let my father out. He stood on the front steps of the building, still in his red-and-white suit and his cotton beard; and now the song felt like it was going to lift us clear off the pavement.

I worked my way in between people's legs to the front steps. My father saw me, and big as I was for my age, he picked me up and put me on his shoulder. The crowd yelled once, without losing the song, and then went into it again as if they wanted to sing and never stop.

I'll never forget it. I've read lots of things people have written about it, college professors and wise men and all, and they call it the incident that marked the end of a bad era, and tell how everything got better for everybody afterward, when the people on the other side of the world finally realized that we meant to be what we are and wouldn't ever change, not for anybody.

But for me it's always that same picture, me sitting on my father's shoulder and looking at all the people standing there in the black night, each one holding a candle and singing, making it sound as if the stones of the city itself were singing that song.

14

Christmas Verse

WEEK BEFORE CHRISTMAS

by Eleanor Alletta Chaffee

God bless all little boys who stand outside
Gay Yuletide windows, with a stubborn pride
Calculating how far present cash
May go; then suddenly resolved and rash,
Darting within to watch with restless eyes
The wrapping of the Annual Surprise.

God bless all little boys who toss and turn
The few nights left to Christmas, and who burn
With agonizing doubt . . . *Would that be better*
Chains them to alternation like a fetter.

God bless all little boys who do not know
That all in vain is indecisive woe.
Their gifts are richer to a mother's heart
Than all the gold man's dreams can set apart.
God bless them all together, in the Name
Of heaven's Gift, and Him through Whom it came.

A CHRISTMAS CAROL

by Gilbert Keith Chesterton

The Christ-child lay on Mary's lap
  His hair was like a light.
(O weary, weary were the world,
  But here is all aright.)

The Christ-child lay on Mary's breast,
  His hair was like a star.
(O stern and cunning are the kings,
  But here the true hearts are.)

The Christ-child lay on Mary's heart,
  His hair was like a fire.
(O weary, weary is the world,
  But here the world's desire.)

The Christ-child stood at Mary's knee,
  His hair was like a crown,
And all the flowers looked up at Him
  And all the stars looked down.

PRAYER

by John Farrar

Last night I crept across the snow,
Where only tracking rabbits go,
And then I waited quite alone
Until the Christmas radiance shone!

At midnight twenty angels came,
Each white and shining like a flame.
At midnight twenty angels sang,
The Stars swung out like bells and rang.

They lifted me across the hill,
They bore me in their arms until
A greater glory greeted them.
It was the town of Bethlehem.

And gently, then, they set me down,
All worshipping that holy town,
And gently, then, they bade me raise
My head to worship and to praise.

And gently, then, the Christ smiled down.
Ah, there was glory in that town!
It was as if the world were free
And glistening with purity.

And in that vault of crystal blue,
It was as if the world were new,
And myriad angels, file on file,
Gloried in the Christ-Child's smile.

It was so beautiful to see
Such glory, for a child like me,
So beautiful, it does not seem
It could have been a Christmas dream.

GATES AND DOORS

by Joyce Kilmer

There was a gentle hostler
(And blessed be his name!)
He opened up the stable
The night Our Lady came.
Our Lady and Saint Joseph,
He gave them food and bed,
And Jesus Christ has given him
A glory round his head.

So let the gate swing open
However poor the yard,
Lest weary people visit you
And find their passage barred;
Unlatch the door at midnight
And let your lantern's glow
Shine out to guide the traveler's feet
To you across the snow.

There was a courteous hostler
(He is in Heaven tonight)
He held Our Lady's bridle
And helped her to alight;
He spread clean straw before her
Whereon she might lie down,
And Jesus Christ has given him
An everlasting crown.

Unlock the door this evening
And let your gate swing wide,
Let all who ask for shelter
Come speedily inside.
What if your yard be narrow?
What if your house be small?
There is a Guest is coming
Will glorify it all.

There was a joyous hostler
Who knelt on Christmas morn
Beside the radiant manger
Wherein his Lord was born.
His heart was full of laughter,
His soul was full of bliss
When Jesus, on His Mother's lap,
Gave him His hand to kiss.

Unbar your heart this evening
And keep no stranger out,
Take from your soul's great portal
The barrier of doubt.
To humble folk and weary
Give hearty welcoming,
Your breast shall be tomorrow
The cradle of a King.

A VISIT FROM SAINT NICHOLAS

by Clement C. Moore

'Twas the night before Christmas, when all through the house
Not a creature was stirring, not even a mouse;
The stockings were hung by the chimney with care,
In hopes that Saint Nicholas soon would be there;

The children were nestled all snug in their beds,
While visions of sugarplums danced in their heads;
And mama in her kerchief, and I in my cap,
Had just settled our brains for a long winter's nap —
When out on the lawn there arose such a clatter,
I sprang from my bed to see what was the matter.
Away to the window I flew like a flash,
Tore open the shutters and threw up the sash.
The moon on the breast of the new-fallen snow
Gave a lustre of midday to objects below;
When what to my wondering eyes should appear,
But a miniature sleigh and eight tiny reindeer,
With a little old driver, so lively and quick
I knew in a moment it must be Saint Nick!
More rapid than eagles his coursers they came,
And he whistled and shouted and called them by name:
"Now, Dasher! now, Dancer! now, Prancer and Vixen!
On, Comet! on, Cupid! on, Donder and Blitzen!
To the top of the porch, to the top of the wall!
Now dash away, dash away, dash away all!"
As dry leaves that before the wild hurricane fly,
When they meet with an obstacle, mount to the sky,
So up to the housetop the coursers they flew,
With a sleigh full of toys — and Saint Nicholas, too.
And then in a twinkling I heard on the roof
The prancing and pawing of each little hoof.
As I drew in my head, and was turning around,
Down the chimney Saint Nicholas came with a bound.
He was dressed all in fur from his head to his foot,
And his clothes were all tarnished with ashes and soot;
A bundle of toys he had flung on his back,
And he looked like a peddler just opening his pack.
His eyes, how they twinkled! his dimples, how merry!
His cheeks were like roses, his nose like a cherry;
His droll little mouth was drawn up like a bow,
And the beard on his chin was as white as the snow.
The stump of a pipe he held tight in his teeth,
And the smoke it encircled his head like a wreath.
He had a broad face and a little round belly
That shook, when he laughed, like a bowl full of jelly.
He was chubby and plump — a right jolly old elf;
And I laughed, when I saw him, in spite of myself.
A wink of his eye and a twist of his head
Soon gave me to know I had nothing to dread.
He spoke not a word, but went straight to his work,
And filled all the stockings; then turned with a jerk,
And laying his finger aside of his nose,

And giving a nod, up the chimney he rose.
He sprang in his sleigh, to his team gave a whistle,
And away they all flew like the down of a thistle;
But I heard him exclaim, ere he drove out of sight:
"Happy Christmas to all, and to all a good-night!"

CHRISTMAS IN OLDEN TIME

by Sir Walter Scott

Heap on more wood! the wind is chill;
But, let it whistle as it will,
We'll keep our Christmas merry still.
Each age has deemed the new-born year
The fittest time for festal cheer.
    And well our Christmas sires of old
Loved, when the year its course had rolled
And brought blithe Christmas back again
With all its hospitable train,
With social and religious rite
To honor all the holy night.
On Christmas-eve the bells were rung;
On Christmas-eve the mass was sung.
Then opened wide the Baron's hall
To vassal, tenant, serf, and all;
Power laid his rod of rule aside,
And Ceremony doffed her pride.
All hailed with uncontrolled delight
And general voice the happy night,
That to the cottage, as the crown,
Brought tidings of salvation down.
    The fire, with well-dried logs supplied,
Went roaring up the chimney wide;
The huge hall-table's oaken face,
Scrubbed till it shone, the day to grace,
Bore then upon its massive board
No mark to part the squire and lord.
    Then came the merry maskers in
And carols roared with blithesome din.
If unmelodious was the song,
It was a hearty note and strong.
England was merry England when
Old Christmas brought his sports again.
'Twas Christmas broached the mightiest ale;
'Twas Christmas told the merriest tale;
A Christmas gambol oft could cheer
The poor man's heart through half the year.

CHRISTMAS AND NEW YEAR BELLS

by Alfred Tennyson

The time draws near the birth of Christ:
　　The moon is hid; the night is still;
　　The Christmas bells from hill to hill
Answer each other in the mist.

Four voices of four hamlets round,
　　From far and near, on mead and moor,
　　Swell out and fail, as if a door
Were shut between me and the sound:

Each voice four changes on the wind,
　　That now dilate, and now decrease,
　　Peace and goodwill, goodwill and peace,
Peace and goodwill, to all mankind.

This year I slept and woke with pain,
　　I almost wish'd no more to wake,
　　And that my hold on life would break
Before I heard those bells again:

But they the troubled spirit rule,
　　For they controll'd me when a boy;
　　They bring me sorrow touch'd with joy,
The merry, merry bells of Yule.

Ring out, wild bells, to the wild sky,
　　The flying cloud, the frosty light:
　　The year is dying in the night;
Ring out, wild bells, and let him die.

Ring out the old, ring in the new,
　　Ring, happy bells, across the snow:
　　The year is going, let him go;
Ring out the false, ring in the true.

Ring out the grief that saps the mind,
　　For those that here we see no more;
　　Ring out the feud of rich and poor,
Ring in redress to all mankind.

Ring out a slowly dying cause,
    And ancient forms of party strife;
    Ring in the nobler modes of life,
With sweeter manners, purer laws.

Ring out the want, the care, the sin,
    The faithless coldness of the times;
    Ring out, ring out my mournful rhymes,
But ring the fuller minstrel in.

Ring out false pride in place and blood,
    The civic slander and the spite;
    Ring in the love of truth and right,
Ring in the common love of good.

Ring out old shapes of foul disease,
    Ring out the narrowing lust of gold;
    Ring out the thousand wars of old,
Ring in the thousand years of peace.

Ring in the valiant man and free,
    The larger heart, the kindlier hand;
    Ring out the darkness of the land,
Ring in the Christ that is to be.

THE MAHOGANY TREE

by William Makepeace Thackeray

Christmas is here;
Winds whistle shrill,
Icy and chill,
Little care we:
Little we fear
Weather without,
Sheltered about
The Mahogany Tree.

Commoner greens,
Ivy and oaks,
Poets, in jokes,
Sing, do you see?
Good fellows' shins

Here, boys, are found,
Twisting around
The Mahogany Tree.

Once on the boughs
Birds of rare plume
Sang in its bloom;
Night birds are we:
Here we carouse,
Singing like them,
Perched round the stem
Of the jolly old tree.

Here let us sport,
Boys, as we sit;
Laughter and wit
Flashing so free.
Life is but short —
When we are gone,
Let them sing on,
Round the old tree.

Evenings we knew,
Happy as this;
Faces we miss,
Pleasant to see.
Kind hearts and true,
Gentle and just,
Peace to your dust!
We sing round the tree.

Care, like a dun,
Lurks at the gate:
Let the dog wait;
Happy we'll be!
Drink every one;
Pile up the coals,
Fill the red bowls,
Round the old tree.

Drain we the cup —
Friend, art afraid?
Spirits are laid
In the Red Sea.
Mantle it up;

Empty it yet;
Let us forget,
Round the old tree.

Sorrows, begone!
Life and its ills,
Duns and their bills,
Bid we to flee.
Come with the dawn,
Blue-devil sprite;
Leave us tonight,
Round the old tree.

YULE-TIDE FIRES

Author unknown

Light with the burning log of oak
The darkness of thy care,
Deck with the scarlet-berried bough
The temple of the fair;
Spread pure white linen for a feast,
Perchance some guest may share.

Give forth thy gold and silver coins,
For they were lent to thee;
Put out to usury thy dross,
One talent gaineth three.
Perchance the hungered and the poor
May pray to God for thee.

Once a pale star rose in the East
For watching herds to see,
And weakness came to Bethlehem,
And strength to Galilee.
Perchance! If thou dost keep thy tryst
A star may rise for thee.

THE THREE KINGS

by Henry Wadsworth Longfellow

Three Kings came riding from far away,
   Melchior and Gaspar and Baltasar;
Three Wise Men out of the East were they,
And they traveled by night and they slept by day,
   For their guide was a beautiful, wonderful star.

The star was so beautiful, large, and clear,
   That all the other stars of the sky
Became a white mist in the atmosphere,
And by this they knew that the coming was near
   Of the Prince foretold in the prophecy.

Three caskets they bore on their saddle-bows,
   Three caskets of gold with golden keys;
Their robes were of crimson silk with rows
Of bells and pomegranates and furbelows,
   Their turbans like blossoming almond-trees.

And so the Three Kings rode into the West,
   Through the dusk of night, over hill and dell,
And sometimes they nodded with beard on breast,
And sometimes they talked, as they paused to rest,
   With the people they met at some wayside well.

"Of the child that is born," said Baltasar,
   "Good people, I pray you, tell us the news;
For we in the East have seen his star,
And have ridden fast, and have ridden far,
   To find and worship the King of the Jews."

And the people answered, "You ask in vain;
   We know of no king but Herod the Great!"
They thought the Wise Men were men insane,
As they spurred their horses across the plain,
   Like riders in haste, and who cannot wait.

And when they came to Jerusalem,
   Herod the Great, who had heard this thing,
Sent for the Wise Men and questioned them;

And said, "Go down unto Bethlehem,
    And bring me tidings of this new king."

So they rode away; and the star stood still,
    The only one in the gray of morn;
Yes, it stopped, — it stood still of its own free will,
Right over Bethlehem on the hill,
    The city of David, where Christ was born.

And the Three Kings rode through the gate and the guard,
    Through the silent street, till their horses turned
And neighed as they entered the great inn-yard;
But the windows were closed, and the doors were barred,
    And only a light in the stable burned.

And cradled there in the scented hay,
    In the air made sweet by the breath of kine,
The little child in the manger lay,
The child, that would be king one day
    Of a kingdom not human but divine.

His mother Mary of Nazareth
    Sat watching beside his place of rest,
Watching the even flow of his breath,
For the joy of life and the terror of death
    Were mingled together in her breast.

They laid their offerings at his feet:
    The gold was their tribute to a King,
The frankincense, with its odor sweet,
Was for the Priest, the Paraclete,
    The myrrh for the body's burying.

And the mother wondered and bowed her head,
    And sat as still as a statue of stone;
Her heart was troubled yet comforted,
Remembering what the Angel had said
    Of an endless reign and of David's throne.

Then the Kings rode out of the city gate,
    With a clatter of hoofs in proud array;
But they went not back to Herod the Great,
For they knew his malice and feared his hate,
    And returned to their homes by another way.

CHRISTMAS EVERYWHERE

by Phillips Brooks

Everywhere, everywhere, Christmas tonight!
Christmas in lands of the fir-tree and pine,
Christmas in lands of the palm-tree and vine,
Christmas where snow peaks stand solemn and white,
Christmas where corn fields stand sunny and bright.
Christmas where children are hopeful and gay,
Christmas where old men are patient and gray,
Christmas where peace, like a dove in his flight,
Broods o'er brave men in the thick of the fight;

Everywhere, everywhere, Christmas tonight!
For the Christ-Child who comes is the Master of all;
No palace too great, no cottage too small.

INDEX